HARVARD HISTORICAL STUDIES   128

Published under the auspices
of the Department of History
from the income of the
Paul Revere Frothingham Bequest
Robert Louis Stroock Fund
Henry Warren Torrey Fund

The Travails of Conscience

THE ARNAULD FAMILY
AND THE ANCIEN RÉGIME

ALEXANDER SEDGWICK

HARVARD UNIVERSITY PRESS

Cambridge, Massachusetts
London, England   1998

Library of Congress Cataloging-in-Publication Data

Sedgwick, Alexander, 1930–
    The travails of conscience : the Arnauld family and the Ancien Régime /
Alexander Sedgwick.
        p.   cm. — (Harvard historical studies ; 128)
    Includes bibliographical references and index.
    ISBN 0-674-90567-9
    1. Arnauld family.   2. Royalists—France—Biography.
3. Jansenists—France—Political activity.
4. Despotism—France—Religious aspects.
5. Religion and politics—France—History.
6. France—History—Wars of the Huguenots, 1562–1598.
7. Fronde. 8. Port-Royal des Champs (Abbey)—History.
9. France—Genealogy.
I. Title.   II. Series: Harvard historical studies ; v. 128.
DC33.3.S44 1998
929′.2′0944—dc21   97-42556

For Kate and Cameron

Acknowledgments

I began work on this book almost twenty years ago. Because it is based to a considerable extent on manuscript sources, I have relied on leaves of absence from the University of Virginia in order to work for extended periods of time in French archives. I am grateful to the University for providing me with a semester's leave in 1978, another semester's leave in 1990, and a year's leave in 1995–96. I particularly appreciate the willingness of the late Hugh Kelly, former provost of the University, to let me begin my tour of duty as the dean of the Graduate School of Arts and Sciences in the middle of the academic year so that I could return to France in 1990 to complete the research after five years in another administrative position.

Librarians at the Bibliothèque Nationale and at the Bibliothèque de la Société de Port Royal were helpful in directing my attention to source materials that I might not otherwise have known about, particularly Odette Barenne of the BPR, who patiently guided me through the masses of materials contained in that library. The bibliographers at the Alderman Library of the University of Virginia were always on the lookout for reprinted works pertaining to the Arnaulds and Port-Royal. Through their acquisitions they have managed to put together a distinguished collection of source materials on Jansenism in seventeenth- and eighteenth-century France.

The Société des Amis de Port-Royal provided me with the opportunity to present two papers relating to the Arnauld family at its annual meetings in 1992 and 1994, both of which have appeared in the society's annual publication, *Le Chroniques de Port-Royal.* Discussions with the distinguished members of the society, particularly Professor Jean Mesnard, for many years the president of the society, gave me a better understanding of the Port-Royal community.

Earlier versions of this book were read by W. W. Abbot, Richard M. Golden, Sharon Kettering, Phyllis Leffler, John Lyons, Elizabeth Wirth Marvick, H. C. Erik Midelfort, Orest Ranum, and Ellen Weaver-Laporte. Their criticisms and suggestions for improvement have made the book much better than it would have been without their help. I will always be grateful to these colleagues for taking time out from busy schedules to provide me with extensive comments on the text.

I would like to acknowledge the courtesy of Professor Philippe Sellier, current president of the Société des Amis de Port-Royal. Others whose help I have appreciated are Albert Hamscher; M. de Leyzour, curator of the Musée National des Granges de Port-Royal; Catherine Maire; the late Jacques Roger; and Allison Weber. Judy B. Mitchell, my secretary during my years in the Graduate School, deserves my thanks for keeping my calendar as free as possible so that I could spend a few hours every day on my book and for being my editorial assistant. And I am grateful to Charles M. Davidson Jr. for designing the genealogy of the Arnauld family.

Finally I would like to thank my wife, Charlene M. Sedgwick, not only for her valuable editorial advice but for her unstinting support and encouragement, especially during times when I began to wonder if this project would ever come to fruition. The Arnaulds have become almost as much a part of her life as they have of mine.

Contents

Genealogy of the Arnauld Family, Fifteenth–Eighteenth Centuries

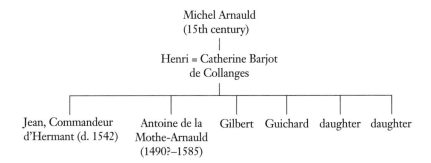

Michel Arnauld
(15th century)

Henri = Catherine Barjot
de Collanges

Jean, Commandeur   Antoine de la   Gilbert   Guichard   daughter   daughter
d'Hermant (d. 1542)   Mothe-Arnauld
                          (1490?–1585)

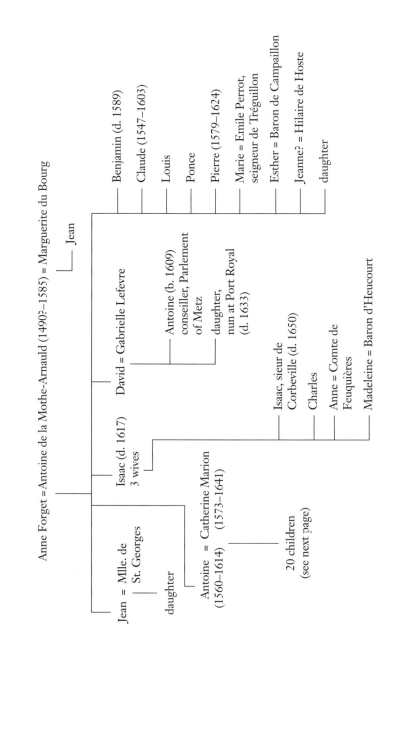

Anne Forget = Antoine de la Mothe-Arnauld (1490?–1585) = Marguerite du Bourg

Jean

Jean = Mlle. de St. Georges

daughter

Antoine = Catherine Marion
(1560–1614)   (1573–1641)

20 children
(see next page)

Isaac (d. 1617)
3 wives

David = Gabrielle Lefevre

Antoine (b. 1609)
conseiller, Parlement
of Metz

daughter,
nun at Port Royal
(d. 1633)

Isaac, sieur de
Corbeville (d. 1650)

Charles

Anne = Comte de
Feuquières

Madeleine = Baron d'Heucourt

Benjamin (d. 1589)

Claude (1547–1603)

Louis

Ponce

Pierre (1579–1624)

Marie = Emile Perrot,
seigneur de Tréguillon

Esther = Baron de Campaillon

Jeanne? = Hilaire de Hoste

daughter

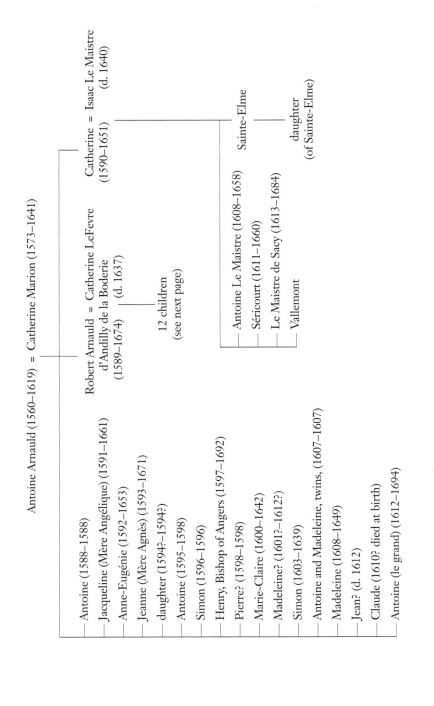

Robert Arnauld d'Andilly (1589–1674) = Catherine LeFevre de la Boderie (d. 1636)

Catherine (1614–1643)

Antoine, abbé de Chaumes (1616–1698)

Marie (1620–1620)

Henri-Charles, seigneur de Luzancy (1624–1684)

Angélique de Saint-Jean (1624–1684)

Marie-Charlotte (1627–1678)

Marie-Angélique de Sainte-Thérèse (1630–1700)

Anne-Marie (1631–1660)

Jules (1634–1660)

Elizabeth (1632–1645)

Claude (1636–1636)

Simon Arnauld de Pomponne = Catherine Ladvocat
(1618–1699)

Nicolas-Simon = Constance d'Harville
(1662–1727)   da Palaiseau

Catherine-Constance

Marie-Angélique (1661–1662)

Marie-Emmanuelle (1663–1686)

Antoine-Joseph (1664–1693)

Charlotte (1668–1746)

Henri-Charles, abbé de Pomponne (1669–1756)

son (1670?–1679)

Catherine (1674–1674)

son (1675–1682)

Catherine-Angélique (1676–1676)

Catherine-Félicité (1679–1755) = J.-P. Colbert, marquis de Torcy

Arnauld d'Andilly and
his wife had 3 other
children who died
in infancy.
Dates unknown.

The Travails of Conscience

1

Introduction

*T*HIS IS THE STORY of the Arnauld family, a family that rose to prominence at the end of the sixteenth century on the basis of loyal service to the French crown. Like other families in similar circumstances—the Bouthilliers, the Colberts, the Fouquets, the Le Telliers and the Séguiers, *grands serviteurs de l'état* as Denis Richet has called them—the Arnaulds advanced the interests of their family by attaching themselves to the king. Their power and influence depended on absolute loyalty and obedience to the sovereign, whose own power they sought to enhance. Their wealth and social status was largely determined by the quality of their service. However, as a result of the religious conversion of Angélique Arnauld (1591–1661) early in the seventeenth century, the family eventually adopted a set of religious principles that appeared to some ecclesiastical authorities to be derived from Calvinist theology. These "Jansenist" principles were condemned by the papacy in cooperation with Louis XIV. By the middle of the seventeenth century the Arnauld family, which had hitherto prided itself on its contributions to the growth of absolute monarchy in France, found itself in opposition to king and pope. Many of its members were moved by conscience to resist every effort of church and state to force them to repudiate their controversial religious beliefs.

At the heart of these beliefs was a profound *mépris du monde* (contempt for the world),[1] which in one way or another pitted members of

1

the Arnauld family against what they had come to believe was a corrupt world. Religious life was for them a perpetual struggle between the forces of good and evil. It was this perception that inspired them and others to involve themselves in the Catholic reform movement in the seventeenth century, and it was this perception that ultimately led them as "the friends of Truth" to resist any and all assaults on that truth by "corrupt" officials of church and state. Like others before and after the era of the Reformation, the Arnaulds, given the choice between obeying duly constituted authority on the one hand and the dictates of conscience on the other, chose the latter in the belief that conscience enlightened by truth must always be the ultimate authority in deciding on any course of action.

The Jansenist controversy in which the Arnaulds became so deeply involved grew out of the Counter Reformation. Indeed Jansenists believed that their religious ideals were indispensable to the reform of both religious institutions and the inner self. Yet during the eighteenth century, long after the most distinguished members of the Arnauld family were dead and their spiritual *seigneurie*, the convent of Port-Royal, destroyed by order of Louis XIV, Jansenism had become essentially a political controversy. As historians Dale Van Kley and Catherine Maire have shown in recent works, Jansenists contributed to the formation of an antiabsolutist political ideology.[2] In this process the Port-Royal community's struggle a century earlier against what one member of the family called "ecclesiastical despotism" was revived in memory through the publication of chronicles, memoirs, and correspondence pertaining to that struggle, much of which was written by and about members of the Arnauld family. Once restored to memory by these publications, the heroic resistance to ecclesiastical despotism of the Arnaulds and other members of the Port-Royal community served as an inspiration to those, including many eighteenth-century Jansenists, who came to regard the monarchy itself as despotic.

The history of the Arnauld family unfolds during a tumultuous period of French history. During the latter half of the sixteenth century, France was torn apart by the Wars of Religion, which greatly weakened the monarchy. When he became king in 1589, Henry IV brought an end to these wars and managed to restore a measure of peace and prosperity to the kingdom. The gradual increase in monarchical power begun under Henry continued under his son, Louis XIII (1610–1643), and grandson, Louis XIV (1643–1715). Unchecked by the violent civil war known as the Fronde, which took place during the early years of Louis XIV's reign, monarchical power, wielded first by Cardinal Mazarin and then by the King himself, expanded even further at the expense of the nobility, the Church, the Huguenots, and provincial and municipal governments during the course of the latter half of the seventeenth century. Monarchical absolutism became the fundamental constitutional principle during this period. The growing power of the king was a significant factor in the Arnaulds' rise to prominence.

The history of the Arnaulds is closely tied to the history of the Reformation. Arnaulds were to be found on both sides of the religious divide. However, the family's notoriety was primarily the result of the involvement of many of its members in activities related to the Counter Reformation—or Catholic reform movement, as I shall call it—which began to make its mark on France at the end of the Wars of Religion. Launched for the purpose of reforming and strengthening the Catholic Church throughout Europe, this movement launched in the sixteenth century produced significant divisions within the Catholic community, not only between those who favored reform and those who did not, but also among the reformers themselves. There were differences of opinion on such contentious theological issues as the relationship between divine grace and man's free will, and there were also jurisdictional conflicts between the regular and secular clergy, the episcopacy and the lower clergy, the episcopacy and the papacy, and the monarchy and the papacy. The French crown was jealous of what were known as its Gallican rights, that is to say, of the authority that it claimed for itself in making appointments to high ecclesiastical offices and in controlling the activities of the clergy. Staunchly supported by the French magistracy, the king had ever since the Middle Ages resisted any exercise of papal authority within the kingdom that did not have his approval. The monarchy continued to do so in the early modern period. The reforming efforts of Angélique Arnauld and other members of her family were often thwarted by these conflicts within the Catholic reform movement in France. Indeed it was the Arnaulds' involvement in the movement known as Jansenism, a movement committed to reforms based on certain theological principles and penitential practices, that inspired the antagonism of the Jesuits and other groups within the Church who were equally committed to reform, and eventually the disapproval of the papacy and the French crown.

The trials and tribulations of the Arnauld family were caused in large measure by the political, social, and religious changes that occurred over the course of three centuries, from the regency of Catherine de Medici to the reign of Louis XV. This collective biography dramatizes the extent to which the family as a unit was able to maintain its cohesiveness across religious divides and in the face of intense political pressures on individual members. The family was the basic social unit under the Old Regime, tied together by bonds of affection, obligations, loyalty, and material interests. Family considerations were often uppermost in the minds of individual members in determining a course of action. In the final analysis it was family loyalty, which took precedence over doctrinal differences or political concerns, that inspired the Arnaulds to stand fast against the combined authority of church and state.

The travails of conscience experienced by the Arnaulds as they found themselves in opposition to that authority created serious tensions within the family. In developing strategies, there were serious differences of opinion between the generations, among members of the same generation, and between the men and women of the family. Gender differences were particularly in evidence in determining the family's response to a given crisis. Among the Huguenots in the family, the men were especially vulnerable to the inclination to convert to Catholicism in order to satisfy their worldly ambitions. During the Jansenist crisis in the middle of the seventeenth century, the same inclination appears among some of the men in the family. In determining whether to reach an accommodation with the authorities of church and state, the opportunity to satisfy ambition was often a factor in the men's considerations. The women in the family, whether Huguenot or Jansenist, were often more loyal to their religious beliefs than were their male relatives.

Throughout the history of Western civilization, women had been the source of religious inspiration within the family. They established their identity as individuals in terms of their religious beliefs to a far greater extent than was the case among men, who were more inclined to identify themselves in terms of social status and political influence. For women, religious belief enhanced their status within the family, but their ability to influence their male relatives diminished as the men's opportunities for success in the world increased.

The history presented in these pages is of one family in particular and not of a family as representative of a group or social order. Nor is it intended to provide a window on the development of Jansenism in general. However, as a history of one family it takes issue with two works published since World War II that interpret Jansenism in light of the concerns of one group in particular whose aspirations were frustrated by the rising tide of monarchical absolutism. These are Lucien Goldmann's *Le Dieu caché* (1959) and Marc Fumaroli's *L'Age de l'éloquence: Rhétorique et "res literaria" de l'époque classique* (1980).[3]

Lucien Goldmann maintained that the Arnaulds and other Jansenists adopted a tragic vision, the essence of which was a pessimistic view of human nature and a God not readily accessible to those in need of his support, because they were members of a social group—the nobility of the robe—whose fortunes were in decline. In the middle of the seventeenth century these *officiers* found themselves adversely affected by a deteriorating economy and by the crown's inclination to rely on the services of *commissaires,* royal officials who served at the king's pleasure, rather than on the *officiers,* who, because they owned their offices, seemed inclined to place their own interests ahead of the king's. Their worldly position threatened, the nobility of the robe adopted that *mépris du monde* that became a basic tenet of Jansenism, which, to Goldmann's way of thinking, was as much a form of political protest as it was an expression of their religious ideals. While Goldmann was right to consider the political and social context in which the texts emanating from the Port-Royal community were written, his social analysis is flawed. As this study makes clear, the Arnaulds were themselves *commissaires,* who prided themselves on the fact that they served at the king's pleasure on the basis of their merits, and did not place their own interests ahead of those of the king. Indeed, as we shall see, there is a close connection between the *commissaire's* ideal of disinterested service to the crown and the Jansenist belief in the efficacy of a disinterested love of God.

In *L'Age de l'éloquence: Rhétorique et "res literaria" de l'époque classique,* Marc Fumaroli also considered Jansenism and the Arnaulds' involvement in it in a political and social context. As members of what he calls *"l'aristocratie gallicane,"* whose political influence manifested itself in the Parlement of Paris, the Arnaulds were steeped in a tradition of civic humanism dating back to the Roman Republic. Barristers such as Antoine Arnauld the Elder and his father-in-law, Simon Marion, used their oratorical skills to defend the integrity of the state against the imperial pretensions of the papacy, whose minions, the Jesuits, used their influence to undermine Gallican rights. However, under Richelieu the *parlementaires* found themselves confronted with an even greater danger—the absolutist inclinations of the crown—which threatened the civic principles to which they subscribed. Just as Cicero and other senators tried to defend the Roman Republic against the imperial pretensions of Caesar, so too did the "senators" in the Parlement resist, without success, the rising tide of absolutism.

Disillusioned with their inability to prevent Richelieu from tightening the crown's control over the kingdom, Antoine Arnauld's nephew Antoine Le Maistre and other barristers withdrew to Port-Royal. There Le Maistre and his family, whose members (male and female) had acquired greater prestige by the middle of the seventeenth century because of their association with Jansenism, abandoned their position within the political elite to become part of a spiritual elite instead. The Arnaulds' renowned eloquence, which they had once put to such good use in advancing *parlementaire* interests, was now put to use in support of religious ideals. In emphasizing the *parlementaire* resistance to papal and royal absolutism, Fumaroli overlooked the fact that Antoine Arnauld, the barrister, was outspoken in his support of the absolutist pretensions of the monarchy that he and his brothers served with such fervor. However, he is undoubtedly right in suggesting that Antoine Arnauld *fils* and his nephew Antoine Le Maistre, although they forsook the ranks of the barristers for the solitude of Port-Royal, nevertheless retained the *parlementaire* distaste for the imperial pretensions of the papacy. Port-Royal's resistance to papal absolutism inspired *parlementaires* in the eighteenth century, many of whom were Jansenist sympathizers, to resist what they regarded as the excessive use of royal power.

The Arnaulds' emergence from provincial obscurity during the latter half of the sixteenth century and their success in obtaining important commissions from the king that enabled them to become prominent figures in the new nobility are not unlike the rise of the families of other *grands serviteurs de l'état* during the same period. What made the family so extraordinary was the remarkable individuals, male and female, who belonged to it. Their emphasis on the spiritual integrity of the individual and on the heavy responsibility that each individual bears in determining the good life in Christian terms helped to shape their personalities. Both the Huguenot members of the family, who played important roles in the political and religious life of the kingdom during the reigns of Henry IV and Lous XIII, and the Jansenist members during the seventeenth century were influenced by the same rigorous Augustinian strain of piety that infused both Protestantism and Jansenism. Indeed it is not unreasonable to assume that the Arnaulds, as they involved themselves in the Catholic reform movement after 1609, were attracted to Augustinian penitential theology precisely because of the individualism inherent in it. It cannot be denied that the momentous political and cultural developments that affected France during the sixteenth and seventeenth centuries did much to shape the ideals and convictions of the Arnauld family. At the same time it must be said that the members of this remarkable family, by means of the strength of their own convictions, the most powerful determinant in their lives, helped shape the history of their time.

⟨~? THE HISTORIAN of the Arnauld family does not lack for sources. In addition to the several cartons of family papers contained in the Bibliothèque de l'Arsenal in Paris, there are important manuscript collections at the Bibliothèque Nationale and at the Bibliothèque de la Société de Port-Royal, only a few blocks from Port-Royal-de-Paris. The notarial records at the Archives Nationales are also useful, as are the smaller manuscript collections in the Bibliothèque Municipale of Troyes and in Utrecht in the Netherlands. There is also an abundance of published sources in the form of correspondence, memoirs, and journals written by several members of the family. The published correspondence of others, including Madame de Sévigné, a close friend of the family, is invaluable, as are the memoirs of the duc de Saint-Simon.

Adequate though these sources are in some respects, they are insufficient in others. We know a lot less about the earlier generations of the family, including that of the parents of Angélique the Reformer, because the French archives contain very little pertaining to them. What we know of them is based on what remains of the public record, on what others, such as Pierre de l'Estoile, had to say about them in their memoirs and correspondence, and what their descendants, for whom the sources are more abundant, wanted to have said about them. And the sources tell us relatively little about the Huguenot branches of the family. The history of the Arnaulds in the sixteenth century is more obscure than that of later generations of the family. However, the sources for the Arnaulds in the next century, while voluminous, are not without problems. The published sources, letters and memoirs alike, constitute attempts on the part of members of the family to present themselves, their relatives, or Port-Royal in the best light. For example, Robert Arnauld d'Andilly published his correspondence in 1645 in order to defend his integrity against public accusations of venality brought against him by political rivals. In his memoirs, a major source for the history of the Arnauld family, he gloried in the illustrious reputation of his ancestors and did not neglect his own. Andilly's account of his family's great deeds on the battlefield and in the king's service were written for the edification of his grandsons, for which reason nothing is said in that account that might diminish his family's accomplishments.

The accomplishments of Angélique Arnauld and other members of the family who contributed to the renown of Port-Royal were recorded by her niece, Angélique de Saint-Jean, to inspire future generations of nuns. It was she, together with her cousin, Antoine Le Maistre, who persuaded her reluctant aunt to write her autobiography, and it was she who assembled the first-hand accounts of the reforming activities of the nuns in the *mémoires* and *relations* that constitute the basic source materials for the history of Port-Royal. As historian Ellen Weaver points out, Angélique de Saint-Jean was essentially a mythographer and not a historiographer.[4] These accounts of the reforming efforts of the elder Angélique in the face of determined opposition and of the heroic resistance of her sister, nieces, and other nuns to the unjust demands of the Archbishop of Paris were intended to inculcate in the hearts and minds of their spiritual descendants a profound respect for the Christian virtues of these women. The "mythic power" of these chronicles, published against the wishes of Angélique de Saint-Jean and her colleagues, sustained this image of the Port-Royal community long after its demise.

Because the published (and unpublished) sources for a history of the Arnaulds, to say nothing of their portraits painted by Philippe de Champaigne and others, were intended to be inspirational, the historian must not mistake these hagiographic representations for reality. He must also treat the deprecatory writings of critics and opponents with caution. The occasional unguarded references to self and to others in the family, and the affectionate but disarmingly frank references to family members by loyal friends such as the *solitaire*, Nicolas Fontaine, and Madame de Sévigné, are of help in presenting a more balanced account of men and women who lived over three centuries ago in a culture and environment so different from our own.

2

The Early Generations

I N H I S M E M O I R S, written in 1667 for the purpose of inspiring his grandsons with illustrious examples provided from the history of his family, Robert Arnauld d'Andilly asserted that the Arnaulds
were of noble stock whose lineage could be traced back to twelfth-cen-
tury Provence. In 1195, according to this account, Bertrand Arnauld
was among the noblemen who attended a ceremony at which the comte
de Forcalquier became the vassal of the comte de Toulouse. A branch of
the family subsequently settled in the Auvergne where, in 1340, one
Gracieux Arnauld accompanied Philip VI into battle. Andilly maintained that he was directly descended from these heroic knights, who
provided exemplary service to their liege lords at court as well as on
the battlefield. His claim to an ancient noble heritage is supported by
a genealogy to be found in one of the early histories of Port-Royal,
Pierre Guilbert's *Mémoires historiques et chronologiques*, published in
1758, which traces the Arnauld's noble lineage as far back as the tenth
century.[1] Unfortunately the substantial genealogical records housed in
the Bibliothèque Nationale do not substantiate these claims. These
records, developed in the seventeenth and eighteenth centuries to vali-
date claims to noble status, trace the family tree only as far back as
Michel, squire, who during the latter half of the fifteenth century
served as a bailiff in the barony of Hermant, not far from Riom, in the
Auvergne.[2] Nothing else is known about Michel other than that he had

at least one son, Henri, the first of Robert d'Andilly's ancestors about whom we know anything at all.

When Henri was born and when he died are unknown. He apparently succeeded to his father's judicial office in the barony of Hermant and held a degree in law. Henri may well have enhanced his wealth substantially in his capacity as manager of the finances of the duc de Beaujeu. According to one account, he provided valuable assistance to the notorious constable Charles de Bourbon, governor of Hermant, in 1523. In disfavor with King Francis I and attempting to escape arrest, the constable arrived at Henri's residence and asked for help in leaving the kingdom. Henri, it is said, suggested the clever ploy of setting the shoes of horses in the constable's company in reverse, thereby misleading the king's troops that were in hot pursuit. Whether or not this story is true, Charles de Bourbon was able to escape to Franche-Comté, then part of the Holy Roman Empire, and not long afterward he offered his service to Francis's mortal enemy, the emperor Charles V. The enraged French king confiscated the constable's lands. Those who helped Charles de Bourbon, including Henri, were brought to trial. Henri Arnauld's property was confiscated but later restored.[3]

Having acquired status and wealth at the provincial level, Henri was in a position to make himself known in the world beyond the Auvergne. Patronage at the king's court was typically secured by favors, usually in the form of loans, to important personages with the right connections at court. There is some indication in the records that the crown was satisfied with unspecified services, presumably a loan offered by Henri, which may explain the restoration of his property. In any event his offspring must have learned from his example that there was ample opportunity in sixteenth-century France for those who, fiercely ambitious, with sufficient resources at their disposal and advantageous contacts, sought to enhance their status and wealth.

In 1480 Henri married Catherine Barjot de Collonges, who bore him six children: four sons and two daughters. One son, Jean, known as the Commandeur d'Hermant, served in the military and died without children in 1542. Another son, Gilbert, was a royal finance official (*controlleur général*) in the Auvergne, and a third son, Guichard, was a canon in the cathedral of Hermant. Henri's offspring remained in the region in which they had been brought up, and they all seem to have married into families of the same social background. The three sons and the one son-in-law who appear in the records held respectable positions in the military, the magistracy, and in the church, but at the provincial level.[4] Nothing more is known of them or of their children.

The records permit us to conclude, however, that the Arnaulds had become what George Huppert has called "bourgeois gentilhommes," an elite social group that had risen above the level of merchant-bourgeois but had not yet attained the status of nobility, a group whose political and social influence increased substantially during the latter half of the sixteenth century as many of its members abandoned the provinces to seek their fortune in Paris. Their rise was greatly facilitated by the acquisition of wealth, often at the expense of peasants and noble families heavily in debt to whom they loaned money and from whom they seized land when repayment of the debt was not forthcoming. The Arnaulds and other families in similar circumstances were prepared to be ruthless as well as diligent in satisfying their ambitions.[5]

⤻ THE MEMBER OF the Arnauld family who made the crucial move from the Auvergne to Paris was Antoine, Henri's second son. Born around 1490, Antoine began his career as a lawyer attached to one of the regional courts of law at Riom, courts that dealt primarily with tax matters. For a man acting in this capacity, the opportunity to satisfy the crown's financial needs while at the same time enhancing his own resources was readily available to one who was prepared to take advantage of his position. Among the family papers is a document attesting to the king's satisfaction with the services rendered by Antoine as his attorney at Riom.[6]

By 1547 Antoine was in Paris, where he continued to represent the crown's fiscal interests before the Parlement. How he got to Paris and under whose auspices is unknown. According to his grandson Arnauld d'Andilly, Antoine was not only a skilled barrister but also a military leader, commanding a company of cavalry during the early stages of the religious wars. Although Andilly preferred to believe that his grandfather had been taken into the king's service because of his military prowess, the mark of a true noble, it is more likely that Antoine's ability to provide financial services to a government badly in need of money brought him to the attention of the regent, Catherine de Medici. Widow of Henry II, who was killed in a jousting accident in 1559, Catherine acted as regent for her two young and feeble sons, Francis II

(1559–1560) and Charles IX (1560–1574). Antoine's appointment to the lucrative position of *procureur général* to the queen mother was undoubtedly a reward for his success as a financial entrepreneur. So useful did he thereafter become to the queen that she had him rescued by a company of soldiers from a mob besieging his house in Paris during the massacre of Saint Bartholemew's Day in 1572.[7]

Antoine's life had been threatened because he was a Protestant and therefore, like others of his faith, the target of a popular uprising on Saint Bartholemew's Day in the summer of 1572 that claimed the lives of three thousand people in Paris alone and many more throughout the kingdom. Family papers indicate that Antoine had become a Huguenot sometime before 1559, but they say nothing about what led to his conversion or whether he was alone among his brothers and sisters in abandoning Catholicism.

Shortly after his rescue, Antoine returned to the faith of his ancestors and in 1577 received the appointment of *auditeur des comptes* (auditor of accounts) in (court of law known as) the *Chambre des Comptes*. It seems likely that a mutually beneficial arrangement had been made whereby he was assured of continued preferment in return for his conversion. The new office was venal and brought with it the status of nobility. It provided Antoine with the opportunity not only to learn more about royal finances but also about the wealth and status of other prominent officials. As a sovereign court the *Chambre des Comptes* had the right to audit the accounts of these officials and to determine the validity of claims for exemption from taxation. Such knowledge was power in the hands of those who had access to it and lucrative as well. The substantial awards received by Antoine in the king's service were further enhanced by opportunities to develop important social connections that would benefit both him and his children.

Over the course of his long career, Antoine managed to acquire a substantial amount of property. In 1540 he purchased the *seigneurie* (noble estate) of La Mothe, not far from Hermant where he had been brought up, and from that time on he bore the name La Mothe-Arnauld. In 1575, shortly before acquiring the office of *auditeur des comptes* over which he had proprietary rights, he purchased a second *seigneurie*, Villeneuve-Pollerande, also in the Auvergne. His house in Paris was located in a fashionable neighborhood, the Faubourg Saint-Germain. It was later sold by La Mothe-Arnauld's children in 1614 to the second

Medici queen mother, Marie, for thirty thousand pounds. The queen had it demolished in order to build the Luxembourg Palace on the site where the Medici Fountain now stands.[8] We do not know the value of La Mothe-Arnauld's other property. Nor do we know much about the income he received from various offices and financial transactions other than the fact that some of it was invested in *rentes* of various kinds, including the salt tax *(gabelle)*, the *hôtel de ville* (what would today be called municipal bonds), and indirect taxes *(aides)*, investments that were typical of persons of his rank in society.

La Mothe-Arnauld was married twice, first to Marguerite du Bourg and second to Anne Forget. Both came from prominent Auvergnat families, members of which, like La Mothe-Arnauld, moved to Paris and served the crown in various capacities. Marguerite La Mothe-Arnauld was a Huguenot, whose cousin Anne, a *conseiller* at the Parlement of Paris, was burned at the stake in 1559 for having protested against Henry II's persecution of Protestants.[9] Anne La Mothe-Arnauld was also a member of a prominent Huguenot family. She remained true to her faith after her husband converted.

One child named Jean was born of the first marriage, but the second marriage produced thirteen children: nine sons and four daughters. All survived childhood, and all were baptized in the Protestant faith. When La Mothe-Arnauld again became a Catholic, his two oldest sons by his second wife, Jean and Antoine, then twelve years old, also converted, as did a younger son named David. Because La Mothe-Arnauld intended for his son Antoine to follow him in his career, he undoubtedly thought it politic, especially after the Saint Bartholemew's Day massacre, for the boy to adhere to the religion of the monarchy. However, La Mothe-Arnauld's son by his first wife and most of his other children remained Huguenots when their father converted, including two sons born before 1572, four sons born after that year, and all four daughters.

The reasons for this schism in the family, which lasted throughout the seventeenth century, are obscure. Jean, the oldest son about whom little is known, may have decided to remain loyal to his mother's faith because her family had produced a Huguenot martyr; or, having remained in the Auvergne, perhaps he saw no need to become a Catholic. The rest of La Mothe-Arnauld's children born before the massacre were all too young to make such decisions on their own. Why were they allowed to remain Protestants? The mother of these children, Anne, who remained a Huguenot despite the massacre, could have persuaded her husband, whose sympathy may well have remained with the Huguenots, to allow most of his children to remain Protestant. Conversions and reconversions with various degrees of sincerity were common in this period. One of Anne's granddaughters resisted similar pressure from her husband to convert a half a century later. As the story of the Arnaulds will bear out, a woman's conscience appears to have been particularly resistant to such pressure.[10]

Several of La Mothe-Arnauld's children remained staunch Protestants throughout their lives. Isaac (d. 1617), his second son by Anne, helped support the Huguenot temple at Charenton outside Paris, and he wrote several essays toward the end of his life that reflect a deep commitment to Calvinist doctrine. His younger brother Louis was also noted for his efforts to promote the faith until his death in 1645. It was said of Louis's sisters that they braved even the coldest weather to make the trip from Paris to Charenton every Sunday to attend services. One of them, Jeanne, a spinster with whom Louis lived, was as distrustful of Catholics as she was ardent in her Protestant beliefs. Born around 1583, she too was active in the Huguenot congregation at Charenton. Especially proud of a bed that she had made with her own hands, Jeanne suggested to a friend of hers who knew Richelieu quite well that the Cardinal might like to have the bed installed in his house. On second thought she withdrew the suggestion because as she said: "I am appalled at the thought that a priest might sleep in a bed made by a Huguenot maiden." Conscious of her virginity even at the age of sixty, she made it clear that she was prepared to defend it with a knife if necessary when, in 1643, it was rumored that there was to be a massacre of Huguenots at Charenton.[11]

Other Huguenot members of the family were less committed to the faith. Jeanne's older brother David, who became a Catholic after Saint Bartholomew's Day, made a visit to Geneva and promptly reconverted to Protestantism. Determined nevertheless to honor a vow he had made as a youth to make a pilgrimage to Rome in the year 1600, he did so and was somehow persuaded to return once more to the Catholic fold. By the second decade of the seventeenth century, it had become increasingly difficult for Huguenots to obtain important positions in the king's service, especially in the army. La Mothe-Arnauld's youngest son, Pierre (1577–1624), decided in 1622, two years before his death in battle, to adopt his father's faith in order to facilitate promotion. Pierre's nephew Isaac, the son of one of the pillars of the Charenton congregation, also an army officer, made a similar decision, although both his sisters remained Huguenots throughout their lives. One of these sisters, Madeleine, married a Huguenot who remained loyal to the faith. After the revocation of the Edict of Nantes in 1685, their son, the great grandson of La Mothe-Arnauld, went into exile in England along with thousands of other Huguenots who chose to abandon their native land in order to preserve their religious heritage.[12] Nothing more is known of Madeleine or her offspring. Neither she or her children remained in contact with the branches of the Arnauld family whose records have survived.

The second daughter of Isaac, Anne, married Manassès de Pas, scion of a prominent Huguenot family. De Pas's grandfather, Jean, sieur de Feuquières, had been a man of considerable political ambition. At some point during the reign of Henry II he became attracted to Protestantism, but hesitated to convert, fearing that in so doing he would be sacrificing his career in the king's service. According to his wife, who, after her husband's death, married the Huguenot leader Philippe Duplessis-Mornay: "He felt himself on the road to advancement in the court and on the point of acquiring honors and wealth which he could never hope to possess if he made confession of the truth." Nevertheless after meditating on the passage in the second psalm in which it is said that "kings and princes more often than not leagued themselves against God and against Christ his beloved King," de Pas decided to convert. Serving the Protestant cause for the rest of his life, he became involved in the conspiracy of Amboise in 1560 and later served in the Huguenot army during the Wars of Religion.[13]

Jean de Pas's grandson, Manassès, apparently suffered no such scruples. When confronted with the choice between his faith and his career in the military, he returned to the Catholic fold early in the reign of Louis XIII and was rewarded for this decision with promotions to the rank of *maréchale du camp* in 1625 and lieutenant general in 1636. For his loyal and honorable service Louis XIII bestowed on him the title of Marquis de Feuquières. Under pressure from their father, the marquis' three sons also converted to Catholicism, although not without some resistance. Writing to his oldest son, Isaac, named for his maternal grandfather, Manassès expressed satisfaction that the boy had finally decided to make a public profession of his conversion in response to his having been appointed to the rank of *maître de camp:* "It scarcely befits someone of your age to live with God incognito, especially after having received a *charge* worthy of a man of fifty, not a child of eight, full of timidity and childish nonsense."[14]

The two younger sons of the marquis de Feuquières, François and Charles, were more resistant to conversion than their older brother. Placed in a Catholic school to assure their conversion, both boys complained to their mother that they were being ill treated by their schoolmasters for their refusal to conform. At the behest of their father, then serving with the French army on the Rhine, their uncle, Isaac, himself a recent convert to Catholicism, placed François and Charles in the Collège de Navarre, an institution that had been recommended by their maternal uncle, Robert Arnauld d'Andilly. "We are being punished by our teacher," wrote François to his mother in May 1634, "who keeps threatening to have us whipped." Even though they were told that they would be placed in the hands of the Jesuits, the boys remained resolute in their refusal to abandon their faith. In another letter to his mother, François reported that he and his brother had received a letter from their father insisting on obedience to his wishes. "I would like to be able to obey him in everything that he asks of me, but we are unable to do anything against the dictates of our conscience. We find our religion to be the best."[15]

The strong commitment of Feuquières' sons to Protestantism was undoubtedly the fruit of their mother's spiritual influence within the family. Austere in character as well as in appearance, the former Anne Arnauld was as unyielding in her resistance to the entreaties of her husband to convert to Catholicism as she was to those who begged her to leave Verdun, where her husband was military governor, when it was under siege by imperial troops in 1640. Her commitment to the faith in which she had been brought up may have been strengthened by her paternal grandmother, after whom she was named. Anne had refused to join the Catholic Church when her husband, La Mothe-Arnauld, did so after the Saint Bartholemew's Day massacre. The marquise de Feuquières' refusal to go against the dictates of her conscience foreshadowed a similar refusal on the part of her nieces, who, as nuns of Port-Royal, were to experience even stronger pressures to alter their religious convictions later in the century. As devoted as she was to the faith of her father, Isaac, she was equally proud of his family name, always signing herself *Arnauld de Feuquières*.[16]

The religious schism that divided the Arnauld family in no way affected the bonds of loyalty and affection that held families together in the early modern period. To be sure, some members regretted the misguided beliefs of their relatives on the other side of the divide. In 1640, Henry Arnauld, the future bishop of Anger, told an acquaintance that he was returning to Paris from a sojourn in the country because his cousin, the marquise de Feuquières, was dying. "I love her like a sister," he wrote, "and it is a great shame that she remains so obstinate in her religious belief."[17] Some members of the family went so far as to try to convert others to their persuasion without affecting family relations. Angélique the Reformer, for example, gave serious thought before her conversion to the possibility of escaping the convent of Port-Royal, where she had been placed against her will by her family. She was encouraged to abandon not only the convent but her faith by two unnamed Huguenot aunts, one of whom may have been Jeanne.[18] Angélique's father, Antoine, a Catholic since the age of twelve, placed his eldest son, Robert, under the tutelage of his Huguenot brother Isaac, an *intendant* in Henry IV's *conseil des finances*. When in 1625 a special *chambre de justice* established to investigate corruption among the *gens de finances* imposed a tax of forty thousand pounds on Robert's Huguenot uncle Louis, Robert successfully intervened with Richelieu to have the tax withdrawn.[19]

With the death of the marquise de Feuquières in 1640, Protestantism no longer remained a prominent feature within the Arnauld family. Although several of La Mothe-Arnauld's children remained Huguenots, none of his grandchildren who bore the name of Arnauld were of that faith, nor after the marquise's death were any of her offspring. For those with the ambition to succeed in the king's service, conversion to Catholicism seemed essential to their prospects. Those women like Anne de Feuquières who remained steadfast in their faith were unable to prevent their male relatives from adopting their sovereign's faith in the hope of retaining his continued favor.

IF THE RELIGIOUS schism in the Arnauld family was nothing out of the ordinary, the long lives of many of its members were somewhat unusual. La Mothe-Arnauld is said to have lived close to a hundred years and was buried in a chapel that he had endowed in the church of Saint-Sulpice. At least two of his children, Louis and Jeanne, lived into their seventies. Whereas Louis's and Jeanne's older brother, Antoine, died at the age of fifty-nine, three of his children, Angélique, Agnès, and Antoine, lived into their seventies. Antoine's oldest son, Robert, lived to be eighty-five, and his second son, Henry, died at the age of ninety-five. Thirteen of La Mothe-Arnauld's children survived childhood. His son Antoine had twenty-one children, ten of whom reached adulthood, including Robert, ten of whose children survived childhood.

Providing for a large family constituted a burden on material resources. Although La Mothe-Arnauld undoubtedly accumulated a considerable amount of wealth in the form of land, urban property, and *rentes* of one sort or another, as well as income from offices, what he was able to leave his children was not entirely adequate. All four of his daughters being Huguenots, he could not place them in convents as his son Antoine did with his "superfluous" daughters, thereby avoiding the need to provide them with adequate dowries. Three of them married, but little is known about their husbands other than that at least one of them, the baron de Chanzillon, a devout Huguenot, was noble. According to Tallement des Réaux, Chanzillon and his wife, Judith, lived simply, which may indicate a lack of means to live nobly. Judith's sister Jeanne did not marry, perhaps because of the lack of a dowry. Her modest means possibly accounts for the fact that she continued to wear clothes that were in fashion during her childhood all her life, not being able to afford a more stylish wardrobe.[20] However, a more likely explanation for the austere and simple style of living preferred by Judith, Jeanne, and, indeed, Anne, the marquise de Feuquières, was a distaste for conspicuous consumption characteristic of the families of their social background throughout the seventeenth century.

La Mothe-Arnauld's oldest son by his second marriage, Jean, inherited the two *seigneuries* in the Auvergne. His nephew Robert notes in his memoirs that Jean travelled extensively as a young man, particularly in the Levant, and that he had "so much zeal for the king's service that Henry III offered to appoint him secretary of state at Blois after the death of the duc de Guise."[21] Whether or not such an offer was made, Jean did acquire the lucrative office of *trésorier de France* for the area around Riom and he also later distinguished himself as a military leader during the early years of the reign of Henry IV. The Auvergne was the scene of constant strife during the Wars of Religion. Troops of the Catholic League destroyed the *seigneurie* of La Mothe, burning its chateau, while its owner was campaigning elsewhere. In 1590 Jean succeeded in weakening the League's hold on the Auvergne by raising the siege of Issoire on the same day that Henry IV won the battle of Ivry and began the siege of Paris, the success of which was to assure him of control over the entire kingdom. Two years later Jean de La Mothe-Arnauld was killed in battle and, according to his nephew, who was never reluctant to proclaim the honor and glory, sometimes imaginary, achieved by his ancestors, was given a hero's burial at Clermont-Ferrand. Married to the daughter of an Auvergnat noble, Jean had only one child, a daughter.

La Mothe's second son by his second wife, Antoine, who along with his father became a Catholic after the Saint Bartholomew's Day massacre, inherited his father's office of *auditeur des comptes* and succeeded to his position as *procureur général* to Catherine de Medici until her death in 1589. Although Antoine and his siblings inherited their father's house in the Faubourg Saint-Germain, Antoine chose to live instead in the house of his father-in-law, Simon Marion, after his marriage in the year of his father's death. Born in Riom in 1560, Antoine spent most of his life in Paris, where he began his education at the recently established College de Navarre. There he encountered a curriculum that was heavily influenced by the classical ideals of the Renaissance. It may be that he continued his education at the University of Bourges under Jacques Cujas, whose studies had done much to revive Roman law.[22] His interest in classical culture was undoubtedly what enabled him to persuade his father to provide him with a generous sum of money to cover the expenses of a trip to Italy.

Antoine's rhetorical skills owed much to his humanist training. He acquired the reputation of being the Cicero of his day because of his command of language and his facility with classical analogies. As Marc Fumaroli has noted, a powerful orator in the "age of eloquence" commanded great respect in political circles. Eloquence was synonymous with wit and intellect, both qualities appreciated by monarchs of the Renaissance.[23] The kings served by Antoine Arnauld saw to it that he was rewarded for his talents. On the basis of these talents, inherited by his progeny, the Arnaulds became known as *la famille éloquente*.

In 1589 Antoine Arnauld sold his office of *auditeur des comptes* in order to devote himself entirely to the practice of law. Almost a century later, his son Robert, in preparing his memoirs, decided to omit any reference to this office of his father, fearing that the questionable financial practices associated with that office might tarnish the family's reputation. Once embarked on a career in the law, Antoine discovered that he was able to earn far more money in this way than from the *gages* (salary) attached to the office acquired by his father.[24] La Mothe-Arnauld's death in 1585 had left Antoine with the responsibility of supporting, in addition to his wife and children, several of his siblings who had not yet reached adulthood. Among his clients were prominent nobles such as the duc de Guise, who in 1611 was involved in litigation with the prince de Condé. He also took on more humble clients, however, among whom was a butcher who was accused of cutting the throat of a young man and then burning him in an oven.[25]

Antoine's oratorical skills made him the ideal person to make the customary formal presentations of the great officers of the kingdom—the dukes and peers, the marshals, constables, and admirals—before the Parlement of Paris. According to his eldest son, Antoine's speeches on these occasions "were of a demonstrative and sublime genre which must contain nothing but the highest, the most illustrious and the most noble [ideals]. To be successful, the speech must be a masterpiece of the sort made in honor of Trajan by Pliny, so well known in antiquity." Antoine enjoyed his practice so much and was so successful at it, both in terms of what he earned and the social contacts that he made, that he turned down lucrative offices such as the first presidency of the Parlement of Provence. Furthermore, we are told by his son Arnauld d'Andilly that he preferred to be his own man, unbeholden to anyone. Andilly claimed that his father was offered his choice of any office or commission he wanted by an unnamed minister of Marie de Medici, regent of France from 1611 to 1617. Arnauld declined the offer, asserting that "I wish to be what I am because I have no desire to pay court to anyone."[26]

Antoine's decision to remain a barrister did not prevent him from serving the crown in other ways. He received several pensions from Henry IV, including one for four hundred *écus* as a reward for persuading the municipal government of Paris to raise a regiment of infantry to bolster the royal army in 1597. But what Antoine's eldest son called "his passionate desire to serve king Henry the Great and his state" most often found expression in various pamphlets written in support of particular policies.

A significant political issue during the reign of Henry IV was whether the Jesuits should be permitted to remain in the kingdom. A powerful force within the Catholic Reformation, the Society of Jesus was committed to turning back the Protestant tide that threatened much of Europe. During the Wars of Religion, the Jesuits supported the Catholic League and used what influence they had to prevent the head of the Huguenot forces, the future Henry IV, from becoming king. Some Jesuit theologians in the sixteenth century, most notably Juan Mariana, went so far as to justify tyrannicide in instances where a heretical (Protestant) ruler had usurped the authority that rightfully belonged to a Catholic king. When Henry III was assassinated by a Dominican in 1589, many believed that the Jesuits were primarily responsible for the act that, ironically, enabled the leader of the Huguenots to succeed to the throne.

During the reign of Henry IV there were those in high places, particularly in the sovereign courts *(parlements)*, who believed that because the Jesuits constituted a clear and present danger to the crown, they ought to be expelled from France. Indeed it was the Jesuit issue that enabled the magistracy to increase its own influence in the political life of the kingdom. Among the more outspoken opponents of the Jesuit order was Antoine Arnauld, who took every opportunity to denounce the disciples of Ignatius Loyola in the most vituperative and flamboyant terms. In 1589, when the king's troops were in danger of being overwhelmed by the Catholic League in alliance with Philip II of Spain and when Paris was in the hands of a municipal government loyal to the League, Arnauld wrote a pamphlet entitled *Antiespagnol, autrement les philippiques touchant les menées et ruses de Philippe Roy d'Espagne pour envahir la Couronne de France* (Anti-Spain, or a Philippic conerning the Intrigues and Utilized by Philip, King of Spain, to sieze the Crown of France) in which he accused the Jesuits of being spies for Spain and of doing all in their power to advance the interests of Philip II. The tone of *Antiespagnol* was so vehement that its author was forced to flee Paris and to establish a temporary residence at Tours. Shortly after an unsuccessful attempt on the life of Henry IV in 1593, Arnauld, on behalf of the university, a bastion of anti-Jesuit sentiment, again demanded the expulsion of the Jesuits. Appealing to the spirit of Henry III, who had been assassinated a few years earlier, Arnauld asked for the late king's divine assistance

> in this cause, and with your bloody shirt continually before my eyes, give me the strength and the vigor to convince your subjects of the grief, the hatred and the indignation that they must feel toward the Jesuits . . . What tongue, what voice is adequate to describe the secret meetings, the conspiracies even more horrible than those of the Bacchi, more dangerous than those of Cataline, that are taking place at [the Jesuit] college in the rue Saint-Jacques and in their church in the rue Saint-Antoine![27]

Grateful for Arnauld's efforts against the Society, which the university regarded as a serious threat to its own rights and privileges, the faculty presented an *acte de reconnaissance envers Monsieur Arnauld* for his having defended the university with such zeal and eloquence: "The University feels itself obliged in return to render with equal zeal such services and duties to [him], his children and all his descendants as are to be expected from a good client to a faithful attorney and to undertake to defend at all times their honor, their goods and their reputation."[28] How ironic this gesture appears in light of the future expulsion of Arnauld's youngest son from the university's faculty in 1655! The king himself was somewhat less impressed with the barrister's endeavor and declined to move against the order until after a second attempt was made on his life in 1595.

The Jesuit issue became even more inflammatory after the assassination of Henry IV in 1610. Antoine Arnauld played a conspicuous role in preparing for the meeting of the Estates General convened in 1614 by the regent, Marie de Medici, and her ministers to deal with various matters of concern to the government. He was chiefly responsible for drawing up an article for the representatives of the Third Estate in Paris that called on the king to declare in the assembly of his estates "as a Fundamental Law of the Kingdom, which shall be inviolable and known to all: that since he is known to be sovereign in his state, holding his crown from God alone, that there is no power on earth whatever, spiritual or temporal, which has any authority over his kingdom, to take away the sacred nature of our kings, to dispense [or absolve] their subjects of the fidelity and obedience which they owe him for any cause or pretext whatsoever. That all subjects, of whatever quality or condition they might be, shall hold this Law to be holy and true as conforming to the word of God, without distinction, equivocation or any limitation."[29]

By describing monarchical power in absolute terms, Arnauld, who like other *parlementaires* believed that the Jesuits were primarily responsible for the late king's assassination, intended to refute the arguments of some, though by no means all, theologians of the Order that the authority of the king was conditional on his commitment to serve the interests of the Catholic Church. The article drawn up by Arnauld was not adopted because of the queen's opposition to it. She and her ministers were trying to reach an accommodation with powerful interests within the kingdom still sympathetic to the ideals of the Catholic League. They regarded the article as too divisive.

Although not endorsed by the Estates General, the spirit of the article, which provides as good a definition of monarchical absolutism as any, survived. It was in the terms embodied in the article that Richelieu and Louis XIV understood the nature of monarchical authority. Royal officials such as Antoine Arnauld and his brothers devoted their careers to strengthening the authority of the crown. The article also constituted a strong assertion of Gallican rights, that is to say, the right of the king and his government to resist any unwarranted interference of the papacy in the internal affairs of France. The quarrel between Gallicans and ultramontanists in the early seventeenth century, an outgrowth of the struggle between the Catholic League and the *politiques* or *bon francais* during the Wars of Religion, was to endure long after the *ancien régime* came to an end. As inheritors of the *politique* ideals adhered to by their ancestors, Antoine Arnauld and his brothers during their years of service to Henry IV and Louis XIII dedicated themselves to sustaining those Gallican rights that were later invoked by their descendants to ward off papal denunciations of their "Jansenist" ideals, and which in the eighteenth century were turned against the absolutist monarchy.

The relatively meager resources inherited by Antoine Arnauld in 1585 were amplified by his earnings and his marriage to Catherine, the only daughter of Simon Marion, baron de Druy, *"première baronnie du Nivernois"* and *avocat général au Parlement de Paris.* Like La Mothe-Arnauld, Marion made the transition from fiscal service at the provincial level to the higher level of the king's service, having acquired the resources to do so by the same means. He began his career in the service of the governor general of the region around Nevers and then moved to Paris, where Catherine de Medici appointed him *avocat général*. For his devotion "to the king's rights, the public liberty and the honor of the kingdom," Simon was elevated to noble status in 1583. Like his son-in-law, he was noted for his eloquence, which he put to good use as a barrister and occasionally in his own behalf. Pierre de l'Estoile reports that he was a bit too vociferous in his plea against the excessive burden of the *gabelle* (salt tax) in the presence of Henry III. The king became so annoyed that he had Marion placed in the Bastille for a brief period.[30] Out of favor only a short time, Marion went on to serve Henry IV and his minister Sully in various capacities and was rewarded by having his granddaughter, Angélique Arnauld, nominated as abbess of the convent of Port-Royal.[31]

There are various accounts of Antoine Arnauld's wooing of Catherine Marion. According to his son Robert, Catherine's father was so impressed by Antoine's oratorical skills that he begged him to take his daughter. On the other hand, Pierre Guilbert, an eighteenth-century chronicler of Port-Royal with access to family documents, maintains that in fact it was Arnauld who was so taken with Catherine that he asked her father's permission to marry her when she was only eleven, a request that was denied.[32] What seems clear is that to Antoine Arnauld the advantages of marrying Catherine outweighed the one disadvantage—her age—whereas to Marion, Arnauld's limited resources, not the age of his daughter, appeared to be a significant obstacle to the marriage. Simon eventually agreed to the union. Undoubtedly he was impressed with his son-in-law's potential to succeed in a career in which he himself excelled.

According to the terms of the marriage contract, Antoine Arnauld provided 24,000 pounds, a sum that he drew in part from the sale of his office of auditor in the *Chambre des Comptes*. His wife brought to the marriage 5000 pounds and 833 pounds a year in the form of *rentes*.[33] The contract stipulated that the couple would inherit Marion's *seigneurie* of Andilly and his town house in the rue de la Verrerie, in the parish of Saint-Merry, after Simon's death. This old quarter between the Louvre to the west and the Marais to the east had in the sixteenth century become the preferred residential area for the nobility of the robe. Antoine further benefitted from the Marion connection because, according to his son Robert, it helped him expand his network of friends and potential patrons beyond the provincial base on which his forebears had relied for advancement.[34] After the marriage the young couple became part of Simon Marion's household in the rue de la Verrerie, where most of their children were born and brought up.

Although Antoine Arnauld's eloquence and oratorical skills gave him his reputation and earned for him a wife and a successful career at the bar, they also on occasion brought him some embarrassment. One of his better known cases involved a dispute between a nobleman and a Genoese merchant over a shipment of goods. During the trial, in one of those flights of oratory that made his pleas so noteworthy, Arnauld not only recounted the misdeeds of the merchant but used the occasion to castigate Genoa for all the hostile actions taken against France since the fifteenth century. Hoping to make Arnauld look foolish, the merchant asked the court what the Republic of Genoa had to do with his money. Finding himself in the unusual predicament of being at a loss for words, Arnauld was unable to respond.[35] Excesses of this sort were duly noted by Pierre de l'Estoile, who described Arnauld's diatribes against the Jesuits as "violent in every respect, for he called the Jesuits 'thieves, corruptors of youth, regicides, conspirators against the state, the plague of republics and disturbers of the peace.' In short he treated them as if they deserved not only to be chased from Paris, from the court and from the kingdom, but thrashed and exterminated from the face of the earth . . . If his address had only been more moderate, less passionate and under control as are most presentations of this sort, it might have been better received by those who do not like the Jesuits and who wish that all of them went to the farthest ends of the earth to convert the heathen."[36] Antoine Arnauld's vituperative attacks undoubtedly contributed to the enmity that existed between the Society of Jesus and the Arnauld family, a sentiment that was to have important consequences for the future.

After the death of his father, Antoine Arnauld assumed responsibility for his younger siblings as well as for his wife and children. He appears to have been successful in launching his brothers in promising careers and in marrying off all but one of his sisters. Three of Antoine's brothers, Benjamin, Ponce, and Pierre, took up careers in the military. Two were killed in battle, Benjamin in 1589 and Ponce a few years later. Pierre, La Mothe-Arnauld's youngest child, began his career as a *conseiller* attached to the *Cour des comptes*, but after Henry IV's death he joined the military as a *maître de camp* and fought in several campaigns during the civil wars that occurred early in the reign of Louis XIII.[37] Valiant according to his nephew Robert, who in his memoirs described his heroic feats in some detail; vain and rather foolish, according to Tallement des Réaux, Pierre died shortly after a siege of the Huguenot stronghold La Rochelle in 1624.

Four of Antoine Arnauld's younger brothers became lawyers, and like Antoine built up a private practice in the early years of their careers. When Sully, a Huguenot, became *surintendant des finances* in 1598, he placed the Arnauld brothers in positions of considerable responsibility in the king's fiscal administration. Although Antoine did not join them, he served as Sully's lawyer, and in 1601, when Sully was presented to the Parlement in his capacity as *grand maître de l'artillerie*, he made the presentation, dwelling at some length on the history of artillery as well as on his client's distinguished genealogy. It was the Arnaulds' good fortune to establish a solid connection with the second most powerful man in France at the time when he and his master, Henry IV, were devoting their efforts to refurbishing the power and influence of the monarchy in the aftermath of the Wars of Religion. The Arnaulds may have been brought to Sully's attention by a cousin of their mother, Pierre Forget de Fresne, Sully's secretary and a *conseiller d'état* in the *conseil des finances*. Forget de Fresne was also one of the authors of the Edict of Nantes, which extended to the Huguenots certain rights and privileges and created, at least during the reign of Henry IV, a more tolerant religious atmosphere that facilitated the advancement of the Arnauld brothers. Sully did not care to what faith his creatures adhered as long as they served him loyally and capably.

The best known of the Arnauld brothers serving under Sully was Isaac, La Mothe-Arnauld's second son. Born in 1566, Isaac became a barrister and as *avocat au Parlement de Paris* acquired a reputation for eloquence and probity. In 1602 Isaac resigned from the bar, protesting the government's decision to tax lawyers' *gages* and to publicize their fees,[38] but by this time he had already been taken under Sully's wing. In 1605 Sully appointed him *intendant des finances* and as such Isaac became involved in efforts to reform the fiscal system. Isaac remained in government after Sully withdrew in 1611, causing some bitterness on the former *surintendant's* part because he had expected his protégé to withdraw with him.

Isaac's brother Claude was also favored by Sully. He too served briefly as the *surintendant's* secretary and for his services received the office of *trésorier de France*. "A young man with a sound mind and excellent prospects, much loved by his patron,"[39] Claude was about to accompany Sully on a mission to England in 1603 when he died suddenly at the age of twenty-nine. His funeral, according to L'Estoile, was extravagant, to say the least, and very uncharacteristic in light of his family's attitude toward conspicuous consumption. Claude's body was wrapped in a dark velvet shroud, and the carriage in which it was taken to the Protestant cemetery of Saints-Pères was accompanied by fifty horses. The black marble tomb that Claude had ordered for himself cost a substantial amount of money, far more than Huguenots usually spent for monuments of that kind. Several weeks after it was erected, the tomb had to be covered over with plaster because it had been defiled by unknown persons. Claude's reputation as a rich financier and the ostentatious manner in which he had himself memorialized may have instigated this act of desecration. So it was, remarked Pierre de L'Estoile, that "a marble tomb becomes one of plaster in the same way that our ambitions are reduced to mud and plaster."[40]

Two other brothers who benefitted from Sully's patronage were David and Louis. David acquired the office of *controleur général des restes* attached to the *Chambre des Comptes* and helped arrange loans to the crown. He too was known for his eloquence and his love of books and of works of art.[41] Louis was reputed to be less talented than his brothers; in his youth he had acquired the unfortunate sobriquet of *"le péteux"* (the farter) because of a tendency to make wind at any time in any place. A friend of the family once made the unkind comment to him: "My poor boy, all the Arnaulds make wind, the difference being that the others make it with their mouths whereas you make your's with your rear end."[42] Despite this handicap, Louis acquired an unusually large number of offices and *seigneuries*, which led to the decision of a special court established under Richelieu's auspices in 1625 to impose a penalty of forty thousand pounds on him. Fortunately for Louis, his nephew Robert was able to persuade the cardinal-minister that Louis's property had been fairly acquired, and the penalty was withdrawn.

Although the sons of La Mothe-Arnauld acquired offices, most of which were venal, they had determined that their interests were best served not by the acquisition of offices, but by receiving commissions such as Isaac's intendancy from the crown. Venal offices were owned by those who held them. To be sure, *officiers* were required to pay an annual tax (the *paulette*) in return for the privilege of ownership. But venal offices could be transmitted to heirs or bought and sold like any commodity. *Commissaires*, on the other hand, held offices from which they could be removed at the king's pleasure. As offices became private property, their owners came to regard them less in terms of public service and more in terms of family assets. To an increasing extent during the reigns of Henry IV and Louis XIII, the crown found it more expedient to rely on persons whose terms in office were determined by the king, particularly in matters pertaining to the royal finances.

A split soon developed within the new nobility between those whose offices were venal, which gave them a measure of independence from the crown on the one hand, and those who, like the Arnaulds, understood that their power and influence was dependent to a considerable extent on the king's satisfaction with their services.[43] Like so many others from similar backgrounds, La Mothe-Arnauld had attached himself to the monarchy at a low point in its history, thereby establishing a family tradition of loyal service. His sons benefitted from the reassertion of monarchical authority under Henry IV by becoming agents of that authority. Isaac and his brothers remained in the king's service after Henry's death despite Sully's desire that they withdraw with him. Loyalty to the sovereign, in their minds, took precedence over loyalty to their patron. Although Antoine Arnauld could have encouraged his eldest son Robert to take up a career in the law and become an *officier* affiliated with the Parlement of Paris, he chose instead to place him under the tutelage of Isaac during the unstable period of Marie de Medici's regency government when the competition among *commissaires* for preferment was particularly intense.

In their *avis au roi* (proposals to the king), unsolicited letters of advice advocating certain policies while at the same time showing off the author's political acumen, the Arnaulds urged the king to select loyal and disinterested counselors (*commissaires*), who would place his interests above their own, rather than to appoint persons whose only interest was to get rich at the king's expense. "Men of honor," wrote Isaac Arnauld in a brief essay on obedience, "must show themselves to be constant and inviolably loyal in the king's service. This is a duty which is imposed on us by the law of God, the requirements of the state and our own best interests."[44] At the same time the king must choose competent officials for positions of responsibility in his government instead of people who were willing to pay him the most for the offices they held. So wrote Antoine in his *Utile et Salutaire Advis au Roy pour bien Regner* for the edification of the young king Louis XIII when he reached his majority in 1617: "Everything gives way to the power of money. The universal complaint of your subjects is that in France virtue, erudition and courage are no longer valued or held in high esteem . . . Today anyone who wishes to acquire an office or, having one already, wishes to acquire one at a higher level must think first about amassing great sums of money [in order to buy it]. But as soon as this pernicious *paulette* and venality [in general] are abolished, then all that a person will need is virtue and not money." These sentiments are echoed in a pamphlet written in 1618 by his brother Pierre *(Propositions au roy sur la réformation de l'état)* (Proposition to the King regarding the reform of his government): "And Sire, regardless of what anyone says, the zeal that your ministers bring to your service is the surest way to improve your Majesty's finances." This kind of zeal, he added, is less likely to be found among the magistrates, for whom the value of their offices is the primary concern.

Having been brought into government by Sully to assist with the royal finances, the Arnauld brothers contended that an essential fiscal reform was the abolition of venality. During the meeting of the Estates General of 1614, Isaac, the *intendant des finances,* called for phasing venality out by retrieving offices that had been vacated by death or resignation.[45] In their *avis au roi,* the Arnaulds also advocated the abolition of dueling on the grounds that nobles should use their swords in defense of king and country. To their way of thinking, the noble who took up arms in his own interest was not unlike the magistrate who bought his office for his own purposes. Other reforms advocated by the brothers included a drastic reduction of pensions awarded by the crown and the discouragement of ostentatious displays of wealth at court.

In strongly opposing venality, the Arnaulds took issue with their former patron, Sully, who as a member of the *conseil des finances* at the end of the sixteenth century defended the custom against another member of that council, Pomponne de Bellièvre, who eventually fell from favor in 1604. By the beginning of the reign of Louis XIII, the power of money, in the Arnaulds' opinion, had become a corrupting influence

on the monarchy and on society as a whole. Antoine and his brothers
were appalled by the extraordinary increase in the cost of offices. Between 1586 and 1621, for example, the value of the office of *trésorier de
France* had increased from 24,000 pounds to 86,000 pounds.[46] Only
those with substantial fortunes were in a position to purchase such
sinecures, thereby depriving those with ability but less wealth of the
opportunity to move up the political ladder. The Arnaulds' disapproval
reflected religious scruples common among Protestants, many of whom
found the elaborate and luxurious courtly culture of the seventeenth
century distasteful. Their disapproval also reflected a distaste for vulgar
displays of wealth common among persons of their social rank.

One of the concerns expressed by Antoine in his *avis* was a revival
of the persecution of Huguenots despite the provisions of the Edict
of Nantes. He was well aware of the pressures, especially from the
Church, on Marie de Medici, and later on Louis XIII, to revoke the
Edict and to impose religious conformity on the kingdom. In fact,
revocation was one of the items on the clergy's agenda during the meeting of the Estates General in 1614. If such a development should come
to pass, Antoine's brothers and sisters would be the victims of renewed
persecution. In his "useful and salutary advice," Arnauld tried to reassure his sovereign that he had nothing to fear from the Huguenots, who
were as loyal to him as any of his subjects. If they were to be converted,
it should be by prayers and not by the sword. At a time when Louis XIII
was preparing a campaign against the Huguenots, Antoine feared that
France would again be torn apart by religious wars.

The family's material interests were as important to the sons of La
Mothe-Arnauld as its political influence. They knew only too well that
their political influence would be negligible without resources sufficient
both to maintain their families in a manner befitting their status as
nobles and to lend to the crown when necessary. Advantageous marriages increased their wealth and brought social and political advancement. Antoine and Isaac acquired *seigneuries* as part of their wives' dowries, and the oldest sons of the two bore the titles of these estates
inherited from their mother's family. David, seigneur of Estry and of
Vitry, took as his second wife Anne Molé, member of a prominent
magisterial family. Her second cousin and the executor of her will was
Mathieu Molé, who became a president of the Parlement of Paris.[47]

Urban real estate was also a source of income. The house once owned by La Mothe-Arnauld was sold in 1614 for thirty thousand pounds to make way for Marie de Medici's Luxembourg palace. Isaac and David joined their patron Sully in a lucrative real estate venture that involved the construction of the Place Royale (today the Place des Vosges) in the fashionable quarter of the Marais. Indeed, Isaac took up residence there in the pavilion that is now the Victor Hugo Museum.

Despite their desire to see the crown reduce the amount of money it spent on pensions, pensions were nonetheless an important source of income for Antoine and his brothers as they were to be for Antoine's sons and grandchildren. How was it possible for the Arnaulds to call for limitations on a source of revenue on which they had become increasingly dependent? One must assume that they looked upon themselves as deserving of rewards for their meritorious service, unlike those who sought rewards out of greed. They were inclined to overlook the fact that greed in the form of usurious loans made to anyone from peasants and local officials to the king himself had helped the Arnaulds make their way onward and upward. Like their ancestors, the Arnauld brothers were fiercely determined to take advantage of what the world had to offer them. In this they were no different from the Maupeous, the Fouquets, the Molés, the Séguiers, and other families who had achieved similar rank and status in the sixteenth and seventeenth centuries. They were able to build on the resources they inherited by means of their evident abilities in fiscal administration and to take advantage of the privileges that accrued to them because of their recently acquired noble status. They also benefitted from family connections and, above all, from favorable political circumstances that enabled them to hitch their fortunes to the monarchy at the right moment in that institution's long history.

Their sons' prospects, as the reign of Louis XIII began, appeared to be brighter than theirs had been at the outset of their careers. This, in their minds, was as it should be. Antoine's oldest son, Robert, was brought into the king's councils by his son Isaac; Isaac's son in turn was provided with resources that enabled him to pursue a career in the military and later to become a client of the Prince de Condé *(le grand Condé)*. David's son Antoine, preferring a career in the magistracy, became a *conseiller* attached to the Parlement of Metz but died before he could advance further.

If the Arnaulds believed that they deserved everything that came their way, there were others who believed that these gains were ill-gotten. One César de Plais, a barrister attached to the Parlement and engaged in adversary proceedings with Antoine, Isaac, and Louis, published several pamphlets in which he accused the brothers of being avaricious slaves who came from humble origins and who had enriched themselves at the public's expense. In amassing a fortune during his term of service in the *conseil des finances*, Isaac, he asserted, was motivated by hypocrisy, deviousness, and cleverness, not by honor, conscience, and modesty. De Plais accused Louis of not being diligent in fulfilling his responsibilities as a fiscal administrator, but he was particularly harsh in his treatment of Antoine, whom he accused of making an excessive fortune at the expense of his clients. He ridiculed "this great pedagogue of princes, who boasts that the advice he gives the king is so salutary and useful that the king has engraved it on his heart, . . . this Cicero-Demosthenes presents nothing but lies and calumnies in his orations." Stung by these accusations, the Arnauld brothers fought back with pamphlets of their own, contending that they had been fair in their treatment of clients and that they had not enriched themselves at the expense of the treasury. Isaac insisted that his only real income was "the liberality shown by their Majesties toward him and his children."[48]

While it is doubtful that the Arnauld brothers were the blackguards that de Plais—and, for that matter, the Jesuits—believed them to be, they were, like their ancestors before them, prepared to act in harsh and cruel ways to make their way in the world. Certainly they were not without character flaws. According to all reports, Antoine was vain, pompous, and ponderous. Although Isaac justified his decision to remain in the regency government after his patron had withdrawn as motivated by loyalty to his sovereign, Sully and others regarded it as crass opportunism. Pierre de l'Estoile and undoubtedly others saw in Claude Arnauld's ostentatious funeral arrangements the sort of vulgar display of wealth that some members of the Arnauld family deplored.

The Arnaulds' wealth and influence were acquired in a highly competitive environment in which one had to be ruthless as well as aggressive in the pursuit of family objectives. But success in obtaining wealth and influence depended in the last analysis on ambition, without which it was impossible to survive in the struggle for place and preferment. Antoine Arnauld, his father, and brothers obviously found that struggle to be exhilarating, and they did not hesitate to do what was necessary to satisfy their ambition. There were those in similar circumstances who did not have the stomach to engage in the competition for honors at court, and there were those, equally ambitious, who were initially successful in seeking preferment but who later saw their fortunes decline as the king or others in high places bestowed their favors on rivals. The Arnaulds had their share of successes and failures at court. Not surprisingly, they attributed their successes to their abilities, and their failures to the malevolence of evil courtiers who had no interest in the public good. Were they hypocrites, or only human?

Although the Arnauld brothers were disliked by some, they were greatly admired by others, including their children. Their primary loyalty was, of course, to the family, and they believed that all that they had accomplished was for its well-being. They also believed that their endeavors were pleasing in the sight of God. The Arnaulds were religious in a conventional sense, the piety of some members of the family, particularly the Huguenots, being more pronounced than that of their Catholic relatives. Isaac, Louis, and Jeanne were prominent members of the Protestant establishment in Paris, and it was Isaac, the *intendant des finances*, who was the first in the family to write a spiritual meditation.

At the end of his life, saddened by the death of his third wife, the *intendant* reflected on a theme that was to become an essential element in the spirituality of his Jansenist nieces and nephews—*"mépris du monde."*[49] "This world," he wrote, "should serve us in no other way than as a step in the ascent to heaven. Therefore while we sojourn here we must constantly elevate our thoughts to heaven . . . our conscience and our concern for our salvation oblige us to do so." One must dedicate oneself to the service of God and work hard at what God calls one to do. Labor is necessary to sustain life. "Whoever would eat must work," contended Isaac. It is God's command that man will eat the fruits of the earth by laboring every day of his life. "And if he wishes to do nothing, he will have nothing to eat . . . The lazy man is like a stone covered with muck . . . He should be compelled to work for fear that leisure will encourage him to pursue evil." By means of hard work man is entitled to harvest what he has sown in the interests of supporting his family. "If I work I attain the blessings of heaven on my labor. I may husband the resources that God has given me, and I may make use of them without exhausting them or wasting them."

Isaac's discourse is full of Calvinist themes—the emphasis on vocation, on the work ethic, and on probity. Like others of his faith, Isaac
believed that one must obey one's calling in order to justify oneself in
the sight of God. What Isaac meant by *mépris du monde* was not a
rejection of the world but a rejection of worldly values in favor of
Christian values. In a very real sense, the ideals that he set forth in his
treatise were as much a justification of his own achievements and those
of his family as they were a justification of his faith. To Isaac's way of
thinking, one should not eschew high office, but one should earn it on
the basis of his ability. To be sure, the true Christian should understood
that "high office is a heavy burden." With this in mind, he should strive
to perform the duties of office in a capable manner.

Isaac's religious beliefs were entirely compatible with his and his
family's desire to move ahead in the world. Although less is known
about the beliefs of his brothers, one may assume that the Huguenot
siblings concurred with the *intendant* that their activities and endeavors, if undertaken in the proper spirit, would enable them to do well
what God had called them to do. Although a Catholic, Antoine appears to have believed much the same thing. Like his father, he rejected
the ideals of the Catholic League during the Wars of Religion on the
grounds that these ideals were inimical to the interests of the king of
France, whose absolute authority was as necessary to the well-being of
the kingdom as it was to the good fortune of the Arnauld family. To
serve the king, to Antoine's way of thinking, was to serve God's representative on earth. He equated obedience to the king and obedience to
God. His vitriolic attacks on the Jesuits were motivated by his conviction that the Society's members were disloyal and disobedient subjects
whose activities violated divine as well as human law. When he and his
father-in-law, Simon Marion, made the fateful decision to place one of
his daughters as abbess of a convent in violation of ecclesiastical law
(she was underage), he clearly believed that the opportunity to bestow
the position on his daughter was a reward to him and to his father-in-
law for good and faithful service to their king and to their God.

↪ 3

Angélique the Reformer

*A*NTOINE ARNAULD's fourth child and second daughter was born in 1591 at a time when he and his family were residing in Tours because of the ill feelings generated against him in Paris by the publication of his *Antiespagnol*.[1] There she was baptized and given the name of Jacqueline. Only after Henry IV secured Paris in 1594 did Antoine feel that it was possible to return to the family house in the rue de la Verrerie still presided over by his father-in-law, Simon Marion. Years later, reminiscing about her childhood experiences, Jacqueline described the household as rather melancholy. Her grandmother, Marion's wife, was sick much of the time and had to be cared for by her daughter Catherine, Jacqueline's mother.

Born prematurely in 1573, Catherine was adored by her father but was never able to please her bedridden mother, from whom she took over the running of the household in 1585, the year in which she married Antoine Arnauld. Her domestic tasks were not made easier by pregnancy and childbirth, which she experienced almost every year from 1588 until 1612, during which time she produced twenty children. According to her eldest daughter, who wrote an autobiographical account of her mother's life, Catherine was a stern and prudent manager who saw to it that nothing untoward occurred to disturb the tranquility of her father's house. She is known to have boxed the ears of one of her maids who had not been able to resist the advances of an unnamed

Portrait de Mère Angélique Arnauld
by Philippe de Champaigne
(Musée Condé). Courtesy Giraudon.

member of the family. When another servant gave her a false account of the linen, she was dismissed on the spot.[2]

Catherine's household duties left her with little time to devote to her children. She appears to have been a loving mother to most, but not all, of her children. In a conversation with her nephew in 1653, Jacqueline asserted that her mother, unloved by her own mother, never loved her, although she apparently adored a younger brother, Antoine, a beautiful child who lived for only three years. In the same conversation Jacqueline insisted that little Antoine "loved only me and was a great comfort to me . . . He loved me so much that he was unable to live without me."[3] The struggle between mother and daughter for the affections of the little boy appears to have foreshadowed future struggles between Angélique and her parents for the hearts and souls of her sisters. As long as Antoine lived, Madame Arnauld suffered her daughter's presence in the nursery because her presence there pleased him. After his death, Jacqueline spent much of her time in her grandfather's quarters while the rest of the children remained with their mother.

Perhaps Catherine Arnauld's lack of affection for her daughter was caused by jealousy aroused by little Antoine's feelings for Jacqueline or perhaps it stemmed from Jacqueline's personality. She was an unruly child, rambunctious and not above disturbing the order imposed on the household by her mother. Late in her life, when abbess of Port-Royal, she still harbored resentment for a beating she had received for having shown a lack of reverence on one of the religious feast days. In any event, Jacqueline enjoyed spending time with her grandfather, who seems to have been devoted to her. She saw herself as set apart from her siblings, frequently referring to herself as Jacqueline Marion in old Simon's presence. When her sisters came to play with her, she chased them away saying that these were her quarters, where they were not welcome. Even as a little girl Jacqueline seemed inclined to go her own way and to define her life on her own terms as much as it was possible for her to do so.

As head of the household, Simon Marion had some serious decisions to make about how best to provide for the growing number of grandchildren produced by his only daughter and her husband. He was accustomed to a much smaller family, a son and daughter, but by 1597 Catherine Arnauld had given birth to ten children, six of whom had survived infancy. Of these six, four were daughters. Antoine Arnauld, whose own father died leaving him with the responsibility of giving support to his mother and numerous brothers and sisters, was quite dependent on his father-in-law's resources in the early stages of his career. He had no choice but to leave important family decisions to Marion. Hence it was Marion who claimed the right to determine the disposition of his granddaughters. The eldest, Catherine, born the year before Jacqueline in 1590, was to be married and would receive a suitable dowry. Jacqueline and two younger sisters, Anne-Eugénie, born in 1592, and Jeanne, born in 1593, were to become nuns. The small dowries required by convents—a fraction of the amount needed to arrange a socially advantageous marriage—made the monastic option attractive to ambitious families with superfluous daughters.[4]

Edmé de la Croix, abbé de Citeaux and an acquaintance of Simon Marion, proposed that Jacqueline become the abbess of Port-Royal, a dilapidated convent affiliated with the Cistercian order located in the valley of the Chevreuse, not far from Paris and near the Marion estate of Andilly. The area in which the convent was constructed in the thirteenth century—today surrounded by the suburban sprawl of the department of Yvelines—was often referred to in earlier times as rather wild and forbidding. Neighboring swamps and a pond that sometimes flooded the fields adjacent to Port-Royal created an unhealthy atmosphere that made the place almost uninhabitable. The convent had an illustrious history, but by the sixteenth century its nuns had become accustomed to leading a lax existence, dressing as they pleased and attending religious services when they had nothing better to do. To remedy the situation, the abbé de Citeaux removed the abbess of Port-Royal, Madame de la Vallée, from her position in 1574 and replaced her with Jeanne de Boulehart. Madame de Boulehart presided over the establishment for over a quarter of a century "without a scandal," Sainte-Beuve informs us, but without any attempt to introduce monastic reforms consistent with the Counter Reformation.[5]

Edmé de la Croix and Simon Marion decided that the old abbess would have to be pressured into receiving Jacqueline as her coadjutrice, who would succeed her as abbess after her death. Jeanne de Boulehart had already refused to have her own niece appointed to the same position, but after some negotiation, she agreed to Marion's proposition. The old lady was no doubt influenced in this decision by Simon Marion's prestige and by assurances that he would help refurbish the buildings and grounds of Port-Royal as well as by the authority of Edmé de la Croix. Having obtained the abbess's consent to the placement of Jacqueline, Simon had no difficulty in securing the approval of Henry IV, who used ecclesiastical benefices as a means of rewarding those who had supported the monarchy during its time of troubles. The king not only agreed to the installation of Jacqueline Arnauld as future abbess of Port-Royal but also consented to a similar arrangement for her younger sister Jeanne as abbess of the nearby convent of Saint-Cyr. Marion's plans were thwarted, at least for the moment, however, when the papacy refused to approve Jacqueline's appointment as abbess, not on the grounds that she was too young under canon law to assume the office, but because she had not yet taken her nun's vows.

Although Antoine Arnauld and his wife were not in a position to object to Simon Marion's arrangements for their daughters, there is some indication that they were not entirely happy about losing them. They no doubt thought that Jacqueline and Jeanne were too young to be separated from their family and placed in an alien environment. Unreformed convents were vulnerable to unhealthy influences of one sort or another, and almost anyone who wanted to do so was able to gain access to these communities of unprotected women. Jacqueline's response to her grandfather's arrangement was more enthusiastic than her parents'. When Marion assured her that she would be an abbess and not merely a nun, she cheerfully accepted it. As she reconstructed the conversation years later, Jacqueline admitted that her one consolation at the thought of being deprived of a future that included marriage and children was the prospect of having "to command others." She then turned to her grandfather and said: "I am only agreeing to become a nun because you are making me an abbess."[6]

Undaunted by the papal refusal to authorize Jacqueline's appointment at Port-Royal, Simon Marion forged ahead with his plans to make her coadjutrice. After brief sojourns at two convents, including Saint-Cyr, where her sister was to become abbess in 1599, Jacqueline was placed as a novice in the convent of Maubuisson, not too far from Paris, hence easily accessible to her family. Its abbess was Angélique d'Estrées, sister of Gabrielle, the notorious mistress of Henry IV. Angélique had once been abbess of a convent near Amiens, where her sister often stayed for the purpose of making herself available to the king. Not wanting to travel so far for the pleasure of seeing Gabrielle, Henry transferred Angélique to Maubuisson, nearer at hand, after he had removed the current abbess from her office. The king continued to be welcome at Maubuisson, as were others, attracted by the abbess, who is said to have given birth to a dozen or more children while in office.

Why did Simon Marion decide to place his beloved granddaughter in the care of an abbess whose living arrangements seemed more attuned to the boudoir than to the cloister? Certainly Madame d'Estrées's behavior in the era of *le roi gaillard* would have seemed less reprehensible to contemporaries than to us. Besides, Marion and his son-in-law were men of the world who would have recognized the social advantages to be gained through a connection with an establishment blessed with royal patronage. Was it to flatter an abbess with powerful connections at court that during Jacqueline's sojourn at Maubuisson, Marion and Arnauld had the girl's name changed to Angélique, the Christian name by which she has been known ever since? Whatever the truth of the matter, both believed a change in name was necessary in order to apply again for papal authorization of the young girl's position at Port-Royal.

An application was made in 1601 after Angélique Arnauld had received confirmation and a month later, in October 1600, had taken her vows as a nun. The girl was now eligible to become an abbess in one sense but, according to canon law, she was still too young to hold that office. Realizing this, Marion, without the slightest qualm, asserted in the request for authorization that his ten-year-old granddaughter was seventeen. Papal approval was received from Rome a few months later, by which time the health of Jeanne de Boulehart, abbess of Port-Royal, had begun to deteriorate rapidly. The old lady died on 4 July 1602, and on the following day the new abbess took up residence at the convent, just short of her eleventh birthday.

Although Angélique was nominally in charge of Port-Royal, the management of the premises and the governance of Angélique herself remained in the hands of her parents. Antoine Arnauld supervised the reconstruction of the buildings, which were in disrepair. Arnauld had been able to incur the expense of reconstruction because his fortunes had taken a turn for the better. In 1605, he became head of the family after the death of Simon Marion. Now a man of some means because of what he had inherited from his father-in-law, he was in a position to provide financial support for the establishment once Angélique was installed as abbess.

Angélique's mother, Catherine, administered the internal affairs of the convent in the same efficient way that she ran her household. She stayed at Port-Royal for several weeks during the summer of 1605. At that time, she had several nuns whom she suspected of being bad influences removed to another establishment. She and her husband obtained permission from the head of the Cistercian order to install a nun from another abbey, who became, in effect, Angélique's governess. This person carefully monitored Angélique's behavior and made regular reports to her parents, who also persuaded the Cistercian authorities to appoint another nun of their choosing as prioress. The prioress's responsibility was to supervise the conduct of the nuns.

As for Angélique herself, she became increasingly unhappy. In her autobiography she wrote: "As I grew older, I became more malicious, and I came to regard monastic life as an unbearable yoke."[7] Taking advantage of the unstructured life at Port-Royal, she diverted herself by playing with other nuns, reading Plutarch's *Lives*, and by taking long walks in the countryside, but she was unable to forget the worldly pleasures that she had become accustomed to in her grandfather's house. She was made even more aware of what she was being deprived of by her occasional visits either to the family house in the rue de la Verrerie or to her father's estate of Andilly. There she admired the fine apparel of her parents and their friends and relatives, and she particularly enjoyed their accounts of life at court. At the same time she resented the fact that her older sister Catherine, whom she believed to be far more devout than herself, was to be allowed to marry. Why wasn't Catherine the nun and she, Angélique, the prospective bride?

As the young girl contemplated her situation, she became so filled with despair that she even considered an escape, encouraged by her Huguenot aunts, sisters of Antoine Arnauld, who undertook to persuade her that her vows were invalid because they violated canon law. As she later wrote, "As much as conventual life displeased me and as great as was my love of the world, I was unable to leave [Port-Royal]. I believed that I could not do so without destroying myself." Yet, as she put it, she continued to lead "a pagan and profane existence," reading anything but devotional literature, visiting neighbors, receiving friends, and flaunting monastic convention in any way that she could. Reports of her rebellious inclinations reached her mother, who immediately descended on Port-Royal for the purpose of rummaging through her daughter's drawers and closet in search of illicit love letters. Although distressed by the attitude of her parents, Angélique continued to read Plutarch "and other profane books" until in 1608 she had what she later described as a religious experience that began the long and painful process by which her life became transformed.[8]

During Lent, Angélique asked one of her nuns to recommend some inspirational work, which, she reported in her memoirs, she read and appreciated. A few days later, during a sermon preached by an itinerant monk in the chapel of the convent, "God touched me in such a way that

I found myself happier to be a nun than I had ever believed it possible."[9] As a result of this experience she came to see

> the necessity for true obedience, distrust of the flesh and all sensual
> pleasures as well as the merits of true poverty. God gave me such
> affection for these virtues that I felt I could not breathe without
> finding the means of putting them into practice. However my
> misery, my rashness, my inability to respond to this first offering
> of grace, despite the fact that my will remained firm in its desire
> to find these means, caused me to commit other faults and infi-
> delities.[10]

Tempted at first to seek guidance from the itinerant monk, she decided against it because he was younger (not yet seventeen) than she
was. She later discovered that the monk had a very bad reputation "*et
qu'il avait fait de grandes sottises en des Maisons religieuses*" (and that he had
behaved badly in several monastic establishments). However, she continued to feel the need for guidance and instruction, and when shortly
thereafter an older and more austere monk preached at Port-Royal,
Angélique spoke to him of her spiritual needs. The monk, a certain
Father Bernard, replied that if she were genuinely committed to reforming herself she was obliged to reform her convent as well. If as a
little girl she had welcomed the prospect of commanding others as
abbess, she now realized that asserting her will over the community
might well jeopardize the monastic vocation that was developing within
her. Her initial inclination was to resign her office and to undertake
what she knew would be her own painful reformation. Her niece, to
whom Angélique described her conversion experience many years later,
recounted her aunt's feelings in this way: "She soon worried about
whether her life was austere and humble enough. She no longer wanted
to be engaged [in activities of leadership] but to install herself instead in
an obscure and reformed convent as its least known and unnoticed
inmate."[11] Even at the age of seventeen she had become aware of the
effect of her powerful will on others. While it might make it easier for
her to get the nuns to do what she wanted them to do, it might make it
harder for her to find favor in the sight of God. Throughout her life,
she was tortured by the thought that her pride in her ability to make
others submit to her will—a sentiment that she was unable to suppress

even in her autobiographical accounts—constituted a major obstacle to her self-reformation.

Father Bernard and others continued to press her to return the convent of Port-Royal to strict observance of monastic rule, from which it had strayed over the course of centuries. Some of the nuns were eager for such a radical transformation, but others, indeed "the most orderly, devout and modest in their habits," including the prioress and the governess, both appointed by her parents, were not. They saw no reason to alter their comfortable life, for which reason they had little enthusiasm for reform. The prioress complained to Angélique's parents that their daughter was too young to take on the responsibilities of a reformer.

In the autumn of 1608, the young abbess paid a visit to her parents at Andilly for the purpose of obtaining their support. Her father, fully informed of her activities at Port-Royal, was adamant in his insistence that she renounce any intention of introducing reforms. Angélique was, he argued, too willing to submit to the influence of monks who, in his opinion, were not as pious as she thought they were. He, like many others in his time, did not have a very high opinion of monks, whom he regarded as more interested in the flesh than in the spirit. "A few days later," she wrote in her memoirs, "I returned to the monastery resolved to do what I could to serve God but at the same time to do nothing that would irritate my father."[12]

In November 1608 a distraught Angélique heard yet another sermon delivered in celebration of the feast of All Saints on the text from the Gospel according to Saint Matthew: "Blessed are they that are persecuted for righteousness' sake." Shortly thereafter one of her maids suggested to her that she, Angélique, might become one of those blessed for having suffered persecution for having done what was right. The abbess's immediate impulse was to rebuke the woman, but on second thought it occurred to her that the woman might be right. Certainly she had been persecuted by the conflict within her between her desire to live a Christian life and her inability to do so, between her wish to do what was right for herself and her community on the one hand and her fear of disobeying her parents on the other, and between her responsibilities as abbess and her personal responsibilities as a sinner. The inner turmoil that she experienced took its toll on her both psychologically and physically. But reflecting on the passage from Saint Matthew's Gospel and on her maid's comment, she now resolved to undertake the reformation of herself and her convent. At the same time she came to understand that religious life, as she had experienced it thus far, involved continuous suffering brought on by the desire to do right in opposition to what the world believed was right. She also became aware at the very moment of her conversion that persecution at the hands of an unregenerate world was in itself an indication of God's favor.[13]

The most difficult reform for the young abbess to accomplish was the reestablishment of cloture, not so much because of opposition from within the community but because of the effect it would have on her family, who were accustomed to going wherever they pleased within Port-Royal. What is more, as Angélique put it, "My mother said that it was necessary for her to enter the inner precincts in order to see if I was behaving myself. She was right in a certain sense, because it was true that what she did was useful and even necessary, given my youth. Because I was only seventeen and a half she didn't trust me very much."[14]

In the autumn of 1609 Angélique learned that her parents were about to visit the convent. Wishing to avoid a painful confrontation, she wrote to tell them not to come because of her determination to impose cloture. Undeterred by this warning, Antoine and Catherine, their oldest son Robert, two years older than Angélique, and their daughter Anne-Eugénie arrived at Port-Royal on 25 September, known in the annals of the convent as *"la journée du guichet."* There they encountered their daughter who appeared before them in a little window (guichet) set in the entry. When she informed them that they would not be admitted, Antoine flew into a rage, telling her that if she did not obey him she would never see him again and accusing her of having become corrupted by evil influences. On previous occasions Angélique had given in to him, not wishing to anger him, but she now held her ground despite the verbal assaults of her father and brother and her mother's entreaties. Responding to Robert's particularly vehement reproaches, she said as calmly as she could, according to her later account, "How strange it is; they [her parents] wanted me to become a nun against my wishes and when I was too young; and now that I want to be a nun, they want me to commit a sin by not observing the rule. I will do nothing of the sort. They did not consult me by making me a nun; I will not consult them now that I wish to live like a nun in order to save myself. They threaten to abandon me."[15] After several hours of a confrontation that Angélique had hoped might be avoided, the Arnaulds withdrew, infuriated by their daughter's intransigence. As their carriage drew away from the convent, Madame Arnauld made a vow never to speak to her daughter again.

The *journée du guichet* constituted a watershed in Angélique's life. Cut off—at least for the moment—from her family, she was able to devote her considerable energy to the reform of Port-Royal and of herself. Having asserted herself against her parents, she was no longer as dependent as she had been on their decisions as to what was right for her. Free to act to a considerable extent on the basis of her own free will, Angélique now understood that she was responsible to God for the choices that she would have to make. The wrong choice would jeopardize her self-reformation.

Throughout the long history of monastic institutions, the convent had provided its leaders with opportunities to exercise their authority and to become independent in ways that were less available to women ensconced in the patriarchal structure of the family. In addition to ordering the lives of the nuns under their jurisdiction, abbesses managed the resources of their convents, while maintaining contacts with the outside world for the purposes of recruiting new members and raising money to support their establishments. During periods of monastic reform, women acted to improve the quality of their communities but, as was the case of Saint Theresa of Avila, also contributed to the revitalization of the Church as a whole. Women such as Madame Acarie (1564–1618), founder of the Carmelites in France, and Jeanne de Chantal (1572–1641), who, with François de Sales, founded the Order of the Visitation, became major figures of the Catholic reform movement in France. After the *journée du guichet*, as she embarked on the reform of her own convent, and later of others, Angélique Arnauld became a leader of that movement. As she became involved in it to an ever greater extent, and as her own reputation as a reformer grew, the dangers that she encountered more than matched the opportunities that presented themselves to her.

Among these dangers was, of course, alienation from her family. Angélique's parents had expressed their disapproval of her reforming intentions in no uncertain terms. They were concerned for her physical well-being, which might not bear up under a regimen of austerity. From their point of view, monastic reform threatened the proprietal rights that gave them access to Port-Royal as well as considerable influence in the governance of the convent. Furthermore, Antoine Arnauld was wary of the Catholic reform movement because it placed the interests of the Church ahead of those of the state. Angélique would find her reforms much harder to achieve unless she could convince her family to accept her decision and at the same time to continue to provide support to Port-Royal.

Another danger was potential conflict with ecclesiastical authorities whose jurisdictions appeared to be threatened by her efforts, or who feared that these efforts might challenge the patriarchal structure within the Church that over the centuries had placed women in a subordinate position. As the history of conventual reform reveals, women who appeared too energetic in the cause of reform and too independent in their activities had always been viewed with suspicion by powerful leaders of the Church, all of whom were male and did not like women who acted like men.

Angélique believed that the recruitment of nuns with a genuine vocation for monastic life was vital to the spiritual well-being of her convent. Before the Catholic reform movement took hold in France in the early seventeenth century, many nuns were placed in convents in return for an endowment provided by their families regardless of a vocation. Her own family had placed her in Port-Royal against her will, but once she became committed to monastic reform she saw to it that those who were admitted to the convent had the potential to live up to Saint Bernard's principles, regardless of dowry. On one occasion she was presented with four young women whose families were anxious to have them admitted to the community. The fathers of three of them were well-to-do, whereas the fourth was having a hard time providing for a large number of children. "As soon as these four girls entered the parlor, I cast my eyes on [the fourth candidate] even though she was the last to enter the room. I was so taken with her that I instantly said to a nun who was with me that she would be the only one allowed to stay."[16] In his brief history of Port-Royal, where two aunts of his were nuns and which he knew well, Racine tells of a young woman who had been admitted to the convent as a novice. Her mother had bestowed eighty thousand pounds on the establishment, which was spent on various charities, on paying off debts, and on reconstruction. After the young woman had spent two years as a novice, Angélique came to the conclusion that she did not have sufficient commitment, whereupon she rejected her. At great cost to the community the eighty thousand pounds was returned to her mother.[17] The admissions policy put in place by

Angélique greatly improved the quality of religious life at Port-Royal. At the same time it compelled the abbess to spend more time seeking out benefactors who would provide financial support for the convent on terms that did no harm to its spiritual mission. This gave her less time to spend on her own needs.

~ BETWEEN 1609 and 1618 Angélique devoted her attention to the needs of Port-Royal. By 1618 her reputation as a reformer had spread beyond the walls of her little abbey tucked away in the valley of the Chevreuse. In that year Dom Boucherat, the head of the Cistercian order at the time, invited her to return to the convent of Maubuisson, where she had spent two years as a novice, to institute reforms. Angélique's former patroness, Angélique d'Estrées, whose namesake she was, had become such an embarrassment to the order that Boucherat decided that something had to be done. However, any disciplinary action against Madame d'Estrées would be difficult to undertake, given her powerful family connections. Her brother was a marshal and her first cousin was Cardinal de Sourdis. Boucherat first sent a representative to Maubuisson to investigate matters. The intractable abbess had the man arrested as soon as he arrived, whereupon Boucherat himself went to the convent to negotiate with the haughty abbess, but to no avail. At last Boucherat obtained an order from the Parlement of Paris to send a troop of soldiers to remove her. Only after the abbess was taken from the convent and placed under house arrest was Angélique Arnauld able to take charge.

Angélique arrived at Maubuisson with several nuns from Port-Royal in February 1618 and began to implement the reforms that she had put into effect at her convent. A year later Madame d'Estrées managed to escape from the abbey where she had been incarcerated. With her own troop of soldiers, commanded by her brother-in-law, she regained control of Maubuisson. Angélique Arnauld and her companions took refuge in the nearby town of Pontoise. She alerted her brother Henry, the only member of her family in Paris at the time, who obtained a royal order to dispatch a company of soldiers to eject Madame d'Estrées from her convent and to reinstate Angélique. These armed confrontations pitting two powerful families against each other, to say nothing of two strong-minded women, suggest the intensity of the quarrels aroused by the reform movement.[18]

During the time that she was at Maubuisson, the tension between

Angélique's public activities as abbess and her own spiritual needs became so unbearable that she decided that she would have to resign her
office and become a nun at a convent affiliated with another order. After
considering several possibilities, including the Carmelites, Angélique
decided to join the Visitandines, an order founded by Jeanne de Chantal. Her interest in the order was greatly increased by her friendship
with the bishop of Geneva, François de Sales, whom she first met at
Maubuisson in 1619. In the same year, Angélique informed Madame de
Chantal of her intention to join the Visitandines in a series of letters in
which she informed her correspondent that she could not live up to her
vocation as a nun unless she gave up her position at Port-Royal. "I
humbly beg of you to have mercy on this poor sister,"[19] Angélique wrote
to Chantal in September 1620, begging her to take her under her wing.
One historian has suggested that Angélique's willingness to submit to
the authority of another woman, older than she but equally committed
to the Catholic reform movement, reflected a yearning on her part to
find a mother who would love her and look after her needs in a way that
her own mother had never seemed able to do.[20] She also may have
wanted to place herself in the hands of an abbess whose spirituality she
greatly admired, never having had that experience. To one who had
assumed the responsibilities of office at a young age, never entirely
confident that she had the proper vocation to exercise those responsibilities, the opportunity to let someone else take at least some responsibility for her own well-being must have been irresistible. Furthermore,
her efforts to rehabilitate Port-Royal and other communities had increased her contacts with the world and, as she believed, had made her
more vulnerable to its influences.

Jeanne de Chantal soon agreed to Angélique's request to become a
Visitandine, but others were very much opposed to the plan, including
Angélique's family, who believed that the abbess should carry on her
activities as a reformer. François de Sales, who by 1620 had become
Angélique's spiritual adviser, was very reluctant to approve the abbess's
plan. He believed that her true vocation lay in continuing her good
works as a leader of the reform movement. However, after consultation
with Madame de Chantal and careful consideration of Angélique's psychological needs, he agreed in late 1620 to support her efforts to join
the Visitandines. A year later, her mother, now a widow and very much
under the spiritual influence of François de Sales, gave her approval. At

this point the long and complicated process of acquiring papal approval began.

The French ambassador to Rome at the time when Angélique's request arrived at the papal court in 1622 was none other than Marshal d'Estrées, brother of the deposed abbess of Maubuisson. Little help in obtaining the pope's approval could be expected from that quarter. Angélique's own brother Henry was also in Rome at the time. A protégé of Cardinal Bentivoglio, the papal nuncio in France, Henry was not without influence, but whether he was willing to use it in his sister's behalf is uncertain. Henry Arnauld at that time was very much a man of the world. He had recently been made the abbé de Saint-Nicolas, a wealthy benefice once coveted by Cardinal Richelieu, and was in the process of launching a diplomatic career when Angélique's request arrived in Rome. He may well have opposed the abbess's decision to resign her office, believing that the office enhanced the reputation of the Arnauld family. Later on, in 1639, he would oppose his youngest brother Antoine's decision to renounce lucrative benefices, and he would also oppose his oldest sister Catherine's desire to resign a prestigious position in the household of the duchess of Nemours for the purpose of becoming a nun at Port-Royal. Assuming that his pride in the worldly honors acquired by his family did in fact prejudice him against Angélique's plan, he would have done as little as he could to support her case at the papal court.

While she awaited word from Rome, the abbess of Port-Royal carried on with her tasks, first at Maubuisson and then at Lys. Upon her return to Port-Royal from Maubuisson in 1623, she was faced with the decision of whether or not to move her community to Paris. The valley of the Chevreuse was an unhealthy site because of the swamps and marshes that surrounded Port-Royal. A number of nuns had died of malaria during Angélique's absence, and those who remained feared for their lives. To make matters worse, the living quarters within the convent were too small to accommodate the growing number of women who had become part of the community. Because an endowment was not required for admission, many women were attracted to Port-Royal and to Maubuisson. The resources at Port-Royal were stretched to the limit because of the addition to the community of thirty nuns whom Angélique had brought with her from Maubuisson.

To transfer the convent to Paris was an enormous undertaking. In the first place, the Cistercians would have to agree to the move, as would the archbishop of Paris, whose diocese included Port-Royal. Second, suitable quarters would have to be found in Paris, which was bursting with new monastic establishments. Finally, substantial funds would have to be raised to construct suitable facilities for the nuns once the new quarters were found.

In 1624, having made the decision to move to Paris in consultation with her mother, who was anxious to relocate the convent in a more salubrious environment, Angélique made the necessary requests for approval from the head of the Cistercians and from the archbishop of Paris. Archbishop Gondi was a friend of the Arnauld family, but he refused to approve the request unless he was given substantial authority over the community. Monastic orders, including the Cistercians, were traditionally exempt from episcopal authority, thereby creating a jurisdictional conflict between the regular and secular clergy that had troubled the Catholic Church for centuries. Dom Boucherat was reluctant to agree to the archbishop's conditions, but when he saw that Gondi was adamant, he gave his own approval in 1625. By this time new quarters in the Faubourg Saint-Jacques were obtained, into which Angélique and eighteen nuns moved in May of that year.

Madame Arnauld had provided the funds necessary to purchase the property in Paris, but Port-Royal-de-Paris was in need of substantial refurbishing. In addition to a new chapel, more dormitory space was required to house all the nuns. The cost of these projects was enormous, and it was to take years before the facility was completed. The chapel was not finished until 1648. Angélique was, of course, the principal fundraiser. Prospective benefactors were not always to her taste. One potential donor, Madame de Pontcarré, recently widowed, had expressed a desire to spend the rest of her life in a small apartment in Port-Royal in exchange for providing an endowment of 84,000 pounds. Not convinced of the lady's religious commitment, Angélique declined her offer. In order to complete the construction the abbess had to borrow enormous sums of money—to the point where, as she later said, the interest payments alone amounted to 136,000 pounds. These financial arrangements "were a great burden to me, not ever knowing how to pay off the interest, . . . which increased all the time."[21]

One of those who encouraged Angélique in her efforts to establish her community in Paris was Sebastian Zamet, bishop of Langres.

Zamet was a member of a wealthy family of financiers, which had moved to France from Italy in the sixteenth century to serve the queen, Catherine de Medici. Like Angélique, he had acquired his office through royal patronage and did not at first take his episcopal obligations seriously, spending much of his time at court. Having undergone a conversion experience of his own, Zamet became committed to the reform movement. In 1622 he visited Angélique at Maubuisson to discuss problems he had encountered while revitalizing the convent of Tard in the diocese of Langres, which was also under the jurisdiction of the Cistercians. Three years after his visit he proposed that Tard and Port-Royal become part of a new order dedicated to the Holy Sacrament that he hoped to establish with Angélique's assistance.

Angélique was favorably inclined toward Zamet's proposal for a number of reasons. The bishop had powerful and wealthy connections that would make it easier for her to raise money for Port-Royal-de-Paris. He was deeply committed to monastic reform. Finally, Zamet's proposal gave her an opportunity to break with the Cistercians entirely. Dom Boucherat, who had been on the whole supportive of Angélique's reforming efforts, had died in 1625, the year that the Port-Royal community had moved to Paris. He was succeeded in that office by Pierre Nivelle, who was far less supportive of Angélique. He had disapproved of the displacement of the convent to Paris and was unlikely to approve her and Zamet's plans for a new order.

As she explained to her nephew Antoine Le Maistre many years later, she had never been satisfied with Port-Royal's affiliation with the Cistercians because she didn't have much use for monks in general. In that conversation she complained of the mistreatment of nuns by monks. "I recognized that this jurisdiction of nuns by monks is pernicious even to the monks themselves, who grow fat in a house full of women. They are so well treated that they become domineering, they intrigue and become unbearable . . . They grow accustomed to ordering women about. [At the same time] this conduct [of the monks] is pernicious to the women. The monks gain control of their minds, they conspire, they undermine the authority of the abbess and prioress in order to become their masters . . . [Such activity] is the very ruin of spiritual life. I know this only too well."[22] Angélique based her harsh criticism of the regular clergy on her own experience both before and after her conversion. To her nephew she made vague references to love affairs, pregnancies, and other misdeeds. Not long after the *journée du guichet* one particular monk who had come to Port-Royal to hear the nuns' confessions spoke to Angélique of a love affair he was having with one of her nuns. She could not recall how many love letters written by Cistercian monks to the women of Port-Royal she discovered in their cells. In another conversation with her nephew in 1652 she remembered that when she began the reform of Port-Royal in 1609 she had refused to discuss her plans with members of the order because she knew them to be on the whole unsympathetic to her intentions. Indeed, her father had learned a good deal about her plans from Cistercians, who denounced those monks—Capuchins for the most part—who encouraged her to carry out her plans as "sneaks, sanctimonious hypocrites and zealots . . . At the beginning of our reform we were regarded by most of the monks as schismatics and innovators intent on destroying the fine old customs of the order."

By the time that Angélique and Zamet requested papal approval for their new order in 1626, the bishop had become her spiritual director, replacing François de Sales, who had died in 1622. The abbess was so impressed with Zamet's spirituality—she found him to be "a man full of zeal, of mortification and devotion"[23]—that she did not hesitate to take him into her confidence in the matter of her joining the Visitandines. Almost five years had passed since she had appealed to Rome to permit her to make the change in her condition, but nothing had happened. Upon learning of her intentions, Zamet insisted that it was her vocation to remain in office and carry on the reforms that God intended her to make. Whether because she realized that she was not likely to receive papal authorization or because she was caught up in the excitement of launching a new religious order, in 1626 Angélique abandoned her attempt to join the Visitandines.

Establishing a new order was a formidable process. In the case of the Order of the Holy Sacrament, it took four years (1626–1630). Papal authorization was required, and in order to receive it, an administrative structure that was acceptable to the pope, the king, and the appropriate episcopal authority was necessary. Since neither Angélique nor Zamet wanted the order to have any affiliation with a monastic order, they decided to place it under the jurisdiction of three prelates: the archbishop of Paris, the archbishop of Sens, and the bishop of Langres. This unwieldy arrangment was to cause trouble for the order in the years ahead as each bishop sought to increase his authority over the estab-lishment at the expense of the others. However, in 1627 the pope, Urban VIII, found the arrangement acceptable and gave the enterprise his blessing. Two years later the convents of Port-Royal and Tard, the latter under the jurisdiction of the bishop of Langres, were linked to-gether as a preliminary step in the formation of the Order of the Holy Sacrament, of which the bishop of Langres was to be the spiritual director.

How was the order to be governed from within? Zamet and Angélique realized that Angélique could not be abbess of Port-Royal and an organizer of the new establishment at the same time. Zamet needed Angélique's assistance in helping him raise money and recruit candidates for admission to the order. The bishop was not satisfied with the location of Port-Royal-de-Paris, situated as it was on the southern edge of the city. He believed that new and more sumptuous quarters near the royal palace of the Louvre would be more attractive to poten-tial recruits and benefactors. Angélique would have to resign her office, not to become a simple nun, but Mother Superior of the Order of the Holy Sacrament. Her successor at Port-Royal would not be appointed by the king but would be elected by the community of nuns, in confor-mance with an ancient monastic tradition that had been usurped by the crown. The right of election would also be restored to the abbey of Tard. Of course, royal approval would be required in order to put into effect this important reform. In 1630, after some hesitation, Louis XIII approved the right of election at both convents, a decision that his son, Louis XIV, would later regret. Angélique immediately resigned her office, and Geneviève Le Tardif was elected to replace her.

In the same year the king approved the Order of the Holy Sacra-ment. He had taken three years to arrive at this decision because of opposition from other orders. The Counter Reformation had spawned new orders and had revitalized old ones. All of these religious estab-lishments required patronage and competed for favor and support at court and among the great nobles. Marillac, the chancellor, who was a patron of the Carmelites, urged his sovereign to reject Zamet's request. On the other hand the proposed order had the support of the king's cousin, the duchesse de Longueville, and of the queen mother, Marie de Medici. Recovering from a serious illness in 1630, Louis XIII, as a gesture of gratitude, decided in Zamet's favor. No doubt he was also motivated to do so by the formidable reputations as reformers of Zamet and Angelique, who were now free to implement their plan.

⟶ ALMOST IMMEDIATELY after receiving the king's approval and the election at Port-Royal, things began to go wrong for the new order. The new abbess, Geneviève Le Tardif, under the supervision of the bishop, introduced changes in the way of life at Port-Royal that appeared at least to Angélique to negate the principles of simplicity, austerity, and poverty that guided her own reforms. The nuns' garments became more refined, the food served in the refectory more elaborate, and the decor in the chapel more sumptuous. Although Angélique said nothing, she was unable to hide her disapproval, as she herself admitted. Zamet was well aware of her feelings and on one occasion remarked to her that her presence was becoming a nuisance.[24] The relationship between the former abbess and the bishop, so promising at first, began to deteriorate. To Angélique, Zamet's religious zeal, which she had once found exhilarating, merely masked worldly aspirations. These aspirations, she believed, were reflected in the recruitment efforts that were directed at wealthy social groups capable of financing the elaborate plans of the bishop of Langres. "The only pensioners he [Zamet] was willing to receive," Angélique later complained, "were the daughters of marquises and counts."[25] In her memoirs she asserted that in order to attract women of high rank, Zamet thought it best to place the new establishment near the royal court, and within the establishment he placed greater emphasis on *politesse* and on speaking well than on piety. To make the environment within the convent less antithetical to the environment at court, she maintained, he encouraged the discussion of worldly affairs, insisting that an awareness of what went on in the world was not incompatible with monastic life.[26]

At the same time that the Order of the Holy Sacrament was experiencing troubles from within, it became the target of attacks from outside. In 1633 the archbishop of Sens, Octave de Bellegarde, one of the members of the troika under whose jurisdiction the Order of the Holy Sacrament had been placed, brought charges against a devotional treatise written by one of the nuns of the order, on the grounds that its mystical aura smacked of heresy. Like the archbishop of Paris, Octave de Bellegarde had never been satisfied with the administrative arrangement. The controversial nature of the treatise now gave him the opportunity to do away with the onerous administrative structure. The Sorbonne, sensitive to the influence of this prominent prelate, agreed to censure the treatise, thereby instigating a furious pamphlet war between Zamet's supporters and his enemies. "We were denounced as heretical visionaries," Angélique later wrote, "and some went so far as to say that we were witches." She was so appalled by the verbal assault on the community that she wrote a letter to Cardinal Richelieu in October 1633 insisting on its orthodox religious beliefs and urging the king's minister to suppress the insulting pamphlets.[27] Afraid that as a result of the Sorbonne's action the order might be condemned by the papacy, Zamet asked an acquaintance of his, the theologian Jean Duvergier de Hauranne, abbé de Saint-Cyran, to write a treatise in defense of the censured work. The abbé's treatise had the desired effect. The papacy refused to condemn the controversial work and the threat to the new order's existence was removed.

The bishop of Langres was so pleased with Saint-Cyran's accomplishment that he encouraged increased contacts between the abbé and the nuns. When in the autumn of 1633 the bishop decided to leave Paris to spend time in his diocese, he asked the abbé to serve as spiritual confessor to the convent until his return. Saint-Cyran had been a close friend of Angélique's brother Robert since 1620 and had become the spiritual director of Madame Arnauld after the death of François de Sales in 1622. He had visited Port-Royal once in 1625, but other than that had no other contact with Angélique or with the community before 1633. As Zamet's temporary replacement at Port-Royal, the abbé preached a number of sermons to the community and received confession from some of the nuns. All who heard him, according to Angélique, were profoundly impressed with his spirituality. As she herself listened to the sermons, she came to realize how great the gap had become between her ideals of austerity, simplicity, and poverty, so emphatically endorsed by Saint-Cyran, and the current practices in the new order.[28]

When Zamet returned to Paris in 1635, he discovered that a number of the nuns, including Angélique, had succumbed to the spiritual influence of the abbé de Saint-Cyran, whom he now began to suspect of undermining his authority. His own relationship with Angélique was strained. Not only did she disapprove of the changes he had instituted, but she also was not, in his opinion, diligent in her efforts to attract influential friends to the establishment. He accused her "of being too withdrawn, of not going often enough to the parlor [where she was supposed to make advantageous contacts] and of talking too little while in the parlor to the point where I was losing friends for the house. I replied as humbly as I could that I was doing what was necessary but that I felt obliged to eliminate superfluous activity because my vows required me to separate myself from the world."[29] Clearly these two very different conceptions of what Angélique was supposed to do posed a serious threat to the Order of the Holy Sacrament.

Matters came to a head shortly after Zamet returned to Paris in 1635. The bishop had in mind to place a certain nun in charge of the novices, a position that was particularly influential in terms of educating the future nuns concerning their religious obligations. According to Angélique, the nun had no vocation whatsoever and had been chosen by Zamet simply because she could "relate well to princesses."[30] When the bishop insisted on his choice in the face of Angélique's objections, she "resolved for the good of my conscience to place the house under the [sole] jurisdiction of the archbishop of Paris," a decision in which most of the nuns concurred. The archbishop, a friend of the Arnauld family, was only too delighted to oblige Angélique, having been waiting for the opportunity to exclude the bishop of Langres from any administrative responsibility within the archdiocese of Paris. Although there were some nuns who continued to support Zamet, Angélique and others were eventually able to convince them that the dissolution of the Order of the Holy Sacrament was in their best spiritual interests. When her sister Agnès was elected abbess in 1636, Angélique persuaded her to write Zamet asking him never to visit Port-Royal again.[31]

Angélique's changed opinion of Bishop Zamet is open to question. It should be said in his defense that launching a new religious order was always difficult, for which reason the bishop needed all the support he could get from prominent families and at court. No doubt it was for this reason that he tried to make the new establishment as attractive as possible to potential recruits and donors. Angélique, who had no difficulty dealing with prominent personages whose spirituality met with her approval, did not agree with what she saw as the introduction of worldly practices in an institution committed to the monastic ideals of austerity and humility. From her point of view, Zamet was repudiating these ideals that he had once espoused. Furthermore, she believed that

Zamet was adopting measures without consulting her. He, in turn, may have felt that Angélique was too inclined to go her own way and to challenge his authority. Very likely he had come to regard her reforming zeal with suspicion, an attitude toward energetic women that was not uncommon among Church officials. Whatever the justification for Angélique's changed attitude toward the bishop of Langres, she did not hesitate to make her feelings known to him despite his superior position within the Church or to take advantage of the clumsy administrative arrangement and her family's close ties to the archbishop of Paris to put an end to an enterprise that did not conform to her ideals.

Once again, Angélique had succeeded in changing the jurisdictional status of Port-Royal. Although the convent was now badly in debt because the network of benefactors developed by Zamet had, for the most part, dissolved along with the Order of the Holy Sacrament, she had nevertheless succeeded in liberating her establishment from the clutches of the bishop of Langres. She and the nuns of Port-Royal, over whom she still had considerable influence, could now reimpose the strict monastic practices that she had put in place. And in the abbé de Saint-Cyran, who replaced Zamet as the spiritual director of the community, Angélique had found a confessor to whom she could bare her soul without any reservations.

∽ ACCESS TO A suitable confessor had been a major concern for Angélique ever since her conversion. She required someone whose spirituality was compatible with her own, who understood her needs, and who was well schooled in Catholic doctrine. She described one of her early confessors, a Cistercian monk, as being so ignorant "that he was unable to say the *pater noster* in French, and he didn't know a single catechism, never having opened a book other than his breviary, his chief activity being the hunt."[32] She never encountered a Cistercian who was able to provide her with spiritual direction, although she admitted that there were some in the order who were competent. Those, however, were reserved as confessors for the monks. As she later told her niece, she found her confessors "too subtle for one who prefers sincerity and frankness," and too limited in their understanding of the monastic tradition.[33] It was not until she met François de Sales that she found the sort of confessor for which she had been looking. The sight of him, she wrote in her memoirs, "produced in me the strongest desire to unburden my conscience to him. For God was truly visible in this holy bishop."[34]

Early in their relationship, as we have seen, Angélique was able to confess to the bishop of Langres, but after he became the spiritual director of the new order, she turned away from him. When Saint-Cyran became temporary director in 1635, Angélique at first refused to confess to him, not because she believed him to be unsuitable but because "his great wisdom made me feel apprehensive about letting him know of my foolishness, and his aura of sanctity [discouraged me from informing him of] my many sins and infidelities. My pain was so great that although I had a real desire to tell him of the state of my soul . . . I found myself unable to confess to him unless God provided me with an extraordinary grace. I begged him as humbly as I could to ask [God] for it."[35]

Eventually Angélique was able to bare her soul to the abbé because she believed that he was motivated by a "genuine spirit of penitence" that enabled him to inspire in those who submitted to his spiritual direction a desire to change their lives by whatever means in order to better serve God. Her willingness to be guided by Saint-Cyran did not always mean that she followed his advice. Profoundly convinced of her own unworthiness, she occasionally refrained for several months from partaking of the sacraments to better prepare herself to receive them in spite of her confessor's advice. On the whole she was inclined to submit to Saint-Cyran because it was her choice to do so, her choice being based on mutually compatible views on penitential ethics. The fact that he was also a close friend of the family helped to sustain the relationship.

Like Angélique, the abbé de Saint-Cyran had himself undergone a process of self-reformation that had altered his life. He was born in 1581 in the city of Bayonne in southwestern France. His father, a wealthy merchant and municipal counselor, had remained loyal to the crown during the Wars of Religion even though there was considerable sympathy for the Catholic League in the region. He began his studies at the Jesuit college at Agen, and then moved on to the Sorbonne and later to the University of Louvain in the Spanish Netherlands. His intellectual abilities and his family connections assured him of a brilliant future in the Church. Ordained in 1618, he was made abbé of the lucrative monastery of Saint-Cyran in central France, and two years later he was appointed almoner to the queen mother, Marie de Medici. At the time of his ordination he underwent a spiritual transformation that caused him to refuse other benefices, some of which were offered to him through the good offices of his friend Robert Arnauld d'Andilly, a man of some influence at court at the time. Over a period of several years, the abbé gradually detached himself from court in order to devote himself entirely to self-reformation and to providing spiritual counsel to those who were willing to receive it.

Saint-Cyran's theological principles, derived from "the Augustinian strain of piety," emphasized man's corrupt nature and inability to achieve redemption and his absolute dependence on divine grace to do good. An awareness of this condition on the part of the sinner inspired humility, "it being impossible to be genuinely pious without humility."[36] An understanding of the human condition also required intense introspection to recognize one's own imperfections. Those who were truly penitent were encouraged by the abbé to change their way of life. In order to sustain that commitment, they had to pray for divine grace, without which even the first step in the process of changing one's life was impossible. To Saint-Cyran's way of thinking, a person had to choose between serving God's interests or serving his own. There was no middle ground, no possibility of compromise, no way to hedge one's bets. The vast majority of mankind, including those who called themselves Christians, chose the way of the world, and only a few hardy souls were prepared to struggle against the world in the hope of ultimate redemption.

Saint-Cyran's profound *mépris du monde* established a common bond with Angélique. For her too the essential truth inherent in the process of self-reformation was an awareness of one's faults. In 1620 she wrote to Jeanne de Chantal: "I am all imperfection, and my grief is that I am unable to see at all the means of perfecting myself." Seventeen years later she confessed to the same person that "I . . . am miserable in the continuance of my infidelities and my resistance to [God's] grace. I am unable to tell you what I suffer knowing as I do that the depths of my soul do not belong to God but to my own selfish interests, against which it never gives any real resistance for the purpose of a genuine submission to God. I believe that my life is nothing but lies and hypocrisy."[37] Saint-Cyran's penitential theology, emphasizing as it did the corrupt nature of the will unsupported by grace, must have had a special appeal to one who was often troubled by the power of her own will.

Religious life for Angélique Arnauld and for the abbé was a never-

ending struggle within the self. Her own experience even before the
journée du guichet involved a struggle against her family's decision to
place her in a convent and against their opposition to reform; afterward
she struggled against her former patroness, Angélique d'Estrées, abbess
of Maubuisson, against the Cistercians, against the bishop of Langres,
and against herself. Her responsibilities as abbess and as a reformer
involved her in activities that she thought brought her into excessive
contact with the world and gave her too little time for solitude, introspection, and prayer. "My misery is so great and my embarrassment
so extreme," she wrote in another letter to Jeanne de Chantal from
Maubuisson in 1620, "that I can't even find time for a retreat. If I try to
set aside time for that purpose it ends up being spent going over accounts with the luminaries of the order [the Cistercians]."[38]

After the *journée du guichet* in 1609, Angélique was in a better position to arrange things on her own terms, be it admitting suitable candidates to Port-Royal, ordering the resources of the household, or solicit-
ing funds from appropriate benefactors. Her reputation as a reformer
had become such that she was called on to rehabilitate other monastic institutions. These accomplishments owed much to her ardent temperament, inherited from her father, her directness, and above all, the
strength of her will. Her sister-in-law, the wife of Robert Arnauld
d'Andilly, said of her that she was like the angels, who terrify one at first
and console one afterward.[39] "The zealous desire she had to reform
the entire world," according to one of the necrologies of Port-Royal,
"caused her to forget sometimes that she was only responsible for the
nuns in her convent."[40] Angélique was, as François de Sales reminded
her, sometimes too impatient and too brusque in her dealings with
others and too demanding of herself.[41] He drew attention to her abrupt
flashes of pride as, for example, when she objected to being addressed as
"ma fille" by Jeanne de Chantal. In his many letters he advised her to be
more gentle in manner and in her dealings with others. She, of course,
was her own severest critic in spite of François de Sales's—and, for that
matter, Saint-Cyran's—pleas that she be easier on herself. She never
ceased believing that the very qualities that enabled her to succeed in
acting for the good in the world endangered her soul, it being impossible to work one's will in the world and at the same time remain humble.
Angélique always kept in mind Saint-Cyran's comment to her that he
had known many abbesses who were able to reform their convents but
not their persons, and this thought filled her with perpetual dread.[42]

In 1636 when Saint-Cyran became the spiritual director of Port-Royal as well as Angélique's own confessor, she was forty-five years old. She had won the admiration of some, who saw her as the worthy friend of the saintly François de Sales, but the enmity of others, including the family of Angélique d'Estrées and Sebastian Zamet, who still had considerable influence at court. There were even those who suspected her and her nuns of being witches. She had developed religious principles that focused on conflict, very different from the principles of her Huguenot uncle Isaac, whose *mépris du monde* was far more accepting of the world than hers. In the struggle for the good against the world outside and within the self, she knew that she had to be willing to suffer persecution, whether from others or from her own tormented psyche, for the sake of righteousness. To her way of thinking, whatever suffering she had to endure was deserved by her, the ever unrepentant sinner. Her *mépris du monde* took root in her consciousness well before she, Saint-Cyran, and indeed her family, became involved in controversy far more serious and dangerous than anything that she had experienced thus far. It was shared by the abbé de Saint-Cyran, whose counsel she would be able to rely on for only a few more years. It was also shared by many members of her family, who in the years following the *journée du guichet* came under the influence of her and Saint-Cyran's spirituality.

4

The Conversion of a Family: The Women

ANGÉLIQUE'S REFUSAL to admit her parents to Port-Royal on the *journée du guichet* did not signify a permanent break with her family but rather a change in her relationship with them, a relationship that thenceforth would be more on her terms than on theirs. Having undertaken her own spiritual reformation, she was now prepared to undertake the reformation of her family just as she had reformed her convent. Her family had placed her in Port-Royal in violation of canon law for reasons that had nothing to do with any religious commitment on her or their part. The spiritual conversion of its members, she hoped, might redeem them in the sight of God. She would also benefit from this conversion in that she would be able to rely on her sisters, her brothers, and her parents for psychological as well as material support as she became increasingly involved in the Catholic reform movement. As Angélique's reputation as a reformer spread throughout France after 1609, so too did her spiritual influence within her own family increase. That influence combined with her forceful personality accounts at least to some extent for the spiritual transformation of the Arnauld family. Whereas before the *journée du guichet* the Arnaulds were caught up in their lives at court, at the Palais de Justice, in the rue de la Verrerie, and at their country estates, after that event they found themselves slowly but surely caught up in the spiritual life of the Port-Royal community. The change in the focus of their lives also resulted from the religious influence of François de Sales and the abbé de Saint-Cyran within the family and from personal experiences that developed in each of them a profound *mépris du monde*. The women in the family were the first to enter Port-Royal, where by 1640 all of Angélique's sisters, her mother, and her nieces had taken their vows as nuns.

The first women to enter the convent were the two younger sisters whom old Simon Marion had decided to place in convents at the same time that he placed Angélique in Port-Royal.

After Angélique's birth in 1591, her mother gave birth to two more daughters, Anne-Eugénie in 1592 and Jeanne in 1593. All three children were born in Tours in their grandfather's household. According to the arrangement that Marion worked out with the crown, Jeanne became the abbess of Saint-Cyr, an office recently vacated by the death of the previous abbess in 1599. Because Jeanne was only six years old at the time, one of the nuns in the convent performed the functions of that office until Jeanne reached the age of twenty.[1] Her parents provided her with a governess (not a nun) to look after her needs, guard her from trouble, and, as was the case with Angélique at Port-Royal, to provide them with reports of her conduct. In October 1599 Jeanne and Angélique were both installed at Saint-Cyr. During the brief time they were together there before Angélique moved on to Maubuisson, Jeanne did not let her older sister forget who was abbess and who was a mere nun.[2]

After Angélique settled in at Port-Royal in 1602, she would occasionally send her carriage to nearby Saint-Cyr to pick up Jeanne, who seems to have become her favorite playmate. Although the two sisters were very different in temperament, they remained close until Angélique's death in 1661. Angélique has been depicted as "passionate, vigorous and tender, capable of humility and *hauteur* as circumstances required, who could make herself feared and loved, capable of creating havoc with her energy and of putting everything to right by her virtues. On the other hand [Jeanne] was of an even disposition, sagacious as well, whose gravity was tempered by sweetness, who inspired confidence and respect, and from whom one learned either from her silence or from her words."[3] The older sister is said to have inherited the temperament of the father and the younger that of the mother.[4]

Unlike Angélique, who after her arrival at Port-Royal remained defiant in her espousal of worldly values, Jeanne never had any doubts about her monastic vocation. By the age of nine she had memorized the psalter and all the chants, and she participated with enthusiasm in all the religious services.[5] Even when Jeanne came to Port-Royal to play with her older sister, she interrupted whatever she was doing in order to attend to her conventual duties. While granting that her younger sister was well behaved and scrupulous in the observance of her duties, Angélique thought her "vainglorious to the point where one might imagine her asking God why he had not made her queen of either France or Spain."[6] During the time that Angélique was undergoing her spiritual conversion in 1608, she often wore the same dirty clothes as a manifestation of her humility. Jeanne was shocked by this behavior.[7] A few years later, when Jeanne became a nun at Port-Royal, Angélique found an occasion to express her contempt for such fastidiousness. When Jeanne spilled oil on her habit, her sister, invoking her *droit d'abbesse*, did not permit her to remove the spot for six weeks.[8]

Yet Angélique's decision to undertake the reform of Port-Royal in 1609 made her realize that she needed Jeanne by her side permanently. She was grateful for her support during the *journée du guichet*. Jeanne, who happened to be visiting Port-Royal on that day, defended her older sister's actions in the face of her indignant parents. Angélique wrote many years later that as "I became strengthened in my desire to give myself to God, he made me see the need to draw her [Jeanne] to me, something that proved to be difficult to accomplish."[9] Jeanne was content with her position at Saint-Cyr, but at the same time she had become attached to Angélique and found it difficult to resist her older sister's earnest requests to join her at Port-Royal. Her father, Antoine Arnauld, was proud of the fact that he could boast of two abbesses in his family. He could easily have exercised his paternal authority and forbidden Jeanne from leaving Saint-Cyr. Instead, he decided to leave to her the decision of whether to leave. Well aware of the difficult choice confronting Jeanne, he refrained from putting any pressure on her. On the other hand, Angélique did not hesitate to resort to pressure, reminding her younger sister that she, like Angélique, had acquired her office under false pretenses.

In 1610, a year after the *journée du guichet*, Jeanne gave in to her sister's wishes that she renounce her office at Saint-Cyr and become a simple nun at Port-Royal. "I let her go for more than a year after she had reached this decision before I would allow her to put on our habit in order to test her," wrote Angélique in her memoirs some forty years later. "And truly she became another person in her submission, her humility and her love of poverty."[10] In 1614 at the age of twenty-one Jeanne Arnauld took her vows as a nun and took the name of Agnès, by which she has been known ever since. For Agnès, there had never been any question about her monastic vocation when she entered Saint-Cyr in 1599. The choice that she had to make between remaining at Saint-Cyr or going to Port-Royal depended on whether she was willing to remain an abbess at the risk of jeopardizing her monastic vows of poverty and humility, a choice that tormented Angélique throughout her life.

Agnès's older sister Anne-Eugénie, in her formative years, was faced with the decision of whether to become a nun at all, given the fact that she was not clear in her mind as to whether she had a true vocation. Born in Tours in 1592, Anne was the third of Antoine and Catherine Arnauld's daughters destined for life in a convent. Evidently Simon Marion did not intend for her to acquire the position of abbess even though she was a year older than Jeanne. Nor did she enter a convent at the same time as her two sisters, but only after Angélique had left Saint-Cyr for Maubuisson in 1600. In that year Anne entered Saint-Cyr, replacing her older sister as Jeanne's companion.

Anne-Eugénie was eight years old when she entered Saint-Cyr. According to Angélique, who saw her quite often when she and Jeanne visited Port-Royal to play with the little abbess, she was quite devout and consequently upset by Angélique's disrespectful attitude toward her religious obligations. Whatever her disposition toward conventual life was in 1605, her parents decided at that time to bring her home. Simon Marion had just died, and Antoine's prospects were much brighter than they had been in the years immediately following the conclusion of the religious wars. His connections at court through his Huguenot brothers, Sully's clients, were solid, his law practice was flourishing, and he had just inherited a substantial amount of property from his father-in-law. He was now in a position to marry off his oldest daughter, Catherine, which he did immediately after Marion's death, and to remove one of his daughters from the convent. Antoine clearly loved his children and seems always to have regretted having to remove them from his household. He and his wife were not unaware of the hazards of the convent and had done all they could to see that the three daughters were properly supervised. Their anxieties were diminished after Anne-Eugénie's return to the safety and comfort of their home.

Anne-Eugénie's return to home occurred before her sister Angélique's conversion. Even though she rapidly became reacclimated to the world outside the convent walls, she defended Angélique's re-forming intentions in the face of her parents' disapproval. "[Anne] had a great love for me and when everyone was against me, she was always on my side defending me as best she could. I believe that God rewarded her [for this support]. I always had a great desire that she become a nun, and I prayed to God with all my heart, but she remained aloof, being vain and extremely complaisant."[11] Although Anne was as loyal to her sister the abbess as Agnès was, Angélique and Anne seemed to be going in opposite directions, Anne embracing the world that Angélique had rejected.

At the age of twenty-one, Anne-Eugénie became so ill from an attack of smallpox that she almost died. Frightened by this experience, she became more attentive to the sermons preached at the family church of Saint-Merry in the rue de la Verrerie and to the advice of her confessor. In September 1615 while listening to one such sermon, she was "seized with the desire to become a nun"[12] in much the same way as Angélique had been a few years earlier, in 1608. The prospect of losing Anne again alarmed her parents, who were not at all convinced that a return to the convent was what she really wanted. Not only did Anne, like Angélique, have to contend with parental disapproval, but she also was subjected to conflicting advice from her sister the abbess, who wanted her to enter Port-Royal, from other devout friends who favored other religious orders, from Huguenot relatives who believed that her spiritual well-being would best be served by converting to Protestantism, and from a lingering inclination of her own to remain in the world and to marry. More infirm of purpose than either Angélique or Agnès, Anne refrained from joining her sisters in Port-Royal until over a year after she decided to become a nun. Angélique was so certain of Anne's vocation that she summoned her to Maubuisson in 1620 to help her with the reforms she was introducing there.[13]

Marie-Claire Arnauld, whose birth in 1600 had precipitated her sister Anne's initial entry into conventual life, also wrestled with conflicting aspirations not unlike Anne's. According to Angélique's recollection many years later, Marie-Claire, the twelfth child born of Madame Arnauld, "was prodigious of mind as well as beautiful. She was able to speak clearly almost from the moment of her birth and to converse with everyone, so taken were they by her delightful appearance."[14] At the age of three, she too was stricken with smallpox that so disfigured her that she was never able to look in a mirror again.[15] Admitted to Port-Royal as a pensioner at the age of seven, Marie-Claire was far more committed at first to monastic life than Angélique had been at her age. Her parents were unhappy at the prospect of losing yet another daughter to the convent. They adored her and enjoyed her visits to the house in the rue de la Verrerie or to the family estate of Andilly. During a visit to Andilly in 1611, at the age of eleven, Marie-Claire began to acquire a taste for the comfortable and agreeable way of life that she encountered there. Her resolve to become a nun became less firm, and when she returned to Port-Royal after the visit she became, according to Angélique, "difficult and disagreeable." Rather than disciplining the pensioner, Angélique, in the words of her niece, "understood only too well how to win her over by being gentle and supportive . . . to the point where she was able to turn her away from the world."[16] Marie-Claire eventually became a nun at Port-Royal in 1615. She was among the small group of nuns who went with Angélique to Maubuisson in 1618, another indication that the abbess of Port-Royal liked to have members of her family with her whenever she could.

Angélique's ascendancy over her sisters is particularly evident in her ability to draw her youngest sister, Madeleine, away from the world and into Port-Royal. Madeleine was born in 1608, only a year after her mother had suffered a painful delivery of twins, a boy and a girl, both of whom died shortly thereafter. Madeleine herself was so weak after a premature birth that she was baptized at home in the expectation that she had not long to live. Despite her frail beginning, Madeleine grew up to become a strong, robust girl, much loved by her parents and entirely acclimated to the world. Neither she nor her parents had any intention of having her join her sisters at Port-Royal. At the age of ten, Madeleine made her feelings on this score all too clear to Angélique during a conversation that took place between the two sisters at their parents' house in the rue de la Verrerie in 1618. The abbess of Port-Royal was on her way to Maubuisson at the time.

> There I found my little sister Madelon [sic], who was pleasure-loving and who enjoyed playing the beauty, which she was. As soon as I saw her I was distressed and said to her, "Why is it, my little sister

Madelon, that you have no wish to become a nun and to come and live with us?" To which she boldly replied, "No, my sister, I have not the slightest desire."—"What do you want to become, my child?"—"My sister, I want to be married."—"And what makes you desire marriage?"—"Nothing more," she said to me "than the affection I have for little children. I love them with all my heart. I am unable to prevent myself from holding and kissing my little nephews. It makes me want to have children of my own." It is true that this simplemindedness of a little girl of ten, who knew nothing of virginity and marriage and who seemed only to want to be the mother of children made me laugh a little at first, but then I was grieved to see her so worldly and so far removed from the desire to give herself to God.[17]

In describing this conversation Angélique appears to have forgotten her own earlier desires to remain in the world and marry like her older sister.

Much as she wanted to draw Madeleine to her and to Port-Royal, she did not have the same easy access to her that she had to Agnès and to Marie-Claire, both of whom were with her during much of the time when they were making critical decisions affecting their lives. In the case of her youngest sister, Angélique was forced to resort to indirect methods. As she explained it to her niece and nephew years later, she was able to work through one of her mother's servants whom she knew wanted to become a nun. Angélique promised the servant that her wish would be realized if she "spoke of God to my little sister and prayed to him to use her [the maid] as the means of obtaining the result that she so much wanted. I also promised the maid that I would receive her not at Maubuisson, where all the places were taken but at Port-Royal, which was entirely reformed and where she would be much better off than at Maubuisson."[18]

Taking Angélique at her word, the maid did what she was told. Her efforts to overcome Madeleine's worldly predilections must have succeeded. Shortly after Angélique made her request, her youngest sister had a dream in which she reportedly saw her patron saint dressed in a nun's garment and covered with thorns. Interpreting this to mean that she was being called to join her sisters at Port-Royal, Madeleine announced to her parents that she too wished to become a nun. Her father refused to take her seriously, but her mother, who had become far more devout than she had been at the time of Angélique's conversion, took her at her word and had her daughter go over her account of the dream several times.

Madeleine's decision to alter the course of her life occurred in 1618, but it was two years before she entered Port-Royal as a pensioner. This delay was undoubtedly caused by internal conflict similar to that experienced by Anne and Marie-Claire. Her father's death in 1619 may also have contributed to the delay. Once having entered the convent, still harboring a lingering desire to remain in the world, she appears to have been recalcitrant during her early years there. Her sister the abbess, who did not shrink from using harsh methods to keep the nuns, including her sisters, in line, mentions having to whip her on several occasions.[19] Five years after entering Port-Royal, Madeleine, confident in her true vocation, took her vows as a nun.

For Angélique and for her sisters Anne-Eugénie, Marie-Claire, and Madeleine, withdrawal from the world was exceedingly difficult. Ironically, the oldest sister, Catherine, had always wanted to become a nun. Born in Tours a year earlier than Angélique, Catherine was intended for marriage according to the strategy determined by Simon Marion, her grandfather. Angélique had been all the more resentful of the decision to place her in a convent because she had believed that her older sister had a real vocation for monastic life whereas she, not Catherine, was better suited for marriage and children. To prepare her for the future that awaited her, Catherine at the age of ten was given the responsibility of assisting her mother in managing the household.[20] When, before the *journée du guichet*, Monsieur and Madame Arnauld visited Angélique at Port-Royal they often brought Catherine with them. "[She] was more devout than I was," said Angélique, "and liked to chant with the nuns, something which I didn't like to do at all."[21]

At the age of thirteen, Catherine received a proposal from Isaac Le Maistre, a *maitre des comptes* (superintendent of accounts attached to the Couv des Comptes), whose wealth was valued at two hundred thousand pounds.[22] Catherine persuaded her father that she was too young to marry, and Le Maistre married someone else. After the death of his wife two years later, Le Maistre proposed to Catherine once again and this time succeeded in winning Catherine's hand. After the wedding, which took place in 1605, the year in which Simon Marion died, the young couple took up residence in the Arnauld household in the rue de la Verrerie, just as her parents had done twenty years earlier. There they remained until the birth of their son Antoine in 1608, at which time they established their own household. Le Maistre seems to have been an unsatisfactory husband from the beginning. When his wife complained of his gambling losses and his indiscreet affairs with other women, Le Maistre became violent and abusive. Catherine Le Maistre spoke to no one outside her household about her unhappy situation, but in 1615 she became so ill that her father insisted on bringing her home as he had done with his other daughters when they became ill at Port-Royal. Safe once again under her father's roof, Catherine broke down and told her parents everything about her unhappy marriage. Monsieur Arnauld decided on the spot to dissolve the marriage and bring Catherine and her five small sons back to his household.

Realizing that he had to proceed carefully, Monsieur Arnauld had his son-in-law placed under surveillance, and when he had collected sufficient evidence he brought suit in the *Chambre des Comptes* to terminate the marriage. Suspecting Le Maistre of being a godless libertine, which would improve the chances of a decision in favor of the father-in-law, Arnauld asked Catherine's husband to declare before the court what his religion was. Le Maistre asked for a delay and after a few days announced that he had converted to Protestantism. By declaring himself a Huguenot, Le Maistre was now in a position to demand, as head of his household, that his sons remain with him after the dissolution of the marriage. The forcible removal of the children of a Huguenot father to the household of his estranged Catholic wife was in violation of rights acquired by the Huguenots according to the terms of the Edict of Nantes. Le Maistre believed that his case was even stronger because it had the support of the chancellor, Guillaume du Vair, and the prince de Condé, both of whom were anxious to establish better ties with the Huguenots in the turbulent years following the assassination of Henry IV. But Antoine Arnauld's connections at court were also strong. His brother Isaac was an influential person in the *conseil des finances*, who, although a Huguenot himself, did not take seriously Le Maistre's change of religion. After much wrangling in court, Arnauld won a favorable decision that enabled Catherine and her sons to live with him.[23] Although Le Maistre tried at least until 1620 to have the decision reversed, he was unsuccessful. He continued his dissolute ways until the end of his life in 1640.

Catherine Le Maistre's responsibilities as a mother made it impossible for her to retire to Port-Royal. Even if she had been able to do so, she could not have taken her vows as a nun until her husband's death effectively dissolved the marriage. When the community of nuns was transferred from the convent of Port-Royal in the valley of the Chevreuse to temporary quarters in Paris in 1625, Catherine withdrew there from time to time, but she did not establish a permanent residence until her sons were old enough to take care of themselves. She served for a time as governess to the children of the duchesse de Nemours, daughter of the duchesse de Longueville, later to become a benefactor of Port-Royal. Despite this opportunity to serve in the household of a princess of the blood, an opportunity that offered women of Madame Le Maistre's rank the possibility of obtaining influential social connections,[24] she yearned to join her sisters at Port-Royal. Indeed she suffered so much whenever she had to leave the convent to tend to her affairs that her sister Agnès became concerned and wrote her a number of letters encouraging her to accept her situation. "I beg you, my sister," she wrote in 1631, "be fair to yourself and be as inventive in consoling yourself as you are in abusing yourself. Don't distress yourself so much by your absence [from Port-Royal] because it will not last long."[25] In another letter several months later, Agnès wrote from another convent that she was visiting: "My dear sister, we have just learned that you have passed some good days at Port-Royal, and I think by now you will have returned to your exile."[26] So strong was the idea of withdrawing from the world in Catherine Le Maistre's mind that she had to be encouraged by her sisters to resume her responsibilities in the world.

Angélique, who was occupied with affairs at Maubuisson and Lys in the years following the dissolution of Catherine's marriage, followed the progress of her sister's life with interest, though from afar. Catherine, in her opinion, was very pious but in need of firm direction. With this in mind, she managed to persuade François de Sales to take an interest in her. In a letter to Catherine in 1619 the bishop of Annecy wrote: "What will I say to you, my daughter, seeing you in such bitterness . . . Courage, I beg of you!"[27] Angélique was also able to interest Jeanne de Chantal in her sister's plight. "My very dear mother," wrote Angélique to Jeanne in 1620, evidently exasperated by Catherine's inability to get a grip on herself, "have some pity on my poor sister; she is a little soft, but she is good and will do well enough. However she must be prodded from time to time. If you will exert a little authority over her and force her to give an account of herself, you will do her a good service."[28] As was the case with her other sisters, Angélique was doing all she could to assert her own authority over Catherine even though her elder sister was not yet a member of her community. After her husband's death, Catherine was finally able to take her vows as a nun in 1640, the first among her sisters to acquire a true vocation for monastic life but the last to actually enter it.

Even her mother, Madame Arnauld, took her vows before Catherine. Madame Arnauld's life in its own way had been as difficult as that of her eldest daughter. Perhaps it was in appreciation of similar experiences that Catherine Le Maistre undertook to write a biographical sketch of her mother. Madame Arnauld had borne twenty children within twenty-four years, the first when she was only fifteen and the last in 1612 when she was thirty-nine. Her last six pregnancies were "accompanied by severe pain in her intestines and other difficulties which never enabled her to relax. Her *accouchements* were so troublesome that she was always in danger of her life."[29] Her piety was of a conventional sort, her primary concern as a wife and mother being the proper ordering of her large household. When, against her own wishes, her daughters were placed in convents, she saw to it that they were properly cared for. Her numerous visits to Port-Royal before the *journée du guichet* attest to her concern for Angélique's well-being despite Angélique's assertion that her mother never loved her.

Madame Arnauld's furious reaction to Angélique's refusal to admit her family to the inner quarters of the convent on the *journée du guichet* was that of a mother confronted with a disobedient child. Vowing never to speak to Angélique again, Madame Arnauld refused to return to Port-Royal even after her husband had obtained a permit for her to enter the establishment from the head of the Cistercian order. Not until 1611, when Agnès Arnauld became a novice at Port-Royal, did Madame Arnauld deign to return and reestablish contact with the abbess. Yet in the years immediately following the *journée du guichet*, Madame Arnauld became more devout, influenced no doubt by Angélique's reputation, which brought honor to the family. She was more responsive to the psychological distress of her daughter Anne, torn between the decision to become a nun or remain in the world, than she had been to Angélique's distress at the time of the *journée du guichet*. When her youngest daughter Madeleine described her dream of her patron saint summoning her to join her sisters at Port-Royal, Madame Arnauld listened with a sympathetic ear. During this time she even consulted with Angélique about her own spiritual needs and permitted the abbess to recommend a confessor to her.[30] By the 1620s she had so impressed François de Sales and the abbé de Saint-Cyran with her piety that they became her confessors.

After Antoine Arnauld's death, his widow presided over a household that now included three sons, a daughter, and five grandsons, all of whom required her attention and imposed a strain on the family resources. Feeling that her responsibility lay at home, Madame Arnauld rejected a prestigious offer to serve as governess to the daughter of the duchesse de Guise, an offer that, taken together with her daughter Catherine's offer to serve in the household of the duchesse de Nemours, is indicative of the social prominence acquired by the Arnaulds. Despite Madame Arnauld's earlier aversion to Angélique, she was clearly drawing closer to the abbess, whom she visited several times at Maubuisson. She opposed Angélique's strong inclination to resign her office to become a Visitandine and only agreed to let her do it at the urging of François de Sales.

In 1623 Madame Arnauld and Catherine Le Maistre spent several weeks at Port-Royal, preferring to go there rather than to Andilly to escape the threat of plague in Paris. During this sojourn Madame Arnauld became convinced that the establishment in the valley of the Chevreuse was too small to accommodate the growing numbers of inmates. It was she who took the initiative to obtain permission from the archbishop of Paris to transfer the community and find a suitable place in the city to install it. When the site in the Faubourg Saint-Jacques was found, Madame Arnauld bought it and the villa located on it for eighty thousand pounds.

It was also during the sojourn at Port-Royal-des-Champs in 1623 that Madame Arnauld began to give serious thought to becoming a nun herself. Like her daughters before her, she resisted the inclination for several years, in part because many of her friends warned her that she was too old to endure the rigors of monastic life and in part because, as she said to Catherine Le Maistre, she had become accustomed to giving orders since she was a girl and was doubtful whether she could learn to obey the orders of others.[31] In spite of her reservations, she found it increasingly difficult to resist being drawn to an establishment that contained all but one of her daughters, an establishment in which she and her husband had invested so much. Among others, she consulted the abbé de Saint-Cyran and her daughter Angélique about her true vocation. In 1626 she finally reached the decision to enter Port-Royal as a novice. At that time she gave over to the nuns for the purpose of relocating the convent in Paris all the property that she had acquired, together with three thousand pounds worth of furniture and the substantial sum of seven thousand pounds. In return, she received residential privileges within the convent for her eldest daughter and her daughter-in-law, Madame Arnauld d'Andilly, as well as the right to have her granddaughters educated there.[32] With Madame Arnauld's generous donation, Port-Royal became an Arnauld family establishment to a far greater extent than it had ever been. By 1629 Port-Royal had become the spiritual citadel of the Arnauld women and, thanks to their intense piety, a symbol of the family's spiritual transformation.

"I granted her her wish," wrote Angélique in her memoirs, commenting on her mother's request to become a novice, "and she had the goodness and the humility to place herself entirely under my direction."[33] Three years later Madame Arnauld took her vows as a nun. The mother who had vowed never to speak to her daughter again after being denied entry to Port-Royal in 1609 was now prepared to submit to the authority of that daughter for the rest of her life. As was said of her in one of the necrologies of Port-Royal, "she resolved to become a nun at the age of fifty-three, receiving her novice's habit from the hands of her daughter whom she regarded from that moment on as her mother, respecting her and obeying her with the simplicity of a child."[34] In submitting to the authority of the daughter whom she had never liked, she "reversed the natural order" within the family, according to Nicolas Fontaine, who knew the Arnaulds well.[35]

The accounts of Madame Arnauld's and her daughters' moves from household to convent are provided by Angélique in her autobiography and in her recorded conversations with her niece Angélique de Saint-Jean and nephew Antoine Le Maistre in the 1650s. In these accounts she attributes the decision of each of the sisters and her mother to join her at Port-Royal to the power of prayer. As she tells the story, God drew the women to her in response to her prayers. Certainly Angélique's spiritual influence within the family increased as her reputation as a reformer grew, making it easier for her to turn the women in her family in her direction. Women had traditionally constituted the spiritual center of the family. In the case of the Arnaulds, Angélique had become that center during the decade following the *journée du guichet*, assuming a role that usually belonged to the mother.

However, there were other reasons for the Arnauld women's spiritual transformations. Each woman had developed a monastic vocation as a result of personal experience or, as in the case of Catherine Le Maistre and Agnès, of their own inclination. Anne-Eugénie and Marie-Claire were disfigured by smallpox, which made them more sensitive to the ephemeral nature of worldly vanity; Madeleine had a dream that eventually drew her to Port-Royal; Catherine Le Maistre had a miserable marriage; and her mother, Madame Le Maistre, was exhausted from the pain and suffering caused by frequent childbirth. The *mépris du monde* espoused by all these women was shaped to some extent by these experiences. There was also the matter of family loyalty. Agnès and Anne-Eugénie felt a strong attachment to Angélique, based on respect for her reforming ideals. As more women in the family became nuns at Port-Royal, others among them were more inclined to join them, identifying Port-Royal with the family as their male relatives were later to do. All the Arnauld women who joined Angélique at Port-Royal came there in response to a true vocation and not against their will, unlike Angélique, who, before she undertook her reforms, dreamed of escaping the convent. Entering Port-Royal with a genuine commitment to monastic ideals, these women were similar to the vast majority of candidates who sought admission to convents early in the seventeenth century in response to the influence of the Catholic reform movement.

ᐸᔆ ONCE HER mother and sisters had become nuns, Angélique behaved very much as a mother toward them, taking advantage of her position to keep them in line. Before they entered her community "she was very tolerant of their faults which it was not yet time to remedy . . . However once inside, everything changed in her efforts to develop their piety. Unyielding firmness became the balm that she applied to the wounds that are caused by pride."[36] Her treatment of Madeleine was typical of this firmness. Contrasting the whippings she administered to her youngest sister with the ones she had herself received as a child from her nurse, Angélique contended that the punishment meted out by the nurse was unjust because it had been done in anger, whereas the punishment she administered to Madeleine was done with good intention.[37]

If her mother and sisters looked to Angélique as the authority figure in their lives, she in turn looked to them for support and encouragement. Madame Arnauld was able to provide much-needed financial assistance in the years between 1624 and 1629, which facilitated the move to Paris and the launching of Angélique's joint venture with Sebastian Zamet, the Order of the Holy Sacrament. Once installed in Port-Royal and committed to monastic life, Anne Arnauld and Marie-Claire helped Angélique institute reforms at both the convents of Maubuisson and Lys. However, it was Agnès who provided Angélique with the most support throughout her career. Shortly after Agnès became a permanent resident at Port-Royal, Angélique put her in charge of the novices, even though Agnès was only a novice herself. When Angélique was preparing to leave for Maubuisson in 1618, she insisted on having Agnès named coadjutrice of Port-Royal even though François de Sales expressed some concern about perpetuating benefices within the family.[38] Angélique prevailed because she believed that Agnès was the person most capable of taking her place while she was away. During the years when the Order of the Holy Sacrament was being organized, Agnès spent time at the convent of Tard in the diocese of the bishop of Langres, where she was elected abbess in 1630. At Tard she prepared the nuns for the eventual unification with Port-Royal in the newly established order. It was Agnès who wrote the religious treatise that led to the charge of heresy against the new order, and it was she who, as the abbess elected in 1636, asked the bishop of Langres at Angélique's bidding to disassociate himself from Port-Royal.

Agnès had not always agreed with her older sister that a break with Zamet was necessary. During the time that Angélique was distancing herself from the bishop, Agnès was far removed from the scene at Tard, where she had no reason to believe that Zamet was undermining her sister's reforms. Her spirituality, akin to that of the bishop's, contained within it a mystical element that was alien to Angélique, more contemplative and more inclined to leave everything to God's will. Angélique was much too impatient and too inclined to the impetuous act to appreciate this attitude, and often criticized her younger sister of daydreaming, but this difference in temperament never affected the close relationship between the two sisters. In 1635 Angélique obtained Zamet's consent to allow Agnès to return to Paris. By the time Agnès got back to Paris she had been briefed by the bishop as to the state of affairs in the new order. Still loyal to Zamet, Agnès rebuked her older sister for having become excessively influenced by the abbé de Saint-Cyran. Wrote Angélique in her memoirs, "I found her [Agnès] so prejudiced against M. de Saint-Cyran, and against me . . . that she seemed to be almost another person." Angélique was so upset by her sister's hostile attitude that she begged Saint-Cyran to speak to Agnès, which he was reluctant to do, fearing that Agnès might think him too forward. However, Angélique insisted, and the abbé, unable to resist her entreaties, eventually agreed to talk to Agnès. Several days later Agnès wrote to Angélique admitting that she had been wrong about Saint-Cyran. "It was a great consolation to me to receive that letter and to find my sister in this disposition."[39]

Another of Angélique's sisters who found it difficult to break with Zamet was Marie-Claire, who until 1635 had been entirely loyal and devoted to Angélique. Indeed Angélique had become somewhat concerned about her younger sister being excessively attached to her. Having found a satisfactory spiritual director in Zamet, Marie-Claire was not happy to find herself at odds with Angélique on the question of his removal and, by 1636, at odds with her mother and all her sisters as well. All the more difficult for her to understand was Agnès's letter to Zamet asking him not to visit Port-Royal again and her request to the nuns not to remain in contact with him. Torn between her loyalty to her mother and sisters and her respect for the bishop of Langres, Marie-Claire was unable to choose between them. Agnès and Angélique were so disturbed by Marie-Claire's state of mind that they even invited their oldest brother, Robert Arnauld d'Andilly, to use his powers of persuasion to bring his sister back into line. Andilly's efforts were successful, in part because he was a man and head of the family.

One of the reasons for Marie-Claire's reluctance to break with Zamet was because he too was a man, as well as a bishop, whose authority over her was legitimate. Thus she was confused by Angélique's request that she in effect renounce that authority. She explained all this to Agnes in a letter asking her forgiveness. In the letter she pleaded with her sister to "forget about her disobedience and her blindness, which had made her resist God's authority."[40] Ironically, the dilemma faced by Marie-

Claire in being forced to choose between loyalty to her family and obedience to a bishop was later to be experienced by Agnès, Angélique, and other members of her family. Marie-Claire eventually became as devoted to the abbé de Saint-Cyran as were her mother and sisters and transcribed his letters written from prison, which were later published by Arnauld d'Andilly. In the last years of her life (she died in 1642), she performed the most menial tasks in the convent in order to atone for her deviation.

Despite the stresses and strains among the Arnauld sisters caused by the Zamet affair, Angélique had succeeded in having them accept the spiritual director on whom she had decided for herself and the community. At the same time, she was able to use her considerable influence to compel two of her sisters, Agnès and Marie-Claire, faced with the choice between submitting to Zamet's authority or to her own, to choose her. Having overcome the troubles that threatened to tear apart the community that she had established and to sow dissension among the Arnauld women, she was in a better position to deal with the troubles that lay ahead, secure in the support her sisters and mother gave her, and secure as well in the support she was now receiving from her brothers and nephews.

5

The Reformation of a Family: The Solitaires

A NGÉLIQUE WAS less directly involved in the reformation of her male relatives than she was in drawing the women in the family to Port-Royal. Despite her belief in the magnetic power of her prayers, she did not have the same easy access to the men that she did with the women. The women were either in residence in their father's household, which she visited from time to time, or at Port-Royal. The men, on the other hand, were out and about at court, in the Palais de Justice, or at the university, and therefore harder to reach. Nevertheless Angélique did have some spiritual influence on the men because of her reputation as a reformer and the growing reputation of Port-Royal, so closely identified with the Arnauld family. The men came to regard Port-Royal as a family shrine to which they were bound at the very least by ties of loyalty and affection. By 1640 the convent had become in a very real sense the center of family life.

The abbé de Saint-Cyran was the key figure in the reformation of the men. By 1625, the year that Port-Royal was moved to Paris, he had become a close friend of several members of the family, including Angélique's older brother Robert Arnauld d'Andilly, Madame Arnauld, and Catherine Le Maistre. When the abbé first became associated with Angélique and Port-Royal in 1633, he had been the spiritual guide and counselor of Andilly for thirteen years and Madame Arnauld's spiritual director for almost a decade. Friendship alone does not explain Saint-

Cyran's influence with the Arnauld men or his charismatic appeal. Like the Arnaulds, he came from an upwardly mobile family and was as ambitious as any of them. Having withdrawn from the world for a life of prayer and contemplation, he could respond sympathetically to the Arnaulds' painful efforts to do the same. Once the abbé became the spiritual director of Port-Royal, he strengthened the bond between the Arnauld men and the convent. Like the women in the family, the *mépris du monde* adopted by the men was shaped to a considerable extent by their experiences in the world—their disappointments, their frustrations, and their desire to be free of the sycophantic atmosphere at court and other places within the public sphere.

In general terms, the men and women in the family had the same choice to make—whether to remain in the world or withdraw from it. For the women it was a choice between their father's household (or the household of a husband) and the convent. Once inside Port-Royal, they followed a well-regulated routine, with the exception of Angélique and, to a certain extent, Agnès, both leaders of the monastic community. In their cases there was always tension between their public roles and their private needs, a tension experienced as well by the men in the family. Having made the decision to withdraw from the world, the Arnauld men did not have the benefit of institutional support in the form of a monastery. Those Arnauld men who did withdraw were on their own in terms of the penitential activities that they undertook. They chose not to become affiliated with any particular order or institution within the Church, preferring instead to conduct their lives according to the simple precepts of the gospel. Hence the magnetic pull of worldly attractions was always strong and the opportunity to satisfy one's ambitions in heroic struggles against the world very real. The Arnauld men and some of the Arnauld women were to discover that the power and influence that they and their ancestors had acquired were hard to give up even after they had renounced the world.

Key to the reformation of the Arnauld family was Antoine Arnauld, Angélique's father. His support, of course, was crucial to Angélique's endeavors on behalf of religious reform, but a spiritual transformation on his part in which he renounced his ambitions for a life of charity and humility would be a significant indication of Angélique's influence within the family and of her influence over him. So much did she desire her father to alter the conditions of his life entirely that she came to believe that he had in fact done so and that the world would have known about it if death had not intervened. Arnauld's final illness, according to Angélique, lasted thirty days, during which time she prayed ceaselessly for his conversion and recovery. As he lay dying, he took a vow in the presence of his son Robert and a priest that were he to live, he would give all his property to his wife and eldest son, keeping only a few books for himself. Although he would continue to practice law, he would do so in the interest of justice rather for his own advantage. He would even go so far as to change his name to René—it is not known why he chose that name—in order to complete the transformation. Unfortunately, he was never given the opportunity to prove himself.[1] Arnauld d'Andilly, who was present at his father's deathbed, makes no mention of this extraordinary vow.[2]

Certainly Antoine was very much involved in the affairs of Port-Royal after the *journée du guichet* in 1609. On that day Angélique had placed limits on his access to the convent and had asserted her own right to govern the establishment as she saw fit. However, her father still maintained parental rights. His approval was required in order to move Agnès from Saint-Cyr to Port-Royal, to engage Angélique in the reform of Maubuisson, and for Angélique to resign her office to become a simple nun, a right that was transferred to his wife after his death. Antoine Arnauld might well have refused permission for his daughters Anne-Eugénie and Marie-Claire to become nuns at Port-Royal. The fact that he did not is as much a measure of his benevolence toward his family as of Angélique's influence on him. Clearly he had become much more sympathetic toward the abbess of Port-Royal's reforms after 1609. Within a year after his abrupt departure from the convent he obtained permission from the Cistercians to enter the premises for the purpose of developing plans for the improvement of the buildings and grounds. He had the exterior walls elevated to discourage intruders, who were a constant menace, and had a floor added to one of the buildings.[3] Angélique depended at times on her father's legal skills. Before she assumed responsibility for the administration of Port-Royal, a substantial amount of land had become alienated from the convent through the Cistercians' real estate ventures. With Antoine's assistance, Angélique reestablished title over much of this property, thereby increasing the convent's revenues.[4]

Antoine Arnauld never became a member of the Port-Royal community in any spiritual sense, although its numerous necrologies recognize him as one of its leading benefactors. He supported his daughter's endeavors after the *journée du guichet*, but he saw these endeavors in terms of the luster they contributed to the family's reputation. He continued to engage in the practice of law and to offer political advice to the king whenever he felt it necessary until his death.[5]

The first male member of the family to become in every sense a member of the Port-Royal community was Antoine's grandson Antoine Le Maistre, whose early career in the Parlement of Paris was modeled on that of his illustrious grandfather but whose later career was in effect a repudiation of his grandfather's achievements. Le Maistre was born in 1608, the son of Catherine and Isaac Le Maistre. At the age of seven he moved with his mother and brothers to the household of old Antoine Arnauld, where he was brought up. There he came under the influence not only of his grandfather but of his uncle Robert Arnauld d'Andilly. Under their tutelage he became interested in a career in the law, but under the influence of his mother, Catherine, and his aunts, particularly after the death of his grandfather, he also gave some thought to a career in the Church. It was through his mother and grandmother that he came to know the abbé de Saint-Cyran, who took interest in his development.

Despite the opposition of his mother and his aunts Angélique and Agnès, all of whom believed that he should devote his life entirely to God, Le Maistre decided to follow in the footsteps of his grandfather and became a barrister. He was helped in this by Arnauld d'Andilly, who brought him to the attention of the *avocat général*, Jerome Bignon, who helped launch his career. Within a few years after arguing his first case at the bar, Le Maistre had acquired a reputation for eloquence that reminded many of his grandfather and his great-grandfather, Simon Marion. It was said of him that when he rose to plead a case in the Parlement of Paris, priests refused to preach sermons for fear of losing their audience to the Grand Chamber of the Palais de Justice.[6] According to the prominent writer Guez de Balzac, who had always been impressed with the eloquence of the Arnaulds, Le Maistre's "powerful, rich and magnificent harangues would have aroused jealousy in Cicero and Demosthenes."[7]

Le Maistre became the protégé of the chancellor, Pierre Séguier, who was responsible for his appointment as *conseiller d'état* in 1633.

Offered the position of *avocat général* at the Parlement of Metz by the chancellor, Le Maistre refused it, believing that he would have better opportunities if he remained in Paris. His career was not without its setbacks, however. In 1634 he expressed a wish to marry Madeleine de Cornouaille, the niece of the *avocat général*, Jerome Bignon. An alliance with a prominent and wealthy magisterial family would benefit him in the same way that similar alliances had benefitted other members of the Arnauld family in that it would increase his contacts in political circles. In a letter to his aunt Agnès, at that time in residence at the convent of Tard, he proudly announced his intention to marry "the richest and the most beautiful young woman in Paris."[8] Agnès's response revealed the profound desire on the part of the women in the family to win Le Maistre over to a total commitment to a religious life. Expressing her disappointment in her nephew's decision, the nun wrote: "You know of my distaste for marriage not in itself but in comparison with the ecclesiastical state."[9]

Angélique's reaction to Le Maistre's announcement was far more blunt. She was determined that her oldest nephew, to whom she was devoted, would enter the clergy, and she was not about to approve the marriage. Le Maistre, on the other hand, was unrelenting in his efforts to obtain her approval. Angélique told him that if he did marry, she would no longer have any affection for him. Infuriated by his aunt's intransigence, Le Maistre replied that her vows as a nun did not free her from the bonds of familial affection and that the Christian faith recognizes "that one must love one's relatives more than others. If you were to renounce your love for me because of an evil deed that I had committed, I would understand. But you have nothing to reproach me for except that I wish to marry, a desire that is perfectly legitimate."[10]

His hopes for an advantageous marriage were soon dashed—not by his aunts' opposition but by Madeleine de Cornouaille's family. Having recently inherited one hundred thousand *écus* from an uncle, Bignon decided, despite his friendship with Le Maistre and the Arnauld family, that his young cousin was in a position to marry someone of a higher rank with a larger fortune. This setback to an otherwise promising career so affected the temperamental young man that he announced to Saint-Cyran and others in 1635 that he wished to withdraw from the world. However, Saint-Cyran urged him to delay such a decision for at least several months until he was more sure of his intentions.

Disappointment caused by his inability to establish an advantageous alliance with the Bignon family undoubtedly contributed to Le Maistre's disillusionment with the world, but his inclination to withdraw from it owed something to the spiritual influence of the women in his family, particularly that of Angélique. His need to obtain his aunt's approval for his marriage and his resentment at her opposition to it reveal his awareness of just how strong that influence was. As he pondered his decision to withdraw from the world, he asked his aunt to support him with her prayers, not as a courteous gesture but in recognition of the important role that she had come to play in his life.[11]

Le Maistre's final decision to renounce his legal career occurred two years later, in 1637. His aunt Catherine, the wife of Arnauld d'Andilly, in whose household Le Maistre resided, became fatally ill during the summer. She was visited frequently by the abbé de Saint-Cyran for the purpose of preparing her for death. On these occasions the abbé emphasized the meaninglessness of life to those gathered around the deathbed, including Le Maistre, who was now convinced that he heard the word of God himself urging him to attend to his own spiritual needs.[12] When he was made aware of the effect of his words on the young man, Saint-Cyran again urged him not to do anything precipitously. Le Maistre returned to the bar with little enthusiasm when the Parlement resumed its sessions in the autumn. His lack of effort was noticed by a colleague, Omer Talon, who was allegedly jealous of Le Maistre's oratorical skills. Talon let it be known that his rival had become lazy with too much success. Le Maistre, when he was told what Talon had said about him, delivered a final harangue in the Palais de Justice "with more force and vigor than ever before . . . [A]s if in this one last effort he had resolved in leaving the chamber to make a sacrifice to God of such a rare talent and to silence forever a voice that had been the admiration of the entire kingdom."[13]

Shortly after this oratorical *tour de force*, which brought to an end his career at the bar, Le Maistre wrote to his patron, Séguier, that he had decided to change his life:

> I would be lacking in the respect that I owe you, and I would be guilty of ingratitude if, having received from you so many extraordinary favors, I carried out a decision of such importance without informing you. I am abandoning, my Lord, a career that you have

been very helpful in promoting, as well as everything that I might hope for or desire in this world. I am withdrawing into a life of solitude in order to do penance and to serve God the rest of my days . . . I do not feel obliged to justify this action, which requires no justification. However I think that I must let you know my most secret intentions so that you may not be misled by rumors that may be circulated against me. You should know that I renounce forever all ecclesiastical as well as civil offices and that I am not simply motivated by a change in ambition; I have no ambition at all. I am even less inclined to enter the clergy and to receive benefices than I am to resume the career that I am renouncing.[14]

In a letter to his father Le Maistre reiterated his intention to undertake a life of penance.[15]

The intentions expressed by Antoine Le Maistre in these letters were similar to those which caused Angélique Arnauld to close the doors of her convent to her parents on the *journée du guichet* twenty-eight years earlier. Just as Angélique had repudiated her family's values, which had made her a pawn in its strategy for worldly success, so too did Le Maistre repudiate the values that had contributed to that success. And as Angélique had freed herself from family control in order to develop herself on her own terms, so did Le Maistre free himself from dependence on the favor of the king and his ministers—a dependence that enabled the crown to establish control over the lives of those who sought its favors—in order to administer to his spiritual needs on his own terms. In asserting his independence, Le Maistre risked the displeasure of his patron Séguier in the same way that his aunt had risked the animosity of her family and other benefactors of her convent by restoring cloture to Port-Royal. Séguier would undoubtedly see Le Maistre's retirement as an act of disloyalty to him.

Le Maistre was undaunted by these risks. Like his aunt, he had adopted a *mépris du monde* that made him contemptuous of everything that he had once cherished. In a letter to Antoine Singlin, Angelique's confessor, several years later, he wrote:

I am well aware, Monsieur, that there are those who look on me with curiosity, with astonishment, with pity or with indignation. Few recognize the effect of divine grace on my transformation or

see the miraculous effect of this first cause. They may see an infinite number of chains which bound me to the flesh, to the world
and to myself broken. It has been a long time since a man in my
place and of my rank, ensconced in the corruption of the Palais de
justice, in the flower of his age, in the advantages of his birth, vain
in his eloquence, with his reputation well established, his fortune
well advanced, his aspirations perfectly legitimate; a man such as I
was suddenly letting go of all these ties, breaking the chains that
imprison men, making himself poor where once he endeavored to
acquire riches, enduring the austerities of penance where once he
pursued the pleasures of the flesh, embracing solitude when once
he was besieged by the affairs of the world, and condemning himself to perpetual silence when once he delighted in speaking to the
applause of those who heard him. This miracle is less common
than those that make the blind see and the deaf hear. Such is the
lack of piety in the age in which we live that most regard such
a transformation as extraordinary rather than as a divine occur-
rence.[16]

Try as he might to insist that his transformation was caused by an
infusion of God's grace, Le Maistre could not conceal an element of
pride—almost of boastfulness—in what he had done. The renunciation
of such a promising career in favor of a life of solitude reminded Sainte-
Beuve of those heroic gestures depicted in Corneille's plays, so popular
at the time.[17] Le Maistre's dramatic renunciation of his career brought
to an end his family's association with the Parlement of Paris.

Having finally secured Saint-Cyran's approval of his decision, Le
Maistre withdrew in 1638 to a small house very close to Port-Royal-de-
Paris in the Faubourg Saint-Jacques. Having cut himself off from all his
former connections, he was now entirely alone, a hermit (*solitaire*), but
only for a brief period of time. He soon became the nucleus of a group
of like-minded men who, inspired by his "*grande action,*" constituted a
community of *solitaires*.

The first to join Le Maistre in his retreat was his younger brother
Simon Le Maistre de Séricourt, born in 1611. Under the auspices of his
uncle Simon Arnauld and his cousins Antoine Arnauld d'Andilly and
Isaac Arnauld de Corbeville, Séricourt had embarked on a career in the
military. Endowed with a gentle disposition and a rather weak physique,
according to Nicolas Fontaine, a close friend of the Le Maistres and

himself a future *solitaire*, the rigors of military life were hard on him, but, as it happened, they prepared him for the penitential discipline that he would soon impose on himself. When he first learned of his older brother's decision to abandon his brilliant legal career, Séricourt was as astonished as everybody else. When his regiment was in winter quarters near Paris, he paid his older brother a visit. In "the lugubrious environ-ment" in which Séricourt found him, Le Maistre was almost unrecog-nizable. "Don't you recognize me, my brother?" asked Antoine. "You are looking on M. Le Maistre of old. He is dead to the world, and he hopes to be dead to himself. I have spoken enough in public, but now I intend to speak to no one but God. I have tormented myself to no avail pleading the cause of others, but now I will plead only my case in secret, in the tranquility of my retreat."[18] So moved was the younger brother by this encounter that he resolved on the spot to join Le Maistre in a life of penance. Antoine was delighted by this decision, as was their mother, Catherine, herself soon to take her vows as a nun. She had always hoped that the favorite of her five sons would devote his life to his religion as his older brother had chosen to do.

Perhaps because he felt the need of institutional support for his life of piety or because he wanted to establish his own spiritual identity inde-pendent of his brother, several years after he became a *solitaire* Séricourt decided to become a member of the monastic order of the Chartreux. Resisting Antoine's efforts to persuade him to remain at his side and his own inclination to remain with his family, he made application to join the order, but his request was refused because of his association with an unorthodox community whose religious ideals were becoming increas-ingly suspect.[19] The refusal came at the moment when Séricourt, ac-cording to Fontaine, was beginning to have second thoughts about becoming a Chartreux. Whatever the facts of the matter, the family tie, which kept the brothers together, remained intact.

The two men were forced to change residences in and around Paris several times because they feared arrest, having aroused the ire of the chancellor, Séguier, and others on account of their unconventional be-havior. As Le Maistre had feared, Séguier was offended by his protégé's abrupt change of career. What was particularly disturbing to the chan-cellor and other officials was Le Maistre's decision not to enter the clergy or enter a monastery, but to reorder his life on his own terms, self-reliant and therefore free of any control or supervision other than that of the abbé de Saint-Cyran. The authorities of church and state viewed with suspicion deviant religious activities such as those displayed by the Le Maistre brothers. These authorities were always alert to unregulated behavior of one sort or another that might get out of hand. The little group of hermits lived a precarious existence until it was disbanded once and for all in 1660. Dispersed from one place, they reassembled in another. At one point, in June 1638, the handful of hermits, no more than ten at the time, were expelled from their residence near Port-Royal-de-Paris by the archbishop of Paris because, as he explained, they were not of good morals. In 1650 they finally settled on a small farm (Les Granges) attached to the abandoned convent of Port-Royal-des-Champs, where they had taken up residence on previous occasions only to be chased out by the king's orders.[20] They gave their worldly goods to the nuns in return for a subsistence pension,[21] and thus in a very real sense became part of the community of Port-Royal.

In 1645 the third of five sons born to Catherine and Isaac Le Maistre became a *solitaire*.[22] Born in 1613, Isaac-Louis Le Maistre de Sacy was raised by his mother, whose spiritual influence on him was even stronger than it was on his two older brothers. Whereas they had first chosen secular careers, Sacy had never wavered in his boyhood desire to become a priest. The chief issue with respect to his career was whether to acquire a doctorate at the Sorbonne and become a theologian as his uncles wanted him to do or, as he preferred, to remain a simple priest. Such was his humility that he feared that in his efforts to become a competent theologian he might compromise his vocation as a priest, an attitude that was looked upon with approval by the abbé de Saint-Cyran.

Saint-Cyran, the confessor of the *solitaires* as well as the nuns, was much impressed with Sacy's piety and with his staunch *mépris du monde*, which was its chief ingredient. "The world is nothing but an insane illusion," the young man wrote to his oldest brother. "We should not give it the slightest thought other than to regard with compassion those who joyfully hurl themselves into the eternal fires of damnation."[23] With the encouragement of the abbé and of Antoine Singlin, who became the spiritual director of Port-Royal after Saint-Cyran's death in 1643, Sacy, who had lived intermittently with the *solitaires* since 1638, became a permanent member of the community in 1645 and was ordained a priest four years later.

Singlin was so impressed with Sacy's vocation that he invited the nuns and *solitaires* to confess to the recently ordained priest. Some within the community of Port-Royal hesitated to submit to someone so new to his position, but all, including Séricourt and his mother, acceded to Singlin's request with the exception of Le Maistre, who was obstinate in his refusal to submit to the priestly authority of his younger brother. The blood tie made it equally difficult for Sacy to judge his eldest sibling. The relationship between the two brothers was made more complicated by different temperaments. Le Maistre was a man of action, of passionate intensity, who, as Fontaine put it, embarked on a life of penance with considerable panache, whereas Sacy was calm and reserved. The difference between them was much the same as the difference between their grandparents, Antoine and Catherine Arnauld, and their aunts, Angélique and Agnès. What Le Maistre disliked most about Sacy was his *"froideur,"* whereas Sacy was put off by the *"chaleur"* of his oldest brother. To be sure, Le Maistre was inclined to the heroic gesture, so much so in fact that he sometimes had to be restrained by Saint-Cyran, always alert to manifestations of false humility. Le Maistre was even jealous of Sacy's ability to endure austerities more than he. Once when they were dining together, Le Maistre devoured his portion almost as soon as it was served, and then was forced to watch his brother "with his gravity and ordinary *froideur* carefully peel a quarter of an apple, eat it without hurrying and then walk away from the table leaving most of his meal untouched," as if he were able to nourish himself solely on spiritual sustenance.[24]

It took a good deal of persuasion on Singlin's part, including mention of his mother's willingness to place her conscience in the hands of her son, to overcome Le Maistre's overweening pride. With Le Maistre's submission to his younger brother accomplished, the natural order within the family, as Fontaine observed, was once again reversed. Sacy became the spiritual father of his mother and older brothers just as Angélique became the spiritual mother of Madame Arnauld. These reversals constitute a dramatic illustration of the extent to which the Arnauld family had become transformed. However, the natural order was never entirely repressed. It reasserted itself in the form of sibling rivalries, clashes of personality, and occasional outbursts of wounded pride.

The conditions of life within the community of *solitaires* was based on

the premise that each man followed the rule of the gospel as he understood it. How the *solitaire* ordered his day was up to him, and he was
free to come and go as he chose. The only authority to which he was
responsible was his conscience. This lack of institutional control at a
time when institutional controls were increasing throughout France, a
trend encouraged by the monarchy, was what aroused the suspicions of
the authorities of church and state. The Jesuits in particular viewed
with alarm the activities of Port-Royal, where members of the Arnauld
family played a prominent role. The Jesuits had not forgotten their old
antagonist Antoine Arnauld, whose vitriolic attacks on the disciples of
Ignatius Loyola still rankled. They were troubled by the fact that the
spiritual director both of the convent and the *solitaires* was the abbé de
Saint-Cyran, who had publicly attacked the Society of Jesus on several
occasions,[25] and whose penitential theology was far more austere than
that advocated by the Society, whose influence with Louis XIII and the
cardinal-minister Richelieu was strong.

Yet the activities of these hermits were innocuous. Once settled at
Les Granges, these *Messieurs de Port-Royal*, as they were often called,
undertook to rebuild the walls of the convent and to cultivate the fields
surrounding it. Much of their time was spent in reading the Bible and
other religious works.[26] They translated some of these works into
French, including, eventually, the Bible itself, and wrote works of their
own. Le Maistre completed a biography of John Chrysostom, the reforming patriarch of Constantinople who became a martyr because of
his efforts to eliminate corruption in the church. He also learned He-
brew, encouraged to do so by Saint-Cyran in lieu of cutting himself
off entirely from all oral communication with others. The best-known
achievement of the *solitaires* was the creation of the Little Schools for
boys, a project much encouraged by Saint-Cyran, who, like the Arnaulds, believed that true piety was based on a sound education. A few,
including Le Maistre de Sacy, were ordained priests, who served as the
spiritual directors of the group as well as of the nuns. All were protégés
of the abbé de Saint-Cyran, whose guidance had contributed to their
repudiation of the world and who might well have become a *solitaire*
himself had he not been arrested and imprisoned in 1638 for, among
other things, encouraging Le Maistre to give up a promising career in
order to form an unauthorized community.

The alarm among political and ecclesiastical officials caused by Antoine Le Maistre's defection and the formation of the community of *solitaires* around him added to the suspicions aroused by Angélique's activities. As a reformer, she had antagonized powerful persons such as the deposed abbess of Maubuisson, Angélique d'Estrées, as well as the prominent and well-connected Sebastian Zamet, bishop of Langres. Furthermore the nuns of Port-Royal had been accused of being "heretical visionaries" and even of being witches by those opposed to the establishment of the Order of the Holy Sacrament. Angélique Arnauld and Antoine Le Maistre, so closely tied together both in flesh and in spirit that she thought of him as her own child,[27] the dominant figures respectively within the female and male communities within Port-Royal, each in their own way contributed to the controversial reputation of the Arnauld family above all because of their independent attitude.

The community of *solitaires* in which male members of the family figured so prominently was eventually to become a refuge for other relatives to the point that in a very real sense Port-Royal became a spiritual *seigneurie* of the Arnauld family, a sacred place where men and women conducted their lives of solitude and prayer and where they died and were buried. As Port-Royal became increasingly controversial during the 1640s, its ideals under attack from various quarters, it seemed to members of the family almost like a fortress. The profound *mépris du monde* adopted by Angélique and, under her influence, by so many other members of her family enabled them and other members of the Port-Royal community to develop a set of theological and psychological defenses that prepared them for whatever sieges lay ahead. Their penitential exercises, which involved each one of them in a perpetual inner struggle between the forces of nature and of grace, together with their willingness to suffer persecution "for righteousness' sake" as a test of their commitment to God's purpose also prepared them for the inevitable confrontation between Port-Royal and the world around it.

6

Robert Arnauld d'Andilly: The Patriarch

*T*HE SPIRITUAL reformation of the Arnauld family was further advanced as a result of Robert Arnauld d'Andilly's decision to join the ranks of the *solitaires* at Port-Royal-des-Champs in 1645. By the time of his death thirty years later he was generally regarded by the men and women there as the patriarch of the community as well as of the family. Ironically, it was he who had been the most offended by his sister Angélique's actions on the *journée du guichet*. At that time Robert was twenty years old and had embarked on what appeared even then to be a successful career in the king's service. Like his father, he initially viewed the Catholic reform movement with suspicion, associating it with the Catholic League that had posed such a threat to the crown during the Wars of Religion. After 1609, as Angélique's reputation as a reformer grew and as Port-Royal came to play an increasingly important role within the Arnauld family, the young man became more sympathetic to the reform movement. After the death of his father in 1619, Andilly established himself as a useful link between the convent and the court of Louis XIII because of his substantial connections. The duchesse de Longueville, the princesse de Guémenée, and Marie de Gonzague, the future queen of Poland, became benefactors of Port-Royal because of their friendship with Andilly. Andilly was the first member of his family to befriend Saint-Cyran, whose association with Port-Royal was made possible in part because of his ties to the Arnauld family.

Robert Arnauld, the eldest son of Antoine and Catherine Arnauld, was born in Paris in 1589 and baptized in the parish church of Saint-Merry. He was educated at home rather than at a college because his father believed that at a college "one learned things that one might as well forget."[1] Steeped in humanistic studies himself, Antoine Arnauld saw to it that his son mastered Greek and Latin and became well versed in "the knowledge of *belles-lettres.*" He also saw to it that Robert was groomed for a position in the king's service at an early age. Meeting with his tutors in the morning, young Arnauld spent the afternoons, even as a small boy, with his uncle Claude, the *trésorier de France*, who undertook to educate him in the art of government. Shortly after his uncle's death in 1602, Robert was asked to accompany the minister Sully on a mission to the Court of Saint-James in London, but the boy was unable to make the trip because of illness. If Robert was disappointed by this turn of events, his family must have viewed the possibility of his being included in Sully's entourage as yet another indication of the favor in which its members were held by the *surintendant des finances*. Two years later Robert became the protégé of his uncle Isaac, about to become an *intendant des finances*, with whom he worked closely until the latter's death in 1617.

The early years of Robert's career coincided with the end of the reign of Henry IV. After Henry's assassination in 1610, the kingdom entered a period of political instability that lasted until Richelieu assumed control of the government in 1624. As regent, governing in the name of the young king Louis XIII from 1610 until 1617, the queen mother, Marie de Medici, gave considerable power and influence to compatriots Concini and his wife Leonora Galigai, who had come with her from Italy at the time of her marriage to Henry IV. The great nobles, including the princes of the blood, Condé and Conti, resented their lack of influence in the regency government and threatened rebellion. The Huguenots, fearful that the new government might seek to diminish the rights that they had acquired under the Edict of Nantes, were prepared to resort to arms in the defense of those rights. The struggle for power and influence was particularly keen during these years. Who was in and who was out, whose favor to seek and whose to shun, were all matters of great concern to an ambitious young man hoping to advance himself in the king's service.

Despite the plots, counterplots, and outbursts of civil war that characterized the regency period, Isaac Arnauld retained his position in the *conseil des finances*, where he was assisted by his nephew Robert, who received his first pension from the crown in 1615 in the amount of 2500 livres.[2] Three years earlier Robert had married Catherine, the fourteen-year-old daughter of Antoine de la Boderie (1555–1615), another client of Sully who had served as ambassador to England from 1606 to 1612 and in the *conseil des finances* from 1612 to 1615. La Boderie's wife was the aunt of the chancellor, Brulart de Sillery. Although, as Robert wrote in his memoirs, he knew that he would inherit "a large enough fortune" and did not have to look for a particularly wealthy heiress, his marriage to the only daughter of the ambassador, which was very much encouraged by both his father and his uncle Isaac, was even more advantageous to the family than his father's had been both in terms of important connections in the political world and of wealth. According to the terms of the marriage contract, Robert's father guaranteed his worth at thirty thousand *écus*, and the young man was promised the inheritance of the *seigneurie* of Andilly upon his mother's death. (He assumed the name Arnauld d'Andilly at the time of his marriage.) Catherine would obtain the *seigneuries* of Pomponne and Briotte after the death of a childless half-brother. The young couple lived with the bride's parents until the death of Antoine Arnauld, at which time they took up residence at the family house in the rue de la Verrerie.[3]

In 1617 Louis XIII came of age. Asserting his independence from his mother, the regent, he instigated the assassination of her favorite, Concini, and had Marie de Medici removed to Blois. At the end of that year Isaac Arnauld died. The *intendant des finances* had hoped that Robert would succeed him in that office, but the duc de Luynes, who had replaced Concini as the dominant figure in the government, was opposed to the appointment because he suspected the Arnaulds of being too close to the Concinis. Nevertheless Arnauld d'Andilly received an appointment as *conseiller d'état* a few months later and in 1619 became the *premier commis* of the *surintendant*, Henri de Schomberg.

The years between the fall of Concini and the entry of Cardinal Richelieu into the government in 1624 were particularly turbulent. The king's favorite, Luynes, remained in power until his death in 1621, at which time the most influential ministers became the chancellor, Sillery, and his son, Puysieulx, members of the Brulart family, to which Arnauld d'Andilly's mother-in-law was related. The great nobles again became restless, intriguing against this minister or that; the queen mother, having returned from her exile at Blois, used what influence she had at court to strengthen her political position, while the Huguenots' military strength continued to pose a threat to the crown in the southwest. In 1621 Louis XIII launched a military campaign against the Huguenots in the Midi accompanied by numerous officials, including Andilly.

During the campaign, Andilly was informed through the king's confessor that Louis wished to offer him the important and lucrative office of *sécretaire d'état* that had been vacated by the death of the Keeper of the Seals. In return Arnauld was to reimburse the heirs of the deceased minister, who were prepared to relinquish the office of secretary, the sum of one hundred thousand pounds. These offices were bestowed on persons destined to play influential roles in the king's council. Ministerial offices were held at the king's pleasure whereas the office of *sécretaire d'état* was venal and by the end of the century worth three hundred thousand pounds.[4] The dominant position of the Brularts and Schomberg in the king's council undoubtedly facilitated the offer, which may have been made in the knowledge that Robert would not be able to afford it. A gesture of this sort on the part of the king was in and of itself a mark of royal favor even though it cost nothing. There is no indication that Louis XIII was prepared to help defray the cost of the office as Louis XIV was willing to do for Robert's son Simon a half a century later. Andilly desired the office above all else, but he could not accept it because the required sum of money would undoubtedly place too great a strain on the resources of the family if he were to die suddenly, as he had almost done a year earlier. As he later wrote in his *mémoires,* he had been brought up to believe that offices should be offered on the basis of merit, not of wealth.[5] This experience served to increase Andilly's distaste for venality, a distaste he shared with his father and uncles.

In 1623 Schomberg was dismissed from office and exiled to his estate outside Paris. He was replaced as *surintendant* by the marquis de Vieuville, who had engineered his predecessor's disgrace. Arnauld d'Andilly, Schomberg's *premier commis,* refused the appointment of *intendant des finances,* the office held by his uncle Isaac and to which he had aspired at the time of Isaac's death, because he regarded himself as Schomberg's friend, making it inappropriate for him to serve Vieuville. Vieuville threatened to put Arnauld d'Andilly in the Bastille a year later in an

effort to purge the government of friends and clients of his rivals. By
that time Richelieu had become a member of the king's inner council
and in August of that year managed the dismissal of Vieuville.

As head of the family after the death of his father in 1619, Arnauld
d'Andilly had to concern himself with his family's interests as well as his
own. In 1624 his uncle Pierre Arnauld died while engaged in the campaign against the Huguenots. He had been awarded several offices,
among them the position of *maître de camp*, for his services. Pierre's
nephew Robert asked the king to award two of them, including the
governorship of Fort-Louis, to the marquis de Feuquières, who had
married Robert's cousin Anne, the daughter of Isaac. The king informed him that his request had come too late; the offices had already
been awarded to someone else. Louis held firm to his resolve in the face
of Andilly's entreaties. "Thus were we deprived of my uncle's offices,"
lamented Andilly many years later, "and the funds which he expended
in the king's service that we had a right to expect as a reward for that
service."[6]

In defense of his family's honor, Robert Arnauld repulsed an attack
on his one surviving uncle, Louis Arnauld. After the dismissal of Vieuville, Richelieu established a *chambre de justice* to look into alleged mal-
practices of financiers. The *chambre* imposed a total of almost eleven
million pounds in fines, including forty thousand on Louis Arnauld. "It
seems to me, *monseigneur*," wrote Robert in a letter to the cardinal, "that
one should be pleased that instead of enriching themselves in the king's
service as so many others do, four of my uncles gave their lives and a
good part of their fortune in serving the king with dignity. Why punish
the only remaining brother for something of which he is innocent?"[7]
The day after receiving the letter, Richelieu, who was favorably disposed toward Andilly, lifted the fine.

The cardinal-minister further favored Andilly by appointing him to
the particularly sensitive position of *intendant* of the household of the
king's brother, Gaston. The duc d'Anjou before 1626 and duc d'Orléans
afterwards, Gaston was heir to the throne. Because Louis XIII and his
wife, Anne, had not yet produced a son, Gaston was regarded by many
as the likely next ruler. As the heir to the king, whose health was always
delicate, and personally more attractive than the king, he had become a
focal point of intrigue. Among the members of the duke's household
was Colonel Jean-Baptiste d'Ornano, a friend of Arnauld d'Andilly, but

one whom Richelieu saw as a potential source of trouble. Hence he required Andilly to keep an eye on both Gaston and Ornano and to report to him anything that seemed out of line. Gaston and Arnauld d'Andilly became good friends. The heir apparent enjoyed erudite men such as Arnauld, who were knowledgeable about politics: "As I had taken pains throughout my life to inform myself of the actions and services of the most important personages—particularly those at court whom I knew well—I gave him [Gaston] as much information as I could about them."[8] Unfortunately, their friendship was jeopardized by Richelieu's continuing suspicions of Ornano, whom he believed to be thwarting his policies. Two issues were of concern to the cardinal: the question of the heir apparent's marriage and his political role. Gaston intended to marry a wealthy heiress, Mademoiselle Montpensier, which to Richelieu's and the king's way of thinking would strengthen Gaston's dynastic position. If he and his wife produced a son and the king and queen remained childless, the Bourbon dynasty would be secured through Gaston. Hence Louis and his chief minister opposed Gaston's intentions. They also opposed any role for the duke in the king's inner councils, in keeping with the crown's policy of excluding the great nobles from affairs of state. Marie de Medici, on the other hand, favored Gaston's marriage as well as a greater political role for her younger son.

To the displeasure of the king and Richelieu, Ornano and Arnauld d'Andilly both favored Gaston's marriage and an increased political role for the heir apparent, although the latter was undoubtedly more discreet about his opinions because of his responsibilities to the cardinal. To make matters worse for Andilly, Gaston became aware that Andilly was a spy for Richelieu. "He no longer talked to me except about unimportant matters and took no further pains to preserve our friendship."[9] In 1626, two years after Arnauld's appointment to Gaston's household, Richelieu had Ornano arrested, an act that so enraged the duke that he dismissed Arnauld from his service.[10] Because of Gaston's antipathy toward him, Andilly was forced out of politics and into private life.

Andilly's political career until 1626 had been very successful. He had powerful connections—his uncle Isaac, the Brularts, and Schomberg—who used their influence on his behalf, he had been carefully trained since childhood in financial administration, and he had the intelligence and social bearing to take advantage of whatever opportunity came his way. He was as ambitious as his forebears, intent on making his way onward and upward to the greater glory of his family and of himself. Andilly's chief weakness was his temperament, which made it hard for him to endure the competition for favors at court. Thin skinned, he was quick to take offense and inclined to lose his temper at inopportune moments. Whatever setbacks and disappointments that he experienced in his career he attributed to the insidious efforts of unworthy rivals, not to any shortcomings of his own. Flattering courtiers and syco-phants were, in his opinion, preferred over persons like himself who were ready and willing to provide loyal and disinterested service to the crown. Of the duc de Luynes, who had prevented him from succeeding his uncle Isaac as *intendant des finances*, he wrote that the duke had hindered his career because he wanted only toadies around him, who thought only of promoting their interests. The best and most worthy counselors thought only of what was best for the king.[11] To his friend and patron Schomberg, who had been temporarily removed from office in 1623, he wrote that at least the former *surintendant* had earned the admiration of persons of merit if not that of flatterers.[12] He blamed corrupt courtiers for his dismissal from the service of Gaston d'Orleans. "It is not surprising," he wrote, reflecting on his experience in the duke's household:

> that those who flatter princes and share their passions are favored by them and have their confidence. But to be agreeable to them and to have their confidence when one opposes their bad inclina-tions, when one encourages them to act virtuously particularly in a century as corrupt as ours, is to make them take pride in the effects of virtuous actions. To counsel rulers in this way is to have true influence over princes. That was the relationship I had with Mon-sieur [Gaston], who was one of those princes who most needed people of merit around him.[13]

There was no doubt in Arnauld's own mind that he was a man of merit whom kings should consult for their own good because he thought only of that good and not of his own. In a letter to a friend in 1623 he wrote: "As for my interests, Monsieur, I have nothing to say to you, being able to swear to you in truth that they are among the things of this world that I think the least about. To be perfectly frank with you, thoughts of

my own salvation, my friends and my books are the only things that oc-
cupy my mind."[14] Arnauld's self-esteem, which in his letters and memoirs he made no effort to hide, appears to us a form of self-flattery,
intended to relieve the hurt caused by the ill feelings toward him harbored by the duc d'Orléans, Cuneo d'Ornano, and others, who thought
him duplicitous because of his behavior in the duke's household.

    Andilly's dismissal from the household of Gaston d'Orleans oc-
curred at a time when he was affected by increasingly powerful religious
sentiments developing within him that changed his attitude toward the
Catholic reform movement. His sister Angélique's accomplishments
and his family's increasing involvement in Port-Royal undoubtedly
contributed to these sentiments. Before his forced retirement in 1626
he had made friends with some of the most prominent figures in the
reform movement, including François de Sales and Cardinal Bérulle.
The friend who contributed the most to his religious development,
however, and the one who helped him to understand that his spiritual
interests were far more important than his worldly interests, was the
abbé de Saint-Cyran, whom he had met in 1620 and to whom he later
introduced other members of his family. At the time of their encounter,
Saint-Cyran was undergoing his own conversion leading to his rejection of his youthful ambitions and was in the process of formulating the
penitential ethics that were to accord so well with those of Angélique
Arnauld. The *mépris du monde* that began to affect his outlook on life
during the 1620s coincided with Andilly's growing disillusionment with
the world of politics brought on by his own disappointments.

For the abbé de Saint-Cyran, there were four impediments to Christian virtue: advantageous birth, wealth, public office, and noble ambition.[15] All four were attributes of Arnauld d'Andilly, who made use of
them effectively during his political career, as had Saint-Cyran before
his conversion. In his letters to Andilly the abbé emphasized the need to
repudiate ambition and seek reward in the kingdom of God. "The great
of this world are incapable of impressing me," he wrote in 1621, and he
admitted that he would be less impressed with his friend "if he did not
have an ambition equal to mine, which aspires to something higher
than those who aspire to a kingdom in this world."[16]

Similar themes appear in letters written to Arnauld from his sister
Angélique in the early 1620s. He had reestablished close ties with the

abbess by the time of their father's death in 1619. In turn, he became as helpful to Port-Royal as his father had been, in preparing for the transition from the valley of the Chevreuse to Paris, in launching the Order of the Holy Sacrament, and in various other ways. Angélique understood the vicissitudes of his career. When Schomberg, her brother's patron, was disgraced in 1623, she wrote: "The turmoil at court and the infinite opportunity to offend God that continuous diversions there provide cannot prevent those of great courage, who are desirous of doing good, from becoming entirely committed to God. Such reversals of fortune test us to see if we understand what true happiness is."[17] When in the following year Schomberg was allowed to return to court after the dismissal of his rival Vieuville, Angélique expressed her satisfaction with this turn of events but added that everything depends on God's will.

> Therefore, my dear brother, for the love of God, if prosperity arrives, one should accept it with modesty, humility and fear of abusing it. If on the other hand the reverse occurs, one should accept that as well with resignation, tranquility and an invincible acquiescence in the divine will, without a murmur or without holding it against anyone. You must forgive my temerity. I am only a poor girl who loves her dear brother with a passion, and for whom she desires perfection. The more I come to understand what perfection is, the more I desire it for you.[18]

Angélique was not unmindful of her brother's temperament. While agreeing with him that the family deserved to retain the offices that had been held by their uncle Louis, she begged him not to lose his temper with anyone in his futile attempt to have the offices awarded to their cousin, the marquis de Feuquières. A few years later she urged him to remain calm in his efforts to obtain a building permit for the construction of Port-Royal-de-Paris. Recognizing in him characteristics similar to her own—a volatile nature, keen ambition, and a strong sense of family loyalty—she believed that he needed to live a more tranquil life. When Andilly was forced to withdraw from public life in 1626, Angélique made the event out to be a real opportunity for him. "I must tell you that I consider that God is bestowing good fortune upon you," she wrote to him shortly after the dismissal, "by enabling you to devote yourself entirely to piety . . . What a happy change from these painful and troublesome affairs of the world, in which one person's happiness is made possible at the expense of another."[19] A few months later she wrote, "I implore you, my dear brother, to devote little time to diversion and to use this precious time to look to the condition of your soul."[20] Agnès Arnauld also advised her brother to use his time well. "I would hope that you will find a better way to spend your time than in the genealogical research on the kings of the earth, who become entirely forgotten in the passage of time. Far better to take as the object of your endeavors the king of all time and of eternity."[21]

Agnès's reference to her brother's researches was directed at Andilly's continuing interest in temporal affairs, an interest that manifested itself in the detailed political journal he had begun at the outset of his career in 1614 and continued to maintain until 1632. In the journals, which he let Richelieu have access to because of the useful information included in them, Andilly describes military campaigns, the comings and goings at court, and political events such as the meeting of the Estates General in 1614. The journals provide unflattering accounts of the irresponsible behavior of the great nobles, more interested in advancing their own interests than the interests of their king. His accounts of duels in particular reflect his strong distaste for an activity that in his opinion displayed a narrow conception of honor that prevented the nobles from seeing that their honor lay in defending that of their sovereign instead of their own. Some of the events that Andilly describes were those in which he participated. In recounting events that occurred after his forced retirement, he had to rely on information provided by others. The journals enabled Andilly to remain in touch with the world of politics after his retirement, much to his sisters' disgust.[22]

As Richelieu set about to prepare for war with Spain in order to ease the threat of Hapsburg encirclement of France and to weaken the most powerful state in Europe, Andilly applauded his efforts from the sidelines even though many of his friends within the Catholic reform movement, including the abbé de Saint-Cyran and Cardinal Berulle, favored an alliance between the two Catholic kingdoms in the interest of protecting the faith. Those in support of a more Catholic foreign policy, known as *dévots*, were in effect perpetuating the foreign policy of the Catholic League during the Wars of Religion. In favoring Richelieu's policy of opposition to Spain, Andilly chose the policy of his father and grandfather, the policy of the *politiques* or *bon français*, who placed the interests of the French crown above everything else. In a letter to the French ambassador to Rome, written from Pomponne, Andilly deplored Spanish designs on the Italian peninsula and blamed the Thirty Years' War on the Spanish king. "Others might be surprised to see that in the middle of my tranquility and amid the pleasures of the country, I am much concerned about the troubles that plague Italy. Louis the Just [Louis XIII], the terror of aggressors and the protector of the innocent will right these wrongs." At the end of the letter Andilly confirmed his continuing interest in affairs of state. "I number myself among those who are inspired by a passion for the public good, which these days most everyone makes fun of."[23] And in letters written several years after his dismissal from Gaston d'Orleans' household, he continued to lament the tendency at court to favor those presumably less worthy than himself.[24]

During his years spent away from court, Andilly gradually came to appreciate life at his country estates. Although he occasionally visited the *seigneurie* of Andilly given to him by his father, he preferred Pomponne, which he was to inherit through his wife. There he enjoyed his books, his gardens, and especially his friends. Friendships that were important to him were those from among the group of nobles, *bourgeois gentilhommes*, and men of letters who frequented the salon of the marquise de Rambouillet. Educated in the humanistic tradition, Andilly regarded himself as much a man of letters as a statesman, for which reason he enjoyed the company of Jean Chapelain, Voiture, Guez de Balzac, and others who made the Rambouillet circle a cultural center of some importance in the development of French literature. The marquise, whose father had been the French ambassador to Rome and whose mother was Italian, encouraged the discussion of literature in both Italian and French. In the *chambre bleue* at the Hôtel Rambouillet there was talk about sun spots as well as about literature, but these subjects, controversial though some of them were, seemed less important in themselves than in the manner in which they were expressed. Wit, eloquence, and the ability to charm were the true marks of distinction in the Rambouillet circle. The marquise and her daughter, Julie, encouraged *galanterie* in the form of courtly poetry that focused on their virtues and their charm. In *La Guirlande de Julie* (1632) for example, a composite work to which Andilly and his cousin, Arnauld de Corbeville (Isaac's son), contributed, Mademoiselle de Rambouillet (Julie) appears as the object of a chivalric love. The poets appear as suitors whose unrequited love has been purified of all sensuousness and whose passions have been subdued by reason:

> *Merveille de nos jours dont les charmes vainqueurs.*
> *Ravissent les esprits et regnent dans les coeurs,*
> *Rare présent du ciel, adorable Julie.*

> Adorable Julie! thou gift from heaven, light of our life,
>   whose vanquishing charm ravishes our minds and rules
>   over our hearts.[25]

During the reign of Louis XIII the Hôtel de Rambouillet became a sort of anti-court that contrasted sharply with the court of Louis XIII. The marquise and her attendants preferred courtly behavior, heroic idealism, purity of thought, and clarity of expression to what they perceived as the coarseness and the lack of cultivation that characterized the royal circle of the early Bourbon kings. At Madame de Rambouillet's salon nobles and others "came there seeking that noble simplicity and honest liberty *(liberté honnête)* that seems to have been banished from the royal palace."[26] As the marquise's *chevaliers*, the men in attendance in the *salon bleue* felt liberated from the atmosphere of obsequiousness that pervaded the palace. One attendant in particular, Guez de Balzac, a protégé of Richelieu, greatly appreciated the liberty that prevailed in the salon. Balzac, whose book entitled *Le Prince* was in effect an encomium to royal absolutism, vacillated during his early career between a desire for favor and preferment at court and a desire to be his own man free of excessive dependence.

Like his friend Balzac, Andilly was torn between his frustrated ambitions and his growing appreciation of his tranquil life among his friends at the Hôtel Rambouillet or at Pomponne. His friends were of his own choosing, with whom he shared common interests, not like friendships at court, which were based on self-interest and therefore less sincere and less stable. Like Balzac, he declined to become a member of the French Academy despite the favor bestowed on it by Richelieu. Even before his forced withdrawal from politics in 1626, he had appreciated the agreeable life that was available to him at Pomponne. "I so love life in the country," he wrote, "because there I lead a life contrary to that which one leads at court. I experience the incomparable pleasures of my family, and I enjoy a quiet life in which I am not idle . . . [T]hat which so many people look for with such intensity does not seem to me to be worthy of the ambition of a man of courage. Therefore I scorn it."[27]

Andilly's appreciation of his new life after 1626, a life conducted on his own terms and not on the terms established by the culture at court, was enhanced by his developing spirituality. His sister Agnès thought that he was undergoing some sort of transformation ("a new birth") that was developing within him an aversion to the world. "You are without ambition, without any cares and hence more dependent on divine Providence . . . Who would have believed that the solitude that so many aspire to but find so difficult is so much cherished by a person of your condition."[28] His new life reinforced the feeling of independence that he experienced as a result of the changed conditions in his life, a feeling not unlike that experienced by Angélique after the *journée du guichet*. Just as she had detached herself from her dependence on the family, he was becoming less dependent on the world at court. Both enjoyed, as did the *solitaires*, the freedom to direct their own lives.

Much as he had come to enjoy the innocent pleasures of his retreat, Andilly accepted an appointment as *intendant* of the Army of the Rhine from Richelieu in 1634. In this first campaign of the long war between France and Spain that did not end until 1659 it would be his responsibility to finance the operation with funds provided him by the *surintendant des finances*, Claude de Bullion. Intendancies were used by Richelieu to maintain royal control over fiscal, judicial, and military activities. Those who received commissions to serve in this capacity did so at the king's pleasure, the office of *intendant* not being venal. In accepting his appointment, Andilly resumed the career marked out for him by his forebears. In his memoirs he recalls that he did so reluctantly.[29] He had been out of public life for almost a decade, and he was no longer young. Besides, he was not in good health. However, his love of public life made Richelieu's offer irresistible to him, all the more so because the cardinal-minister's favor was important to him and his family. After the Day of Dupes in 1630 Richelieu strengthened his control over the king's government. Among his creatures was Claude Bouthillier, whom Richelieu had appointed *co-intendant des finances* in 1632. The Bouthilliers, a robe family from Brittany, had been closely associated with Richelieu since early in the seventeenth century. Early in his political career Andilly had befriended the Bouthillier family. Indeed it was a brother of Claude, Sebastian le Bouthillier, bishop of Aire, who had introduced Andilly to the abbé de Saint-Cyran in 1620. The friendship between the Arnaulds and the Bouthilliers was helpful in securing Andilly's appointment as *intendant* of the Army of the Rhine in 1634.

From the moment of his return to the king's service to the very last years of his long life, Andilly continued to be torn between what he called his passion for the king's service and his desire for a private life. The tension created within him by these conflicting desires was similar to that within Angélique, torn between her responsibilities as a reforming abbess and her own spiritual needs. Agnès understood this reluctance on her brother's part to tear himself away from the life that he had come to enjoy so much. Although she had approved of Andilly's retirement, she now felt that he should return to the king's service.

> For several years now you have lived for yourself. Jesus Christ was pleased with you because he had asked you to lead a retired life somewhat removed from the world and you had accepted this, loving your solitude. Now he no longer requires of you this desire for withdrawal, and if you continue to yearn for it you do so against his will . . . I appear to be preaching to you, my dear brother, as if I had forgotten that I am a woman and younger than you at that, but you have instructed me on numerous occasions not to think of my condition in regard to you.[30]

To Andilly's concern that in accepting the office he would be motivated by his own material interests rather than by grace she responded that one might serve both God and king as long as there were no conflict.

In approving her brother's return to public life while at the same time disapproving of her nephew Antoine Le Maistre's determination to remain in it, Agnès was not contradicting herself. Rather, she understood that the two men were different in terms of their potential for a life of prayer and solitude. Le Maistre had from an early age been inclined toward that kind of life, whereas her older brother had pursued his career too long to renounce it easily. She knew him well enough to believe that he would never become a recluse, that he would always have, as he himself put it, a passion for public service. Agnès and her sister Angélique also thought that Andilly's return to public service would increase his influence at court at a time when Angélique and Bishop Zamet needed that influence to launch the Order of the Holy Sacrament.

At the time he received his appointment, Andilly was forty-five years old. He had been out of public life for almost ten years. He departed for the Rhine with armies under the command of marshals de la Force and de Brézé, where he spent a year before returning to France. His stint with the army was cut short by continuing ill health. Also, he may have heard that there were complaints at court about his performance as *intendant* and felt the need to defend himself there. When he reported to Bullion, *surintendant des finances*, Andilly was informed that he was being accused of mismanaging his accounts and that he would have to explain himself to the king. The exact nature of Bullion's allegations are unclear. It may be that they were the result of the competition between him and Claude Bouthillier for Richelieu's favor. In any event, Andilly refused to resign his commission and insisted on defending himself before the king and cardinal.

Andilly's brief tour of duty had certainly not been satisfactory from his point of view. To be sure he had made important social contacts who would be important to his family, including the commander of the Army of the Rhine, Marshal de Brézé, Richelieu's brother-in-law; and Turenne, just beginning his illustrious military career at the time. But his honor had been offended by Bullion's allegations as it had been by Gaston d'Orléans accusations of hypocrisy after his last period of service. Again he experienced the discomfiture inherent in the jockeying for power and influence at court. Looking forward to his return to private life, he found that once he got there he had to deal with difficult family matters. His cousin Isaac Arnauld de Corbeville, the son of the old *intendant des finances* who had done so much to advance Andilly's career a quarter of a century earlier, was in the Bastille, preparing his defense against charges that he had not done his duty as an officer in the royal army. Corbeville had been recently appointed governor of the fortified city of Philipsburg on the northeast frontier of the kingdom. In the winter of 1635 troops of the Holy Roman Emperor laid siege to the town and took advantage of a frozen moat to enter it. Unable to obtain reinforcements that might have secured the town, the governor surrendered. After three months as a prisoner, Arnauld de Corbeville escaped and made his way to Paris. Though much relieved that his cousin and two other members of his family, including his oldest son, had not been killed at Philipsburg despite rumors to the contrary, Andilly realized that because of the charges leveled against Corbeville, the family honor was at stake. Once again he found himself at court, this time defending his cousin's reputation. Although Corbeville was eventually exonerated, this distasteful experience intensified Andilly's desire to return to private life.

Two years later Andilly suffered another blow with the death of his wife. As we have seen, the death of Madame Arnauld d'Andilly had helped determine Antoine Le Maistre to become a *solitaire*, It also caused his uncle in his grief to give serious thought to joining his nephews in a life of prayer and solitude. When his sister Angélique learned of this inclination, she warned him not to act too hastily.

> Take care, my dear brother, to heed the words of M. de Saint-Cyran that it is sometimes an evil spirit which prompts such a change in those who would convert themselves from the world to a life of piety. The change may be nothing other than amusing oneself with pious discourse instead of with the idle amusements afforded by the world. A change of occupation of this sort is even worse in that one believes that one is entering into the way of true virtue when in fact one is entering the way of falsehood and self-deception.[31]

Angélique, like Agnès, realized that her brother derived too much pleasure from the more worldly aspects of private life to impose on himself a strict regimen of penitential discipline. Furthermore she feared that Andilly's withdrawal from public life might weaken the family's influence at court.

Nine months after the death of his wife, Andilly, his family, and the community of Port-Royal suffered yet another devastating blow. On 14 May 1638, the abbé de Saint-Cyran was arrested on Richelieu's orders. The abbé had made numerous enemies over the course of his career, including the Jesuits, the bishop of Langres, who had not forgiven him for his role in destroying the Order of the Holy Sacrament, and the chancellor Séguier, who blamed him for causing Antoine Le Maistre to withdraw from public life. More important, Saint-Cyran was associated with the *dévot* opposition to Richelieu's foreign policy. Now that France had become involved in a war with Spain, Richelieu feared that those who disapproved of a war against another Catholic country in alliance with Protestant states constituted a danger to the security of the kingdom. Finally, Richelieu looked with disfavor on Saint-Cyran's theological opinions, which were controversial and, some said, heretical.

Saint-Cyran's arrest and imprisonment at the chateau de Vincennes, which was to last five years, caused consternation among those who looked to him for spiritual guidance and who believed that his penitential theology was vital to the spiritual mission of the Catholic Church. Angélique wrote of Saint-Cyran after his arrest that "he is the only person in the Church today who in the purity of his doctrine and his piety and in the persecution [which he is experiencing] has achieved the same stature as the holy fathers of antiquity."[32] To a friend who enquired after Saint-Cyran in 1639 she remarked that "time is very short and eternity very long. Those who are prisoners in time will be free in eternity, and those who are free in this world will be prisoners for an eternity."[33] The imprisonment of the abbé only strengthened Angélique's view of religious life as "a continuous war on earth" between those who were obedient to the divine will and those who were obedient to their own selfish interests. It also reinforced her belief in the efficacy of persecution as a test of faith.

Andilly too was horrified by "this unjust imprisonment,"[34] and he used what influence he had to have the man whom he had come to regard as his dearest friend released from the chateau de Vincennes, where he was to remain until Richelieu's death even though the charge of heresy was never substantiated. All the more shocking to him was the fact that imprisonment was ordered by Andilly's patron, Richelieu, with whom he had had close ties for almost twenty years. As he wrote to a friend who was also in prison for having displeased the cardinal-minister: "It is time to arouse ourselves from the sleep in which most men are buried and realize that your travail and my ill fortune, which pass for evils to those who judge things according to the senses, are the best things that can happen to us. They cause us to turn our attention to ourselves and enable us to think seriously about ourselves and to view with contempt those fleeting pleasures. It would be inexcusable for us to be dazzled by them after having come to recognize them as empty and vain."[35]

Although Andilly began to think about becoming a *solitaire* in 1637, he did not in fact join Le Maistre and the others until 1645. Family responsibilities made it impossible for him to retire until that time. A year after Saint-Cyran's arrest, Andilly's brother Simon was killed in the battle of Thionville and his cousin by marriage, the marquis de Feuquières, taken prisoner. Released a few months later, the marquis subsequently died of a wound received in that battle. His promising career, aided no doubt by his family ties to Père Joseph, Richelieu's *éminence grise*, was thus cut short at a time when he was under consideration for the position of governor to the dauphin.

These events, attributed by Andilly's oldest son to "the prevailing and unfortunate star that hovers over our house,"[36] were distressing to the family. A strong bond of affection existed between the children of Antoine and Isaac Arnauld despite the differences in their religious beliefs. Isaac had sponsored Andilly's early career in the king's service, and Andilly felt obliged to return the favor in the form of support for his uncle's grandchildren. A major problem caused by the deaths of three members of the family within the space of two years was the disposition of the offices that they had acquired. The Arnaulds relied on the income from venal offices in spite of their dislike of venality. Andilly and Corbeville managed to secure most of the military offices, including the governorship of Verdun, for Feuquières's oldest son, who inherited the marquisate as well.[37] The offices held by Simon Arnauld, on the other hand, were less easy to secure for the family because Simon left no heirs. A lucrative *charge de distribution de sel*, which produced income from the salt monopoly held by the crown, became yet another contentious issue between Andilly, who wanted it given to the young marquis de Feuquières, and the *surintendant* Bullion, who had disapproved of Andilly's handling of public funds. Bullion, no friend of the Arnaulds, complained that Andilly and his relatives were being too greedy in their efforts to retain the offices of the deceased. Andilly was, of course, much offended by this attitude. The young marquis eventually obtained the office, but Andilly's efforts on his young cousin's behalf only strengthened his intention to become a *solitaire*.

Andilly had also to think of his own material interests and those of his progeny as he prepared for his final retirement. In 1640 his pension had been reduced from eight thousand *livres* a year to six thousand because of the government's efforts to retrench in the face of the mounting costs of the Spanish war. Attributing the reduction to Bullion's malevolence,

Andilly wrote to Richelieu in October that "While he [Bullion] may believe that the security of France depends on cutting the pension of a man who has been made poorer in the king's service while others have become prodigiously wealthy in that service, I know that Your Excellency does not share that sentiment."[38]

In a memoir addressed to his children drawn up in 1652 Andilly provided an account of his material resources that, though not comprehensive, makes clear his dependence on royal generosity. By this time he had acquired Pomponne after the death of his brother-in-law in 1649 (according to the terms of the marriage contract of 1613), but because of extensive damages caused by the Fronde, the estate cost him more than it produced in the way of income. Six years earlier, in 1643, Andilly had sold the estate of Andilly for 150,000 *livres*, which was needed to pay off debts inherited from his mother-in-law as well as debts of his own. His total indebtedness, including repairs on Pomponne, amounted to 197,800 *livres*, which he paid from 198,550 *livres* put together from the sale of Andilly and the smaller *seigneurie* of Briottes. Neither estate had produced much income during the time that they belonged to Andilly. Andilly itself brought in about 1000 *livres* a year and Briottes 750 *livres*, unless there was an increase in the *taille* or damage done to the *seigneurie* by marauding troops or malicious neighbors, in which case no income was forthcoming. The memoir concludes with the assertion that "I have brought up my children well, as everyone knows, and I have supported my family honorably. This would not have been possible without the pensions and other emoluments that I was awarded for having served the king faithfully, without having taken advantage of one *écu* that can not be accounted for."[39]

The pensions received by Andilly came not only from the crown, which had been awarding them to him since 1615, but also from Gaston d'Orleans, to whose good graces he had returned several years after his dismissal from the heir apparent's household. In 1637 the duc d'Orleans awarded him an annual pension amounting to three thousand *livres*, making his annual income approximately eleven thousand *livres*.[40] By 1643, as he was making final arrangements for his children before withdrawing to Port-Royal-des-Champs, Andilly needed to make sure that the pensions would be inherited by his progeny. Such gifts from the king were not venal and depended entirely on his good will, upon which *commissaires* necessarily relied.

After her marriage to Arnauld d'Andilly in 1613 Madame Arnauld d'Andilly gave birth to fifteen children; the last, born only three months before her death in 1637, had died almost immediately. Ten children survived childhood, of whom six were female and four were male. According to the oldest son, Antoine, Andilly was not an attentive father, preferring his friends to his children,[41] an assertion with which Andilly himself agreed. "Like you, I prefer the sentiments of virtue to those of blood and nature," he wrote to the marquise de Sablé in 1668, "I know that one must do all that one can for one's children, but I must confess that I do not understand this stupid blindness which prevents one from seeing their faults, or this bestial passion which makes us love them even though they may be unworthy of one's love. True friends may take the place of everything, but if children do not have the qualities that merit their being considered as friends, they should only be considered as children."[42] Andilly's arrangements for his children reflect these sentiments.

Like his father before him, Andilly had to consider the effect of a large number of daughters on his resources, a number large enough, said his sister Angélique, "to make one's hair turn white."[43] All six were placed in the convent of Port-Royal at an early age. Only one, Marie-Charlotte, appears to have resisted the career being imposed on her by her father. She left Port-Royal in 1643 but returned a few years later. Andilly's decision to make his daughters nuns was based as much on his religious sentiments and on the wishes of his mother and sisters, especially Angélique, as it was on material considerations. As for the daughters, they were made aware at an early age of the reputation of Port-Royal and of the involvement of their aunts in the reform movement and were drawn toward monastic life in much the same way as Angélique's younger sisters had been.

In considering his sons' careers, Andilly decided to advance the political career of only one, Simon, born in 1618, and to invest most of his resources in that career. Simon was not the oldest son. Antoine, born two years earlier, was never liked by his father. In his own memoirs Antoine blames "the little love my father bore me" and his father's stinginess for his own inability to launch a successful military career.[44] When his mother died, the young man claimed that he had lost everything in losing her. "She always served as an influential mediator between my father and me. Whatever distance she kept from me out of

deference to my father disappeared as is made clear in the most affectionate letters I received from her."[45] There is no doubt that Andilly
wanted to keep his oldest son at a distance. Writing in 1641 to his
cousin, the young marquis de Feuquières, he asked him not to bring
Antoine with him on his next visit to Paris unless it was only for a short
time.[46] A quarter of a century later, when Andilly was writing his memoirs, his son Simon implored him to include Antoine in his account of
the family. "Not only do I think it necessary, but I beg of you in all
humility to make mention of him in a way that indicates your love for
him so that your grandchildren will come to understand that one of the
great blessings of the family is to have a grandfather who loves his
children equally." When announcing to his father a prospective visit of
Antoine to Pomponne to visit his nieces, Simon again urged Andilly not
to shun his oldest son.[47]

Andilly was never able to overcome his antipathy toward his son
Antoine. To his way of thinking Antoine had not earned his affection,
although he never explained why. Antoine had wanted to pursue a career in the military under the auspices of his cousins, the marquis de
Feuquières and Isaac Arnauld de Corbeville. Indeed he had been with
Corbeville at Philipsburg and escaped with him to Paris, but his father
was not impressed with his military feats and refused to give him the
money necessary to advance his career.[48] When Andilly withdrew to
Port-Royal-des-Champs in 1645, he took with him more than enough
to live on, according to Antoine, but he still required his son to reduce
his expenditures. In 1644 the young man became a secretary to his
uncle Henry, who was soon to become bishop of Angers. Had he been
able to order his life in his own way, he would have remained in the
world, serving the king in the army as other members of his family had
done. He leaves no doubt in his memoirs that psychologically at least he
always remained very much a part of the world that so many members
of his family rejected, but without the resources necessary to take advantage of what the world had to offer.

Andilly's two oldest sons received religious instruction from Martin
de Barcos, the nephew of the abbé de Saint-Cyran, and subsequently
attended the College de Lisieux. In 1637, at the age of nineteen, Simon
received an appointment similar to his father's last, *intendant* of an army
operating in northern Italy under the command of Turenne, a friend of
the family who was to play an important role in his career—a career

that embodied the ideals and aspirations of Arnauld forebears who had made their fortunes in the king's service. Simon Arnauld had moved to Catalonia, where he was serving in a similar capacity, when his father wrote him in October 1643 of his intention to withdraw to Port-Royal-des-Champs.

> I have been pressed by God for several years to renounce the world entirely in order to lament my sins and to spend the rest of my life in solitude. Since the death of my incomparable friend [Saint-Cyran, who had died earlier in the year] I have at last received the grace to strengthen my resolve. However I will defer its execution for about a year so that I may put in order the affairs of my family and especially yours since you are the only one remaining in the world.[49]

Simon was not at all pleased to learn that he might lose his father's active support at the beginning of his career. To his brother Antoine he wrote a few weeks later: "Whenever I find a ray of happiness from outside, I am overcome by a domestic misfortune which destroys in a moment the little hope that I was beginning to have. I fall, having lost the only support that I had and lose all hope of raising myself up." And to his father he wrote: "Please forgive me for not having enough virtue to bear with you in the resolution you have taken. I do not have enough strength to bear losing you."[50] Simon's fear of losing his father's assistance proved to be groundless. Long after Andilly retired, he continued to do what he could to promote his son's interests including transferring his pensions to him.

Andilly's third son, Henri-Charles Arnauld de Luzancy, born in 1623, was of delicate health and not particularly adept at his studies. At an early age he was appointed a page in Richelieu's household. Close to his sister Angélique de Saint-Jean, who influenced his spiritual development, which was further enhanced by his education in the Little Schools established by the *solitaires,* Luzancy was torn between a desire to pursue a military career and to become a *solitaire.* A nasty head injury received from a fall caused him to give up his position in the cardinal-minister's household. Although he joined a regiment under the command of his cousin Arnauld de Corbeville, he finally decided, on the advice of the abbé de Saint-Cyran, who continued to provide spiritual direction to all his protégés from prison, to retire to Port-Royal-des-Champs in 1643, where he found his cousins, the Le Maistre brothers, and where his father was to join him less than two years later. There he engaged in manual labor, which he preferred to the scholarly pursuits of the other *solitaires*.[51]

The youngest son of Catherine and Robert Arnauld d'Andilly, named Jules, was born in 1634. He was only a boy when his father retired. Like his brothers Antoine and Henri-Charles, he was eager to serve in the army. His father approached his friend Marshal Abraham Fabert, whom he came to know during the campaign on the Rhine twenty years earlier, for help in securing a position for his youngest son. "My youngest son is about twenty-one years old," he wrote Fabert from Port-Royal in 1655:

> He has shown some facility in the study of languages, philosophy and other subjects, but I don't respect his judgment . . . He does not understand that he is not equipped with a becoming physique, and he has a manner of speaking that makes him appear somewhat foolish. But what I find particularly objectionable about him is that these drawbacks notwithstanding he has an agreeable opinion of himself, and he is shortsighted enough to believe that he can make his fortune . . . Thus have I given you, Monsieur, a true picture of this boy. If it is not particularly attractive, at least you will understand that I do not flatter myself in regard to my children.[52]

Despite his father's unfavorable character reference, Fabert eventually found a place for *"le petit Jules"* as a lieutenant in one of the regiments under his command. There he carried on without any particular distinction until his death from illness in 1660.

Of Andilly's four sons, only one—Luzancy—became entirely immersed in religious life. The others, including the abbé Arnauld, remained in the world in one way or another. But if Andilly preferred a life of solitude, or at least of privacy, he did all that he could to encourage the worldly ambitions of Simon as if they were an extension of his own. And his own were not entirely suppressed even after his wife's death and the imprisonment of Saint-Cyran. The possibility of his return to public life arose after the death of Richelieu in December 1642. Louis XIII, close to death himself, had to reorganize his council of ministers, causing a power struggle between two of the late cardinal's associates with close ties to the Arnaulds, Jules Mazarin and the comte de Chavigny, son of Claude Bouthillier. Chavigny supported the admission to the *conseil d'état* of Gaston d'Orleans, no longer the heir apparent because of the birth of the dauphin in 1638, a sentiment shared by Andilly and his brother Henry. The competition for preferment and place is described in a series of letters written by Henry Arnauld, Andilly's brother, who lived with him, to his friend Henri Barillon, the *prévot des marchands* and a member of a prominent robe family, exiled to Amboise by Richelieu for being critical of the crown's fiscal policies.

Writing from Pomponne just after Richelieu's death in December 1642, Henry informed Barillon that he had returned to Paris from Pomponne to learn more about what was happening and that he had high hopes that political prisoners, including, presumably, Barillon and Saint-Cyran, would soon be liberated. "I pray to God with all my heart for an improvement in the public welfare and for our friends."[53] In subsequent letters Henry also expressed the hope that the king would become his own first minister and that the duc d'Orleans would soon be arriving in Paris from his place of exile at Blois. "M. de Chavigny is working hard to arrange this," he wrote on the last day of 1642. In February of the following year Saint-Cyran was released from prison, only to die a few weeks later, much to the dismay of Henry and other members of his family. Louis XIII also died in that year. Henry was pleased to inform his friend Barillon that the king had named Gaston d'Orleans as Lieutenant General of the kingdom in the regency government.[54]

The revived political fortunes of the Arnauld family at the death of Louis XIII was also commented on by the abbé Arnauld in his memoirs. According to the abbé, everything had changed at court with the death of the king. The queen, Anne, "who had been for so long without credit became all-powerful." Andilly, who had always been attached to the queen, now regent, began to receive indications of her favor.[55] Hoping to impress the regent with his political acumen, Andilly addressed two *mémoires* to the queen mother in which he set forth principles of good government that were reminiscent of the advice given to Louis XIII by his father and uncles during and immediately after the earlier regency period. In them Andilly emphasized the importance of awarding offices and commissions on the basis of merit rather than wealth, thereby inspiring competition among worthy candidates as to who might best serve the king's interests. Andilly undoubtedly had in mind his own earlier inability to accept an appointment as *secretaire d'état* because it was too expensive even though he believed himself to be well qualified for the position. In the *mémoires* he also expressed his opposition to venality as well as to dueling and luxurious habits at court. Like his forebears he disapproved of the duel, which, he said, killed nobles whose swords might be put to better use in the king's service. Concluding his advice to the queen-regent, Andilly urged her to alleviate the excessive tax burden imposed on all elements of society by the crown in its efforts to finance the war against Spain, particularly its effects on those least able to bear it.[56]

Taken as a whole, the *mémoires* reflect not only Andilly's self-esteem, which always expressed itself in the distinction that he made between persons of merit and persons with too much money, but also the values of his family. Throughout the reign of Louis XIII, the Arnaulds had championed the loyal *commissaire* at the expense of the self-serving *officier*, for which reason they consistently opposed venality as a corrupting element in the body politic. Although quite wealthy themselves, they, like many others of their rank, deplored the influence of money in political life, a sentiment that was widely expressed during the Fronde. The Arnaulds' distaste for conspicuous consumption, expressed in their *avis* and *mémoires* during the two regency periods, may also have been a vestigial remnant of their Huguenot heritage—high thinking and plain living—or of their bourgeois origins.

The favor that Andilly apparently sought from Queen Anne was the position of tutor to Louis XIV, who was six years old at the time of his father's death. In an interview described in his memoirs, the queen mother told Andilly that if it were up to her she would "place the King in my hands to educate him as I saw fit. 'For,' she added, 'what better thing could I do than to place [him] in the hands of a man to whom God has given the heart of a king?'"[57] As it turned out, Andilly's final opportunity to return to public service was short-lived because of opposition to the appointment from some unknown quarter in the royal household or in the *conseil d'état*, where the influence of the family friend Chavigny was in decline.

The competition for office after the deaths of Richelieu and Louis XIII had become at least as fierce as it had been in the years immediately following the assassination of Henry IV. The queen mother's favorable attitude toward Andilly had aroused jealousy among rival courtiers.[58] In an effort to sow dissension among the supporters of the duc d'Orleans, one pamphlet making the rounds during the 1640s accused Andilly of being the venal slave of Richelieu, who in 1626 had destroyed the close relationship between the duke and his governor, Ornano.[59] Deeply offended by yet another attack on his integrity, Andilly published his entire correspondence from the beginning of his career to show that he had never been dependent on any one except the king. The vicissitudes of life at court had clearly taken their toll on him. In the last letter in the published collection, written to his friend Abel Servien, who had for years supported his interests at court, Andilly decried "the constant shifts in the affairs of state, the extraordinary changes in the condition of the most powerful people on earth; all that one calls happiness is mixed with so much bitterness and discontent. Death terminates insatiable desires in an instant, and ambition devours the hearts of the most eminent among men."[60]

Of his own ambition, he writes in his memoirs, "I had none because I had too much, not being able to suffer the severe limitations that dependency imposes on those whom God intended to perform great deeds glorious to the state, deeds inspired by zeal for the public good rather than by self-interest." As always, Andilly derived some comfort from his good opinion of himself, which enabled him to believe that if the world in which he had been brought up had been less corrupt, he would have received the honors he was sure he deserved. The *mépris du monde* that affected his outlook to an increasing extent was shaped by both his political experience and by the religious ideals that he had come to share with the abbé de Saint-Cyran and the community of Port-Royal. He had learned that the corrosive influence of self-interest in political life was but another manifestation of the human condition without the vital support of efficacious grace. What ambition he had left he was now prepared to invest in his son Simon, who might yet achieve what he was never able to.[61] Aware of Andilly's sentiments, his friend Valentin Conrart saluted him in verse "upon his wise retirement." Andilly, Conrart wrote, was wise to the intrigues at court and secrets of state and never engaged in them, realizing the influence of fickle favor in political affairs. Furthermore Andilly understood that the fearsome reputation of Louis XIII, wrought by the success of

Richelieu's foreign policy, had been achieved at the expense of heavy taxes on the people, "their fields abandoned, their houses ruined." Moved by these misfortunes, Andilly "has turned [his] eyes from terrestrial objects to contemplate the heavenly life."[62]

At the end of 1645 Andilly at last joined the *solitaires* at Port-Royal-des-Champs, where for his remaining years he translated patristic works, worked on restoring the gardens of the old convent, and submitted to a regimen of penitential discipline. He did not cut himself off from the world, though, maintaining a correspondence with old friends, promoting the careers of his sons Simon and Jules, and serving as a liaison between Port-Royal and the world outside. Although he had espoused the ideals of the *solitaires* and of his sister Angélique, which had seemed so offensive to him at the time of her conversion, he had done so in his own way. And even though he had arranged his life to suit himself, he continued to experience a conflict within him between his temporal and spiritual interests.

It is perhaps because he felt this conflict so intensely that he undertook in 1649 to translate the *Confessions* of Saint Augustine, a work that spoke so poignantly to the turmoil within himself. *"Ainsi j'avais deux volontés, l'une ancienne et l'autre nouvelle, l'une charnelle et l'autre spirituelle qui se combattaient, et en se combattant déchiraient mon âme."* (Thus I found myself with two wills, one old, the other new; one carnal, the other spiritual, which struggled against each other, and in the struggle tore apart my heart.)[63] This inner predicament, described in such dramatic terms by Augustine, was experienced, as we have seen, by Angélique, Antoine Le Maistre, and other members of Andilly's family. Augustine confessed that he had longed to acquire a reputation for eloquence, a reputation that the Arnaulds had already won, but he had come to understand that this longing was a manifestation of damnable ambition *"qui ne travaille que pour s'élever dans l'éclat et dans la gloire"* (which only endeavored to enhance one's (worldly) estime and glory).[64] The one person who tried to restrain Augustine in his efforts to satisfy his ambition was his mother, Monica, who by her prayers and exhortations *"tachait de m'enfanter à Dieu par l'esprit,"* tried to make me a child of God in spirit.[65] just as Angélique and the women of the family had done in regard to the Arnauld men. How ironic that this translation, undertaken as an act of penance for his own vainglorious career, earned him a second invitation to become one of the immortals of the Academie Française, an invitation that he again declined.[66]

Like Saint Augustine, Andilly was a passionate man. He enjoyed the sensuality of eating a well-cultivated peach, and, so we are told by Tallement des Réaux, a fellow member of the Rambouillet circle, made love to his wife several times a night while at the same time asking God to forgive him for over-indulging his carnal appetite.[67] In keeping with these inclinations, Andilly fashioned a life for himself at Port-Royal-des-Champs that enabled him to become a *solitaire* while at the same time remaining a courtier at least in spirit. How he was able to do this is perhaps best explained by that acute observer, Nicolas Fontaine. "He managed to combine two almost antithetical qualities, *la politesse du monde*, with a pure innocence, a penetrating mind, with an unbelievable simplicity, and a heroic generosity with a profound humility."[68] These attributes made it possible for him to work and pray with the *solitaires* while maintaining contact with his friends at court. Not surprisingly, the fruit he cultivated at Port-Royal, *"fruits bénis,"* to use Cardinal Mazarin's expression,[69] graced the tables of both the nuns and the queen mother.

The ability to reconcile the attributes of the hermit with those of the courtier was much harder for Andilly to accomplish than Fontaine and others realized. The turmoil within was never really overcome. As a *solitaire* he had always to keep an eye on his son Simon's career, and as a courtier in spirit he had always to worry about the adverse effect of his worldly concerns on the ultimate disposition of his immortal soul. To be both *solitaire* and courtier was important to him, however, because it made him more independent. Living at Port-Royal-des-Champs freed him from the claustrophobic atmosphere at court and gave him an aura of disinterestedness that, he hoped, might increase his political influence should he need to use it in the interests of Port-Royal or of his son Simon. Andilly managed to retain the respect of friends and associates in both worlds despite the fact that Port-Royal was viewed with increasing suspicion by the authorities of Church and state. The *solitaire* Fontaine provides us with a portrait of the patriarch many years after his retirement that reflects this respect.

I must confess that I am still aroused when I think of the brilliant flame which burns inside this holy *solitaire*. Old age, which weakens most people, seems to redouble his strength. I seem to see and hear him speak to me with those piercing eyes, with those animated words and gestures that belie his great age. He acts like a boy of fifteen with a body that is eighty years old. His bright eyes, his firm and quick step, his voice of thunder, his sound and upright body, full of vigor, his white hair which suits his ruddy complexion so well, the grace with which he mounts and holds his horse, his accurate memory, the quickness of his mind, the firmness of his hand either in holding a pen or in pruning a fruit tree, provides one with an image of immortality, in the words of Saint Jerome, an image of the resurrection, and, if one may say it, these characteristics seem to be the reward for a singular virtue.[70]

Among his younger brothers the one for whom Andilly felt the most affection was Henry, born in 1597. The two brothers lived together for many years, in the house in the rue de la Verrerie and at Pomponne. Both were members of the Rambouillet circle, and both became increasingly involved in the affairs of Port-Royal although in different ways and at different times. After Henry became the bishop of Angers in 1649 and decided at that time never to leave his diocese, the brothers lived apart but maintained the close ties of affection. As was the case with all her male relatives, Angélique Arnauld was eager to have Henry devote his life to pious activities. In 1619 she asked François de Sales, who by that time had become a close friend of the family, about the spiritual condition of her brothers Henry and Simon, born in 1603. The abbess of Port-Royal hoped that both would enter the clergy. On the subject of Henry the bishop replied, "My daughter, M. de Trie [Henry] after turning hither and yon will enter the Church."[71] Although his father had him tonsured in 1615, he intended his second son for public service. Henry's advancement as a young man was due to his brother Andilly's connections. In 1620 he received a pension of 1200 *livres* from Louis XIII "in consideration for the useful services provided the late king, my father, by Monsieur Antoine Arnauld, *avocat au Parlement*" in order to encourage Henry to follow in the tradition of his family. Two years later the king named him abbé of the monastery of Saint-Nicolas in Anjou, a lucrative benefice.[72]

In 1621, again owing to Andilly's connections, Henry became the secretary of the papal nuncio, Cardinal Bentivoglio, and in that capacity spent several years in Rome, where he became familiar with Italian politics. While in Rome he was ordained in Bentivoglio's private chapel. Returning to Paris in 1625, Henry led a secluded life similar to that of his older brother, who a year later was dismissed from the service of Gaston d'Orleans. He too frequented the Hôtel de Rambouillet in Paris, where he resided in the family house in the rue de la Verrerie, spending his summers at Andilly or at Pomponne. "He had many friends because of his pleasing manner and his gentle disposition. He particularly liked men of letters and was liked by them because he was very well read, particularly in history, which few people knew as well as he." His was a well-ordered life: He devoted the early morning to prayer and study, the late morning and early afternoon to social calls, and the evening to contemplation. "He was born generous and liberal; although a most sober man of the world, he would not have been happy without his friends."[73] In 1637, through his family ties to the marquis de Feuquières, governor of Toul, and to Richelieu's creatures Claude Bouthillier and his son Léon, comte de Chavigny, Henry was appointed bishop of that fortified city by the king. However, because of a quarrel between France and the Vatican, Pope Urban VIII refused to ratify the appointment. Henry withdrew his name from consideration and returned to private life.

Henry Arnauld's letters to President Barillon, written almost every day between 1639 and 1643, contain a detailed account of public affairs similar to that found in Andilly's journals for the period 1614–1630. Henry dwelled at some length on the excessive cost of the war with Spain, opposition to the government's fiscal policy, and other issues that reflect concerns similar to those expressed by Andilly in his *mémoires* to the queen mother in 1643. They also contain news of the family, illnesses and deaths, the comings and goings of Henry and his older brother between Paris and Pomponne, and the impact on the family of the imprisonment of the abbé de Saint-Cyran. Among other things he reports his older sister Catherine Le Maistre's taking of vows at Port-Royal. "I would have preferred," he wrote, "to have her remain in her former condition."[74] In this correspondence Henry states his preference for tranquility of life in the country to the noise and confusion of Paris. "I must confess to you that I have a passion for the solitude of the country and a hatred for Paris," he wrote on 8 October 1642.[75] He appears to have disliked life at court as well. In a letter written in the summer of 1639 he describes a visit to the court, then at Saint-Germain-en-Laye, to secure one of his brother Simon's offices for the family. "There I experienced the worst humiliation, having spent the entire day being buffeted about, so that I returned with a fever and the firm resolve never to return there."[76]

Although he was clearly sympathetic to Port-Royal and was endowed with a temperament that might easily have inclined him toward a life among the *solitaires*, Henry did not join their ranks. Indeed he tried to discourage Antoine Le Maistre from abandoning his career and, later on, Sacy from joining his older brothers. If it had been up to him, they and his oldest sister, Catherine Le Maistre, would have remained in the world of which he was a part by inclination if not by temperament. Lacking the ambition of his older brother, Henry continued to enjoy his quiet life in Paris or at Pomponne until he was again sent on a mission to Rome by Mazarin in 1645. Religious in a conventional sense, there is no indication that he had any intention of transforming his life in the turbulent 1640s. Like Andilly he was disillusioned with the politics of his time, a sentiment that became more intense after his failure to receive the bishopric of Toul and the arrest of Saint-Cyran. His letters to Barillon indicate that Henry was entirely content with his private life. He seems only to have realized Angélique's prayers and François de Sales's prediction that he would "come to the Church" to the extent that he became a member of the clergy.

François de Sales's predictions in regard to Simon Arnauld were also realized. He told Angélique that he saw no indication that Simon would enter the Church. Simon apparently led a profligate life in the army as a *maître de camp*, frittering away most of his inheritance and frequently becoming involved in duels without regard to Andilly's opinion that such activity was against the public interest. Despite the prayers of his mother and sisters that he abandon this way of life, he continued in it until his death in battle outside of Verdun, where he was serving under the command of his cousin Feuquières. By way of an epitaph Angélique said of him without compassion that "he was a man of the sword and entirely given over to the world."[77]

All three of Angélique's brothers—Robert, Henry, and Simon—remained in the world in one way or another. Simon was the most unregenerate of the three, but Henry, though critical of the world in which he lived, remained a part of it in his own quiet way. As for Robert, the patriarch of the family, he became disillusioned with the world, to be sure, and joined the *solitaires*, who were only too glad to receive him at Port-Royal-des-Champs but maintained his contacts at court. Unfortunately, Andilly's withdrawal to Port-Royal occurred at a time when his friend the abbé de Saint-Cyran's penitential theology was again under attack because of his association with a relatively obscure Flemish bishop by the name of Cornelius Jansen. The most ardent defender of that theology was the youngest child of Antoine and Catherine Arnauld, Antoine, who in his own way would contribute to the family renown by involving it in a controversy that incurred the displeasure of both church and state.

7

Le Grand Arnauld *and the* Origins *of* Jansenism

ANTOINE ARNAULD was the last of the twenty children born to Catherine and Antoine Arnauld. His birth occurred in 1612, three years after the *journée du guichet*, by which time Angélique was well on her way toward reforming Port-Royal, his brother Robert had already begun his political career, and the influence of his father and uncles at court and in Paris was at its height. The youngest Arnauld came to be known as *le grand Arnauld* because of his diminutive stature, although some among his relatives and acquaintances referred to him as *le petit oncle* because he was younger than three of his Le Maistre nephews.

Only seven years old when his father died, Antoine was brought up by his mother and oldest sister together with his nephews. Because of the close ties between the Arnaulds and the Catholic reform movement that were established after Angélique's conversion, greater attention was paid to Antoine's spiritual development than had been the case with his older siblings. He was fortunate enough to receive the blessing of François de Sales during one of his visits to the house in the rue de la Verrerie. By the time he began his formal education at the College de Calvi, his mother had committed herself to Port-Royal, leaving Catherine Le Maistre and Henry Arnauld, who had taken up residence in the family house after his return from Rome in 1625, in charge of the boy's upbringing.

Unlike Antoine Le Maistre, young Antoine Arnauld was not at first a dedicated student. Tutored at home with his nephews before they all went off to school, *le petit oncle* never did his homework. After the others had recited the lesson of the day, he merely parroted without error what they had said. Although he appears to have decided early on that he would enter the Church, his decision was based entirely on worldly considerations. As a young man he was by no means as pious as Le Maistre, who agonized over whether to become a member of the clergy or undertake a career in the law, or Sacy, whose sole ambition was to become a simple priest. Antoine Arnauld *fils* had no such scruples. Desirous of winning a reputation for eloquence as a member of the theological faculty, he enrolled in the Sorbonne.

According to Nicolas Fontaine, who knew him as well as he knew the Le Maistre brothers, Arnauld was quite the young man about town. Scion of a distinguished family, he enjoyed being seen taking a drive in his carriage in the fashionable quarters of the city. He lived comfortably on his inheritance, which was managed for him by his older brother Henry. Eager to win a reputation for himself, he went to great lengths to impress his teachers and fellow students with the power of his intellect, and although there were some among them whose intellectual abilities were greater than his, they were often cowed by him, only too aware of his inclination to enter into a dispute "with his head down," ready to charge into the fray before he had thought his position through.[1] Like his father, who had reveled in the verbal joustings of the Palais de Justice, young Antoine, even at an early age, enjoyed the thrusts and parries that characterized the theological debates of his time. One such debate occurred at the time when Arnauld submitted his dissertation to the theological faculty in order to complete the requirements for the doctorate. One of his professors objected to Arnauld's excessive reliance on Augustinian theology. This objection delayed the young theologian's admission to the ranks of the faculty of the Sorbonne until 1641.

In 1639, while Antoine Arnauld was working toward his doctorate, he made the decision to renounce his worldly ambitions and join the ranks of the *solitaires*. By this time he had come under the influence of the abbé de Saint-Cyran, then a prisoner in the chateau de Vincennes. Arnauld had been acquainted with the abbé from childhood. His mother and sisters had encouraged him to seek his counsel during his formative years, but Saint-Cyran apparently took little interest in him[2] until the young man began to visit him in the chateau de Vincennes from time to time and exchanged numerous letters with him. Writing in early 1639, Antoine admitted that his interest in theology had initially been inspired by the desire to amuse himself rather than by any religious zeal. Perhaps, he said, he would be better off joining the *solitaires* except that if he absented himself from the Sorbonne, he might arouse suspicion "and renew the persecution against you and the monastery [Port-Royal]." In any case, such a radical course of action would require the approval of his brother Henry, his legal guardian, who was not likely to give it.[3]

Saint-Cyran urged young Arnauld, despite his reservations, to continue his studies and to complete the requirements for the doctorate. This advice was quite different from that which he had given Sacy, but the abbé realized that the two men were very different from one another in terms of temperament and vocation. Sacy, in his opinion, was best suited to the role of simple priest and confessor to the Port-Royal community; *le petit oncle* would best serve the cause of truth by employing his rhetorical skills and his theological training in its defense. Saint-Cyran also advised his protégé to retain two benefices that had been given to him through the influence of his cousin, the marquis de Feuquières. As governor of Verdun, the marquis was in a position to bestow on Antoine the offices of subdeacon and cantor in the local chapter, both of which Antoine wanted to refuse. Upon hearing that the other candidate for the positions was disliked by the cathedral chapter at Verdun, Saint-Cyran advised his protégé to hold on to them.

It was not until Arnauld received his doctorate from the Sorbonne in December 1641 and was ordained as a priest a few days later that Saint-Cyran instructed him to join the *solitaires*. In one of his early letters to the abbé, Arnauld admitted that residence at Port-Royal would be better for him because he was "too susceptible to commerce with the world." At the end of the same letter he wrote "that God has called on me to engage in a struggle which may cause me great harm, and maybe even death, and I understand what is expected of me in the defense of truth."[4]

What was the truth that Saint-Cyran wanted Antoine Arnauld to defend? In the first place, those principles pertaining to penitential discipline: an awareness of one's own corrupt nature and a commitment to serve God's interests rather than one's own, an understanding that such a commitment would have no effect whatsoever without the impetus provided by efficacious grace, a willingness to struggle against those forces both within and without the self that sought to undermine the good, and above all, a *mépris du monde*. The abbé had enunciated these principles to those who submitted themselves to his guidance, but they were controversial within the Catholic community. Some Catholic theologians, including Richelieu, who prided himself on his understanding of such matters, believed that the penitential ethics espoused by Saint-Cyran and others were too harsh. A total conversion from love of self to love of God was more than should be expected of anyone but a saint. To their way of thinking, a sinner had only to confess his or her sins out of fear of God's punishment and perform the penance prescribed by the priest in order to receive absolution. For Saint-Cyran, such an attitude reflected a greater concern on the part of the sinner for his own well-being than a genuine commitment to serve God in that his repentance was based merely on a fear of punishment and not on a genuine change of heart.

The quarrel over penitential ethics had a profound effect within the French Catholic community in the middle of the seventeenth century. There were those—among them the Jesuits—who believed that a penitential ethic that seemed excessive might hamper the work of the Catholic reform movement because of its discouraging effect on the ordinary Christian. Louis XIII, whose conscience was especially sensitive, was much alarmed by the ethics ascribed to Saint-Cyran and others. Cardinal Richelieu, always suspicious of troublesome issues that divided public opinion, decided to arrest the abbé de Saint-Cyran in part because of the controversial nature of his penitential theology. In short, powerful interests—the king, the cardinal, and the Jesuits—were lined up against the abbé and his followers on this critical issue.[5]

The abbé de Saint-Cyran's penitential ethics touched on another controversial issue—the role of God's grace in the process of redemption. The abbé came to believe that man, corrupted as he is by original sin, is entirely incapable of any meritorious act without an infusion of grace. During his time in prison, the abbé received a book entitled *Augustinus* written by a friend, Cornelius Jansen, the bishop of Ypres in the Spanish Netherlands, who had died two years before its publication in 1640. Jansen and Saint-Cyran had met as students at the University of Louvain and had worked together to develop a sound penitential theology that would provide doctrinal support for the reform movement as they understood it.

The role of God's grace in the process of redemption had generated debate within the Church from its earliest times. In the sixteenth century, Protestant leaders had focused on this issue, insisting that man on his own was incapable of redeeming himself in the sight of God and was entirely dependent on the workings of divine grace within him to achieve salvation. Even within the Catholic Church there were continued debates on the issue after Luther's break with Rome. Some Catholics, including the Society of Jesus, insisted on an active role for the human will in the quest for redemption. In so doing they became vulnerable to the accusation that they were reviving the Pelagian heresy, which in effect gave too much credit to man and too little credit to God. The assault on Pelagianism had been led by the great theologian Saint Augustine, who argued that the will was corrupted by original sin and therefore entirely dependent on the power of grace to achieve the good in the sight of God. Those Catholic theologians in the sixteenth and seventeenth centuries who took a similar stance were themselves vulnerable to the accusation that they were crypto-Protestants. The debate among Catholic theologians on the issue had become so intense at the beginning of the seventeenth century that the papacy issued decrees in 1611 and again in 1625 prohibiting further public discussion of these contentious issues.

In spite of the papal ban, Bishop Jansen undertook to write what he hoped would be the definitive work on the Catholic doctrine of grace, the *Augustinus*. After explicating the Pelagian heresy and declaring emphatically that Saint Augustine was the ultimate authority in matters pertaining to grace, he addresses the relationship between grace and free will at length. Vitiated by original sin, the will is incapable of choosing between good and evil. Without an infusion of grace it inevitably acts on the basis of love of self *(amour-propre)*. By means of grace, the will is liberated from the debilitating effects of original sin, enabling the love of self to become converted to a love of God.[6]

The Augustinian doctrine of grace as interpreted by Jansen and Saint-Cyran appealed to a number of Catholics, including the Arnaulds. It appealed to Angélique, whose pessimistic view of human nature was instilled in her by her sense of her own weakness and unworthiness in the sight of God. It appealed to Robert Arnauld d'Andilly, increasingly disillusioned with a political system based on self-interest rather than the public good. Jansen's insistence that without an infusion of grace, man's will acted entirely on the basis of self-interest provided a theological explanation for the politics of selfishness and greed. All the more reason, in his opinion, to withdraw from that world and devote oneself to prayer and introspection. But if one cut himself off from the world, how was true doctrine to be expounded? How would withdrawal affect the work of religious reform? The abbé de Saint-Cyran was well aware of the problem. Confident in the theological training, the rhetorical skills, and the religious commitment of his young protégé, Antoine Arnauld, the abbé called on him to defend "the truth" against the powerful forces within the Church that regarded that truth as heretical. Arnauld did not underestimate the forces arrayed against him, but he had come to understand, like his sister Angélique, that religious life is a perpetual struggle and that a willingness to suffer persecution for righteousness' sake at the hands of one's enemies was a test of one's commitment to the defense of "the truth." He was undoubtedly aware of Saint-Cyran's prophetic opinion, expressed in a letter to Angélique in 1643, that it was better that Port-Royal itself be destroyed than its penitential discipline undermined.[7]

The form of persecution that Saint-Cyran experienced was imprisonment without term at the chateau de Vincennes on the outskirts of Paris even though nothing explicitly heretical had been found among his papers. Whether he would ever be released was by no means certain despite the efforts on his behalf of Arnauld d'Andilly and other friends. His incarceration in 1638 occurred at a time when Richelieu was making every effort to silence potential enemies of the state in order to unite the kingdom against Spain. As long as he remained in prison, he could not speak out on the issues of importance to him. The bright and energetic young theologian who had placed himself under his tutelage, Antoine Arnauld, member of a family closely associated with Catholic reform, had no such handicap. By training, temperament, and inclination he was ideally suited to the task of lifting his voice, as the abbé put it, on behalf of the true doctrine of the Church. "It is certain that our efforts to maintain our silence and our modesty have done us harm," Saint-Cyran wrote in one of fifty letters written from the chateau de Vincennes to his protégé.[8]

One must not remain silent or dissimulate out of fear of jeopardizing my release from prison . . . I have come to understand how much we should condemn the silences and the omissions that have done us harm in this affair. The time has now come for vigilance and continual action . . . We must have the courage to defend grace and penitence against any and all, for this defense is in itself an act of repentance and meritorious in its own right . . . Even if I had committed every crime I would have confidence in my salvation if God gave me the grace to defend [his] grace not only against heretics but against those Catholics who discredit it, who are all the more dangerous in that they have assumed the right to speak in the Church.[9]

The same militant tone appears in another letter written in October 1642. Saint-Cyran reminded Arnauld that it was his duty as a theologian to speak out in support of the doctrine of efficacious grace, "which is not just that of the bishop of Ypres or of Saint Augustine but of the Church as a whole," even if forbidden to do so by ecclesiastical officials at the highest level.

Arnauld's defense of that doctrine took the form of two *apologies*, the first published in 1644, the second in 1645. Both were written in response to an attack on Bishop Jansen's *Augustinus* by Isaac Habert, a prominent Parisian cleric who, in his sermons and a polemic entitled *Défense de la foy de l'église*, maintained that Bishop Jansen's theology contained heretical propositions closely resembling the Calvinist doctrine of predestination. At the same time, Habert denounced the little group of *solitaires*, disciples of Saint-Cyran, gathered together around Port-Royal as a cabal organized for the purpose of disseminating heretical beliefs.

In the preface to the first *apologie* Arnauld reiterated Saint-Cyran's point that it is not always possible to maintain peace within the Church "when it becomes necessary to uphold the cause of truth." It is not just the Huguenots whom we must combat, he asserted, again echoing his mentor, it is also Catholics "who like vipers tear at the breast of their mother." Taking issue with Habert's contention that the proposition contained in the *Augustinus* that Christ gave his life only for the purpose of redeeming the elect was essentially Protestant, Arnauld responded that although Christ died to save all Christians, most of those who called themselves by that name were not worthy of his sacrifice because they were not genuinely repentant of their sins. Those "who live like Christians and persevere in the good life until the end are predestined to become members of the elect." In other words, redemption is possible only for hardy souls who, like Angélique Arnauld and Antoine Le Maistre, had transformed their lives by rejecting the world and dedicating their efforts to the service of God.[10]

In the second *apologie* Arnauld underscored the difference between Jansen's doctrine of predestination and Calvin's. In the former, man is held responsible for his corrupt nature, whereas in the latter God was made to seem responsible for original sin. Therein lay the heresy. In this polemic Arnauld also attacked the Jesuits for subscribing to a penitential ethics that smacked of the Pelagian heresy, thereby launching a life-long campaign against his father's old nemesis, now among the abbé de Saint-Cyran's severest critics. By defending the doctrine of the bishop of Ypres in such a forceful manner, Arnauld and other like-minded persons came to be known as "Jansenists," a term applied to those who defended the bishop's treatise on the doctrine of efficacious grace.[11]

In 1643, before the appearance of the *apologies*, Antoine Arnauld had published another controversial work entitled *De la fréquente communion*, which elaborated on the penitential ethics espoused by Saint-Cyran and Angélique Arnauld. In its preface *le grand Arnauld* again justified the need to defend the truth especially when it is under attack, adding that to remain silent is to betray God. "It is far better to cause trouble and to shock the community than to abandon the truth." The specific issue of concern to the author was whether abstinence from the sacraments upon occasion was beneficial to the sinner. Some theologians advocated frequent participation in the sacraments because of their healing quality, but Arnauld argued that in certain instances it was better for the sinner to refrain from partaking of them until he or she was in a proper frame of mind. Such had been the practice of his sister Angélique, who occasionally refused to participate in the sacraments in spite of Saint-Cyran's advice to do so.

> For what penance would be more pleasing to God . . . than to break entirely . . . with the world and to renounce forever the pleasures or rather the follies of this century; to give up all sorts of pretensions in order to take up a holy and religious life; to withdraw in solitude following the example of so many great saints, or

to choose the depths of a monastery for the purpose of satisfying God's justice with continuous tears.

These words speak to the experiences of several members of his family as well as to his own intentions.

How was the sinner to know whether he or she was moved to take communion by love of self or love of God?

> If we feel at the bottom of our heart a detachment from worldly considerations and attachment to God; a contempt for the pomp and vanity of this century and a delight in the expectation of eternal benefits; a mortal fear of having fallen into disgrace [in the sight of] God and a pressing desire to please him in all things, and the firm intention of fleeing from all occasions in which we might commit a sin; and finally the veritable disposition to abandon father, mother, sisters, brothers, relatives, friends, goods, grandeur, honors and esteem rather than to abandon the service of Jesus Christ; if we feel all these dispositions in our hearts at least in some degree . . . we may have reason to believe that we love God.

In other words, if the sinner is prepared to adopt a profound *mépris du monde*, he might feel somewhat confident that he is inspired by efficacious grace.

At the same time, the issue of frequent or infrequent communion was directly related to the abbé de Saint-Cyran's belief, viewed with such suspicion by Richelieu, that the truly repentant sinner must be inspired by a love of God rather than a love of self. Far from being an innovation, this belief was rooted in the practices of the early Church, which Arnauld contrasted favorably with the corrupt practices of his own time. How very different were the penitential practices of that time from the doctrine and discipline subscribed to by so many in this century when the "abuse of the sacraments is common, . . . when so many people want to cover their profligacy with this veil."[12] By contrasting the practices of the early Church with those of the Church in the seventeenth century, Arnauld, by implication, points up the difference between the penitential ethics of the Jansenists and what he regarded as the devious ethics espoused by the Jesuits.

Whereas most of the issues contained in Bishop Jansen's *Augustinus* were intelligible only to well-schooled churchmen, those contained in

De la fréquente communion were of concern to laymen as well as clergy. What was troublesome to many about the demands made on the Catholic conscience by Saint-Cyran and Antoine Arnauld was that these demands seemed to place the possibility of redemption beyond the reach of ordinary mortals. Arnauld's work was made all the more controversial by its introduction, written by Martin de Barcos, Saint-Cyran's nephew, who referred to Saints Peter and Paul as "the two heads that make but one," which seemed to question the primacy of Peter, the rock upon which Christ intended to build his church. Not surprisingly, the current heir to the Petrine tradition, Pope Innocent X, condemned Barcos's proposition in 1645.

By the time he had published *De la fréquente communion*, Antoine Arnauld had resigned his benefices and given a portion of his inheritance (twenty thousand pounds) to Port-Royal in return for an annual stipend,[13] as his cousins the Le Maistre brothers had done. He served as a confessor to the nuns of Port-Royal together with another protégé of Saint-Cyran's, Antoine Singlin. Because of his controversial doctrine and his association with the imprisoned abbé and the *solitaires* of Port-Royal, he was forced to spend much of his time in hiding. Despite this hardship, Arnauld, like the other *solitaires*, was able to live on his own terms, speaking out when he thought it necessary without regard to its effect on his worldly condition. In choosing to conduct his life in this way, one becomes aware of that same spirit of independence displayed by other members of his family.

Although associated with the *solitaires* for much of his adult life, Antoine's commitment to defend the truth publicly put him at odds with the Le Maistre brothers. The life of the *solitaires* as established by the first among them, Antoine Le Maistre, involved a complete withdrawal from the world. For Le Maistre this meant no further commerce with the world, "which will think me lost." How, if one were to remain out of communication with the world, was he to defend the truth in the struggle against the forces of evil? Saint-Cyran had urged Antoine Arnauld to speak out on behalf of the true doctrine of the Church. So too had his mother, who, on her deathbed in 1641, having received the last rites from her confessor Singlin, the only person with whom she had communicated in several months, begged Singlin "to tell my youngest son whom God has engaged in the defense of the truth that I exhort him, I urge him to uphold it fearlessly, even if it costs him his life."[14]

Le Maistre clearly disapproved of a public defense of the truth, as did his brother Sacy, because such activity engaged one in too much commerce with the world. This sentiment was not unlike that of his aunt Angélique, who regarded her public responsibilities as a distraction from a life of prayer and solitude. In a letter written to his aunt Agnès in 1645, Antoine Le Maistre complained of having to live with his cousin Antoine Arnauld in Paris. Life with *le petit oncle* involved him in too many polemics. "I have thought it best to disengage myself from these activities, which I would have to continue were I to remain with this doctor.[15]

Sacy also lived with his uncle Antoine for a few months after the appearance of *De la fréquente communion*. Well aware of *"la vivacité de son feu,"* in the words of Sacy's intimate companion Fontaine,[16] Sacy sought to temper *le petit oncle's* ardor as he frequently did with his older brother Antoine. Sacy and Arnauld, in Fontaine's opinion, were well suited to each other.[17] Arnauld served the cause of truth by defending it against its enemies, whereas Sacy, who was not combative by nature, preferred to edify and console those who sought spiritual sustenance from him. Angélique Arnauld, who kept a careful eye on her younger brother's activities, was also concerned about his combative tendencies. Endowed with a nature similar to his and to Andilly's, she knew that he would have to suppress his inclination to remain engaged in the world because she was always trying to suppress it in herself. She had always worried about her own activities as abbess, fearing that her involvement in the world in the interests of promoting reform, which often involved her in conflict with others, was inimical to her spiritual requirements. Returned to the office of abbess by election in 1642 as the controversy over Jansen's *Augustinus* was just getting under way, she was affected more than ever by the tension created by her public responsibilities—supervising the construction of the chapel at Port-Royal-de-Paris, cultivating benefactors, and administering the resources of the convent—which brought her into frequent contact with the world.

Angélique was well pleased with the decision of her youngest brother, whom she often referred to as *le petit frère*, to give up his benefices and become associated with the *solitaires*, a decision that she had been encouraging for a long time. She was impressed with his spirituality and believed that he was ideally suited to be a confessor to her nuns, although she herself remained under the direction of Singlin.[18] Like Saint-Cyran, she believed that her brother's theological training would be put to good use in support of the penitential ethics to which she was committed. Thus she encouraged him to write *De la fréquente communion,* but she had serious reservations about his engaging in polemics against those who were attempting to discredit Jansen's work. In a series of letters written to *le petit frère* during the early 1640s, she expressed her concerns about his disposition as she had done to Arnauld d'Andilly at the time of his dismissal from the service of the duc d'Orleans two decades earlier.[19] "I cannot refrain from saying to you that I am mortified to have learned that you have set aside that excellent work so necessary to [understanding the workings of grace] in order to defend yourself against a man [Habert] so ill thought of among decent people who disapprove of your amusing yourself in combat with an unworthy champion," she wrote in one of these letters. "Cut short this unfortunate work as soon as you can in order to resume work on your book about grace." In another letter she lamented "the unhappiness to the point of tears that I often experience when I think that they [your adversaries] will never leave you in peace and that unless a miracle occurs, your whole life will be painful. At the same time I praise God with all my heart that [such pain] may the best thing that can happen to you. I often think of the blessing that our good mother gave you at the time of her death, to die for the truth."

The real issue, as Angélique saw it, was whether to suffer persecution in silence as a gesture of humility or to engage one's enemies in a public debate in order to have the truth prevail within the Catholic community. Engaging in a polemical duel with Habert and the Jesuits involved a knowledge of theological traditions and a rhetorical skill that might impress the public but at the same time inflate the ego of the polemicist. "I confess to you," she wrote again, "that I have always been uneasy when I have seen you [afflicted by] this persecution out of fear that you will not bear it as humbly as our good father [the abbé de Saint-Cyran]." Although convinced that God had chosen her family "to participate in a happiness that is as rare as it is glorious," she worried that "we will not be humble enough [to deserve] such favor." And in a letter written to him while he was in hiding, she reminded him that the early Church fathers often found themselves in similar circumstances, "but I pray to God that you have their modesty, humility and charity." She urged her youngest brother to pray every time he took up his pen, to read scripture frequently "because I fear that you don't know it well enough and that your activities make you forget to read it," and to ignore the praise he was receiving from many quarters for his book on the sacraments.

Much as Angélique worried about the spiritual well-being of *le petit frère*, she herself was outraged by the attacks on "the truth." Whether she actually read the controversial *Augustinus* is not known, but she was certainly aware of the theological issues involved, despite the claims of the nuns of Port-Royal later on that as nuns they were supposed to be ignorant of such matters. In a letter written to an acquaintance in 1643 she complained: "From their pulpits the Jesuit fathers denounce Monsieur d'Ypres [whom she referred to as "a saintly bishop"] as a Calvinist." In the same letter she also referred to efforts underway in Rome to have the *Augustinus* censured.[20] "You will undoubtedly find [the tone] too bitter in the second *Apologie* [of Antoine Arnauld]. This is the opinion of several people, but others believe that it is necessary to repulse with force and vigor that which is said with such insolence against the truth," she wrote two years later, "but those who know the truth must not be slack in their defense of it. Forceful [arguments] that confuse the enemies of God and the Church are not unChristian. If they had treated [the fathers of the Church] as they have M. d'Ypres . . . wouldn't we have every right to defend them with vigor?"[21] Again and again she asserted, as did other Jansenists, that the doctrine of efficacious grace was not that of Jansen "whom I have never met," or of Saint-Cyran, but the long-established doctrine of the Church. Every Christian, she asserted, must resist the revival of the Pelagian heresy in the form of the Jesuits' penitential ethics.[22] Her own resistance was expressed in an appeal to the archbishop of Paris to condemn a pamphlet written by a Jesuit that described the nuns of Port Royal as heretics.[23]

By 1650 the assault of the Jesuits and their allies on Jansen, Antoine Arnauld, and the Port-Royal community had become so furious that Angélique appeared to be willing to throw caution and fear for her youngest brother's immortal soul to the winds when she wrote him: "If I were in your place I would make known to all France the sentiments of the popes on grace in the vernacular as well as the treatise of our father, Saint Bernard, on grace and free will . . . And too the sentiments of men and women saints entirely in conformance with Saint Augustine . . . This is the best way to enlighten the world."[24]

To enlighten the world meant to remain in contact with the world, to engage in public debate. If Angélique's feelings about this contact were ambivalent, her brother Antoine's were not. Mindful of Saint-Cyran's instructions and the last words of his mother concerning defending the truth, words that were inscribed on a piece of paper he carried with him for the rest of his life, Antoine castigated the penitential ethics of the Jesuits, Huguenot theology, scholastic rhetoric, and libertinism in books and pamphlets that amount to over forty volumes of his collected works. Although he spent much of his time with the *solitaires,* he was never really one of them any more than was his oldest brother, Robert. Harassed though he was throughout much of his life by those who sought to have him condemned as a heretic, he enjoyed, as always, the admiration of others such as Charles Perrault and Pierre Bayle for his eloquence, clarity of expression, and the power of his intellect in the same way his father, the lawyer, had been admired for similar adversarial skills. Just as a lawyer defends a client against one allegation or another, Antoine used his training as a theologian to defend "the friends of truth" against the various accusations levied against them by the authorities of church and state. In a very real sense Antoine Arnauld *fils* became the lawyer for his family and for the Jansenists as a whole. He clearly enjoyed adversarial proceedings in much the same way as his father did, and, of course, both shared a common adversary in the Society of Jesus.

For *le grand Arnauld,* his career as a theologian was what he had hoped it would be when he embarked on his studies, eager to win the respect and admiration of his contemporaries. His decision to give up his benefices and his inheritance in order to engage in his sister's struggle with the world did not change the course of his life as he had determined it as a young man. Even as a schoolboy he had delighted in verbal combat. By becoming the principal spokesman for the Jansenists, he had ample opportunity to take up his pen in the same way his warrior cousins took up their sword. He was thus able not only to sustain, but to enhance, the Arnaulds' reputation for eloquence. Early on, Antoine Arnauld seems to have realized that a theologian had considerable autonomy, and that he could use his knowledge and training to speak out on doctrinal issues of concern to him even in the face of higher authority within the Church.[25] He may have understood that a career in the Church offered more opportunities than might have been available to him in the law or at court. He must have been aware, when he began to give serious thought to his future, of his older brother Andilly's frustrations with his political career. What is certain is that Antoine Arnauld *fils* acquired greater renown as a theologian than his father or grandfather had ever been able to acquire as lawyers. It is ironic that in renouncing the world and its ways he became involved in a struggle that earned him what he may always have wanted—the world's respect and admiration.

Efforts to suppress Bishop Jansen's *Augustinus* began almost immediately after its publication in 1640. Richelieu and a number of French bishops tried to have the work condemned both by the Vatican and by the faculty of the Sorbonne, but the conduct of the war with Spain, whose armies were threatening Paris from the north, was of more pressing importance at the time. Besides, the highest sovereign courts, the parlements, and many bishops were wary of any pronouncement from Rome that might jeopardize the Gallican rights of the French Church. Thus little attention was paid in France to the papal encyclical *In eminenti* issued in 1643 denouncing the *Augustinus* for having violated the ban on public debates over grace and free will.

Realizing that a more precise condemnation of Jansen's theology would have to come from Rome, opponents of that theology looked for a new opportunity to approach the Vatican. In 1649 the faculty of the Sorbonne was asked to consider the heretical implications of several propositions allegedly drawn from students' theses. These propositions were remarkably similar to those drawn from the *Augustinus* and refuted by Isaac Habert, now bishop of Vabres. When the theologians of the Sorbonne declined to condemn the articles, the articles were forwarded to Rome in 1651 by Habert and others, on appeal. Because of the alacrity with which Habert appealed to Rome, many theologians believed that Habert was in effect asking for a condemnation of the *Augustinus*. After some hesitation on the part of Pope Innocent X, who was afraid of arousing Gallican sensibilities, the encyclical *Cum occasione* was issued in 1653 condemning five of the propositions forwarded by Habert.

The propositions, although not attributed to Jansen by the pope, were nonetheless directly related to the central theme of the *Augustinus*, reiterated in Antoine Arnauld's *Apologies*, that grace is necessary for the will to accomplish anything good in the sight of God.[26] Small wonder that Angélique, in a letter written two months after the appearance of the encyclical, urged her brother Antoine to enlighten a world mis-guided by false doctrine. The intense debate within the Church over the issues raised by Bishop Jansen's *Augustinus* reveal divisions that hampered the work of the Catholic reform movement in France. Al-though there were reformers on both sides of the issue—those, like Arnauld, who believed that reform was impossible without adherence to the penitential theology expounded by Jansen and the abbé de Saint-Cyran, and those, like the Jesuits, who believed that the doctrine ex-pounded by the late bishop of Ypres was merely a restatement of the Protestant heresy—their profound disagreement on what they re-garded as crucial issues prevented them from uniting in support of reform.

The reform movement was further hampered by the Gallican issue. As Innocent X rightly suspected when he considered speaking out on the propositions submitted to him, the French crown and a number of French ecclesiastical officials were reluctant to accept pronouncements from Rome on the grounds that they encroached on the rights of the state or the rights of the French Catholic hierarchy. Finally, as we have seen, French Catholics were divided on policy issues. There were those *dévots*, among them Saint-Cyran, who opposed the war with Spain, believing that the interests of the Counter Reformation would best be served by an alliance between the two Catholic powers. These divisive issues, in evidence at the time that the controversial articles were taken under consideration by the papacy, were exacerbated by the impact of civil war that threatened to undermine the regency government of Anne of Austria.

⟿ 8

The Arnauld Family during the Fronde

$\mathcal{T}$HE CONTROVERSY over whether Bishop Jansen's book on efficacious grace was heretical took place during the era of civil war in France known as the Fronde. Every segment of society had been adversely affected by the heavy tax burden that had been imposed by the crown to cover the cost of the war with Spain begun in 1636. Richelieu's death in 1642, followed six months later by the demise of Louis XIII, had aroused widespread hope that the regency government would bring an end to the conflict. After his appointment as first minister by the queen-regent Anne, Cardinal Mazarin concluded that the war must continue until the objectives established by his patron, Richelieu, had been achieved. The early years of the regency (1643–1645) were marked by popular revolts and conspiracies instigated by discontent over high taxes, food shortages, and a general dislike of Mazarin, a foreigner who had become the dominant figure in the government.

The Fronde itself began in 1648 when Mazarin ordered the arrest of several magistrates of the Parlement of Paris because of what he regarded as their obstructionist reaction to his government's fiscal policy. The popular response to these arrests caused Mazarin and the queen to remove the court from Paris and to assemble an army for the purpose of restoring order in the city. Although a temporary compromise between the crown and the Parlement was reached in early 1649, other rebellions occurred that involved at one time or another some of the most prominent nobles, among them the princes of the blood, Condé and Conti, and the king's uncle, Gaston d'Orléans. The Fronde lasted until 1653 when Mazarin, having triumphed over the shifting coalition opposed to him and to his policies, returned from a second brief exile to take over the reins of government once again until his death in 1661. The political upheaval coincided with a series of harvest failures and an outbreak of the plague in several parts of France, which, when added to the impact of war both within and beyond the frontiers of the kingdom, had a devastating effect on France, particularly on Paris and the surrounding area.

The Fronde intensified Mazarin's desire to crack down on rebellious activities of any kind. It was his opinion, shared by the queen mother, Anne of Austria, and the young king, Louis XIV, that Jansenism was a potentially rebellious movement that might lead to another schism in the Church, to the detriment of social order and stability. They were not unaware of accusations made in pamphlets written by the opponents of Jansenism that the Jansenists were *frondeurs* bent on destroying the monarchy.[1] Thus the extent to which the Arnaulds were involved in or sympathized with the Fronde becomes an important question. Even if they were not *frondeurs* in any sense of the term, they and the Jansenists as a whole would undoubtedly experience even greater pressure from the king's government to submit to the commandments of the Church.

The ravages caused by war and economic crisis are vividly described by Angélique Arnauld in a number of letters to the queen of Poland, the former Marie de Gonzague, a benefactress of Port-Royal, and to others. During the Fronde, Angélique spent some time at Port-Royal-des-Champs, which had been reopened in order to accommodate the growing number of nuns who sought to become members of the monastic community or who were refugees from convents that had been victimized by marauding troops. Her presence there enabled her to manage more effectively the resources upon which both Port-Royal establishments depended. Thus she observed at first hand the impact of the civil war on Paris and the surrounding countryside. "Our farmers, entirely ruined by the *taille*, have left us," she wrote in 1647, but fortunately the *solitaires*, who lived on the estate, were able to harvest the crops.[2] Nevertheless, she wrote two years later, the convent was "surrounded by the most brutal troops in the world, who have ravaged the entire countryside with all sorts of cruelties, sacrileges and [other] malicious [acts]. But God in his mercy has preserved for us our good hermits *(solitaires)*, who have taken up their swords in order to protect us and have constructed solid barricades which would be difficult to breech."[3] From Port-Royal-de-Paris she wrote to Antoine Le Maistre in 1652: "We live in fear of a new siege; flour is three times the price it was three years ago, and even if one goes to great lengths to obtain some, the *pain de Gonesse* is no longer available; the sick grow in number, the dead multiply, and so there is nothing but misery."[4]

Nuns from other convents who sought refuge in Paris, she wrote, were "in direst poverty . . . and forced to beg from friends and relatives. In such a way is religion destroyed and the enemies of truth become triumphant."[5] Overcrowded conditions caused by the increase in the number of inhabitants at Port-Royal-des-Champs, she wrote after a visit there in 1652, were such that nuns and livestock shared the same living quarters, and crops were stored in the chapel already crammed with books belonging to the *solitaires*.[6] Although many nuns dislodged from convents in the countryside around Paris sought refuge at Port-Royal, others declined to do so because of the aura of heresy that hung about the convent.[7]

In all her letters to the queen of Poland written in 1652 (she wrote the queen at least once a month between the years 1646 and 1660) she provided a vivid description of the appalling conditions that prevailed not only in Paris and at Port-Royal-des-Champs but also at Pomponne, the estate inherited by her brother Robert through his wife. There "my brother's house has not only been pillaged by soldiers from Lorraine but almost demolished, the trees torn down and the poor peasants killed or maimed." The only reason Port-Royal-des-Champs had escaped such destruction, she explained, was because of the fortified chateau that the duc de Luynes, a patron of the establishment and friend of the *solitaires*, had built on the premises, which facilitated the defense of the convent. However, in the surrounding countryside "everything is ruined, wheat is no longer being sown because the soldiers have taken away the peasants and their horses."[8]

Angélique expressed great concern about the pervasive fear of a total breakdown of law and order, which she attributed to the irresponsible behavior of the leadership on both sides, who seemed to prefer their particular interests and their pleasures to the common good. "I know only too well the evils at court, where the dissimulation and guile with which one undertakes to waste the time of kings and queens has a corrupting effect." Those who preach the need for penitence are persecuted, she complained, by those who prefer to spend their time at gaming tables or at balls. "The terrible evils that I see wrought by *les grands* of this world, whose power is guided by their own judgments and not by the holy spirit, makes me tremble. How terrible it is that these men let themselves be controlled by passions which blind them to the miserable conditions which prevail today in France, now become a tragic theater where demons exert their cruelties, which are in effect the just judgment of God." The "cruelties" that she referred to included crimes of all sorts—libertinage and atheism, all of which were tearing apart "our wretched France." "Everyone, and especially kings," she reminded the queen, sensitive as always to her responsibility as spiritual counselor to the rulers of Poland, "must recognize by the evils they are unable to avoid that there is a sovereign on whom they all depend and to whom they owe a perfect submission."[9]

Although Angélique was critical of the attitudes and activities that prevailed at court and in the great houses of France, an attitude she shared with her brothers Robert and Henry, there is no indication that she sympathized with the *frondeurs* despite a widely held view among their opponents that Jansenists were involved in the rebellion. She was critical of at least one *frondeur,* Cardinal de Retz, a close friend of the family, who, in her opinion, preferred intrigue to his Christian responsibilities.[10] According to Jean Racine, a former student in the Little Schools, "it was the doctrine of Port-Royal that under no circumstances could a subject in good conscience rebel against his legitimate prince and that even if [he] were unjustly oppressed, he was obliged to suffer oppression and to demand justice only from God, who alone may call rulers to account for their actions. These [principles] have always been taught at Port-Royal."[11] Racine went on to say that the community had not been entirely discreet in its association with some *frondeurs.* The young Louis XIV "was convinced that [the members of the community] were not favorably disposed either toward his person or toward his state; and without thinking, they strengthened this conviction by their association, however innocent, with . . . many people who sought consolation from people who were either disgusted with the court or in disgrace."[12]

Racine was right in pointing out that a number of prominent bene-factors of the convent were involved in the Fronde or in conspirato-rial activity of one sort or another during the regency period. After the collapse of the Order of the Holy Sacrament in 1636, Port-Royal was encumbered with a heavy debt. Fortunately Angélique was able to count on the financial support of the Gonzague family, including Marie, who left France in 1645 to marry the king of Poland after par-ticipating in a foiled conspiracy against Mazarin in 1643 (the so-called *cabal des importants*). Another prominent benefactress and *frondeuse* was the duchesse de Longueville, the sister of the prince de Condé, for whose grandchildren Catherine Le Maistre had at one time served as governess. The duchess and her husband contributed seventeen thou-sand pounds to help Angélique pay off a debt of forty-four thousand pounds in 1641,[13] and it was the duchess who laid the cornerstone for the chapel at Port-Royal-de-Paris in 1645. During the time when she was actively involved in the Fronde with her brothers, husband, and lover (La Rochefoucauld, another friend of the family sympathetic to Port-Royal), she continued to support Port-Royal. In her later years she had quarters constructed for herself at Port-Royal-des-Champs, where she intended to devote a good part of her time to prayer and meditation. Yet another noble patron and *frondeur* was the duc de Luynes, the son of Louis XIII's favorite, whose mother, the duchesse de Chevreuse, was a congenital intriguer and for a time the mistress of one of the leaders of the Fronde, the Cardinal de Retz. Luynes's first wife had come under the influence of Angélique and had persuaded her husband to withdraw from court and to build a chateau near Port-Royal-des-Champs. It was Luynes's protection and support that had enabled the convent to escape the ravages of civil war.

Many of the patrons of Port-Royal—the duchesse de Longueville, the queen of Poland, and Retz in particular—had close ties to the Ar-nauld family, which also continued to benefit from the largesse of that "prince of conspirators," Gaston d'Orleans, whose remarkable daugh-ter, *la Grande Mademoiselle*, paid at least two visits to Port-Royal-de-Paris during the 1650s. The family also benefitted from its association with the Bouthillier family. Claude Bouthillier, a minister in the *conseil d'état* under Richelieu, was an old friend of Arnauld d'Andilly. His son Léon, comte de Chavigny, a member of the regency council, had been governor of the chateau de Vincennes at the time of Saint-Cyran's imprisonment there and had seen to it that the abbé was given comfortable quarters in response to Andilly's pleas. According to Henry Arnauld, who asserted it in one of his letters to Barillon, the minister was influential in obtaining the release of Saint-Cyran from prison in 1643.[14]

Such was Chavigny's intense dislike of Mazarin and the resentment he felt at his dismissal from the ministry in 1648 because of his rivalry with the cardinal-minister that Chavigny engaged in the Fronde on the side of the prince de Condé. "His declaration in favor of the party of the Princes astonished everyone of good sense," wrote an acquaintance, Valentin Conrart, in his memoirs, "considering that he owed his entire fortune, which was very large for a person of his condition, to the late king and to Cardinal Richelieu. What profound ingratitude to have contributed as he has done to the ruin of France."[15] Whether because he saw that Condé's cause was doomed or because he came under influence of a priest affiliated with Port-Royal, Chavigny broke with the prince in 1652. In a rather desperate attempt to atone for his actions he offered eight hundred thousand *livres* to Port-Royal, an offer that was refused.[16] He died in the same year.

Like the Arnaulds, the Bouthillier family had acquired power, status, and influence because of its attachment to the king and his principal minister, Richelieu.[17] Little wonder that Chavigny's friends were astonished when he attached himself to one of the leaders of the rebellion against the king's government. However, among the Arnaulds themselves, Isaac Arnauld de Corbeville, the son of Andilly's former patron, Isaac Arnauld, had also become a client of the prince de Condé. The prince's enormous wealth and his impressive reputation as a military leader caused numerous ambitious officers to seek his patronage. Having survived the disastrous siege of Philipsburg in 1635 and having cleared himself of charges of cowardice with the help of Arnauld d'Andilly, Corbeville resumed his military career. He participated in numerous campaigns in the war against Spain during the 1640s at the side of the prince de Condé, and by the time the Fronde broke out he had become a trusted associate of the prince. The abbé Arnauld, Andilly's eldest son, who served with Corbeville at Philipsburg and who remained in close touch with him thereafter, describes in his memoirs the difficult choice that Corbeville had to make when Condé became involved in the Fronde in 1650. "Monsieur Arnauld, because he was attached to Monsieur le Prince, was bound in honor to follow him . . . but with a profound sense of shame at being the first in his family to have taken up arms against the king."[18] Sent to Dijon by *le grand Condé* to command the garrison there, Corbeville died of jaundice in 1650, "consumed by a secret sense of remorse which he was unable to over-come."[19]

There were, of course, other members of the Arnauld family who loyally served the king's government during the era of the Fronde. In 1645 Mazarin called Henry Arnauld out of retirement and sent him to Rome to represent Mazarin's personal interests as well as the interests of France. Accompanied by his nephew the abbé Arnauld, who had become his personal secretary, Henry remained at the papal court for two years, during which time he devoted his efforts to winning Inno-cent X's support for the French cause in the war against Spain. In 1648 Henry returned to France and a year later was named bishop of Angers as a reward for his services. Consecrated at the chapel of Port-Royal-de-Paris, a gesture that symbolized the family's ties to the convent, Henry took up his episcopal duties at Angers in 1650. There he discov-ered a considerable sympathy within the clergy, as well as among other segments of society, for the prince de Condé and his allies. In Novem-ber 1651 Angers was captured by one of the leaders of the Fronde, the duc de Rohan. Rather than compromise himself by remaining in the city, the Bishop withdrew to Saumur, where the king, his mother, and Mazarin were then in residence. As Mazarin prepared to lay siege to Angers, Henry was able to provide him with useful information con-cerning the movements of the enemy gathered for him by the abbé Arnauld, who had remained in the city. At the same time he ordered his clergy not to give absolution "to anyone who under any pretext whatso-ever bore arms against the king."[20] However, when Henry learned that the queen mother, Anne, intended to impose harsh conditions on the Angevin *frondeurs*, he interceded on their behalf. "Madame, I beg of you from the depths of my heart to show mercy to my people."[21] Moved by the bishop's plea, Anne of Austria agreed to a more lenient treatment of the rebels.

While Henry was giving what help he could to the crown, his nephew Simon was doing the same as an *intendant* of the army of Catalonia. In September 1651 Simon received a letter from the king asking him to monitor the activities of Marsin, one of the generals in that army, long a friend of the prince de Condé. Unfortunately the letter arrived too late for Simon Arnauld to take any action. Marsin had already joined the prince in the Auvergne, bringing troops and money with him. The king's (and undoubtedly Mazarin's) favorable opinion of Simon was expressed in a letter from Le Tellier, one of Mazarin's counselors, to another *intendant* requesting him to work closely with young Arnauld, "whom his majesty values for his ability and adroitness."[22]

What were Robert Arnauld d'Andilly's sentiments during the Fronde, in which kith and kin were to be found on both sides of the conflict? Upon their return from Rome in 1648, Henry Arnauld and his nephew the abbé visited Andilly at Port-Royal-des-Champs. "We had left him there three years earlier," wrote Abbé Arnauld in his memoirs, "in a condition of real solitude, but because of the expenses he had laid out for the purpose of draining the swamp and planting the gardens, he had so changed the place that the nuns in residence . . . no longer had to fear from the bad air that forced them to abandon the site years earlier."[23] Andilly invested a great deal of time, energy, and money in rehabilitating the rustic convent, as his father had done a half a century earlier. Old Antoine's reason for doing so was to make the place fit for his daughters to live in, whereas his eldest son's efforts were inspired by the ideals of the *solitaires*, for whom tilling the soil was part of their spiritual regimen. But Andilly also prided himself on his knowledge of horticulture, which he put to good use in restoring the gardens at Port-Royal. In 1652, even as civil war was destroying the countryside around him, Andilly published a treatise entitled *La Manière de cultiver les arbres fruitiers*. In it he wrote that "one cannot have plants without loving them; for it is neither the richness of the soil, the quantity of fertilizer or a favorable location that makes trees grow. Rather it is the affection of the gardener who gives life to them and who makes them strong and vigorous. Without that loving care trees die." Trees, like friends, required proper cultivation.

Tending to the gardens of Port-Royal or engaging in other pietistic activity did not take up all of Arnauld d'Andilly's time. In his correspondence during the 1650s with Abraham Fabert, his old friend and comrade-in-arms during the campaign on the Rhine in 1634, Andilly revealed not only a keen awareness of the political scene but also that same disillusionment with the political atmosphere that had caused him to retire from active life. Fabert, who was made a marshal in 1658, had remained loyal to Mazarin despite a close friendship with Chavigny, whose defection the marshal deplored. Fabert, like Andilly, and indeed like Angélique, was appalled by the condition of the country caused by the long war with Spain and by the Fronde, as well as by the climate at court where preferment, in his opinion, was given to those who placed their own interests ahead of the public good. He admired his friend Andilly for his disinterested service to Louis XIII, a sentiment that Andilly returned.[24] "I love the state and the public welfare too much," wrote Andilly to Fabert in 1659, "and I know too well how much we need people like you. We must have extraordinary men to accomplish extraordinary things and to remedy the evils caused by the corruption of the times. Where does one find persons like you who have the ability, the generosity, the disinterestedness and the love of country necessary to achieve this?"[25]

Like Fabert, Andilly was distressed by Chavigny's decision to join the cause of the prince de Condé. Chavigny paid Andilly a visit at Port-Royal, according to Conrart, for the purpose of explaining his reasons for opposing the king. So persuasive was the former minister that after the interview Andilly assured everyone that what his friend "had done was very beneficial for the welfare of France."[26] Conrart comments that Andilly, who never liked to think ill of a friend, was deceived by Chavigny. Andilly certainly cherished the friendships he had cultivated as much as the fruit trees he labored over, but he had other reasons for being sympathetic to his old friend. Like Chavigny, Andilly believed that the war with Spain was draining French resources and that the only way to restore order and stability to the kingdom was to seek peace.

In the two *mémoires* Andilly addressed to Anne of Austria in 1643, he had complained of the excessive tax burden imposed on the king's subjects because of the war. During the Fronde he expressed his views of the political situation in two pamphlets *(Mazarinades)*. The first, entitled *Avis à la reine*, was published in 1649 and signed by *le solitaire* writing from "the desert," a term often used to refer to Port-Royal-des-Champs. Many of the problems confronting France, he wrote, were caused by fiscal incompetence, unacceptable appointments to the higher offices of the state, and the unnecessary continuation of the war. These problems would be resolved if the queen dismissed Mazarin, who had usurped the powers of the crown, and if she sought the advice and counsel of persons renowned for their virtue and merit. In the second *Mazarinade*, entitled *La Vérité toute nue, ou advis sincère et désintéressé sur les véritables causes des maux de l'estat et les moyens d'y apporter le remède* (The Naked Truth, or Sincere and Disinterested Advice as to the True Causes of the Ills that beset the State and How to Remedy them), Andilly asserted that the Fronde was a form of divine intervention by means of which God was punishing France for her sins. In uncompromising terms he condemned the disastrous fiscal policy of the king's government and the tyrannical first minister who together with courtiers and financiers wallowed in the luxurious appurtenances of the royal palace while the rest of the population suffered the ravages of war. Andilly was also critical of the Parlement of Paris, which he believed had done very little to improve the situation, and of the prince de Condé, who, while he was publicly attacking the cardinal-minister, was secretly negotiating with him. Insisting that he disapproved of any form of rebellion against the king, Andilly nevertheless asserted that the Fronde was the inevitable result of Mazarin's ruinous policies. Appealing to the king, Andilly urged the dismissal of the cardinal: "Choose for ministers the great and virtuous personages of your kingdom. Hold the name of favorite in horror, remembering the evil caused by those who have served in that capacity that has had fatal consequences for your kingdom. Reestablish order in your finances, banish luxury, and enrich your provinces by land and sea."[27]

To be sure, the themes contained in these *Mazarinades* were played and replayed throughout the course of the Fronde by those wishing to denigrate the policies of the regency government. Indeed, corruption in government and at court had become prominent political issues not only in seventeenth-century France but in England as well, utilized by those who hoped for a change of policy if not of government. We find them in Andilly's pamphlets written in 1643, in Angélique's letters to the queen of Poland, and in the several *avis* written by Andilly's father and uncles during the regency of Marie de Médici. These themes also reflect attitudes and values that the Arnauld family had cherished for at least two generations, most important among them a distaste for conspicuous consumption and disapproval of fiscal disorder. The pamphlets also reflect various experiences of members of the family during the reigns of Henry IV and Louis XIII. To these experiences may also be attributed the dislike of favorites such as the first duc de Luynes and Mazarin, both of whom on different occasions had frustrated Andilly's

political ambitions. Disillusioned though he was with the political atmosphere that pervaded France at mid-century, Andilly nevertheless
eschewed open rebellion, confining his *frondeur* activity to discreet
pamphleteering, seeking anonymity as he did so. While he may have
sympathized with his friend and patron Chavigny, as well as with his
cousin Corbeville, he himself was unable to go that far because of the
scruples that he expressed in *La Vérité toute nue* and because it was
clearly in his interest not to break with Mazarin publicly lest he jeopardize his son Simon's career.

The Fronde came to an end with Mazarin's return to court in 1653,
the same year in which Pope Innocent X issued the encyclical *Cum
occasione* condemning the five propositions allegedly drawn from the
late Cornelius Jansen's theological treatise, *Augustinus*. The cardinal
was not particularly interested in the issues involved in the Jansenist
controversy, but he did not want that controversy to get out of hand.
For this reason and because he needed the support of the papacy in
the war against Spain, Mazarin was prepared to use the power and
influence of the crown to enforce adherence to Innocent's decision
throughout the kingdom. He was all the more prepared to do so when
he realized that the encyclical had not put an end to the controversy.
Antoine Arnauld and other Jansenist theologians had determined that
the Augustinian doctrine of grace as they interpreted it was not in
jeopardy because the bull made no specific reference to Jansen's work,
and so the quarrel continued. In response to the Jansenist position,
Mazarin managed to persuade Innocent X that in order to avoid a
possible schism he must write a letter to the bishops of France attributing the five propositions to Jansen.

Mazarin's efforts to suppress Jansenism were complicated by the fact
that in 1654 one of the leaders of the Fronde, Jean-François Paul de
Gondi, Cardinal de Retz, had become the archbishop of Paris. Retz was
the nephew of the previous archbishop, Jean François de Gondi, under
whose jurisdiction Angélique Arnauld had placed the convent of Port-
Royal after the demise of the Order of the Holy Sacrament. The elder
Gondi had been protective of the establishment, condemning some
of the more vitriolic attacks on it when they appeared, and he had
also opposed the arrest of the abbé de Saint-Cyran. The Arnaulds had
long maintained ties with the Gondi family. In one of his letters to the

exiled magistrate Barillon, written in 1642, Henry Arnauld rejoiced at the prospect that the elder Gondi might name his nephew coadjutor bishop,[28] and a year later his brother Andilly also wrote Barillon: "I have learned that Monsieur the Coadjutor (Retz) has been sick. Thank God he is cured! You know how much I honor him, and I beg you from the bottom of my heart to tell him . . . that neither he or his family have a more faithful or more devoted servant than myself."[29]

Retz was hardly the good and faithful servant that Andilly thought he was. He had been involved in conspiratorial activities throughout his life, first against Richelieu and then against his successor. Believing that he might be chosen by the regent to replace the increasingly unpopular Mazarin, the coadjutor bishop became one of the leaders of the Fronde. Shortly after being himself named a cardinal, Retz was arrested. While in prison, his uncle, the archbishop of Paris, died, and much to Mazarin's chagrin, Retz, as coadjutor bishop, automatically succeeded him. Two years later the new archbishop of Paris managed to escape from prison and make his way to Rome.

The presence of one of the leading *frondeurs* in Rome further complicated Mazarin's diplomatic efforts to gain papal support for France in the war against Spain. At the same time, the archbishop's absence from his diocese complicated Mazarin's efforts to suppress Jansenism within the archdiocese. Many of Retz's staunchest supporters in Paris were parish priests who resented any attempt on the part of the government to undermine Retz's episcopal authority. A number of priests, including the curé of the Arnaulds' parish church of Saint-Merry, were Jansenists, thus strengthening Mazarin's conviction that the Jansenists were *frondeurs*. While Andilly shared the curés' resentment at Mazarin's efforts to undermine Retz's authority, he denounced Retz's boundless ambitions in *La Vérité toute nue*, an opinion that he shared with his sister Angélique.

As long as Cardinal de Retz had the ear of the pope he constituted a serious threat to Mazarin, both because he was in a position to influence the Vatican against the French cause and because he could use his supporters in Paris to put pressure on the king to dismiss Mazarin and end the war. To this end Retz and the new pope, Alexander VII, appealed to the French clergy to do what it could to achieve peace regardless of the cardinal-minister's determination to continue the war. It was therefore incumbent on Mazarin to put an end to what some historians have called the religious Fronde by suppressing Jansenism.[30] By associating Retz with Jansenism, disapproved of by both Innocent X and Alexander VII, Mazarin hoped to diminish the archbishop's influence at the papal court.

Jansenists, as we have seen, had been under attack well before the Fronde began in 1649, but efforts to suppress the movement intensified during the Fronde. Port-Royal felt the brunt of these attacks not only because of its close association with the late abbé de Saint-Cyran and with the leading Jansenist spokesman, Antoine Arnauld, but also because of the growing number of women who sought admission to the convent and the unorthodox nature of the *solitaire* community at Port-Royal-des-Champs. One of the more scurrilous attacks on the convent and on *"les Arnaudistes"* was made by a Jesuit, Jean Brisacier, who in a polemic entitled *Le Jansénisme confondu* (Jansenism Confounded) (1651) accused the nuns of being *"viérges folles"* (mad virgins) who no longer believed in the sacraments and who refused to pray to the Virgin or the saints.[31] These allegations of heresy, echoing those leveled against the same nuns a decade earlier at the time of the dissolution of the Order of the Holy Sacrament, were roundly condemned by Archbishop Gondi. Nevertheless, the attacks continued throughout the period of the Fronde.

In one of her earliest letters to the queen of Poland, written in 1647, Angélique asserted: "We are still in disgrace, but we respect God's decision to permit it, and we rejoice that [disgrace] separates us all the more from the world." In the same year she complained of an order from the *conseil d'état* to disperse the *solitaires* assembled at Port-Royal-des-Champs. The group included some forty or fifty persons according to government figures, when, according to Angélique, there were only ten. "This should make you believe, Madame, that sovereigns are obliged not to let themselves be misled by slanderers but to inform themselves carefully of the truth before acting against people accused of wrongdoing." In another letter written a year later, Angélique informed the queen that in addition to forming "an heretical sect" the *solitaires* were accused of using the Little Schools to indoctrinate the young with false beliefs. Referring to the encyclical *Cum occasione*, Angélique, who was familiar with her brother's opinion on the matter, assured the queen that the Augustinian doctrine of grace as interpreted by Jansen was unharmed. Her brother Antoine, she wrote in 1654, would be able to respond more effectively to the unfair charges brought against the community of Port-Royal if he and the other *solitaires* were not forced to move from place to place to avoid "persecution."[32]

Antoine Arnauld was quick to challenge the anti-Jansenist campaign early in 1655. He was outraged when he learned that a Jansenist sympathizer, the duc de Liancourt, was denied the sacraments by an anti-Jansenist priest. In response to this incident, he wrote two polemics[33] in which he insisted in uncompromising terms that the five condemned propositions were not to be found in Bishop Jansen's *Augustinus*. Under pressure from the chancellor, Séguier, the faculty of the Sorbonne voted in February 1656 to exclude Arnauld from its ranks, sixty-one years after the same faculty had publicly thanked his father for defending its rights against the Jesuits. Were the learned doctors assembled for the purpose of disciplining the son aware of the university's obligation, assumed under oath, "to render services to Monsieur Arnauld and to his children with the same zeal that good clients owe to a defense counsel who has defended their honor, rights and reputation"?[34]

As the Sorbonne was in the process of determining Arnauld's fate, Cardinal Mazarin asked the Assembly of the Clergy, then meeting to consider its usual *don gratuit* to the crown, to endorse the papal encyclical of 1653 together with Innocent X's letter to the French bishops attributing the five propositions to Jansen. Although the assembled ecclesiastical dignitaries were reluctant to respond to this first ever request to deal with doctrinal issues, they found themselves unable to resist the cardinal-minister. In a letter to an acquaintance written a year earlier, Angélique excoriated those "courtier bishops . . . unworthy of respect because they are the slaves of the court, where the Jesuits are their masters."[35]

Angélique was of two minds about Mazarin's assault on the Jansenist movement and on her younger brother in particular. "There are already six polemics written against M. Arnauld," she wrote to the queen of Poland in May 1655, "one of which calls for a new Saint-Bartholomew [a massacre of Jansenists similar to the massacre of Huguenots on Saint Bartholomew's Day, 1572], at least that is what they tell me . . . One must die no matter what, and the best and most beneficial way of doing it would be to die for God as victims of persecution."[36] A year later she wrote to the same person:

> M. Arnauld is in hiding with three others somewhere in Paris. He has become the principal focus of hatred . . . They hate him without out knowing him. I assure you that he uses his pen reluctantly because he feels himself called upon in good conscience to defend the truth. He endangers his life in order to satisfy his sense of duty, but if they would only stop persecuting and slandering him, he would cease his attacks and devote his energies to devotional works instead of polemics.[37]

Yet she continued to harbor doubts about her brother's public utterances. As he was preparing his defense of the duc de Liancourt, she told him that although she agreed with the opinion that "the outrage committed at Saint-Sulpice" justified a response, she did not want copies of the letter sent to her convent "because it will only make people talk when they should be praying."[38] A few months later, at the time when the faculty of the Sorbonne was considering disciplinary action against her youngest brother, she implored him "not to let yourself be carried away by what men do no matter how zealous, because patience and Christian humility are the most effective means of glorifying God and defending his truth." And when he was expelled from the faculty, she reacted sympathetically, reminding him of the natural love and tenderness that she bore her "*pauvre petit frère* . . . But if your name no longer appears among the doctors, it will nevertheless be inscribed in the book of God." Again counseling patience and humility, she asserted that it was better to defend God's truth "by suffering rather than by one's writings."

Angélique admitted to her brother that she found it difficult to endure "the insolence with which one attacks the truth . . . I realize that it is very hard to suffer as one should the attacks not only on the truth but against one's friends. The rebelliousness that I feel within me makes me tremble." For her the difficulty was, as it had always been, to act energetically on behalf of one's belief without violating her monastic vows. If her patience was stretched thin by the attacks of those whom she regarded as the enemies of truth, it was tried as well by "the various attempts at accommodation" on the part of well-intentioned persons who believed that the Jansenists were being too intransigent. Such proposals, she believed, would only be turned against them sooner or later. When her niece, Angélique de Saint-Jean, sent her a libelous pamphlet, she replied: "It is not its eloquence or its lack of a compelling argument that is disturbing, but the insolent tone in which it denounces us as heretics who should be consigned to flames." Yet she complained that no one was taking the trouble to respond to the libel. Many of our friends "while admitting that we are upholding truths that are important to the Church, accuse us of lacking in charity toward [our accusers], at the same time excusing our accusers' insolence and slander. What a painful crown of thorns!"[39]

Angélique's *pauvre petit frère* had no qualms about taking up his pen to assault his enemies. Writing to his sister in the spring of 1655, after having issued his spirited defense of the duc de Liancourt, Antoine seemed entirely confident that he was doing what was required of him by his mother and by Saint-Cyran. "This prayer came to mind this morning: *Exurge deus judica causam tuam*," he wrote her. "However you must pray to God, my dear mother, that he sustain me and that he not permit my unworthiness to be prejudicial to the defense of his holy and divine truths."[40] A few months later, after having been expelled from the faculty of the Sorbonne, he sought to reassure her from his hiding place that he was prepared to abandon everything to the cause "for which I am being persecuted."[41]

To his brother, the bishop of Angers, then in the process of reforming his diocese in the face of strong opposition from various religious orders, including the Jesuits, he wrote words of encouragement. "We are told that your monks are pamphleteering against you, but you mustn't take that too seriously. It is not your cause but that of the clergy as a whole. You need not undertake anything new but simply make certain that your ordonnances are carried out and that you make no accommodations with those monks who are rebelling against your lawful jurisdiction."[42] He also informed Henry without any apparent distress that as a result of Jesuit machinations in Rome, his works had been placed on the Index, a move that would not be taken too seriously in France, where papal censure was usually regarded as an infringement on Gallican rights.

Antoine Arnauld's combative spirit is most clearly revealed in a letter written to his niece Angélique de Saint-Jean, a nun at Port-Royal who was to become a close ally in the struggle against the enemies of "the truth."

> In truth, my very dear niece, it is not from any fear of wasting my time that I have refrained from getting you involved in the struggle. Rather it is because it seems to me that human exhortations are pointless given the fact that it is God himself who animates those whom he wishes to enlist in his cause. It also seems to me that the conflict is of such a nature that our conscience must bear witness that it is the movement of God within us that engages us rather than any mortal persuasion.[43]

Whereas his sister Angélique feared that the call to do battle was inherent in human nature and therefore to be eschewed, Antoine believed the call came from God himself and therefore required obedience.

Mazarin's efforts to suppress the Jansenist controversy placed Robert Arnauld d'Andilly in a difficult situation. While he had wished for Mazarin's dismissal during the Fronde, he undertook to improve his relations with the cardinal after the latter's return to power in 1653. Mazarin's favor was necessary, Andilly believed, in order to put an end to the persecution of his youngest brother and of the Jansenist movement in general. The cardinal's support was also essential to the advancement of the career of his son Simon. He sought to assure Mazarin in a letter written in January 1654 that the *solitaires* were not engaged in subversive activities of any kind but were instead engaged in charitable works and in laboring in the fields around the convent to increase its revenue. "And as service to the king is inseparable from service to God in that one cannot be faithful to one while at the same time being unfaithful to the other, I can assure you, Your Eminence, that there is no place on earth [Port-Royal-des-Champs] where one prays with greater ardor for the king and for the queen."[44] While admitting that his brother Antoine and his Le Maistre cousins had taken up their pens "in defense of Catholic truths," he asserted that they were in no way involved in political activities of any kind.[45] After the faculty of the Sorbonne had voted to expel Antoine Arnauld from its ranks early in 1656, Andilly wrote to Mazarin that his brother "hopes that God will not condemn him since he would rather die a thousand times than believe in any doctrine not based on the orthodox sources of the Church."

Later that year Andilly and other *solitaires* were expelled from Port-Royal-des-Champs where, Mazarin persisted in believing, seditious activities were continuing. From Pomponne, where he had taken up residence, Andilly wrote indignantly to the bishop of Coutance, a close associate of Mazarin, that he deserved better than to be treated like a criminal. Instead of honoring one who had devoted his life and much of his fortune to the king's service while others were enriching themselves at the king's expense, "here I am at the end of my life being chased from a saintly establishment where my mother died a nun among twelve of her daughters [he meant by this daughters and granddaughters], and which was restored by my father and again made habitable by means of the resources I have invested in it."[46]

Although Mazarin allowed Andilly to return to Port-Royal-des-Champs at the end of 1656, he continued in his efforts to suppress the Jansenist controversy by obtaining the adherence of the French clergy to the condemnation of the five propositions extracted from Bishop Jansen's *Augustinus*. The supporters of the late bishop of Ypres were heartened by an event that took place in March 1656 at Port-Royal-de-Paris. A nun suffering from an ocular abscess experienced a sudden recovery after a fragment from Christ's crown of thorns—one of the relics contained in the convent—was applied to her eye. Jansenists interpreted this event as a miracle intended by God to show his favor to their cause. "Thus in every quarrel that has taken place in the Church," proclaimed Antoine Arnauld, "and during persecutions that princes have sometimes launched against those who uphold the verities of the faith, God has only performed miracles in favor of those who are defenders of his truth."[47] The miracle could not have happened at a better time, proclaimed Arnauld d'Andilly,[48] and in a letter to his friend Fabert he wrote that God "has visibly declared himself to be the protector of the truth and of the innocent victims of oppression."[49] The so-called Miracle of the Holy Thorn was only one of several, reported Angélique to the queen of Poland, all of which must be regarded as signs of divine favor. "I don't know what to tell you of our affairs," she wrote in August 1656. "We continue to be threatened, but at the same time God continues to protect us. Miracles are occurring with such frequency that we are all astonished and confused. God knows what he is doing, and we await in peace whatever it pleases him to ordain."[50] At the end of that year she informed the queen that the threat of persecution was greater than ever. "The miracles that God has made and continues to make only serve to further irritate them [our enemies]. They say that they will do us great harm as if they [the miracles] were our own inventions to protect ourselves."[51]

Certainly the miracle did nothing to abate Mazarin's desire to put an end to the Jansenist controversy. His efforts were intended in part to placate Pope Alexander VII, who loathed Jansenism as much as he loathed Mazarin. Alexander had gone so far as to suggest to the French ambassador at the papal court that the nuns and *solitaires* of Port-Royal be dispersed, and he was considering the issuance of another encyclical condemning Jansenism. Having come to the conclusion at the end of 1656 that Mazarin's position as the head of Louis's government was impregnable, he promulgated *Ad sacram* in March 1657. In this third anti-Jansenist encyclical Alexander VII asserted unequivocally that the five propositions condemned by his predecessor, Innocent X, were to be found in Jansen's *Augustinus*.

One of the more vehement critiques of *Ad sacram* came in an anonymous pamphlet entitled *Lettre d'un avocat au parlement à un de ses amis.* Its author was none other than Antoine Le Maistre who, although he had vowed to have no further commerce with the world, felt compelled to join his relatives and friends in defense of his ideals. Deploring the involvement of the papacy in French affairs, the former barrister insisted that the encyclical should have no effect in the kingdom until it had been approved by the Parlement of Paris.[52] Both he and his uncle *le grand Arnauld* went so far as to maintain that Alexander VII, by intruding on Gallican rights, was in effect attempting to establish the Inquisition in France.[53] Undaunted by Gallican sentiment, Mazarin presented the bull to the Parlement, which, with considerable reluctance and after some delay, approved *Ad sacram*. The cardinal-minister had now succeeded in arraying the highest authorities of church and state against the Jansenist movement. With Cardinal de Retz no longer a significant influence in Rome, Mazarin was free to bring the long war with Spain to a successful conclusion in 1659. In that year he saw to it that the Little Schools of Port-Royal were closed permanently. No longer would the young be susceptible to evil influences at that foyer of heresy.

Despite Mazarin's hostility toward Port-Royal and Jansenism, Arnauld d'Andilly did what he could to advance his son's career in the king's service. During the era of the Fronde, Simon Arnauld continued to serve as an *intendant* with French armies in Spain and in Italy and had continued to impress Mazarin with his abilities. When an important position in the household of Louis XIV's younger brother became available, Andilly used what influence he had to obtain it for his son. He asked his friend Abraham Fabert, recently promoted to marshal, to intercede with the minister, and he himself wrote not only Mazarin, whom he congratulated on the victorious conclusion of the war, but the queen mother, Anne of Austria, as well. Assuring her of his family's fidelity to the crown, Andilly went on to say that it was his last great hope that his son would be permitted to carry on the family tradition.

Responding to Andilly's request for support in June 1659, Fabert informed him "that there is a strong cabal against you" at court. Mazarin in turn wrote that however much he personally wanted Simon to have the position in the duc d'Anjou's household, the queen was adamantly opposed to it. Finally Queen Anne herself wrote that although she was well aware of past services rendered to the crown by the Arnauld family, her responsibility to her youngest son required her to make certain that he was brought up in the true faith. Denying Andilly's assertion that Jansenism was a chimera manufactured by those whose faith was impure, the queen continued:

> You are in the midst of Jansenists and instigators of heresy . . . You have asked me to enlighten you as to what a Jansenist is. I will give you the same response that I gave to a bishop who asked me the same question. A Jansenist is one who refuses to submit in all humility and without any reservation whatsoever to the decision of the Holy See, which has since been followed up by the universal consent of the entire church. A Jansenist obstinately insists that Jansen's doctrine has not been condemned by the bull.

Stung by Anne's denial of his request to admit Simon to the duke's household, Andilly replied that "those dear to him" were entirely prepared to renounce any doctrine clearly shown to be heretical. He and they agreed that the five condemned propositions were undoubtedly heretical but maintained that they were not to be found in bishop Jansen's work. "Given that fact, Madame, I cannot regard their belief as suspect without violating Jesus Christ's commandment as it appears in the gospels that one must not condemn our brothers as long as we have reason to believe them innocent. Nor can I separate myself from them as long as I see them united to the church by the ties that attaches all Catholics to it."[54]

Andilly, his family, and the Jansenists in general believed themselves to be the innocent victims of the Jesuits and other impure Catholics who had succeeded in persuading the highest authorities of church and state that they should be persecuted for harboring heretical beliefs. From Port-Royal-des-Champs and elsewhere, Antoine Arnauld and others tried to defend their ideals. In vigorous polemics such as the *Provincial Letters*—written by that "friend of Port-Royal," Pascal, with Arnauld's help—they castigated the Jesuits for their corrupt penitential ethics and asserted in the strongest possible terms that they were prepared to suffer persecution rather than renounce their own penitential ethics.

Innocent victims though they thought themselves to be, the Arnaulds' religious ideals seemed to invite persecution. The text from the gospel of Saint Matthew, "Blessed are they that are persecuted for righteousness' sake," had helped to inspire Angélique's conversion. From the time of her conversion, religious life was for her a perpetual struggle against the forces of evil within her order, within the Church, and within herself. Persecution was not only the means by which the forces of evil sought to destroy her and her family and friends but also a means by which her own faith was tested. To her way of thinking, to suffer for one's beliefs was the way to win divine favor. What she feared was not persecution, which she saw as a divine and not a human instrument, but the temptation to lash out at her persecutors, a temptation that, she believed, revealed her flawed nature. She viewed the persecution suffered by her family and by the Port-Royal community during the era of the Fronde in personal terms. It was part of the struggle she had been engaged in since her conversion, a test of her faith that would end with her death.[55]

Antoine Arnauld had no fear of persecution, which he interpreted as a call from on high to do battle. Persecution was a test of his commitment to the vows that he had given to his mother and Saint-Cyran that he would defend the truth against all those who sought to undermine it. To him it made no difference that "the enemies of the truth" included the highest officials in the church in which he held a privileged position or the highest authorities of the crown that his family had served for so long. As long as he believed that the condemned propositions were an erroneous construction of Jansen's—and Saint Augustine's—doctrine of grace, Arnauld argued that no authority in the world could force him to renounce that opinion. "One may not in good conscience," he wrote to an acquaintance shortly after the publication of Alexander VII's encyclical, "make a public statement contrary to one's personal beliefs or even engage in equivocation when lawful authority presses us to declare ourselves. Nor, contrary to what some are saying, do I believe that one should submit to [that authority] as a matter of deference if not of consent."[56]

For the patriarch of Port-Royal, Arnauld d'Andilly, Mazarin's efforts to suppress Jansenism were particularly painful, for reasons that pertained at least as much to family honor as to religious belief. He was torn between his loyalty to those of his relatives who were members of the Port-Royal community and to the crown to which his family had given so much. Port-Royal had become in his mind a family shrine, and thus he felt himself in honor bound to uphold its integrity. However, he also believed that he was in honor bound to advance the political career of his son Simon. For this reason, he was particularly distressed by the hostile attitude displayed at court toward him and those dear to him. The queen, who two decades earlier had told him that she would have been honored to have him as a member of her household, was now unwilling to offer a similar position to his son, even though Simon was in no way involved in the religious dispute. Regardless of the material stakes involved, Andilly was unwilling to repudiate the beliefs of the nuns and *solitaires* because of his loyalty to them and to the memory of the abbé de Saint-Cyran, and because he shared these beliefs.

The Arnaulds' defense mechanisms were inherent in their *mépris du monde*. Conflict was a test of their religious commitment and a demonstration of their hostile attitude toward the world. In their minds Port-Royal had become a citadel against which the enemies of the truth were arrayed. Racine was right in saying that the members of the Port-Royal community were indiscreet in their choice of benefactors, whose *frondeur* activities cast aspersions on Port-Royal itself. However, he was wrong in asserting that the Arnaulds and other members of the community were not themselves *frondeurs*. When Angélique Arnauld admitted that she harbored "rebellious sentiments," she spoke for the "friends of truth" as a whole. The Arnaulds believed that they lived in a particularly corrupt age and that they were bound by conscience to resist those forces contributing to that corruption. Their willingness to defend their religious ideals regardless of the stature of their adversaries and the cost to themselves made the Arnaulds *frondeurs* in spite of themselves.

The lines were drawn well before Innocent X promulgated *Cum occasione* in 1653, between the Arnaulds and the other supporters of Jansen's theology on the one hand and those on the other who regarded what had become known as Jansenism as potentially injurious to public order as well as to the Catholic faith. A confrontation between the two sides was made all the more inevitable because of the social and political tensions aroused by the Fronde. Mazarin had succeeded in lining up the formidable powers of the papacy, the French episcopacy, and the crown against those who came to be known as Jansenists, but he died in 1661 before he was able to extirpate the movement.

9

The Confrontation

When Cardinal Mazarin died in 1661, he left the kingdom of France at peace both within and beyond its frontiers. Louis XIV, then twenty-three years old, moved quickly to assert his personal control over his realm and was applauded for so doing by Robert Arnauld d'Andilly, who wrote him a long letter shortly after Mazarin's death. After congratulating the young king on his decision "to take the affairs of state in his own hands," Andilly urged him to maintain the ban on dueling, to discourage excessive displays of wealth among his subjects, to ignore flatterers, and, above all, to appoint only persons of merit to positions of responsibility. "Only the lack of esteem for men of virtue dampens the affection of those who are the most worthy of your beneficence." Royal favor bestowed on subjects who deserved it, asserted Andilly, would encourage a healthy competition for office among the best and most able of the king's servants.[1]

Now that Louis XIV had determined to become his own first minister, Andilly hoped that Simon's career might advance, a hope that was cruelly dashed soon thereafter by the arrest of Nicolas Fouquet, *surintendant des finances* under Mazarin.

In order to establish his absolute control over his own government, Louis had Fouquet arrested in November 1661 for enriching himself at the expense of the state. A year earlier Simon Arnauld had married a cousin of Fouquet's, Catherine Ladvocat, and because of this associa-

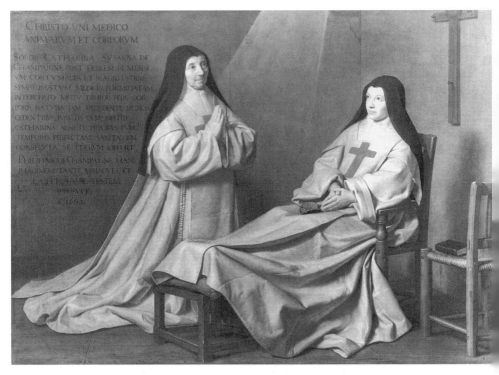

Portrait de la Mère Catherine Agnes Arnauld et de la Soeur Catherine de Sainte-Suzanne
by Philippe de Champaigne
(Louvre). © RMN Réunion des musées nationaux.

tion, he was exiled to Verdun. His father was devastated by this turn of events, which threatened to put an end to his son's continued advancement as it increased the court's suspicions of the Arnauld family. Simon's uncle Antoine complained that the young man was being unjustly accused of being involved in Fouquet's machinations. At the same time, he and other members of the family viewed with considerable alarm the king's decision to suppress Jansenism once and for all. As Louis later wrote in his *Mémoires for the Instruction of the Dauphin:* "I dedicated myself to destroying Jansenism and to breaking up the communities where this spirit of novelty was developing, well-intentioned perhaps, but which seemed to want to ignore the dangerous consequences that it could have."[2] The communities to which he was referring, of course, were the two convents of Port-Royal, from which boarders and postulants were expelled. *Lettres de cachet* were issued to secure the arrest of the convents' confessors. Once again, Le Maistre de Sacy and Antoine Arnauld were forced to go into hiding, as was Angélique's confessor, Singlin.

The chief instrument by which the king sought to obtain a general acquiescence to the papal decisions with respect to Jansen's doctrine was a formulary that had been drawn up by the Assembly of the Clergy in 1657. Mazarin had secured the formulary but had not used it. Now in April 1661, only a few weeks after the cardinal's death, the *conseil d'état* decreed that all members of the clergy must sign the document, including nuns and lay schoolteachers. The text of the formulary read as follows:

> I submit sincerely to the encyclical of Innocent X of 31 May 1653 [Cum occasione], according to its proper meaning as set forth in the constitution of our Holy Father, Alexander VII, of 16 October 1656 [Ad sacram]. I recognize that I am obliged to obey these constitutions, and I condemn with heart and mouth the doctrine contained in the five propositions of Jansenius in his book entitled *Augustinus* that two popes and the bishops have condemned, whose theology has been misinterpreted by Jansenius.[3]

By requiring adherence to the document from each and every member of the clergy including nuns, the king hoped to end the Jansenist controversy that had lasted for twenty years in spite of papal condemnation. To end the quarrel was to prove more difficult to achieve than the king, the pope, or the vast majority of French bishops ever imagined.

When the formulary was first drawn up in 1657, Antoine Arnauld, while admitting that the five propositions were heretical, denied that they were to be found in the *Augustinus*. All Catholics, he argued, might agree that the propositions were heretical, but clearly there was disagreement among Catholics as to whether they were contained in the *Augustinus*. The Church, according to Arnauld, had the right to require adherence to its judgments on doctrinal matters, on the *question de droit*, as Arnauld put it, because these matters pertained to the faith, over which it had absolute authority. However, on matters of fact—the *question de fait*—the Church had no such authority. "She has often permitted her children to maintain a respectful silence and even to hold opinions contrary to what she has decided with respect to matters of fact."[4]

In other words, the Church was infallible on matters pertaining to the faith, but in matters pertaining to fact, which depended not on revealed truth but on human judgment, the Church was fallible. Using his training as a theologian and the skills of a lawyer that would undoubtedly have made his father proud, Arnauld hoped to prevent Jansen's supporters from condemning the late bishop of Ypres' doctrine of efficacious grace. Jansenists might sign the formulary as required, he argued, but with certain expressed reservations as to the *question de fait* attached to the signature.

At the time that the signature of the formulary was decreed by the *conseil d'état* in 1661, Cardinal de Retz was still in exile. The affairs of the archdiocese of Paris were being administered by two vicars-general, both of whom were sympathetic to Jansenism. After consulting with Arnauld and others, the vicars-general agreed to permit a statement of reservation as to the *question de fait* to be appended to the signatures of those who chose to do so. By permitting this procedure, the vicars-general greatly facilitated signature within the archdiocese, even in parishes where Jansenist support was strong. The nuns of Port-Royal signed the formulary in June 1661 without any difficulty. When the pope learned of the vicars-general's arrangement, he ordered them to withdraw it; at the same time the *conseil d'état* ordered new signatures without appendages of any sort.

Jansenists responded in several ways to this new demand. Some, including Singlin, Angélique's confessor, and Saint-Cyran's nephew, Martin de Barcos, maintained that one might sign the document with mental reservations as to the question of fact. Barcos urged the nuns of Port-Royal to take this course of action, insisting that the theological issues involved were of no concern to women. Nuns ought not to make their own decisions in these matters but should obey their superiors. "It may seem a sign of strength to bring ruin on your house," he wrote to one of the nuns at Port-Royal, "but this strength can only be considered as presumptuous if you exceed the limits of your knowledge by making yourself the judge of matters that are beyond your understanding, persuaded as you seem to be that you have the right to prefer your own judgment to that of your superior."[5] Others, including Pascal's sister Jacqueline, a nun at Port-Royal, refused to sign at all on the grounds that a signature, even if there were a reservation attached, implied the condemnation of fundamental tenets of faith. Finally there were those, led by Antoine Arnauld, who urged Jansenists to sign with a statement appended that the person signing preferred to maintain a respectful silence as to the question of fact.[6]

The controversy aroused by the formulary became so intense that the king authorized the bishop of Comminges, a friend of Arnauld d'Andilly's, to work out a compromise that would meet the requirements of church and state and at the same time satisfy Jansenist consciences. In a letter to Henry Arnauld, bishop of Angers, Comminges suggested that one should sign the formulary out of respect for the authority of the pope even if he or she had doubts about whether the condemned propositions were to be found in Jansen's work. To openly express any reservations one might have as to the *question de fait* reflected a lack of respect for duly constituted authority that would inevitably disrupt "the peace of the Church."[7] In order for his proposal to have adequate endorsement, the bishop insisted, it would have to be approved by Antoine Arnauld, the leading Jansenist theologian. The bishop of Angers in turn urged his youngest brother to adhere to the compromise. Agreeing with his fellow bishop that it was important to maintain peace in the Church, Henry Arnauld, with what seems remarkable prescience, warned that further disputes would eventually lead to the destruction of Port-Royal.[8]

Arnauld d'Andilly, who was kept abreast of these proceedings, attempted to use his own influence within the family to obtain Antoine's endorsement of the bishop of Comminges's proposal. According to Andilly, the proposal in no way jeopardized Jansenist doctrine or obliterated the distinction between the *question de droit* and the *question de fait*. One might maintain a mental reservation as to the fact of the five propositions being in the *Augustinus* while appending one's signature to the formulary out of respect for papal authority. His youngest brother was being too squeamish, in Andilly's opinion, and excessively scrupulous in not endorsing the proposal. Such an attitude, asserted the patriarch in a rather patronizing tone, was never very helpful in dealing with affairs of state. In pressing his case, Andilly went so far as to assert his *droit d'ainesse* (right as an older brother), to which Antoine ought to defer. "How is it possible, my dearest brother, to separate the love of truth from the love of peace? Should one be favored over the other? Is not the God of truth also the God of peace?"[9]

Stung by the tone of Andilly's appeal to accept the arrangement worked out by the bishop of Comminges, Antoine responded in similar fashion. Andilly, he contended, was so dazzled by his friendship with one of the more influential bishops in the country that he preferred the flawed arguments of the bishop to those of a member of his own family. "Have I no longer a place in your heart? Has your esteem for me entirely vanished?"[10] Why didn't Andilly take the trouble to read what he, Antoine, had to say on the subject of the *question de fait* instead of accepting uncritically the opinion of a prominent friend? As to the attitude one should have in dealing with worldly affairs, Antoine reminded his brother, reasserting the basic premise of the religious ideals of Port-Royal, that "there can be no accommodation between the affairs of the world and the affairs of Jesus Christ."[11]

The strong differences of opinion among the three brothers over the bishop of Comminges's proposal reflected their different concerns. Henry feared that if the compromise were not endorsed by all parties, great harm would come to Port-Royal, which meant so much to him and other members of the family. And although he did not say it openly, he believed that because the compromise had been worked out by a brother bishop, it ought to be treated with respect. Andilly too approved of the arrangement because he not only feared the effects of continued controversy on Port-Royal, but also its effect on the career of his son Simon, now jeopardized by his ties to the disgraced Fouquet. If a compromise of some sort could be reached, Simon's situation might be improved.

In Antoine's opinion, the compromise may have satisfied his brothers, but it did not satisfy the consciences of the more scrupulous supporters of the late Bishop Jansen. He resented Andilly's attempt to push him into endorsing the plan against the dictates of his own conscience, and he took issue with the bishop of Comminges on two other points inherent in Comminges's proposal. It was an insupportable assumption, Arnauld maintained, that one must accept the opinion of the pope on a matter of fact if one disagreed with that opinion. He also maintained that it was not "scandalous behavior" to challenge papal encyclicals just because one assumed that they were drawn up "with great circumspection, wisdom and piety."[12] For Antoine Arnauld, any sort of peace in the Church or, for that matter, peace within the family, must in no way compromise the religious truths that he had promised both his mother and his mentor, Saint-Cyran, he would uphold.

The three brothers were equally concerned about the effect of the formulary on the nuns of Port-Royal. Immediately after the decree of the *conseil d'état* in 1661, Antoine assured the nuns that God had caused the Miracle of the Holy Thorn to occur as a sign of his protection. "God provides the greatest protection to those he loves the most at the very moment when, in the eyes of ordinary mortals, he appears to have abandoned them. In this way he strengthens the hearts of those whom he intends to save to make it possible for them to repel their enemies."[13] Henry Arnauld, who really believed that the acceptance of Comminges's compromise was the only way to protect Port-Royal from destruction, soon realized that the nuns themselves adamantly refused to accept the proposal. In a letter written to his brother bishop at the end of 1663, Henry admitted, albeit reluctantly, that the proposal was dead because of the nuns' attitude. He had tried to get the nuns to agree, he assured Comminges, because he feared renewed persecution of Port-Royal, "where God has assembled a great number of people who are the closest and dearest to me."[14] However, he had come to understand that the nuns were unable in good conscience to sign without any express reservation as to the question of fact because to do so was to condemn the doctrine of efficacious grace. To compel the nuns to sign the formulary against their consciences was, in Henry's opinion, a form of persecution in and of itself. Once they realized that Comminges's proposal was unacceptable to the nuns, Henry and his brother Andilly rallied to the support of Port-Royal. The spiritual influence of the nuns, most particularly those who were members of the Arnauld family, had prevailed once again over those political considerations that had caused the two brothers to accept Comminges's compromise. And in yielding to the uncompromising attitude of the nuns, the two brothers accepted the inevitability of confrontation between Port-Royal and the highest authorities in the kingdom.

↪ WHATEVER misgivings they may have had as to the outcome of such a confrontation, neither Andilly nor his younger brother were able to resist the appeal of Port-Royal, which had affected the lives and fortunes of so many members of their family since Angélique had become abbess at the beginning of the century. By 1661 the community, which had once consisted of thirteen nuns and six *solitaires* who were members of the Arnauld family, had been reduced to four nuns and four *solitaires* who were members. Death had removed Angélique's mother, four of her sisters, and one of her nieces as well as Antoine Le Maistre (1658) and his brother Séricourt (1660). And in May of 1661 Angélique, always the dominant personality within the family, succumbed after a long and painful illness at the age of seventy. Writing to his one remaining sister, Agnès, Antoine admitted that despite his clerical rank, he considered himself to be Angélique's "son in so many ways." Now that Angélique was among God's elect, as he believed her to be, she was now "united with them in demanding vengeance against their enemies."[15]

The last months of Angélique's life coincided with the renewed persecution instigated by Louis XIV. She had been at Port-Royal-des-Champs, her favorite habitat, all winter, but when told of the expulsion of the pensioners, she returned to Paris. *"Mon frère, mon frère, soyons humble"* were her parting words to Andilly as she left *les Champs* for the last time.[16] Writing to one of the nuns at Port-Royal-des-Champs from the convent in Paris, the aged matriarch declared that she and the nuns had been too pleased with themselves for being on the side of truth and therefore less inclined to mortify themselves. Insisting as always that religious life was essentially painful, Angélique welcomed the repressive measures undertaken by church and state as a means of turning one's attention toward God. "The time of the martyrs is long passed," she wrote in her last letter to her sister Agnès, "but the time to suffer and to be reduced to powder in body as well as in soul is with us as always."[17] Although she bitterly resented the assault on the Jansenists and complained of the inadequate support of their friends, she was determined during the last weeks of her life to suffer in silence. Deprived of her confessor, Singlin, who had been removed from Port-Royal, Angélique preferred to devote her last moments attending to her own spiritual needs. A few years earlier she had described to her brother Antoine how she would like to spend her last hours: "I have always asked God to enable me to spend my last days in a cell in which I would shut myself up with only a pair of glasses and some lancets, the one for reading and the other for caring for the sick; the one for truth and the other for charity. I would maintain a profound silence, and they would be deceiving themselves at court if they believed that I would engage in dogmatizing, for I would talk only to God, thereby enjoying a perfect repose." She would be able to console herself, she said, even if they destroyed her convent because she had come to understand that the essence of religious life was rooted in the inner self.[18]

In spite of her determination to minister to her spiritual needs, she found herself unable to abandon the nuns to the mercy of their oppressors. Only days before her death she made an appeal to the king's mother. "I fear that I may offend Him to whom I look for justice if I neglect to justify myself before Your Majesty, his representative on earth, and if I fail to do justice to my sisters, worn down by affliction and grief, by not bearing witness to the sincerity of their consciences."[19] This perpetual concern for the welfare of the community, which she had led for over fifty years, always placing it above her own, inspired Fontaine to say of her that she had *"une grandeur d'âme au dessus de son sexe"* (a greatness of spirit not characteristic of her sex).[20]

Angélique died before the signature of the formulary became a real issue for the nuns. However, she was certainly aware of the debates over the *question de droit* and the *question de fait*, which she undoubtedly regarded as the sort of dogmatizing that she was determined to eschew. She had always been wary of the polemical tendencies of Antoine, and she had frequently warned him that he was too often governed by his pride. Whether she would have signed the formulary, as Singlin thought the nuns ought to do, cannot be known for certain, but it seems safe to surmise that she would not have signed a document that had been drawn up by people whom she believed to have no religious integrity, a document that appeared to question the integrity of those—Jansen and Saint-Cyran—whose ideals were similar to hers. Not to sign and to suffer the consequences in silence was in keeping with the ideals that she had cherished since the time of her conversion.

Her sister Agnès, the only one of Antoine and Catherine Arnauld's six daughters to live through the crisis over the formulary, maintained that Angélique's legacy to the nuns was her will to suffer, which only strengthened the nuns' will to resist all efforts to destroy the ideals that they cherished. "A word from her," she wrote in August 1661, "gave courage even to the faintest heart because it put matters in such a way that it was impossible not to come around to her point of view. She made those who feared persecution come to look on it as a sign of divine favor. She used to say that we are dignified by our afflictions and that it made her tremble to think that God has chosen us to suffer for his truth."[21]

Among the nuns most influenced by Angélique's legacy, one who was to become the dominant figure among the nuns after her aunt's death and a powerful force within the Arnauld family in her own right, was her niece, Angélique de Saint-Jean. The second Angélique was the fifth child and second daughter of Robert and Catherine Arnauld d'Andilly. Born in November 1624, she entered Port-Royal as a pensioner in 1630. Indeed, all of Andilly's five daughters received their education at Port-Royal. Unlike her namesake, Angélique adjusted easily to religious life within the convent. When offered the opportunity to return to her father's house to see a younger sister who had just been born, Angélique declined, believing that her place was with her spiritual rather than with her natural family. Perhaps the adjustment was made easier by the presence within the convent of so many relatives. As she grew older, the distinction between her two families became blurred in her mind to the point where they seem to have become one and the same. It was said of her in one of the necrologies of Port-Royal that "she loved her family and honored her house [Port-Royal] both of which served the cause of truth."[22]

Angélique de Saint-Jean's education was supervised by her aunts Angélique and Agnès. So great was the power of her mind and her capacity for learning that her instructors began to fear that her education was doing her more harm than good. Always alert to any manifestations of pride, her aunt Angélique wondered whether her niece would acquire the humility necessary to become a nun.[23] Despite any qualms she may have had about the younger Angélique's religious vocation, she permitted her to become a novice in 1641. In that year the abbé de Saint-Cyran wrote the young novice from prison that he was pleased to learn of her intention to become a nun. Such a calling "reveals a desire to withdraw from the ordinary life of Christians, who, it grieves me to say, have become so lax as to bring tears to the eyes of those who live by the principles laid down in the gospels."[24] Thus, at an early age the second Angélique was alerted to the corrupt influences within Christendom against which her aunt and Saint-Cyran had struggled for many years and against which the younger Angélique would struggle for the rest of her life.

In 1644, at the age of twenty, the young novice took her vows as a nun and assumed the name Angélique de Saint-Jean. She was placed in charge of the pensioners, supervising their education despite her aunt's concern about her excessive learning. The elder Angélique had always believed that nuns should be well educated so that they would not be misguided by superstition or by false doctrine of any sort. Angélique de

Saint-Jean was perfectly equipped for the task of instructing her pupils in the proper articles of the faith because she was looked upon within the convent as enlightened, serious, and firm. Some even thought her too serious and too firm. She had "an inimitable facility of writing and speaking well," a facility that owed much to the education she herself had received as a pensioner, and she had come to know "what was most important and useful in the ecclesiastical sciences" and in the other sciences as well.[25]

As a student at Port-Royal, the girl read Saint-Cyran's *Coeur nouveau* (an explication of the mass) as well as his catechisms. Other readings included the *Imitation of Christ*, the meditations of Saint Theresa of Avila, and the lives of various saints and *"pères du desert."*[26] However, her reputation as a person of considerable learning—it was even said of her that she knew Greek—must have been based on an education far more expansive than what she had received as a pensioner. Sheltered though she was, she did have contact with the *solitaires*, who had at their disposal a library consisting of religious writings, works of history, *belle-lettres*, and treatises on various subjects including the law. The collection was built around the library that had once belonged to Antoine Le Maistre, which he had placed at the disposal of the *solitaires*, who were themselves teachers at the Little Schools at Les Granges, their residence close by Port-Royal-des-Champs.[27] The *solitaire* closest to Angélique de Saint-Jean was her cousin Sacy, who served as her confessor. Although he disapproved of learning for learning's sake, Sacy, like Saint-Cyran and the elder Angélique, believed that the responsible Christian should be well informed. It seems likely that it was he, Antoine Le Maistre, and perhaps her uncle, *le grand Arnauld*, who exposed the young woman to many of the sources that became the basis of her learning and the learning she imparted to her own students.

Not only did Angélique believe that the younger members of the convent should receive proper religious training, she believed as well that the entire community should be made aware of her aunt's achievements as a reformer. To this end she began to collect relevant documents and to interview older nuns for the purpose of developing a historical account of all that had taken place at Port-Royal since Angélique's installation as abbess. What emerged from her efforts were the basic source materials on which so much of the history of the convent and of Jansenism has been based, the *Mémoires pour servir à l'histoire de Port-Royal,* the *Mémoires pour servir à la vie de la Réverande Mère Angélique de Ste Madeleine Arnauld, réformatrice de Port-Royal,* and several of the necrologies.

Angélique de Saint-Jean realized that no account of the events that had taken place at Port-Royal during the first half of the seventeenth century would be complete without the testimony of the Reformer herself. The elder Angélique was reluctant to write an account of her own life, although she did not mind describing various incidents in conversations with her nephew Antoine Le Maistre. Convinced that these conversations were *"grands trésors de grace et de lumière,"* Le Maistre encouraged Angélique de Saint-Jean to put together a biography while at the same time both he and Angélique pleaded with their aunt to write her autobiography. She refused even to consider it until her confessor, Singlin, ordered her to do so.

> She [Angélique] was very worried about it, and perhaps she feared the use we would make of it, for what she feared most in the world was that after her death there would be anything said or written to her advantage. However, being constrained to do it, she retired to a small, isolated cell . . . [where] giving more time to praying than to writing she produced this account with such distaste that it was impossible for her to finish it. Under pretext of other business she let it remain unfinished.[28]

The *Relation écrite par la Mère Angélique Arnauld sur Port-Royal* was begun in 1654.[29] It describes the abbess's life up to the arrest of the abbé de Saint-Cyran. One reason for not wanting to carry the story further may have been a reluctance to describe the Jansenist controversy that had begun during Saint-Cyran's imprisonment and had reached a peak at the time she began writing the *Relation.* Whatever the reason, the project was set aside in 1655, the same year that she complained to her brother Antoine of "the rebelliousness that I feel within me" brought on by the oppressive measures taken by the authorities of church and state. Fearful that such sentiments might involve her in activities that belied the spirit of humility, she may have decided that the less said about her life during the turbulent decade since the death of Saint-Cyran the better.

Angélique may have had no interest in preserving her reputation for posterity, but her niece believed that the future of Port-Royal depended on its preservation. As the persecution of Port-Royal and of Jansenism increased after the Fronde, the younger Angélique concluded that the nuns' will to survive would only be sustained by their awareness of the great abbess's accomplishments. Her aunt's account of the conflicts in which she became involved would undoubtedly inspire them to continue the struggle against the corrupt forces of the world. As Angélique de Saint-Jean continued collecting materials pertaining to the history of the convent, she came to realize that some of the documents that she discovered might cause more harm than good if they fell into the wrong hands. Writing to her aunt in 1657 not long after the publication of Alexander VII's encyclical attributing the five propositions to Bishop Jansen, Angélique de Saint-Jean mentioned the need to prepare oneself for more oppressive acts on the part of church and state. Among the preparations she recommended was the removal "of papers that serve no useful purpose and which might cause a great deal of harm if they fell into the hands of those who wish to do us harm."[30] Angélique the elder replied that there was good reason to be concerned about the papers. Professor Ellen Weaver maintains that Angélique de Saint-Jean burned the letters of Geneviève le Tardif, abbess of Port-Royal during the 1630s, when Port-Royal first came under suspicion for heresy.[31] The profoundly mystical nature of Tardif's religiosity was of the sort that had contributed to these suspicions, and Angélique probably felt that it would be unwise to revive them at a time when the convent was again under attack for harboring unorthodox beliefs.

If to many of those in the outside world Port-Royal appeared to be a hotbed of heresy, to Angélique de Saint-Jean it seemed to be "only Port-Royal and the places attached to it that are free from the corruption that pervades the world today."[32] Like her aunt she saw religious life in terms of a struggle between the cloister and the world outside, between the pure and the corrupt, and between the willingness to suffer pain and the pursuit of pleasure. Her aunt Angélique had once written her that "the bane of Christians is consolation, pleasure and satisfaction. In order to be truly happy, Christians should imitate their master, who bore the weight and yoke of the cross. Like Christ, they should bear the tears and afflictions of body and soul."[33] This view of Christian life was the essential ingredient in Angélique's legacy to the nuns and to her family, a legacy that inspired them to defend her ideals during the crisis over the formulary.

Although Angélique de Saint-Jean had the greatest respect for her aunt and came to believe that her main task in life was to perpetuate her ideals, she was never as close to Angélique as she was to her other aunts, Agnès and Marie-Claire. The latter's death in 1642 was a great blow to her. Angélique the elder, as we have seen, had misgivings about her niece's powerful intellect and undoubtedly made her aware of this. Angélique de Saint-Jean at the age of thirty complained to her aunt that she still treated her like a child, adding with some resentment that she "understood full well that persons in positions of authority are able to do what they pleased, while we are obliged to submit to them and to remain silent." Her aunt replied, in a tone that must have served her well in maintaining a distance between herself and the other nuns, that good children "do not find occasions to complain."[34]

At the time of her aunt's death, Angélique de Saint-Jean was thirty-seven years old. The necrologies (written by the nuns) describe her as deeply committed to the ideals of Port-Royal and loyal to family and friends. Her critics were somewhat less charitable. Racine describes her as "headstrong . . . a little too erudite *(un peu scientifique)* and someone who disliked being contradicted."[35] Her *hauteur* and her brusque manner irritated some of the nuns.[36] Angélique herself agreed with Madame de Sablé's opinion that, unlike her father, Angélique did not understand the art of friendship. In dealing with people, she maintained, "firmness is better than tenderness. I would go so far as to say that I prefer my simplicity and my brusque manner to the caresses and gentle behavior of some people we know."[37] Her austere personality seemed to conform to the religious ideals that she espoused. All who knew her were impressed with her intellect and her strength of character. "She had none of the weaknesses of her sex," wrote one of her male acquaintances after her death in 1684. "She radiated strength and masculinity. Her mind was so superior to others that even men believed her to be one of the greatest intellects of her time."[38]

Both Angéliques, in the opinion of their contemporaries, had "risen above their sex." Their greatness would have been impossible had they remained "mere women." Both Angéliques had intimidating personalities, but the elder was more emotional and capable of greater warmth than her niece, whose reserve reminded some of her grandmother Catherine Arnauld and of her uncle Henry Arnauld. Whereas the aunt was always torn between her desire to dominate those around her and her desire to withdraw from the world entirely, between the certainty of her faith and the gnawing uncertainty of her merits, the niece seems almost always to have been sure not only of her faith but of herself. There was a pride and arrogance inherent in her that belied her monastic vows.

At the time of Angélique the elder's death, the women in the family were still very much in evidence at Port-Royal. Her sister Agnès, then sixty-eight, was the only daughter of Antoine and Catherine still alive, but three of her nieces, including Angélique de Saint-Jean, were also members of the community. Of the five daughters of Robert and Catherine Arnauld d'Andilly who had been placed as children in Port-Royal, two were dead (Catherine in 1643 and Anne-Marie in 1660). Among the nuns' confessors who had been removed from their positions just before Angélique's death were Antoine Arnauld and Le Maistre de Sacy, but both remained in contact with the community, as did Henry Arnauld, bishop of Angers. These family connections and her own strong personality enhanced Angélique de Saint-Jean's influence within Port-Royal at the time that the crisis over the formulary began.

Angélique de Saint-Jean did not hesitate to use this influence on her male relatives to defend the ideals of Port-Royal. "The sacred fire of episcopal charity, which seemed to be extinguished is rekindled in your person," she wrote Henry in 1661.

> Other bishops will surely be inspired by your example, no longer fearing that they may risk something by defending the truth . . . You have known only too well the suffering that we have endured for two months, but I assure you that God could not have given us a stronger indication of his favor toward us, which will only invigorate our confidence and our courage to suffer even more, than in choosing you to protect our innocence. You cover yourself with glory as you prepare to do battle alone while others retreat.[39]

The same militant tone appears in a letter to Antoine a few months later after the vicars-general had been compelled to withdraw their order permitting signature of the formulary with reservations as to the *question de fait*. Those outside the cloisters, she said, complained that the nuns more than anyone else should protect themselves by obeying the king and the pope. How little they understood the nuns' commitment to suffer persecution for the truth, she continued, reasserting the theme from the gospel according to Saint Matthew that had inspired the elder Angélique to launch her reforms in 1609. This commitment was not only a part of the elder Angélique's spiritual legacy, it was also an expression of their religious vocation, which required submission to the will of God and not of men. In remaining true to their vocation, Angélique de Saint-Jean concluded, "God provides them [the nuns] with the arms necessary to resist evil. Nothing animates them more than to think that if there are wolves among the sheep, Jesus Christ is their shepherd, who follows them everywhere and who will not abandon them." Contemplating the physical destruction of Port-Royal as her aunt and the abbé de Saint-Cyran had done, she concluded that all those who had helped to make the establishment the sacred refuge that it had now become should take comfort in the thought that the act of destruction itself would be an indication of divine favor. Far better for Port-Royal to be destroyed in a good cause than preserved in a bad one.[40] Given this intransigent attitude, Antoine Arnauld was all the more inclined to refuse the compromise worked out by the bishop of Comminges. Bombarded by letters from his niece, whom he had encouraged in her militancy, letters in which she implored him to maintain the explicit distinction between the *question de droit* and the *question de fait*, he was never allowed to forget his mother's dying wish that he devote his life to defending the truth.

Angélique de Saint-Jean was well aware of pressures within the family to yield on the matter of explicit reservation. Even though she praised Henry Arnauld for his willingness to protect the nuns, she knew that he thought it inappropriate for them to become enmeshed in the complex doctrinal issues pertaining to the *question de fait*. She also knew that her brother Simon, disgraced because of his ties to Fouquet, strongly disapproved of the nuns' resistant attitude. Nevertheless, she was convinced that she and the nuns were obliged to express their reservations on the contentious issue. Not being well versed in the intricacies of theology, the nuns might compromise the doctrine of efficacious grace if they unwittingly attached their names to a document that they little understood. To do so would undermine the religious principles that they cherished. "If one understands that the nuns always act with sincerity and with a proper regard for the truth, one should know that they would not dare lie to the Holy Spirit before the whole church by signing with the hand and not with the heart."[41] She could never bring herself to sign without explicit reservations, she told her uncle, because she was afraid of jeopardizing "the integrity and the innocence of a saintly bishop [Jansen] whose virtue I revere and whose doctrine I esteem."[42]

Both those who thought that the nuns should sign without reservations out of respect for authority and those who thought that they should not out of respect for their vocation emphasized their weakness as nuns and as women. Although Angélique de Saint-Jean herself did not refrain from referring to these weaknesses as justification for attaching a reservation as to the *question de fait* to their signatures, she was made uneasy by her male relatives' constant reference to the nuns' "innocence" and their "ignorance."[43] "Ignorance excludes intelligence and discernment," qualities that were important to the responsible Christian. "We are capable of making distinctions and we are able to explain that which ignorant people do not understand."[44] Actively involved in the controversy over the formulary herself, Angélique refused to view either herself or the other women in the community as pawns in the strategies developed by men on either side of the issue.

Angélique herself did not hesitate to suggest to her uncles strategies that should be adopted to protect their ideals. Even though Antoine was her superior in the Church as well as her uncle, she spoke her mind in no uncertain terms when she learned—erroneously as it turned out—that Antoine was prepared to accept Comminges's proposal. In another letter on the same subject she asserted that God would not approve of any effort to restore peace to the Church based on false premises. Taking issue with the contention of her father and her uncle the bishop of Angers that the overriding concern of all those involved in the controversy should be peace within the Church, which therefore required acceptance of Comminges's compromise, Angélique declared that peace on terms such as these was unacceptable because it compromised the truth.[45]

A MAJOR problem for Louis XIV in moving against the Jansenists was the confused situation that existed in the archdiocese of Paris. Even though its affairs were in the hands of the vicars-general because the archbishop, Retz, was in exile, the King was sensitive to the continuing influence of the cardinal in Paris, for which reason he was careful not to arouse the ire of Retz's supporters among the Parisian clergy. In 1662 Cardinal de Retz suddenly resigned his office, thereby facilitating his return to France and enabling the king to appoint a staunch anti-Jansenist to the office. Pierre de Marca, the archbishop of Toulouse and an outspoken anti-Jansenist, received the appointment, but he suffered a fatal stroke before he was able to take office. Louis next turned to his former tutor, Hardouin de Péréfixe, who, although he was nominated in 1662, was unable to take office until 1664 because of continuing quarrels with Pope Alexander VII. As long as there was no clearly established authority in the turbulent diocese, the crown was not in a position to make a concerted effort to suppress Jansenism there. Once Péréfixe was in place, the situation changed dramatically.

After being installed in office in the spring of 1664, the new archbishop issued an order to all the clergy under his jurisdiction demanding signature of the formulary without reservation. In the order he made the distinction between *droit* and *fait*, stating that obedience on the *question de droit* was a divine obligation and on the *question de fait* an obligation based on respect for one's superiors in the Church. Well aware of the strong feelings on the subject that permeated Port-Royal, he spent several days at the convent in Paris interrogating the nuns individually and demanding the signature of each.

"The hour of combat is at hand,"[46] proclaimed Angélique de Saint-Jean to her father shortly after the archbishop's initial visits. She, of course, refused Péréfixe's order, and fearing disciplinary action, she urged Andilly to come to Paris from Pomponne. Like her aunt Angélique, she needed the support of her family. Earlier in the year she had written Antoine Arnauld that she was grateful for the ties that bound her in so many ways to "persons whom [God] has chosen to defend his truths."[47] Expelled from Port-Royal-des-Champs with all the other *solitaires* including his son Luzancy, Andilly had taken up residence at the family estate of Pomponne in the Marne valley. When he realized that no compromise on the formulary was possible, the patriarch, then seventy-five years of age, rallied to the side of the nuns. Writing to the marquise de Sablé at the end of June, he expressed his horror at the thought of "the great storm that is about to fall on an establishment that is as dear to you as it is to me . . . We must do our best to try by means of our approbation to participate in the sacrifice that so many saintly virgins are offering to God by exposing themselves to any danger rather than to offend their consciences or betray their principles because of a cowardly apprehension of transitory punishments."[48]

Andilly was on hand at Port-Royal-de-Paris when Archbishop Péréfixe arrived there on 26 August 1664 with a company of archers to take action against the twelve nuns who had refused to obey his order to sign the formulary. The twelve included Agnès Arnauld and her three nieces, Angélique de Saint-Jean, Marie Charlotte, and Marie-Angélique de Sainte-Thérèse. In a scene dramatized by Henry de Montherlant in his play *Port-Royal* (1954),[49] the archbishop entered the convent and commanded the archers to remove the recalcitrant nuns from the premises. Deprived of the sacraments until such time as they were prepared to sign the formulary, the twelve nuns were to be placed in various convents in the city. Assuring the prelate that they would not resist removal, they walked out of the convent on their own and entered the carriages that were waiting for them. Leaving the building, Angélique encountered her father, who was waiting beside one of the carriages. Throwing herself at his feet, she asked for his blessing. As she climbed into the carriage she was asked her name by the captain of the archers. "I said it [the family name] in a forceful tone without blushing, for in such a situation it is almost like pronouncing God's name to pronounce our own when it is being dishonored in his name."[50]

By associating the Arnauld family name with God, Angélique expressed not only her own concept of family honor but that of many members of her family. The aspirations of her aunt and namesake, who had exerted all her influence to win her family over to what she regarded as the cause of righteousness, were in her mind fulfilled. And because most of the family had come to identify themselves with that cause and the enduring conflict that resulted from it, the Arnaulds now found themselves in a confrontation with the crown in whose service the family had acquired honor and glory in the past. In a very real sense, the family's conversion to Angélique's spiritual ideals had begun on that day in 1609 when she had barred her parents and her oldest brother from entering Port-Royal. Ironically that conversion resulted fifty-five years later in Angélique's sister and three of her nieces being expelled from the convent that had become the center of their family's life.

Robert Arnauld d'Andilly, who had objected vehemently when his sister had forbidden him and his parents entrance to Port-Royal-des-Champs because of his opposition to the Catholic reform movement, was again at the gates of the convent, this time to provide moral support for the nuns, including another sister and three daughters, to whom the doors of the convent were now closed. A few weeks later in a letter to a friend, Andilly categorically denied that he had tried to arouse the bystanders who witnessed the expulsion of the nuns by appealing to their sense of compassion "in the face of such an extreme act of violence."[51] According to Angélique's account of events, the old man, after blessing his daughter, escorted her to her carriage through the crowd of archers and onlookers milling about the courtyard.[52]

By order of the archbishop, Angélique was placed in the convent of the Annunciades, an establishment with close ties to the Jesuits, in the Marais, not far from her family house in the rue de la Verrerie. There she was shown to her room by the abbess, who told her that she would be allowed to attend services in the chapel, but that she was to have no other contact with the other nuns. Reflecting on her situation once she was left alone in her room, Angélique felt the pain of separation from the community in which she had spent almost her entire life. "Port-Royal in its affliction had always nourished me, and I was now cut off from all those whom I loved so much."[53] After eight days spent entirely alone, Angélique decided to write the archbishop to learn more about what his intentions were. In her letter she pointed out that she was being made to suffer imprisonment and separation from her convent in addition to being deprived of the sacraments, and she asked that he at least permit her to partake of them again.

Péréfixe's response to the letter was a visit to the convent of the Annunciades on 6 September. When Angélique was brought before him, he told her that he had the greatest respect for her family and for her uncle Antoine, who had been his colleague at the Sorbonne. He went on to say that he very much regretted the situation in which they both found themselves, a situation that would be much improved if she would only sign the formulary on his terms. All he was asking of her was submission on the *question de fait* as an act of obedience to the judgment of the Church, to which she replied that she was prepared to accept the condemnation of the five propositions but not the fact that they were to be found in the *Augustinus*, "because we know that it is still open to question." To her the *question de fait* was a matter of conscience that prohibited her from subscribing to something of which she was not certain. He replied in turn that he was unable in good conscience to allow her to participate in the sacraments, and with that the interview came to an end.[54]

Two days after Péréfixe's visit Angélique experienced an acute crisis of faith, a crisis involving a struggle not between herself and others, but within herself. It was, she wrote, as if there were two persons within her, one who gloried in her suffering because she believed that her ability to endure it was an indication of divine favor, and the other who believed that her suffering was a punishment for her faults. It was a struggle that her namesake had experienced throughout her life but which was now affecting Angélique de Saint-Jean apparently for the first time. Although she later provided an extensive account of this crisis, which lasted for several days, in her *Relation*, she omitted its most significant aspect.[55] In a letter written to Antoine three years later, she admitted that although she had said in the *Relation* that she had seen *"les portes ténébreuses et les portes d'enfer"* (the gates of darkness and the gates of hell), she had not said what she had meant by this. She found it painful to think back on the crisis, but she now felt that she should mention it to him. *"Les portes ténébreuses"* represented an absolute skepticism in "everything pertaining to faith and providence." This made her feel uncertain about everything that she had until that moment believed to be the truth. Even "the immortality of the soul" seemed dubious to her.[56] She went on to say that "in this state of mind, prayer and an avowal of my sins before God whose justice I revere were all the arms I needed [to combat these sentiments] which, if they had lasted much longer, might well have destroyed me."[57]

Angélique's crisis of faith resulted within a few hours in a triumph of the stronger over the weaker self, a triumph of grace over nature that enabled her to endure continuing persecution, firm in the conviction that she had survived the test of her faith that God had demanded of her. Certainly she was not the first person, nor would she be the last, whose religious, philosophical, or political ideals were strengthened by a sojourn in prison. Psychologically reinvigorated by the crisis,

I made a church of my prison, and I chanted the offices alone during the day at the usual hour. I even chanted what the choir sings at high mass when I knew them well enough and at least the *Kyrie*, the *Gloria*, the *Credo*, the *Sanctus* and the *Agnus dei*, and I followed in my mind everything the priest said during the mass because I had been allowed to have a missal. In this way the time that I devoted to participating in the mass passed quickly. I had no time to become bored. My time was as filled as it would have been were I still at Port-Royal.

The longer she was left to her own devices, the stronger she felt within herself. "I wish one could see how beautiful and holy it is to find oneself alone in a prison at night singing God's praises without being heard by anyone but him."[58]

The strength of Angélique's convictions was sustained not only by these solitary acts of piety, but also by the genteel debates she engaged in with Madame de Rantzau, the widow of a German general who had served in Louis XIV's army. A former Lutheran well versed in theology, Madame de Rantzau had entered the convent of the Annunciades after the death of her husband. She had been encouraged by her abbess and the archbishop to try to persuade Angélique of the error of her ways. In the *Relation*, Angélique records several encounters between the two women. In one, which took place immediately after Archbishop Péréfixe's interview with Angélique, at which Madame de Rantzau had been present, Rantzau insisted that the archbishop had a right to be concerned about her spiritual welfare because she, Angélique, was in error in making the distinction between matters of fact and matters of faith. To support her argument, she cited the disciples of Origen, who in the third century were obliged to repudiate Origen's teachings because the Church had declared them heretical. In response to this argument Angélique cited Saint Jerome, who gave John of Jerusalem the choice either of condemning Origen's doctrine or, if he did not wish to condemn him, of denying that the errors attributed to him were to be found in Origen's writings. When Rantzau referred to the fourth council of Chalcedon, Angélique countered with the fifth and sixth councils of Constantinople. In her *Relation* Angélique asserted that she was better versed in theology than her opponent who, she said, "was not sufficiently versed in these controversial subjects. Therefore I did not have to worry about her pushing me too far."[59] During one of these dogmatic encounters Madame de Rantzau told Angélique that she had it on excellent authority that Bishop Jansen had always kept a volume of Calvin's writings on the desk in his study, to which Angélique retorted that the bishop was an intimate friend of the abbé de Saint-Cyran, who would have ended the relationship if he had any suspicion that his friend was sympathetic to Protestant doctrine. "Even though we never knew the Bishop of Ypres, it was enough to know that he was a friend of the abbé to be certain that neither had any sympathy for a heresy that they had both fought against."[60]

At the heart of these discussions was the question of authority. To Madame de Rantzau, papal authority within the Church was absolute, and the faithful were therefore obliged to submit to the judgment of the pope on matters pertaining to fact as well as to the faith. To her way of thinking, Angélique's attitude was not only scandalous, it bordered on heresy. Angélique in turn accused Madame de Rantzau of adhering to the doctrine of papal infallibility "which is not universally accepted and which certainly does not extend to matters of fact that are determined by the senses."[61] Furthermore she was critical of "the blind obedience"[62] to each and every pronouncement by an official in the Church who, being human, was capable of misjudgments. The well-educated Christian was capable of making the proper distinction between what one ought or ought not to submit to. "It is not hard to understand," she wrote "that one must be submissive to the authority of the Church and at the same time realize that one need not obey it in matters that are subject to human error over which it [the Church] has no infallible authority."[63] In such matters one could not in good conscience submit to a judgment that one believed to be wrong.

Self-sufficient as she felt herself to be in many ways—in her ability to stand up to Madame de Rantzau, to say nothing of the archbishop, and to recreate the chapel of Port-Royal in her mind—Angélique was nevertheless keenly aware of her separation from her family. She was deeply moved when the abbess brought her a note from her father because "I knew for the first time since my captivity that my father was thinking of me and that he was still alive." She asked permission to reply because she knew that Andilly would not be certain that she was all right unless he heard from her directly. In her note she sought to reassure her father that she was faring well. She also asked to be remembered to her uncle the bishop of Angers and her brother Luzancy. A day or two later the abbess returned the note to Angélique and told her that she had been given explicit orders by the archbishop not to allow anything to pass between Angélique and her father or uncle. Although disappointed, Angélique took heart at the thought that the prohibition was undoubtedly an indication that Péréfixe was angry at the bishop of Angers, who continued "to protect the innocence" of the nuns of Port-Royal.[64]

Angélique was not pleased to learn from Madame de Rantzau that when her brother Simon, who had recently been permitted to return to Pomponne from his own exile, had paid a visit to the convent to ask after his sister, he had asked Rantzau to convey to Angélique his wish that she obey the archbishop and sign the formulary. The whole affair, he said, was "a mere bagatelle;" what Péréfixe was asking was for the nuns to sign the formulary as a gesture of respect for his authority. Angélique replied indignantly that the matter was far more serious than her brother believed, that "he was speaking as a man of the world, involved in politics, about something that was none of his business. He shared the view of those who agreed to sign without thinking of anything other than their own interests."[65]

Of all the members of her spiritual family from whom she was separated, her aunt Agnès was the person whom she missed the most. She learned from one of her "jailers" that Agnès had finally agreed to sign the formulary. She had been told of others who had given in to the various forms of pressure being brought to bear on them, but their recantation did not affect her to anywhere near the same extent as the news of her aunt's surrender. She saw in it "something inexplicable." Yet the more she thought about Agnès's "piety, understanding and humility," the more unlikely she thought it was that God would abandon her. How could one have any faith in God's mercy if it were denied to someone as good and faithful as she? Just as Angélique had managed to overcome her earlier crisis of faith, she overcame her doubts about her aunt's constancy. "By means of a blind faith in God's promises," she concluded that Agnès could not possibly have given in to the archbishop's demand, a conclusion that turned out to be right.[66]

After almost eleven months in captivity, the recalcitrant nuns were removed from their "prisons" and returned to Port-Royal-des-Champs. Their release was brought about for a variety of reasons, among them the cost to the Church of providing for them in the host convents and a fear that the nuns in captivity might infect other nuns with their disobedient attitude. All the nuns who refused to sign the formulary were now together at the older establishment, while those who signed remained at Port-Royal-de-Paris. Those at Port-Royal-des-Champs included Agnès Arnauld, who had never once considered signing the formulary. Seventy-one years old and in poor health at the time of her removal from Port-Royal-de-Paris, she endured her captivity in good spirits. Like her older sister Angélique, she recognized the need to suffer persecution for righteousness' sake. As she put it in her own *Relation*, "affliction is nothing but a form of consolation."[67]

The group at Port-Royal-des-Champs also included Angélique's two sisters, Marie-Angélique and Marie-Charlotte, both of whom had signed and then retracted their signature during their captivity. Marie-Angélique had been placed in the same convent as Agnès, not far from Port-Royal-de-Paris. There Marie-Angélique "experienced spiritual pains so intense that only God knows about them." Unable to communicate with her aunt, who was ill for much of the time, she began to have doubts about her refusal to sign. When he learned of her doubts, Archbishop Péréfixe assigned a confessor to her who managed to persuade her that if she was having second thoughts, she would be well advised to sign. Soon she was brought again before the archbishop, to whom she declared that she was only willing to sign on condition that he understood that she was doing so out of respect for him and not because she had any intention of condemning Jansen's doctrine. Péréfixe, of course, agreed to accept her signature in that spirit as long as no explicit reservation was attached to it. Despite her act of obedience, Marie-Angélique continued to suffer, becoming increasingly convinced that she had in fact condemned Jansen with her signature. Unable to endure the continuing pain and anguish, she informed the archbishop in a letter that she was retracting her signature. "Perhaps I needed the experience in order to learn how little assurance one receives from putting one's trust in humans. No matter how hard I tried to follow the advice that people gave me, I was unable to escape the reproaches of my conscience, which had become my accuser as well as my judge."[68]

Marie-Charlotte's experience after having signed the formulary was similar to her sister's. She was particularly troubled by the thought that Agnès and other incarcerated members of her family would think ill of her for having given in to Péréfixe. In her own way she saw that the honor of her family was involved in resisting the archbishop's demands, for which reason she retracted her signature as well. Thus did the Arnauld women within the convent remain united in their resistance.

Shortly after their return to Port-Royal-des-Champs, the nuns decided to write down accounts of their several experiences both as a form of confession (they were still deprived of their confessors) and as a means of edifying the community as a whole. Antoine Arnauld wanted to have these accounts circulated beyond the walls of the convent to give greater publicity to the sufferings of innocent victims, but Angélique de Saint-Jean objected on the grounds that the publication of private confessions was a violation of cloture.[69] In spite of the nuns' wishes, these *relations* were eventually published after the destruction of Port-Royal in 1711 for the purpose of sustaining the memory of the defiant community in the eighteenth century.

The release of the nuns from their captivity did not mean an end to the efforts to suppress Jansenism. The confessors to the nuns were either in hiding or in exile, which meant that either the nuns would have to confess to priests who were assigned to them by the archbishop or not at all. They were still denied the right to participate in the sacraments, and they were also denied the ability to replenish their ranks, not being permitted to admit pensioners, postulants, or novices to the convent. As Angélique wrote to her uncle Antoine, still in hiding, shortly after her release: "We expect salvation from no one but our Savior, and we are more convinced than ever that he will not deliver us unless we defend his truth. Being made captives in doing so, we will not receive our freedom except in doing so. Our friends must understand that the greatest good that they can do for us is to respect our consciences."[70]

The various deprivations experienced by the nuns at Port-Royal-des-Champs did not cut them off from spiritual sustenance. In a small volume on the shelves of the Bibliothèque de Port-Royal entitled *Réflections de la Mère Angélique de Saint-Jean pour préparer les soeurs à la persécution* one finds the characteristic assertion that it was not the nuns' oppressors who were denying them the sacraments but God himself in order to test their commitment to him and their repentance. As Antoine Arnauld maintained in *De la fréquente communion*, abstinence from the sacraments enabled the sinner to devote more time to the contemplation of his iniquities. As to the loss of their confessors, Angélique maintained that without the mediating role of the spiritual director, each nun was drawn closer to God. Angélique, and presumably the other nuns, was even prepared for the possibility of excommunication. The threat was made by a confessor sent to her shortly before her release from captivity, to whom she replied that no matter how great the authority of the pope, she was not able to submit to it if in doing so she was forced to disobey God's law.[71]

Left entirely to their own spiritual devices in their rustic convent, the nuns had become virtually self-sufficient in the conduct of their religious lives, which in effect became an extension of the life that Angélique de Saint-Jean created for herself alone in her cell at the convent of the Annunciades. "The situation in which we find ourselves," wrote Angélique to Antoine in 1667, "cut off as we are from everyone is beneficial to us."[72] Alienated from the world that they had been taught to believe was entirely corrupt, the nuns seem to have convinced themselves that they had become united with God. Under the impact of persecution they came to make a distinction between the true Church of Christ and his apostles, to whose truth they were committed, and the false Church represented by the archbishop of Paris and other ecclesiastical officials whose authority they felt bound to resist.[73]

Instead of putting an end to the Jansenist controversy, the crisis over the formulary had only exacerbated it. Several bishops sympathetic to Jansenism, including Henry Arnauld, refused to circulate the formulary in their dioceses. In response to this action, the king invited Alexander VII to issue yet another encyclical, which he did in 1667. Comparing the Jansenist heresy to a serpent whose head was crushed but whose body was still writhing, *Regiminis apostolici* again demanded unconditional signature of the formulary by every member of the French clergy. The pope also ordered the recalcitrant bishops to comply with his orders, but in so doing he raised another sensitive issue, namely the degree of autonomy that every bishop enjoyed in his diocese. Once again a papal encyclical condemning Jansenism had encountered obstacles, this time in the form of episcopal jurisdiction. Although the pope believed that in pronouncements of this sort he spoke for the Church as a whole, there were bishops throughout the Catholic world who maintained that in order for an encyclical to have the proper imprimatur in a given diocese, it required the approval of the bishop of that diocese. Any attempt to impose an encyclical without the approval of the bishop constituted a violation of episcopal rights. The refusal of several bishops to endorse *Regiminis apostolici* pointed up the delicate balance between papal authority, the king's authority, and episcopal rights. Not long after the promulgation of the latest anti-Jansenist bull, Alexander

VII died and was replaced by Clement IX, who, fearing a possible schism within the French Church, actively encouraged an accommodation on the formulary that would satisfy all parties.

By this time Jansenists were able to rely on a formidable support system that included a handful of bishops, prominent nobles such as the duchesse de Longueville, the king's cousin, and a significant element of the lower clergy. And although the magistrates of the Parlement of Paris were not for the most part Jansenist sympathizers, they were deeply suspicious of the crown's appeals to the papacy to condemn the movement, appeals that from the Parlement's point of view constituted a threat to Gallican liberties. In the face of this coalition, Louis XIV, preparing for war against the Dutch, determined that he must reach some sort of compromise that would relax tensions within the kingdom. He again encouraged several prominent bishops to work out a universally acceptable compromise. Negotiations began at the end of 1667 and lasted until the spring of 1669. Participants included Henry Arnauld and eventually Antoine Arnauld himself, who was encouraged both by the attitude of the new pope and the apparently more flexible attitude of the king. Upon learning of these negotiations, Angélique wrote her uncle Antoine several anxious letters in which she made clear once again her opposition to accommodation. Any compromise, she believed, would inevitably undermine the truth. "For an accommodation would likely include the promise to remain silent on the *question de fait* in order to prevent further disputes. In this way the truth would be silenced while the voice of falsehood would be heard throughout the land."[74]

Whereas Antoine Arnauld had been unwilling to reach a compromise in 1663, he was far more amenable to one five years later. In response to his niece's letters, he pointed out that silence on the *question de fait* would in no way jeopardize Jansen's doctrine. He also emphasized the fact that a number of bishops of the highest integrity, whose authority the nuns should respect, were involved in the negotiations. Not only was Angélique under pressure from Antoine, with whom she had collaborated so closely in developing a strategy for resistance to what both regarded as unjust authority, but also from one of those closest to her, her cousin and confessor Le Maistre de Sacy. Imprisoned in the Bastille for his own refusal to sign the formulary, Sacy, like *le grand Arnauld*, had come to the conclusion that the interests of the Jansenists were best served by an accommodation. In several letters written from prison, Sacy warned Angélique that there was a difference between being intransigent in defense of the truth and being stubborn, and that her behavior (and that of the nuns) verged on the latter. Reiterating his point that the accommodation being worked out had the support of ecclesiastical officials of the highest integrity, he implored her "to consider not only your commitment to the truth but also the authority of persons in the Church whom you ought to esteem for their dignity, their virtue and their understanding." To disobey such authority would cause a real scandal in the Church.[75]

Under pressure from two spiritual directors of Port-Royal whose authority she respected, both of whom were members of her family, Angélique and the nuns eventually acquiesced, albeit reluctantly, to the accommodation that came to be known as the Peace of the Church. It went into effect in 1669. Its terms, as Angélique suspected, included signature of the formulary with the right to append a statement to it to the effect that he or she was prepared to maintain a respectful silence on the *question de fait*. In so doing, a Jansenist was able to make clear that he or she was in no way asserting that the five propositions were to be found in Jansen's work. At the same time the archbishop of Paris and other bishops were able to construe "respectful silence" as a statement of submission to their authority. Under the terms of the compromise all further public debate on issues pertaining to Jansenism was prohibited by king and pope. As soon as the Peace of the Church went into effect, Le Maistre de Sacy and others were released from prison and the nuns permitted once more to partake of the sacraments. Sacy and Antoine Arnauld returned to the convent to administer to the spiritual needs of the nuns, who were again authorized to admit pensioners and postulants.

If Port-Royal benefitted from these arrangements, it suffered from the separation of the two houses imposed on it by the archbishop of Paris. As the result of the separation, Port-Royal-de-Paris, which housed those nuns who had submitted to the archbishop's authority in 1664, retained two-thirds of the establishment's wealth. Yet the confrontation, which had pitted the nuns against the highest authorities of church and state and lasted for almost a decade, had come to a halt at least for the moment. Against their better judgment, the women endorsed the terms of the Peace of the Church out of respect for the authority of those to whom they were willing to submit, namely, the handpicked disciples of the abbé de Saint-Cyran.

The confrontation that took place in the 1660s had its origins in the religious ideals of Angélique the elder to which she had subscribed a half a century earlier. One's religious commitment was tested by means of persecution, and the conflicts resulting from persecution constituted, to her way of thinking, the very essence of religious life. Angélique had been involved in a number of confrontations—with her family, with Angélique d'Estrées and her company of archers at Maubuisson, with the Cistercians, with the bishop of Langres, and with the opponents of Jansenism (albeit vicariously through her nephew Antoine). She had also confronted within herself the weaker side of her nature. As a result of the influence of her ideals and of Port-Royal, which had become an especially sacred place for members of her family, her family had been drawn into her lifelong struggle with the world. Inspired both by her aunt's ideals and by her family's commitment to those ideals, Angélique de Saint-Jean, with little of her namesake's self-doubt, carried the struggle to a higher level, against the archbishop of Paris supported by the king's archers. Whereas her aunt had frowned on public forms of resistance, Angélique de Saint-Jean took pride in her family's public role as defenders of the faith and urged them on until she herself was discouraged from further resistance by the male members of her family.

During the period of negotiations leading up to the Peace of the Church, a more subtle conflict emerged between the Arnauld women within the cloister and the Arnauld men outside. For the women there could be no compromise between the ideals of Port-Royal and those of the corrupt world, which manifested itself in many forms—in the form of the archbishop, the king, or the pope, all part of the patriarchal structure of the society that existed beyond the walls. In the conduct of their spiritual lives they had become self-sufficient, capable of sustaining themselves without confessors and without the sacraments. On the other hand the Arnauld men, each in his own way, remained in the world. Henry Arnauld, although energetically engaged in reforming his diocese, never leaving it even to visit Port-Royal, was by the very nature of his duties involved in the world. Committed to bringing the regular orders within the diocese under his control, he was never entirely happy with the refusal of the nuns of Port-Royal to submit to the authority of the archbishop of Paris. Thus it was in the interest of preserving episcopal authority that he used his influence on the convent to keep it from becoming entirely independent of any and all authority in the Church. If Henry was disturbed by the nuns' challenge to the patriarchal authority of the bishops, his younger brother, Antoine, worried about their resistance to patriarchal authority within the family. In urging his niece Angélique to accept the terms that were embodied in the Peace of the Church, he gave as the most important reason for doing so "the terrible scandal that your continued intransigence would cause, which would in turn prejudice the cause of truth. For you would appear to be the most stubborn and foolish people in the world if you did not accept the terms endorsed by those [Antoine and Henry Arnauld] in whom you have had confidence, at least until now."[76]

The small band of nuns in seclusion at Port-Royal-des-Champs had attained the ideal monastic condition. Their intransigence reflected a *mépris du monde* that brooked no compromise with the world. They had borne the brunt of the assault of church and state on Jansenism during the 1660s. As a result of this experience they had come to realize that the only relief from oppression would have to come from God. On the other hand, the men—even Sacy, in the confines of the Bastille—were never able to achieve that degree of isolation and, being more exposed to worldly pressures, were more inclined to compromise. For Antoine Arnauld the world in 1669 seemed to have become a better place. The new pope was less hostile to Jansenism, and the king apparently more accommodating to the Jansenists. Indeed the political environment had changed so much that Antoine went so far as to accept an invitation to appear at court shortly after the Peace of the Church was concluded, and he took advantage of his new-found freedom to become more actively involved in the social and cultural life of Paris. He hoped that if he and other Jansenist leaders were restored to favor, they would be able to increase their influence in religious and political matters. Certainly the Arnauld family's political influence was on the rise again with the return of Simon Arnauld to royal favor in 1665. The highly successful career of Arnauld d'Andilly's second son, although viewed with alarm by his relatives among the nuns, was a consideration that was undoubtedly taken into account among the male members of the family as they endeavored to restrain Angélique de Saint-Jean from further acts of disobedience to the authorities of church and state upon whose beneficent attitude Simon's career depended.

Angélique de Saint-Jean's intransigence depended on the degree to which she and the other nuns were able to maintain their independence from the world beyond the cloister. As it turned out, she could not free herself from the bonds that tied her to her family. Unable to disobey her uncle and cousin, whom she had chosen as confessors, or her uncle the bishop of Angers, to whom she and her aunt had always looked for protection, Angélique felt that she had no choice but to yield. Although willing to challenge the highest authority within church and state for the sake of her religious ideals, she found herself unable to challenge patriarchal authority within the family. To have done so would have compelled Angélique to break with her family also, something that she clearly had no intention of doing. She remained in touch with her father and her brother Luzancy all during the period of negotiations, delighting in the fact that her father had taken charge of the education of his grandchildren and worrying about his health and that of her brothers. She even sent Luzancy some peaches from a tree that he had planted during the time that he and the other *solitaires* resided in Les Granges[77] to remind him, no doubt, of the bond that tied the family to the convent in the fields, a bond that Angélique the elder had refused to break in 1609 and that her niece wished to sustain.

By 1669 the fortunes of the Arnauld family had improved considerably from what they were at the beginning of the decade. The nuns at Port-Royal-des-Champs, including Angélique de Saint-Jean, her aunt Agnès, and her sisters, were able to conduct their affairs without further harassment. Simon Arnauld, whose political career seemed to have been destroyed as a result of Fouquet's disgrace, was once more in favor at court. As his power and influence in the world increased after 1665 so too did it increase within the family, to the point that by the middle of the next decade Port-Royal, having superseded the rue de la Verrerie and Andilly as the focal point of family activity in the 1640s, had in turn yielded that place to Simon's *seigneurie*, Pomponne.

~ 10

Pomponne: The Rise and Fall of a Minister

*T*HE PEACE of the Church that went into effect in 1669 occurred at a time when the political fortunes of Simon Arnauld de Pomponne were looking up. Many members of his family had withdrawn from the world, but Simon's successful career dramatized the extent to which the Arnauld family remained a presence in that world. His father, Robert Arnauld d'Andilly, had renounced his own worldly ambitions to become a *solitaire* in 1645, but he continued to do all in his power to nourish his son's. "No one has more ambition than he," he wrote in his memoirs, "to advance [his career] without compromising himself in any way.[1] Pomponne's revived fortunes together with the relaxation of tensions after the Peace of the Church encouraged the male members of the Arnauld family to adopt a more favorable disposition toward the world.

In his own quest for preferment, Pomponne had the advantage of the friendship of Michel Le Tellier, minister of war under Mazarin; Hugues de Lionne, another of the cardinal's close associates and a friend of Henry Arnauld; and Marshal Turenne, an old friend of Andilly's from the campaign on the Rhine in 1634. He had at his disposal the material resources with which his father provided him at the time of his retirement.[2] Finally, Pomponne could rely on his own administrative and political skills, which had impressed Le Tellier at the time of the Fronde, as well as his family's long tradition of devoted service. On the other hand, the Arnaulds' involvement in the Jansenist movement proved to be an obstacle to his career. The queen mother, Anne of Austria, as we have seen, refused to appoint Pomponne to the household of the duc d'Anjou, the king's brother, in 1659 because of her distaste for the Arnauld family's religious ideals.

Fortunately for Pomponne, the queen's refusal proved to be only a temporary setback. A year later Simon married Catherine Ladvocat, the daughter of Nicolas Ladvocat, a *maître des comptes*, and cousin of Nicolas Fouquet, the powerful *surintendant des finances*. Indeed Fouquet had suggested the marriage to Ladvocat in order to establish Simon Arnauld as a client. Ladvocat was a rich man who was in a position to advance his family's interests by marrying his daughter advantageously. To persuade Ladvocat to give Catherine's hand to Simon, Andilly compelled his sons Antoine and Henri-Charles to give over their inheritance, which included the *seigneurie* of Pomponne and the house in the rue de la Verrerie, to Simon in return for modest pensions from Simon. Simon, in turn, was required to provide Port-Royal with twelve thousand pounds. As proprietor of the *seigneurie* that had given his father so much pleasure, Simon assumed the name of Arnauld de Pomponne. His older brother, Antoine, gave up his rights to his father's estate with some reluctance. All these provisions were included in the marriage contract, which also stipulated that the bride's father would provide a dowry of two hundred thousand pounds, eighty thousand of which was to given over immediately.[3]

Recognizing the advantages of his son's marriage in augmenting his resources and establishing a fruitful political connection, Andilly wrote to the *surintendant des finances* at the time of the wedding, ardently assuring Fouquet of his family's loyalty to him. "I make so bold as to assure you that no one will be as committed to you as we will be for the rest of our lives. I make this pledge to you not in the usual terms that are customary in these times, but in the language of truth which ceases to contain the truth if it includes even the slightest dissimulation."[4] Little did he realize as he wrote these words that the connection with Fouquet would come close to destroying Pomponne's career.

Seventeen months later, in September 1661, the king ordered Fouquet's arrest on the grounds that he had enriched himself at the expense of the royal treasury. Louis took this step in order to remove a threat to his own authority in the months following Mazarin's death. As a client of the *surintendant* and a member of his family, Pomponne inevitably suffered the consequences of Fouquet's fall from power. His brother Antoine, then residing with his uncle Henry the bishop at Angers, was stunned by this sudden reversal of his brother's fortune.

> It was for him [Pomponne] a lightening blow that dashed all his hopes . . . We had seen him at Angers a few days earlier [before Fouquet's arrest] in such a glorified condition *(état de gloire)* that, from the peak where he believed himself to be, everyone else appeared so low that he scarcely saw them. M. d'Angers came to greet him, and I accompanied him. He barely looked at us. Nor was his wife less cold or more polite. It would have been hard to imagine at that moment that he would soon be humiliated and condemned to a long and harsh penance. One may say to their credit, however, that their misfortune strengthened their virtue, which had been smothered under the weight of *grandeur* and riches.[5]

Several months after Fouquet's arrest Pomponne was served with a *lettre de cachet* banishing him to Verdun. There he received a letter of consolation from his sister Angélique de Saint-Jean taking advantage of his adversity for the purpose of strengthening his religious sentiments. Their aunt Angélique had sent the same sort of letter to their father at the time of his dismissal from the household of Gaston d'Orleans in 1626. "In the unhappy situation in which you find yourself, your solitude is advantageous in that it provides you with time for reflection, which you do not have when your life is taken up by worldly activities and distractions."[6] Despite his own misfortunes, Pomponne was not unmindful of those affecting the nuns of Port-Royal during the crisis over the formulary. "I must confess to you," he wrote to Angélique de Saint-Jean in the summer of 1662,

> that I am not able to rid myself of the apprehension that I have for you even when I think of the reward that you expect [from your suffering]. I am only too aware of my inability to give the proper value to anything and to overcome that which the world regards as evil . . . God, who has given you sufficient grace to proportion your strength to your suffering, may one day make them cease, and al-

though I see things in a very different way, I am unable to lose my hope for this. I do not doubt that whatever he does will be advantageous for his glory and for you, and I beg him to do it with all my heart. I try to accept the situation in which he has placed me by keeping in mind that it is this way with all the disgraces with which he afflicts us. I also try to persuade myself that the best way to make them bearable is to believe that nothing can harm us because nothing can happen to us except by his command, and his commands are always good. With this in mind I try to endure my banishment, the perils that threaten my affairs and anything else he might cause to happen.[7]

In spite of Angélique's hope that her brother's disgrace might detach him from the world and enable him to devote more time to his spiritual needs, Pomponne yearned for his return to the king's favor. In letters to various friends and associates at court, he complained of the enormous costs of renovating Pomponne after the ravages of the Fronde, the money the king owed him for services rendered in the past, and of that part of his wife's dowry that he had not yet received.[8] More than anything else, he deplored the loss of the king's confidence.

These difficulties notwithstanding, Pomponne was able to rely on influential friends at court, including Le Tellier, Claude Le Peletier, a prominent magistrate (*président à mortier*) in the Parlement of Paris, and the maréchal de Turenne. These men did what they could to obtain the king's permission for Pomponne to take up residence closer to Paris, where he would be in a better position to supervise his affairs, but the king, who feared the possibility of a revolt on the part of Fouquet's friends, was adamant about Simon's remaining at Verdun. "We must await the end of the Fouquet business," wrote Le Tellier to Le Peletier, and so Pomponne grew "older and sadder," telling those who visited him that he "did not see where it would end and [that he] was bored to the point of madness."[9] Eventually, at the end of 1663, Pomponne received permission to move to La Ferté-sous-Jouarre, within easy reach of his family, and a year later to Pomponne. Like his father, Simon appreciated the value of friendship, as he later made clear to one of his supporters at court: "The generous spirit which you have shown in trying to relieve the recent disgrace of my father and my long lasting suffering by making it possible for me to return to Pomponne is rarely seen in these times. Few people undertake to combat the ill fortune of their friends or to ease the difficulties which they encounter."[10]

In December 1664 Fouquet was condemned to life imprisonment in the remote fortress of Pignerola in the Alps, not far from Turin. Any danger of an uprising of Fouquet's supporters having receded by February 1665, Louis XIV allowed Pomponne to return to Paris. Arriving in the city from which he had been absent for three years, Pomponne reported to his father, then residing at Pomponne, that he had paid a visit to the Hôtel de Nevers, the town house of Anne de Gonzague, where he met many old acquaintances, among them Madame de Sévigné, Madame de Lafayette, La Rochefoucauld, and Boileau, and enjoyed Racine's reading of one of his plays. The Arnaulds had formed friendships with many of these persons at the marquise de Rambouillet's *chambre bleue*. Pomponne inherited from his father an appreciation of the Rambouillet circle, where "a noble simplicity and an honest liberty" prevailed to a far greater extent than at court. "There was no one in the group who did not inquire after you. Everyone asked me to convey to you the friendliest sentiments."[11]

Pomponne made other calls upon his return from exile, including one to the convent of the Annunciades where his sister Angélique was incarcerated, for the purpose of persuading her through Madame de Rantzau to sign the formulary. Such a gesture would perhaps restore him to the king's good graces, but it turned out to be futile. Shortly thereafter, Pomponne appeared at court accompanied by the maréchal de Gramont, a cousin by marriage. The king refused to see him at first, but pressed by Gramont, he grudgingly admitted him to his presence. "I bowed to the king. He turned his head toward me and said nothing. The expression on his face was non-committal, but reassuring to one who had returned from exile." He received a much warmer reception from the queen mother, who, prompted by Jehannot de Bartillat, a member of her household and friend of the Arnaulds, assured Pomponne of her special affection for his family, whose association with Jansenism she now seemed willing to overlook. Others whom Pomponne felt obliged to see were the king's brother and Gaston d'Orléan's daughter, the duchesse de Monpensier, better known as *la grande Mademoiselle*. His father's dismissal from Gaston d'Orléans' household had long since been forgotten. Andilly had even received a pension of three thousand pounds from the duke, which he had managed to pass on to his son. The former *frondeuse* did not refrain from discussing the "fracas de Port-Royal." She told Pomponne that she had visited the convent where Agnès Arnauld and one of Agnès's nieces had been placed after their expulsion from Port-Royal-de-Paris. She did this, the duchess explained, "not out of curiosity but because they were members of a family for which she had the greatest affection."[12]

The Arnauld family's connections in high places and the esteem in which it was held by members of the royal family apparently overcame the king's reluctance to return Pomponne to his service. Within a year after his return from exile, Louis offered him the position of ambassador to Sweden. Louis XIV may have been willing to overcome his antipathy toward Jansenism and appoint a member of the Arnauld family to an important position because of his realization that he was in a better position to control the family's religious activities by satisfying its worldly ambitions.

Even though Pomponne was pleased by the king's offer, he almost refused it. As he explained to his father, he had relatively little wealth and a large number of children to support. The cost of maintaining an embassy in Stockholm, he believed, was too much for him to bear. Pomponne found himself in a real dilemma: Either he could refuse the ambassadorship and offend the king or accept it and ruin his family.[13] Writing to the minister Colbert a few months later, he pointed out that travel expenses and the cost of living for an ambassador, who was expected to be lavish in his treatment of prominent persons at the court to which he was accredited, were too much for a person in his financial condition to take on even though he might later be reimbursed for some of these expenses. "If I were fortunate enough to be better known by you, which I am not," he said to Colbert, who had been largely responsible for Fouquet's downfall, "you would know how difficult it is for me to speak of my own interests. Thank God that I have neglected them too much in the services that I have had the honor of rendering. I have never sought any advantage other than what any honest man might seek, namely the opportunity to acquire esteem and to discharge his duties well."[14]

Pomponne's account of the parlous condition of his "own interests" seems excessive given the advantageous marriage he had made to the daughter of a wealthy financier, but he had not received the full amount of his wife's dowry, nor would he receive it until a few years before his death. His father-in-law, Nicolas Ladvocat, who died shortly after the arrest of his cousin Fouquet, had been closely associated with the former finance minister's fiscal schemes designed to support the king's government in the last stages of the war against Spain. In 1648 Ladvocat had loaned the crown 500,000 pounds, less than half of which had been repaid at the time of his death. When Colbert assumed control of the treasury after Fouquet's disgrace, he made every effort to recover funds from those whom he had charged with having enriched themselves at the state's expense. Because of Ladvocat's close ties to Fouquet, his estate was taxed an additional 350,000 pounds. For Pomponne, the connection with the Ladvocat family had turned out to be a serious liability—all the more so because he had to deal with Fouquet's implacable enemy Colbert to obtain relief.[15]

In letters to various dignitaries, including the king, Pomponne complained of 80,000 pounds being owed him by an official in the king's employ who had promised to pay it back but had not yet done so. "My family's entire ruin or its relief depends on this debt," he wrote to the duc de Luynes, Colbert's son-in-law, a former *solitaire* who had returned to court.[16] To make matters worse, he declared, the pensions and salary that he and his father had received had either been reduced or paid irregularly. Although he had been appointed a *conseiller au roy* in 1644, he had never received a regular income from this office. While in exile at Verdun, Pomponne estimated that the king owed him 14,800 pounds for services rendered over the past twenty years.[17] Pomponne, in turn, was required by his marriage contract to pay his family's debts; 1200 pounds to Port-Royal, which he paid in 1665; and annual pensions to his father and to his brothers, the abbé and Luzancy, in the amount of 3500, 2000, and 500 pounds respectively.

The cost of renovating the *seigneurie* whose name he bore, badly damaged during the Fronde, added further to Pomponne's expenses. The restoration of the chateau, based on designs by Mansart, cost six thousand pounds,[18] this at a time when landed income throughout the kingdom was in decline. What was received in the way of revenue went toward supporting a troop of gendarmes lodged on the estate as additional punishment imposed on Pomponne because of his ties to Fouquet. In July 1666 Pomponne wrote Le Peletier a letter thanking him for his successful efforts in having the gendarmes removed. "I assure you," he wrote, "that it was very hard on me to lose not only the pleasure but also the use of a possession that means so much to me."[19]

The precarious condition of Pomponne's material resources was not unusual for persons of his rank with similar sources of income. Having devoted their lives to the king's service, they found that the cost of that service to them was often more than they were able to afford. Thus they were faced with the choice of devoting themselves to the cultivation of their landed estates at a time when income from that source was affected by adverse economic conditions or begging the king for increased pensions and salary. Pomponne's circumstances in 1665 were not unlike those of his grandfather Antoine, whose large family required him to renounce service to the crown in favor of developing his law practice, or of his father, who had refused the office of secretary of state early in his career because it was too expensive. Even when forced into private life after his dismissal from the household of Gaston d'Orléans in 1626, Andilly apparently had little difficulty in supporting himself and his family on his pensions, his investments in the salt tax and the Hôtel de Ville, and on income from his estates. To be sure, the more favorable economic climate during the first three decades of the seventeenth century favored old Antoine Arnauld and his son Robert, but both complained in their various *avis au roi* of the high cost of office that excluded people of merit. Theirs was the complaint of the *commissaire*, whose power, influence, and wealth depended entirely on the king's pleasure. These complaints were echoed by Pomponne, who, as he contemplated the further advancement of his career at the end of 1665, realized that he was dependent on the largesse of the crown to an even greater extent than his ancestors had been and that the only way of supporting his family was to continue to provide the king with valuable service.

In order to secure Pomponne's services, the king agreed to provide him with a *gratification extraordinaire* of six thousand pounds, which was supplemented by an additional two thousand pounds a year later. At the same time he assured his new ambassador that he would not have to bear the burden of the cost of his embassy himself. He "wished that I serve him not with my wealth, but only with my head."[20] Pomponne accepted the prestigious position and set out for Stockholm in the middle of winter, arriving there on 27 February 1666. His wife and children remained at Pomponne in the company of Andilly and Luzancy, both once again in exile from Port-Royal. Although pleased with the royal encouragement he received from the king, Pomponne continued to complain about his finances. Writing to Le Peletier from Stockholm in July, the ambassador compared himself to a ship that had just weathered a terrible storm but was still some distance from port.[21]

The distance between Stockholm and Pomponne seemed very far to the ambassador, especially in winter. "No one from the rest of Europe has passed through Sweden in over a month," he lamented in a letter to Andilly a year after his arrival there, "and the ice prevents our letters from leaving the country. You may judge for yourself how hard this is on one who relies heavily on letters from friends and loved ones."[22] The purpose of his mission was to detach Sweden from her alliance with the Netherlands and England, an alliance that threatened French interests. His official duties were not demanding, however, and Pomponne found himself with a lot of time on his hands. "You have no idea how bored I am," he complained to his father in the same letter.

In order to relieve the boredom and loneliness, Pomponne devoted a considerable amount of time to writing a detailed account of his diplomatic mission, to be found among the family papers housed at the Bibliothèque de l'Arsenal.[23] He also edited his father's memoirs, which were sent to him in segments over the course of the year. Andilly asserts in the first paragraph of the memoirs that he had been asked by his son "to write something that might be useful to my children, that would encourage them to be virtuous by examples from the family, and that would inspire in them a contempt for false goods that most men pursue at the expense of their honor and their salvation."[24] "I was right in asking you to write [your memoirs], which will be a treasure of great value to your grandchildren,"[25] Pomponne wrote in January 1667. He was dismayed, however, by the scant references to his older brother, the abbé Arnauld. "All that he did in the king's army and his change of career ought to be mentioned. Because he is the oldest of your children, you ought to say more about him. If you mention only me, he will be much offended."[26] A week later Pomponne wrote again to say that he had heard from his brother, who, although pleased with the idea that their father was in the process of writing his memoirs, "was deeply hurt by your overlooking him (that is the expression he uses rather than something worse), your having mentioned all the others without any reference to him."[27] Andilly paid no attention to his son's request. The memoirs contain no reference to his eldest son. The abbé's own account of his *"vie malheureuse"* (unfortunate life) also describes his unhappy relationship with his father, who clearly wanted to have as little to do with him as possible.[28]

The abbé Arnauld was not the only person slighted in his father's memoirs. Andilly makes no mention of his own brother Simon, killed in battle in 1639, who, according to Angélique the elder, was too much given to the world and therefore not worthy of emulation. Andilly's two youngest sons, Luzancy and *"le petit Jules,"* are barely mentioned except for a reference to Jules having died young and Luzancy being "the companion of my solitude." In keeping with his intention—and that of his favorite son—to include only those members of the family whose lives might serve as illustrious examples for Pomponne's grandsons to follow, Andilly extols the valor of the Arnauld warriors: the "remarkable firmness of courage" of his uncle Jean la Mothe Arnauld, the "extraordinary understanding for military affairs" of his uncle Pierre, and the courage and "the impressive valor" of his cousin Isaac. He praises the virtue and sagacity of the Arnauld statesmen: the judiciousness of his uncle and patron Isaac Arnauld, the "marvelous capacity for the affairs of state" of his uncle Claude, and the diplomatic skills of his brother Henry. As for Andilly's father, "the best in all the world," his virtues enlightened the age in which he lived. All of these men were worthy of higher offices that they were never able to obtain. Pierre might have been a marshal of France had he not been killed too soon, Isaac might have been a *surintendant des finances* had he lived long enough, and the king once gave thought to appointing *"le meilleur père du monde"* chancellor, according to Bassompierre, except that "he was too able."[29] In recounting the illustrious deeds of his noble family at a time when his son Pomponne had been restored to royal favor, he may have foreseen as early as 1667 that Pomponne would one day earn the high honors that had eluded earlier members of the family.

Andilly's memoirs include very little about his sisters and daughters who had such an influence on the religious life of the family. Six of his father's daughters, he said in his only account of them, "have finished or will finish their days in the sacred house of Port-Royal," and of his six daughters who became nuns, "three have died holily, and I will be only too grateful to God if the others follow their example."[30] All of them had a saintly vocation that manifested itself on the occasion of the archbishop of Paris's removal of the twelve nuns from Port-Royal-de-Paris in August 1664, an event that Andilly describes briefly as "an action terrible in itself and in the manner in which it was executed."[31] Two women among his acquaintances whom he singled out for special praise were the marquise de Maignelay, a cousin of Cardinal de Retz, whose virtues in his opinion resembled those of Saint Paul, and the marquise de Rambouillet: "No one in our time has received more praises than she, all of which she deserved."[32]

The omission of any account of the reforming activities of his sister Angélique, to whom he never refers by name, or of his other female relatives in the convent or of their influence within the family perhaps may be explained in light of Andilly's main purpose, which was to provide illustrious models for his grandsons. Perhaps he feared that to pay tribute to the influence of the Arnauld women within the family might have made him and his male relatives appear less strong. After all, his sister Angélique and his daughter Angélique de Saint-Jean had been described as being more than women. The best explanation for Andilly's failure to mention the women in his life, however, is that the women were not in the world of which he wanted his grandsons to be a part. It was his intention to inspire them not to withdraw from the world but to emulate their ancestors' military and political careers. In writing his memoirs, Andilly seemed to anticipate a better time, when his favorite son and after him his grandsons would have the opportunity to serve the king to the best of their ability and to receive their just rewards for that service. While Andilly was writing his memoirs, he sat for the portrait by his friend Philippe de Champaigne that now hangs in the Louvre. In the portrait, one of Champaigne's best, he is shown holding his *brevet* of *conseiller au roi*, a reminder of his years in public life rather than as a *solitaire*.

Work on the memoirs sustained the close ties between Andilly and his son at a time when the ambassador felt somewhat isolated and cut off from his family. Pomponne took pleasure in the fact that his oldest son, Nicolas-Simon, was under Andilly's tutelage. Writing to his brother Luzancy in the autumn of 1667, Pomponne explained that the education that his son was receiving would enable him to become both *"un homme de bien"* with respect to his religious responsibilities, and an *"honnête homme* (that is to say, a man of refinement who knows how to live)." Pomponne recalled what he himself had learned from his maternal uncle, Pomponne-Hacqueville, about the politics of the various European states and from his uncle Henry about history and genealogy.[33]

Pomponne believed that as a result of his grandfather's instruction, young Nicolas-Simon would come to appreciate the family's reputation for eloquence and would be better prepared to advance the family fortunes in the face of the corrupting forces that afflicted society and politics.

Before he left France for Stockholm, Pomponne wrote to Hugues de Lionne on behalf of his cousin Isaac Le Maistre de Sacy, who had been imprisoned in the Bastille in 1664 because of his refusal to sign the formulary. He continued to press Sacy's case during his sojourn in Sweden, making sure that Lionne understood that he was acting in the interests of his family and not because of any sympathy for Jansenism, a movement "in which I am not now or ever will be involved, but whose unfortunate victim I seem to have become."[34] That he did not adhere to Jansenist tenets is reflected in his inability to understand why his sister and the other nuns were so adamant about not signing the formulary. Nonetheless, he shared the Jansenists' and his family's antipathy to the Jesuits. In writing Le Peletier on behalf of Sacy in July 1667, he maintained that his efforts to release his cousin would increase "the hatred that the most influential body in all of Europe bears against the name that I bear."[35] Pomponne's grandfather Antoine had antagonized that prestigious order because he regarded it as a threat to the prerogatives of the French crown, a sentiment Pomponne shared. Because he supported these prerogatives, Pomponne was offended by Pope Alexander VII's efforts to suppress Jansenism. A staunch Gallican, in the tradition of his family, he resented what he regarded as the unwarranted encroachment of the papacy in matters for which the king was solely responsible.[36]

Under the provisions of the Peace of the Church, which Pomponne enthusiastically endorsed, Sacy was released from prison. The ambassador, who was recalled to the French court in July 1668, went with his wife and older brother to the Bastille to inform his cousin that he was a free man. Sacy's freedom taken together with *le grand Arnauld's* presentation at court were further indications of Pomponne's return to royal favor. Several weeks after his return from Stockholm he was appointed ambassador to the Estates General at The Hague, the capital of the Dutch Republic.

The king was becoming increasingly preoccupied by the problems caused by the Dutch, the allies of France during the Thirty Years' War. At the time when Pomponne received his new appointment, the two countries found their interests in conflict in the Spanish Netherlands, on which Louis made territorial claims based on his marriage to the Spanish princess Maria Theresa. The Dutch viewed these claims as a threat to the security of their country. The Estates General relied on the so-called Triple Alliance with England and Sweden, which threatened French interests. As ambassador to Sweden, Pomponne had tried without success to detach that country from the alliance. In his new position, he had as his responsibility to observe the diplomatic activities of the Dutch government and to win it over to the acceptance of French claims in the Spanish Netherlands.[37]

The official duties of the ambassador did not prevent him from monitoring his own affairs, albeit from a considerable distance. Writing to the duchess de Chevreuse to thank her for interceding with Colbert to provide further "gratifications" for the support of his embassy, he reiterated his reliance on the king's generosity. "Whatever appointments it pleases the king to bestow on me provide little support for a man of limited resources."[38] As a result of his pleas and those of his friends at court, Pomponne managed to recover eighty thousand *écus* of what was owed him for past services, as well as his father's pension of four thousand pounds from Anne of Austria, which, he feared, might have been terminated at the time of her death in 1666. Andilly turned that pension over to Port-Royal-des-Champs, badly in need of financial support after its separation from the convent in Paris.[39] The cessation of hostilities between the Jansenists and their enemies was a great relief to Pomponne. Writing to his father from The Hague, he expressed his satisfaction that the nuns of Port-Royal were no longer deprived of the sacraments and that the convent could once again admit pensioners and postulants. He allowed two of his daughters, Marie-Emmanuelle and Charlotte, to enter Port-Royal as pensioners.[40]

Pomponne's sojourn at The Hague came to an end in the spring of 1671. As relations between France and the Estates General deteriorated, Louis and his minister of war, Le Tellier, believed that it was more than ever necessary to lure Sweden away from the Triple Alliance.

Impressed with Pomponne's diplomatic abilities, Le Tellier urged the king to send him back to Sweden, where he arrived for his second tour of duty in September 1671. However, a week before his arrival in Sweden, his patron, Hugue de Lionne, minister for foreign affairs, died. The king decided to bestow the office of secretary of state on Pomponne and to admit him to the *conseil d'en haut*, the king's highest council: "Thus I saw myself suddenly elevated to one of the most important posts in the state, with no obligation but to the king himself."[41] Only six years after his return from exile, Pomponne had attained what his father had only aspired to, elevation to high office through the king's favor and, presumably, his own merit.

Pomponne's influential connections at court—Lionne, Le Tellier, Le Peletier, and the duc de Luynes, among others—had secured the end of his exile and later the ambassadorial posts, but in appointing Pomponne to the office vacated by Lionne, the king apparently consulted no one but himself. Louis was undoubtedly impressed with Pomponne's abilities and with his knowledge of Dutch affairs, both of which would be useful to him as he prepared for war against the Netherlands. He was aware of the tradition of loyal service to the crown of the Arnauld family. The Peace of the Church now made it possible for him to favor a member of that family despite its involvement in the Jansenist quarrel. By elevating Pomponne to one of the highest administrative ranks, the king may also have thought that he could blunt any rebellious inclinations on the part of the family.

Fifty years earlier Pomponne's father had been offered a similar office but could not afford to accept it. To become secretary of state, Pomponne would have to pay eight hundred thousand pounds to Lionne's son. In his letter of appointment of September 5, 1671, the king offered to provide Pomponne with three hundred thousand pounds toward the cost as well as an additional five hundred thousand that would be deducted from the annual income he would receive as secretary. Pomponne would have to make do with this arrangement "until such time within a few years as I am able to find the means of relieving you of the embarrassment of being too much in debt."[42] In order to prevent himself from acquiring excessive debts, the new minister would have to arrange loans at a favorable rate of interest. The rewards of high office came at a high price.

Before he left Stockholm to take up his new position at court, Pomponne informed his cousin, the marquis de Feuquières, that he was recommending him for the office he was leaving behind. The grandson of Isaac Arnauld, under whose auspices Pomponne's father had entered public service sixty years earlier, Feuquières was the son of the first marquis of that name, who had died of wounds received in battle in 1640 when he was being considered for a post in the king's household. "The position [of ambassador] is not particularly remunerative," wrote Pomponne to Feuquières at the end of October 1671. "It will not improve your affairs, given the condition they are in, but it will keep you busy and will make your abilities known to a master as good and as just as ours is, who knows how to reward those who serve him."[43]

Pomponne and his wife looked after Feuquières's interests while he was in Sweden. Catherine de Pomponne, who had dealt with her husband's accounts while he was in exile and on duty abroad, was in an excellent position to advise the marquis in these matters. Her letters to him reveal the precarious condition of those who depended on the king's largess. In May 1673 she informed him that most ambassadors had received no payments for their services, only those which had been approved by Colbert, the finance minister. "If I had not sent M. de Colbert your memoir, I assure you that you would have received nothing for more than three months."[44] Feuquières's finances seem to have been in even worse condition than Pomponne's were when he returned from exile, but Pomponne, perhaps forgetting his own impatience when in similar circumstances, admonished his cousin that "patience is a virtue at all times, but particularly in these times under a king who does not forget to reward those who serve him."[45] How confident he now was of the king's beneficence when only a few years earlier he had almost convinced himself that service to the crown might well lead to his financial ruin!

Writing to her daughter a few days after his appointment, Madame de Sévigné expressed sentiments undoubtedly shared by many who knew Pomponne: "What think you of M. d'Andilly's gratification to see M. de Pomponne become minister and secretary of state? In truth, the king must be praised for such an excellent choice . . . What marvels will he not accomplish in this position and what joy for all his friends."[46] Andilly was, of course, delighted by his son's elevation. Writing to congratulate Pomponne on his achievement, he took the occasion to warn him not to be seduced "by the vain honors of the world that seduce most men." By keeping in mind the honors reserved for him in heaven, Pomponne would better serve the king.[47] Andilly's old friend Bartillat, the former treasurer in the household of the late queen mother, proposed that Andilly pay his respects to the king. Eighty-four years old at the time, Andilly was reluctant to make the trip from Pomponne, but he did so only a few days after the appointment was announced.[48]

After he was presented to the king, Andilly reminded Louis of his family's "hereditary passion" for public service, "which induced the late king, his father, to offer me the office of secretary of state at Béziers in 1622, vacated by the death of the keeper of the seals." The king replied that Pomponne would have to pay a lot more for the office than Andilly would have had to pay in 1622, but that everything would work out for the best. Before he took leave of the king, Andilly availed himself of the opportunity to compliment the king on his firm stand against dueling, a policy that had always been favored by the family.[49] Even Pomponne's brother Luzancy, who had long since abandoned the world to become a *solitaire*, congratulated him on his elevation: "Now that his Majesty has honored you with the office of secretary of state, we are now assured that there will always be someone from the family near the king to receive his commands and carry out his orders."[50]

One member of the family who was far from pleased with the news of her brother's promotion was Angélique de Saint-Jean. Writing to Luzancy on September 8, she deplored the perilous situation confronting Pomponne, "whom I love very much indeed. Others, who think in terms of the interests of church and state are struck by the advantages of his appointment for both."[51] If one served the state, Angélique maintained, one became too much influenced by worldly considerations. "To remain humble in such a high office, poor when surrounded by such wealth, and a disciple of the cross of Jesus Christ amid the temptations of this world is almost impossible," she wrote Madame Périer, Pascal's sister.[52]

Angélique was appalled when she learned that Pomponne had offered Luzancy a position as an aide. "A man who has rid himself of the world," she wrote the minister, "and has of his own choice consecrated himself to God by a life of penance, may not turn back with impunity. You would not permit a vase consecrated for use on an altar to be utilized for profane purposes, and yet you are thinking of taking his [Luzancy's] heart from him which is far more precious than an ordinary vase."[53] Much relieved to learn that Richelieu's former page turned *solitaire* had rejected the offer, she assured Luzancy that he was among those "who have wings to fly higher [than most mortals] and who find their security in their contempt for the world *(dans le mépris qu'ils font du monde)*."[54]

Pomponne's appointment as minister and secretary of state revealed two different interpretations of *"mépris du monde"* that affected the attitudes of various members of the Arnauld family toward Pomponne's advancement. In the minister's own opinion—and in his father's as well—one might serve the king as long as one did so in a Christian manner. Fortified by a genuine commitment to religious principles, the public servant would be able to defend himself from worldly temptations. In Angélique de Saint-Jean's opinion, on the other hand, no matter how conscientious that public servant might be, he would almost certainly be seduced by these temptations, thereby jeopardizing his soul. Andilly's conception of *"mépris du monde"* was not unlike that of his uncle Isaac, who had written a treatise on the subject earlier in the century. Neither man believed that service to the king was incompatible with service to God if one were properly motivated. Indeed, enlightened rulers and their ministers might provide the kind of government that improved the quality of life, unlike governments headed by indifferent monarchs surrounded by self-serving sycophants. Angélique's *"mépris du monde,"* like that of her aunt and of her cousin Antoine Le Maistre, derived from monasticism and meant a rejection of the world and a total commitment to a life of penance, solitude, and contemplation. Angélique the elder had hoped to commit her family to these ideals, a hope that was not entirely realized, at least as far as some of the male members of the family were concerned. Angélique de Saint-Jean used the occasion of Pomponne's elevation to remind him and other members of the family of these ideals once again. But just as she was unable to prevent the compromise of these ideals that led to the Peace of the Church, so too was she unable to persuade her brother that the only way to achieve true happiness was to reject the appointment offered to him by the king. Angélique's inability to persuade her brother of the efficacy of the ideals of Port-Royal is further evidence that the influence of the Arnauld women on the men decreased as the possibility of the men acquiring worldly honors increased. This had been the case with the Huguenot women in the family during an earlier period: They were unable to prevent their male relatives from converting to Catholicism for the purpose of satisfying their ambitions.

The Peace of the Church facilitated Pomponne's elevation and enabled the nuns of Port-Royal to carry on their duties, which included the education of young girls. Angélique, who throughout her career devoted herself to this, was delighted that Pomponne, whose sons were being tutored by Andilly, had sent his daughters to the convent to be educated by her. In her letters to her father at Pomponne, she reported on their progress. She also expressed concern that Andilly was working too hard. "I fear that because you want to get everything done, you do more than you should. When one is as old and as feeble as you are, that is not right. In the name of God, nothing is more important to us than your preservation."[55] Now that the *solitaires* were permitted to return to Port-Royal under the terms of the Peace of the Church, she also expressed the hope that he and Luzancy, health permitting, would take up residence there as well "and that you return to your life of solitude from which you were so unjustly removed."[56] When she learned that her father and brother had decided to return so that the patriarch could spend his last days at Port-Royal, she informed him that his two granddaughters "can't wait to embrace you."[57]

The addition of Pomponne's daughters to the community hardly offset the loss of their great-aunt Agnès, who died on 19 February 1671, only a few months before Pomponne took up his new duties. Angélique had been concerned about her aunt's deteriorating health for several months. Now, at the age of seventy-eight, Agnès faced her death, as she had her exile from the convent, with equanimity. Writing to a friend less than two weeks before she died, she informed him that "I would have preferred to die rather than to rid myself of this bad cold that has bothered me for so long. For although I must confess that all that I have done is obscure in the sight of God, I believe nevertheless that death, if accepted in good faith as the end of a sinful life, is more likely to satisfy God than all that we are able to accomplish in this life."[58]

In all the chronicles and memoirs pertaining to Port-Royal, Agnès appears less conspicuous than either of the two Angéliques. Nonetheless, Agnès was a powerful influence within the community in her own right. When Angélique the elder undertook her reform of Port-Royal in 1609, she made every effort to have her sister join her at Port-Royal because she had come to depend on her for advice and support. Indeed Angélique would have had a far more difficult time in breaking with the bishop of Langres over the Order of the Holy Sacrament without that support. In noting the difference between the two sisters, Angélique de Saint-Jean contrasted Agnès's serenity with Angélique's volatility. Undoubtedly it was this quality in Agnès that drew the niece closer to her than to her other aunt. Angélique de Saint-Jean's own dependence on Agnès revealed itself in her account of her captivity at the convent of the Annunciades.

Agnès's firmness is exemplified in her response to the government's order to remove the uniforms of the pensioners before their dismissal from the convent in 1661. The costumes worn by the girls were a matter of conventual discipline, she insisted, over which the government had no authority whatsoever. The pensioners left Port-Royal in proper attire. Her supportive nature, on which the members of her family relied so much, is perfectly illustrated in one of the best-known paintings of Philippe de Champaigne that hangs in the Louvre, which portrays Agnès praying at the bedside of a sick pensioner (the painter's niece). The expression on her face reflects a tenderness and serenity that gives warmth to the ascetic surroundings in which the two personages are placed.

Antoine Arnauld presided over Agnès's funeral, but her oldest brother, Andilly, was too unwell to attend. He did not feel strong enough to make the move from Pomponne to Port-Royal until May 1673, when he and Luzancy again took up residence at the neighboring farm. His friend Madame de Sévigné made her first visit to Port-Royal to see him in January 1674. "I must say that I was very pleased to see that divine solitude about which I have heard so much," she wrote her daughter. "It is a frightful little valley entirely appropriate for one's salvation." There she spent six hours with the old man, "experiencing all the joys that a conversation with such an admirable person gives one."[59]

A few months after this visit, on 27 September 1674, Andilly at the age of eighty-four died of a sudden fever in the arms of his son Luzancy. Present at the deathbed were his brother Antoine, his sons Pomponne and Luzancy, his daughters Angélique, Marie-Angélique, and Marie-Charlotte, his nephew Sacy, and two granddaughters. Luzancy was appointed the executor of his estate. His one remaining pension of six thousand pounds was left to Port-Royal.[60] The epitaph on his tomb in the convent described him in much the same terms as he described himself in his memoirs:

> In his youth he was worthy of the most important appointments. In the very important positions in which he served he did so with ability and with integrity. In his person he had all that the world admires, and he always held the world in contempt *(il a toujours méprisé le monde)*. He was blameless at court and incorruptible in situations in which he had the opportunity to enrich himself and unwavering amid the pleasures and the temptations of the century.[61]

Angélique de Saint-Jean was "overwhelmed" by the loss of her father.[62] "Those who attribute to me greater strength than I have do me an injustice because they deprive me of the support of their prayers."[63] Now she was deprived of Andilly's suport at a time when she was becoming increasingly uneasy about the hostile attitude toward Port-Royal and its supporters that persisted at court and within the Church despite the Peace of the Church. "One has need of a good deal of faith and charity in order to accept with equanimity the result of such long-lasting intrigue, which will only succeed in destroying this poor house," she wrote shortly after the death of Andilly,[64] but she continued to derive comfort from the belief, always reassuring to the nuns, that "it is a good sign when the world is opposed to that which one would do for God's sake."[65] For her, Port-Royal was what it had always been, a dwelling place "for a small number of God's elect,"[66] where those whom the world persecuted might expect redemption.

Angélique's fears of renewed persecution were justified. Though preoccupied with his war against the Dutch throughout most of the decade, Louis continued to be suspicious of the Jansenists, whom he believed were bent on creating a new schism within the Church. He was particularly concerned about the activities of *le grand Arnauld,* whom he persisted in believing was the head of a cabal that threatened to create new disorders within the kingdom. After the promulgation of the Peace of the Church, Arnauld divided his time between Paris and Port-Royal, free to move about as he chose and to speak out on religious matters as long as he did not touch on Jansen, the five propositions, or the contentious issues pertaining to the doctrine of efficacious grace. As if to prove his Catholicity, he polemicized against the Huguenots and expressed satisfaction at the revocation of the Edict of Nantes in 1685. He also attacked the longtime enemies of his family, the Jesuits. "Despite what the Jesuits say, the face of the earth has not changed since [the order] came into existence. There is no less simony, usury, impurity, injustice, or violence. Merchants cheat as usual, judges continue to embezzle and distort, and soldiers blaspheme and steal as much as they ever did."[67] Far from improving the moral tone of society, the Jesuits, according to Arnauld, made it easier to commit such crimes. The king, whose confessor was a Jesuit, was distressed by these attacks on the influential order and by the report that Arnauld's brother, the bishop of Angers, permitted the explicit distinction to be made between *fait* and *droit* to be appended to signatures of the formulary. In the middle of a campaign in Flanders, he issued an order rebuking the bishop and demanding signature without reservations.

In order to control Antoine's activities, the king held Pomponne responsible for the behavior of his family's members. Pomponne in turn realized that his career depended on the loyalty and obedience of the members of the family. His uncle Antoine Arnauld for his part insisted that he was indeed a loyal and obedient subject. "I have received with great respect that which you have instructed me to do on behalf of the king," he wrote his nephew in 1677. "I hope that I have not given him reason to suspect me of wanting to renew the quarrels that the Peace of the Church has put an end to." That peace, he went on to say, was endangered not by him but by his enemies, who had continued to attack and insult him and his family and friends with impunity since 1669.[68] Arnauld's assurances did not satisfy Louis. Two years later Pomponne informed his uncle that the king was of the opinion that Arnauld was holding meetings of dissidents at his house in the Faubourg Saint-Jacques in Paris. He was henceforth forbidden to have any gatherings at his home. Arnauld admitted to entertaining numerous people, but he maintained that these social events were entirely innocent.[69]

Antoine Arnauld resented the fact that his liberty had been curtailed and that he was held accountable for his behavior by his nephew Pomponne. Shortly after being informed by his nephew of the king's concerns, Antoine Arnauld wrote to inform him that he had decided to make no more public appearances. "It was only because I did not want to involve you in our wretched affairs that I didn't tell you of my intention sooner. It will be better in every way if you are able to say that you know nothing about my plans."[70] On June 17, Antoine left Paris and three days later arrived at Mons in the Spanish Netherlands. This was his first trip beyond the frontiers of France, to which he never returned.

Rumor had it that Antoine intended to settle in Rome where the new pope, Innocent XI, far more kindly disposed toward Jansenists than his predecessors, intended to make him a cardinal. He never had any such intention, however, having learned from his brother Henry and from Pomponne, both of whom had spent time there, that the atmosphere was not much more hospitable than that of Paris. He made his decision to take up residence in the Spanish Netherlands because of the more favorable attitude toward the theology of the Flemish bishop Jansen within religious circles there and because a number of his friends and associates had settled there.[71] By going into self-imposed exile, he would no longer be an embarrassment to Pomponne, nor would he risk jeopardizing the minister's career. At the same time, he was able to free himself from his nephew's control and to speak out on matters of concern to him, associating with whomever he pleased. In a very real sense, his self-imposed exile became his liberation.

Louis XIV's continued hostility toward the Jansenists made itself felt by the nuns of Port-Royal as well as Antoine Arnauld and his friends. Angélique de Saint-Jean, who had been elected abbess of Port-Royal in 1678, appears to have had some intimation of a revival of attacks on the convent early in the fateful year 1679. "It seems to me that we may have some hope in Christ's assurance that we should be happy when men speak ill of us in violation of the truth," she wrote, "and we should look upon it as an effect of God's mercy toward us in that he makes use of the injustice done to us to make room for us in his kingdom."[72] Two months before Antoine Arnauld's abrupt departure from France, Port-Royal lost the protection of a powerful benefactress, the former *frondeuse* and princess of the blood, the duchesse de Longueville, who had built a house for herself attached to the convent. There she devoted herself to *"pénitence extérieure et intérieure,"* so the necrologies inform us, until her death in April 1679. Deprived of this protection, Port-Royal became vulnerable to renewed assaults. Within weeks after the demise of the duchess, the archbishop of Paris, Harlay de Champvallon, journeyed to the convent to inform them of the king's command that the pensioners once again be expelled and the recruitment of new nuns be prohibited. Included among the pensioners were two of Pomponne's daughters. At the same time the archbishop ordered the removal of the few remaining *solitaires*, including Le Maistre de Sacy and Luzancy, both of whom returned to the chateau de Pomponne.

With no additional revenue from bequests and dowries or new blood to sustain it, it would only be a matter of time before the community, once so vigorous, would wither away like the leaves during what Sainte-Beuve called the "autumn of Port-Royal." Describing the archbishop's visit to the bishop of Angers, Angélique de Saint-Jean said that he had taken pains to explain that he was acting under the king's orders. However, "we are accustomed to hearing words of this sort from the mouths of prelates, who are so unlike the bishops of the early church."[73] In response to a sympathetic letter from her brother Pomponne, she admitted that she found it difficult to believe "that a Prince who has made all Europe tremble should have anything to fear from a group of small children and four or five priests who serve the community of nuns."[74] In an effort to defend the establishment, Angélique appealed to Innocent XI, who, though unable to countermand the king's orders, succeeded in preventing the convent from being deprived of its right to elect abbesses.

The year 1679 saw not only the collapse of the Peace of the Church, which had turned out to be only a truce, and renewed persecution of the Jansenists, but also Pomponne's dismissal from office in November. The reasons for his removal were not directly related to his family's religious affiliations (although the end of the Peace undoubtedly made the minister's situation at court uncomfortable to say the least) but to differences of opinion with respect to policy. Pomponne, who certainly had helped his sovereign prepare for war against the Dutch, was less enthusiastic about the war itself than was Louvois, the minister primarily responsible for the conduct of the war. The heavy price that war exacted from the kingdom's resources had concerned Pomponne's father during the era of the Fronde, when France was at war with Spain as well as within itself. Clearly this was Pomponne's growing concern as the war against the Dutch, which everyone thought would be brief, dragged on. The effect of protracted conflict on persons of his condition is revealed in Pomponne's letters to his cousin Feuquières. Feuquières was eager to sell his office of governor of Verdun, but Pomponne advised against it because he would not get a high enough price as long as the war continued.[75] His own affairs, he admitted, were adversely affected because of the irregular payments he received from the king. The honors and awards that he had received were not enough, he complained, to avoid ruin.[76]

As the Dutch war continued, Pomponne employed his diplomatic skills to prevent the German princes, threatened by the proximity of the French armies, from joining the alliance against France. He tried and failed to persuade the king and Louvois to participate at a peace conference to be held at Cologne in 1673. After 1676, when Louis XIV at last agreed to negotiate an end to the war, Pomponne was primarily responsible for arranging the terms of the Treaty of Nimwegen (1679). Although under its terms France received the province of Franche-Comté from the Spanish, the Dutch emerged from the war as well off as before. Louvois persuaded the king that France might have won more if Pomponne had not been so inclined to give in to the Dutch.

Although Michel Le Tellier had been one of those responsible for reviving Pomponne's political career after the disgrace of Fouquet, his son Louvois, whose influence in the *conseil d'en haut* was on the rise, had always been Pomponne's rival in the council. In urging Pomponne's dismissal Louvois found himself in agreement with Colbert, who hoped to replace the minister in charge of foreign affairs with a member of his own family. After Louis had informed Pomponne that his services were no longer needed, his office was given to Colbert's brother Croissy.

Pomponne's dismissal was the result of the jockeying for place and favor that his father Andilly had disliked so much about political life. Furthermore, his dismissal demonstrated the perilous situation in which the *commissaire* often found himself, vulnerable as he always was to the loss of the king's favor. To the *commissaire*, loss of favor meant loss of status and influence. Pomponne had no choice but to retire to private life, as his father had done after his dismissal from the household of Gaston d'Orleans in 1626.

✑ *11*

Toward the Destruction of Port-Royal

$\mathcal{T}$HE FORTUNES of the Arnauld family, which seemed so bright at the time that the Peace of the Church went into effect in 1669, took a turn for the worse after the collapse of that agreement ten years later. In 1679, Arnauld de Pomponne, whose career had seemed so promising at the time the Peace went into effect, was dismissed from ministerial office. Like his father Arnauld d'Andilly in similar circumstances after his removal from the household of Gaston d'Orleans, Pomponne now had the opportunity to reflect on his experiences in public life. His career having suffered a serious setback, would he adopt that contemptuous attitude toward the world that would enable him to seek redemption from God, as other members of his family had done, or would he yearn for a return to the king's good graces? His sister Angélique de Saint-Jean, recently elected abbess of Port-Royal, had little hope for the future now that the archbishop of Paris had deprived the convent of the right to admit postulants and pensioners. Their uncle Antoine Arnauld received at court by Louis XIV in 1669, was in exile ten years later.

Pomponne's reduced circumstances were obvious to his friends and relatives. Madame de Sévigné visited the fallen minister a few days after he left court. Describing her visit to her daughter, she expressed concern for his diminished resources. The king, she reported, had agreed to continue Pomponne's pension of twenty thousand pounds, but that was hardly enough on which to support his children. "My God! What a change! What retrenchment! What economies are being made in this household! Eight children!" Nevertheless she assured her daughter that "M. de Pomponne is more capable than anyone else to bear this misfortune with courage, with resignation and *beaucoup de christianisme.*"[1] Pomponne's young cousin, the son of the marquis de Feuquières, informed his father at Stockholm: "I returned yesterday from Pomponne where I found M. de Pomponne more stoical than Seneca except when he gave thought to his numerous children whom he pities. He accepts everything else with a firm mind."[2] Writing himself to Feuquières, whose career depended on his cousin's influence, Pomponne referred to the deplorable condition of his affairs. "I try to make good use of the pain I feel and to understand that men often ignore what is good for them, and they apply the term 'evil' to things which should be called 'good.' How different is the order of Providence from their thoughts and desires."[3]

In trying to find some good in the adverse circumstances in which he now found himself, Pomponne could draw on his father's experiences during the 1620s and the advice and counsel that he was receiving from his sister Angélique. Now that her brother's fortunes were in decline, her spiritual influence on him was likely to be greater, in the same way that her aunts' influence had been on Arnauld d'Andilly when he had been out of favor. The fluctuating spiritual influence of the women within the Arnauld family depended on the worldly affairs of the men. Angélique de Saint-Jean was much relieved that his disgrace had removed him from "a position in which ruin is far too common. He is not yet saved, but certainly this is an indication of his salvation *(marque de son salut).*"[4] She had always feared that his elevated position in the world "would place him among the lowest orders in the kingdom of Jesus Christ, a kingdom in which so many members of his family have attained exalted positions on account of their virtue."[5] As always, her conception of her family's mission, to serve God by repudiating the world and its ways, stood in sharp contrast to the more worldly conception that had contributed to the Arnaulds' success in the world. It was a conception shaped by the only world that she had ever known—the cloister. "No man may serve two masters," she wrote Pomponne, "or pursue two conflicting objectives, the glory of the world and the glory of heaven at the same time."[6]

Pomponne was grateful for his sister's belief "that such a terrible blow is a sign of God's mercy toward me. I know I must make good use of it, and that in itself will require a powerful infusion of his grace. I don't dare ask for that in my prayers, but I put my trust in yours, my dear sister, and in those of your sacred community." Try as he might to make the best of what had befallen him, he was unable to rid himself of worries about his large family. "The sight of your nieces [his daughters, who had been expelled from Port-Royal]," he wrote, " pierces my heart more than I can say. It is indeed unfortunate that they are now separated from you! I would not complain if they were still with you. It fills me with grief to think of what will become of them. May God pity them!"[7]

Angélique too was saddened by the departure of her nieces from Port-Royal, but she remained in contact with them as they resumed their studies at another convent. She had become particularly close to Charlotte, then fifteen years of age, who intended to become a nun, and in her letters she encouraged the girl in her belief that she had a genuine monastic vocation.[8] How painful it must have been for her to realize that Charlotte would very likely never join the community that had included so many members of her family and that had been for so long the focal point of its religious life! Deprived of the resources necessary for its survival, the convent was slowly dying. "We are threatened with the greatest evils," wrote Angélique to an acquaintance in 1680. "Our ruin is too slow for those who await our death."[9]

This sense of foreboding pervades all of Angélique's letters written during the last years of her life. To her brother Luzancy, in residence at Pomponne, she declared that she was not one of those who believed that the storm had passed and that Port-Royal would be left alone.[10] What made matters even worse for the nuns was the difficulty of finding acceptable confessors to replace Arnauld and Sacy. Angélique derived some comfort from expressions of concern not only from the *solitaires* residing at Pomponne but also from the former minister himself. Pomponne went so far as to assure the nuns that he would use what little influence he had at court to protect the community from further harm.[11] Brother and sister shared similar worries. His, the limited resources available to his family; hers, the support necessary to sustain the convent. Both were in their own way victims of the king's displeasure. Angélique, however, knew that her brother was unable to do much for

Port-Royal, but as she explained to a friend, "we are like birds who in winter nourish themselves on air, for we are reduced to relying on certain attitudes, words and behavior that amount to nothing. But that amuses us from time to time and makes us hope for the best—I laugh as I say this—in the situation we are in."[12] Upon hearing the news of the birth in 1682 of the king's grandson, the duke of Burgundy, on the anniversary of her aunt Angélique's death, she "prayed for him in the hope that in fifty years he will rebuild the walls of Jerusalem and the ruins of Port-Royal . . . We pray that he may receive from God a love of truth and of justice."[13] She did not have to add that these were qualities that she believed were lacking in the duke's grandfather, who had willed the destruction of her convent. She knew well enough that she could expect little in the way of relief from any temporal power, "but God has given me tranquility to face this uncertainty. In the midst of our present dangers and those yet to come, I look upon death as a great deliverance."[14] In this she differed from her brother, for whom deliverance could only come from the king.

Four years after these words were written, death delivered from the "evils" that surrounded them not only Angélique but Sacy and Luzancy as well. Sacy, the last of the three Le Maistre brothers who had become *solitaires*, died at Pomponne on 4 January 1684, in the arms of his cousin Luzancy. According to his longtime companion Nicolas Fontaine, he sustained himself in his last hours with the thought that death was a cathartic force that purified the sinner "before he appeared before God. That is why he said so often on his deathbed, *O bienheureux purgatoire!*"[15] Sacy was buried at Port-Royal, where three weeks later on 24 January, Angélique, sixty years old and serving in her second term as abbess, died after a short illness. She had been particularly close to Sacy, her spiritual director at the time of his death. His death had affected her even more than had the rumor that her aunt Agnès had signed the formulary. After Sacy's funeral she spent many hours beside his grave. Although seemingly a self-contained and self-sufficient person who weathered adversity with unusual composure, she was now, as she had always been, psychologically dependent on her family.

Angélique, more than anyone else among her relatives, believed the family to have been singled out by God to suffer persecution for righteousness' sake. Whereas her aunt, the elder Angélique, had believed that suffering and persecution were a test of one's faith, she was never certain that she or anyone else, with the possible exception of François de Sales, Jeanne de Chantal, and the abbé de Saint-Cyran, had passed the test. Angélique de Saint-Jean believed, however, that she, her family, and the Port-Royal community in general, had braved the ordeals that they had encountered in defense of their religious beliefs and that they were undoubtedly among God's elect. Before her death she had made herself in effect the chronicler of Port-Royal so that the deeds of the nuns and *solitaires* might inspire future generations in the community. In her struggle against those whom she regarded as the enemies of the truth, she needed her family by her side. She had called on her father to be on hand when the archbishop appeared at Port-Royal-de-Paris to remove the nuns, on her uncle Antoine to remain as intransigent as she was, and on Antoine and Sacy to serve as her confessors. Now, with Sacy dead and Antoine in exile, she must have felt more than ever alone.

With her death in 1684, to use Sainte-Beuve's words, "Port-Royal lost the last of its noble figures [*Port-Royal perdit sa dernière grandeur*]."[16] Only one member of the Arnauld family, Marie-Angélique, remained in the convent, Marie-Charlotte having died in 1678. Twelve days later, on 10 February, Luzancy, the last of the Arnauld *solitaires*, died at Pomponne and was buried at Port-Royal as well. Of the children of Antoine and Catherine, only Henry and Antoine were still alive; and of those of Robert and Catherine Arnauld d'Andilly, Pomponne, his older brother the abbé, and the one sister remaining at Port-Royal.

Antoine Arnauld was living in Brussels when he learned of the deaths of his nephews. Sacy and he had been brought up together and had lived together at the farm attached to Port-Royal-des-Champs, serving as confessors to the nuns during difficult times. Antoine received the news "with profound grief and strange surprise." The night before he had dreamed of seeing Sacy and Angélique de Saint-Jean lying side by side in twin coffins. The prophetic nature of the dream became clearer when he learned of his niece's death several days later. Since Arnauld left France he had been in constant communication with her on various matters pertaining to the administration of the convent, and he had continued to encourage her as she at other times had encouraged him. When, in 1680, the king decided to abolish the right of election of abbesses, Arnauld reminded his niece that "the nuns must remain firm in refusing to recognize the king's nominee . . . I believe that they are obliged in good conscience not to give in to such an act of violence and to provide the world, grown used to cowardice and weakness, with an example of firm resolve."[17] His sense of loss was aggravated by the death of Luzancy, also a companion at Port-Royal, who had performed secretarial duties for him as he had done for Andilly.

During his years in exile Antoine Arnauld was compelled to move from place to place—Mons, Brussels, Liege in the Spanish Netherlands, and Utrecht and Amsterdam in the United Provinces—because he was aware that he was under observation not only from the spies of Louis XIV but from the Spanish government, the Vatican, and the Jesuits. In hiding as much as he had been in France, Arnauld nevertheless felt free to associate freely with whomever he chose and to express himself on sensitive issues as his conscience dictated.[18] He moved from place to place, he said, so as "not to do anything that might dishonor me or that might cause me to reproach myself for having preferred my own wellbeing to the truth and the interests of the Church."[19]

By the time he left France in 1679, Arnauld had become a citizen in what was then known as the Republic of Letters, in constant communication with Leibniz, Huygens, Malebranche, and other citizens. He was almost as interested in philosophy and mathematics as he was in theology. As a theologian he had emphasized the purity of belief and customs of the early Church, but as a philosopher he was on the side of the Moderns against the Ancients. Natural philosophy, he maintained, had made progress since antiquity as a result of the work of Copernicus, Huygens, Galileo, and others, and he refused to be tyrannized in this area of knowledge by the authority of the Ancients any more than in theology by the Church. Extending the distinction between the *question de droit* and the *question de fait* to the realms of grace and of nature, Arnauld continued to insist that in matters pertaining to faith one was obliged to submit to the authority of the Church (although his definition of the Church was much broader than that of the pope or of the king). In the realm of nature, however, one must rely not on the authority of others, but on one's own judgment, a position that put him at odds with the official doctrine of the Church. In order to acquire a better understanding of natural phenomena, he wrote, "we should not consider those passages [from the Scriptures] wherein natural things are spoken of in such a way as to oppose demonstrable truths. We believe that the Holy Spirit made the canonical writers speak of those things in terms of commonly-held opinion rather than in terms of the exact truth."[20] By insisting on greater freedom for the human mind in its efforts to understand natural phenomena and by drastically reducing the authority of the Church in such matters, Arnauld anticipated a theme that was to become an integral part of the eighteenth-century Enlightenment.[21]

Arnauld's preoccupation with the nature of authority in philosophical and theological matters, a preoccupation shared with his niece Angélique, who had discoursed at length on the subject in her debates with Madame de Rantzau, is not surprising considering his own experiences. His commitment "to defend the truth" made at the time of his mother's death compelled him to attack any authority that sought to compromise it. He had refused to sign the formulary because he believed that the questionable authority of the archbishop of Paris threatened to compromise Jansen's theology. Free to speak out on the issue now that the Peace of the Church had collapsed and he was more or less out of the king's reach, he complained again that the "atmosphere of domination over the faith in those things that do not pertain to faith is not likely to make the government of the Catholic Church more charitable. It is scarcely suitable to the successor of him who said: 'Non dominantes in cleris.'" To declare that one must accept a matter of fact out of respect for the authority of the Church was just as wrong as to submit to that authority in matters pertaining to the movement of the earth and the structure of the universe.[22]

In considering the proper government of the Church, Arnauld was strongly opposed to the doctrine of papal infallibility because the doctrine gave too much power to one man. "One must not suppose that the pope is the absolute master of the Church and that he has the power to command as he pleases, the bishops being nothing more than the executors of his wishes, without any right to determine what is just or unjust or what is in conformity with or contrary to Scripture and tradition in what he says."[23] Resorting to the traditional Gallican argument, so much a part of French political culture, Arnauld favored conciliar government within the Church. Only a council made up of the highest authorities of Church and state—the fifteenth-century Council of Constance being the best example of such a council—had infallible authority in matters pertaining to doctrine. He further believed that the pope had no right to assume an interim authority when no such council was

in session. Any formal pronouncement by the pope on theological issues required the endorsement of the bishop before it could be promulgated in that bishop's diocese. This, of course, had been the position of
his brother Henry Arnauld, the bishop of Angers, in regard to the
formulary and the anti-Jansenist encyclicals issued by the Vatican. At
the same time, Arnauld was sensitive to excessive pressure brought to
bear on the Church by the state. Toward the end of his life, he suggested the possibility of a French council of bishops, the function of
which would be to resist unwarranted encroachment on the rights of
the Gallican Church by either the king or the pope. Only too aware of
the deleterious effect of political interests on episcopal appointments,
Arnauld favored a return to the practice of electing bishops by cathedral
chapters. Although his views on ecclesiastical government were never
fully developed, they nevertheless reveal his dislike of absolutism in the
form of papal power or the absolutist pretensions of the crown in regard
to the Gallican Church.

From exile, *le grand Arnauld* also spoke out against abuses of authority in the temporal sphere. Like his father, uncles, and oldest brother,
he believed that the king was far more likely to govern wisely and justly
if he chose as ministers and counselors those who served his interests
without regard for their own and who for that reason were not afraid to
speak out against unwise policies. Arnauld was vehemently opposed, for
example, to Louis XIV's attempt to assert his "regalian rights" to revenues in dioceses where vacancies occurred because of the death of the
bishop. Pope Innocent XI rejected this claim, but only a handful of
French bishops sided with him. The regalian rights controversy became
acute at the time that Arnauld moved to the Spanish Netherlands, but
from Brussels he publicly attacked his sovereign for violating episcopal
rights, no doubt because of his brother Henry's position, but also because he believed that as in the case of the formulary, royal authority
had gone too far. He did so in spite of a warning he received from his
nephew Pomponne to remain silent on the issue.[24] Arnauld was also
critical of the French king's aggressive foreign policy. "Kings should
cure themselves," he wrote, "of their passion for glory and of their
foolish ambition to become conquerors."[25] Louis XIV's suspicion that
Arnauld was the head of a dangerous cabal was only heightened by
the theologian's stance on the regalian rights question. Fearful of Arnauld's pernicious influence within France, the king encouraged his

police agents to be on the lookout for Arnauld's books and pamphlets smuggled across the French border.

Le grand Arnauld's concerns were not limited to public issues. Personal needs also required his attention. Since 1643 he had lived on an income that was not always enough to support him, given his charitable inclinations, and he often spoke of being too dependent on his friends' largesse. One possible source for additional funds was his brother Henry, the bishop, who was supposed to pay him annual interest on a sum that he had received from his youngest brother in 1638, a payment that was made only irregularly. By 1673 the bishop owed Antoine 6,895 pounds, taking into account arrears in payment. Writing from Brussels in 1682, Antoine expressed regret at having to remind Henry of the debt: "What must I do? I have to live, and I have debts to pay. Is it right that I should live on the charity of others when those who owe me won't pay me? . . . The sale of our books [abroad] has helped to support us, but that source is drying up because the books are not permitted in Paris, and those books that get in are confiscated."[26]

Rather than blame his brother for his financial woes, Arnauld chose to blame his nephew the abbé Arnauld instead. The abbé acted as secretary to the bishop of Angers, and having given up most of his inheritance to support Pomponne's career, was dependent on his uncle the bishop for support. What disturbed Antoine Arnauld about his nephew was his standard of living, which, he firmly believed, cost the bishop so much that he was unable to pay his debt to Antoine. Provided with several benefices, the abbé lived "with a *valet de chambre*, two lackeys, a coach and two horses."[27] (Clearly Antoine had no more love for the abbé than Arnauld d'Andilly, his father, had.) He thought his nephew was egotistical and selfish, and entirely oblivious to the mortal dangers he risked "in contenting himself with living an honest life according to the standards of the world, without thinking of his fundamental Christian responsibilities."[28] Ten years after these words were written Antoine was still complaining of the irregular payments received from the bishop. Were the bishop to die, the abbé would be the beneficiary of his will, and there would be little chance of ever recovering the debt.[29]

Antoine Arnauld was also irritated with the abbé's brother Pomponne. Toward the end of 1683 the theologian began to give serious thought to returning to France. He felt cut off from his family and worried about the future of Port-Royal. Various possibilities presented themselves to him including taking up residence at Pomponne, a possibility that he rejected. Finally he decided, in consultation with various friends, to ask the king's permission to install himself at the monastery of Hautefontaine in eastern France, where the abbé, a staunch Jansenist, was eager to receive him. He would be allowed to continue writing on religious matters but would be willing to have his work reviewed by the prominent bishop Bossuet, though not by the official censors. Pomponne would have to seek permission from the king for his uncle to return. Much to Arnauld's annoyance, Pomponne refused, suggesting instead that the archbishop of Paris present the case for Antoine's return. In January 1684, the month in which both Sacy and Angélique de Saint-Jean died, Arnauld conceived of the idea of returning to Paris secretly, but he would not do so, he told his friends, without Pomponne's approval. Pomponne was agreeable to his uncle's return, but only on condition that he live at Pomponne and curb his activities, terms that were entirely unacceptable to Arnauld.

Antoine Arnauld was also displeased with Pomponne for not upholding the honor of the family when it came under attack. As the Jansenist controversy flared up again after the breakdown of the Peace of the Church, a number of pamphlets appeared, undoubtedly under the auspices of the Jesuits, attacking not only Port-Royal but members of the Arnauld family including the Jesuits' nemesis, old Antoine, of whom it was said that he had never really converted to Catholicism in the wake of the Saint Bartholemew's Day massacre. Antoine's children had done so only for political reasons, remaining crypto-Huguenots (that is, Jansenists) in their hearts. The occasion of these public assaults on the Arnaulds' Catholicity was the revocation of the Edict of Nantes in 1685, which led to renewed persecution of the Huguenot community. One of the few remaining Huguenot Arnaulds, the marquis d'Eucourt, grandson of Isaac Arnauld and son of his second daughter, Madeleine, about whom nothing else is known, had recently settled in England with his three sons rather than convert to Catholicism, an incident that gave rise to renewed assaults on the family's religious beliefs.[30]

To the mortification of Antoine Arnauld, Pomponne refused to ask the king's permission to defend the integrity of his grandfather Antoine against "the calumnies of the Jesuits," a responsibility Arnauld believed he ought to have undertaken as the head of the family. Taking note of

Pomponne's fear of further disgrace, Arnauld proclaimed that "even if the whole world abandoned me, I would defend with no less vigor the honor of my family."[31] Writing in 1692 to a close friend of the family, Madame de Fontpertuis, a year after Pomponne had returned to the ministry, Arnauld again took issue with his nephew's refusal to use his influence to defend the reputation of Port-Royal. "Believe me, your friend [Pomponne] has the obligation to speak out on behalf of one of the most saintly convents in Christendom. How can he allow it to be destroyed without saying a word in its defense? Is he not obliged in good conscience to tell his Majesty that it would be worthy of his bounty and justice to have this sacred house investigated by disinterested but pious persons in order to verify its orthodoxy?"[32] What particularly irritated Arnauld was the minister's apparent willingness to place his own self-interest above that of his family, Port-Royal, his God, or even his king. A faithful counselor ought never to be afraid to tell his sovereign what he might not want to hear for his own good.

Pomponne, to be sure, had never neglected his own interests, which, over the course of his life, had been buffeted about considerably. His interests, as with any *commissaire*, inevitably lay on the side of the king and not on the side of his uncle, whom the king regarded with disfavor. Were Pomponne to respond favorably to his uncle's requests, he would undoubtedly forfeit any possibility of regaining the king's favor, to the detriment of his wife and children. Brought up by his father, Arnauld d'Andilly, to be a good and faithful servant of the king, he believed that he had no choice but to deny the requests, and all the more so given various indications that he was regaining Louis's favor. The king not only let the former minister keep his pension, but he also permitted him to return to court within a year of his dismissal. "He made his obeisance to the king," wrote Madame de Sévigné to her daughter. "The press of courtiers must have seemed strange to him since he has always been either an exile, an ambassador, or a minister. It might have been easier for him not to return, but a pension of 20,000 pounds and the prospect of an abbey for one of his sons must have made it clear to him where his duty lay."[33] In 1682, the king made him a marquis, and in that year Pomponne purchased a second *seigneurie*, Chambrais, in Normandy. A few years earlier, the marquis had moved from the family house in the rue de la Verrerie (which remained in the family but became rental property) to a more fashionable residence in the Place des

Victoires. The king's generosity extended to Pomponne's three sons, two of whom received regiments and the third a lucrative abbey. In her brief account of Pomponne's life, his granddaughter, the marquise d'Ancezune, wrote that he received more honors and rewards from Louis after his fall in 1679 than he or his family had ever received before.[34]

The king's generosity toward Pomponne clearly indicated that he liked the minister whom he had dismissed and was not willing to let Pomponne suffer too much from his loss of office. His prospects brightened by his sovereign's continuing favor, Pomponne was not at all inclined toward that *mépris du monde* that would have caused him to reject the graces bestowed by the king in favor of God's grace. The improved circumstances of the former minister also had the effect of strengthening his determination to control the activities of his family. Two former *solitaires*, Sacy and Luzancy, resided with him at Pomponne, where he could keep his eye on them. When Antoine Arnauld asked him for his approval to return to France, Pomponne made it a condition of his return that he too establish his residence on his estate. Whether he was aware of it or not, Pomponne had become an instrument of the king's authority within his own family.

Pomponne accepted his dismissal from office with far greater equanimity than he had his earlier setbacks, buoyed up as he was by the king's favorable disposition toward him. Although he was at first worried about what he would do with his time, he managed to fill it by writing accounts of his embassies in Sweden and in the Netherlands, managing his estates, and looking after his children, two of whom died in the early 1680s, much to the distress of both parents. The king's largesse enabled him to live comfortably. His friends received no further complaints from him about imminent ruin or about other misfortunes. The disposition of the marquis during the 1680s was similar to that of his father, Andilly, after his disgrace at the hands of the duke of Orléans. Both men occupied themselves with their writing—Andilly with his journals and genealogies, Pomponne with his accounts of his embassies—their books, and their families and friends. Both enjoyed the freedom of living on their country estates away from court, and both, at that point in their lives, believed that their public lives were at an end. Pomponne returned to court from time to time, but he knew that the *conseil d'en haut* was dominated by Louvois and Colbert de

Croissy, both of whom had benefitted from his dismissal, and that there was little likelihood of his return. As it turned out, he was mistaken in this assumption.

In July 1691 Pomponne's rival in the *conseil d'en haut*, Louvois, died, and on the same day the king offered Pomponne his place in the ministry. "What extraordinary events have happened in the last few days," wrote Madame de Sévigné to a friend a short time later, "the death of M. de Louvois and the glorious return of M. de Pomponne."[35] Her sentiments were shared by most of the marquis's family and friends, but *le grand Arnauld* took a different view. Admitting to a friend that he, like everyone else, was surprised by the news, Arnauld went on to say that his nephew

> will find many obstacles to doing good, and it may be that he will please neither God or man. I doubt if he fully understands the obligations imposed on persons in positions such as his to make clear to the king what manifest injustices are being done to exiled or imprisoned ecclesiastics for no legitimate reason. One might excuse this by saying that [such an act] on his part would serve no purpose and that it is the responsibility of the archbishop and not ministers to speak on such matters and that the king would not appreciate a minister's giving his opinion on matters that he has not been invited to consider. However I believe that if one tried hard enough, he would find an opportunity to get the king's attention without offending him. I don't hold out much hope for this. Although many people expect wonders, they will soon be disabused of the excessively high opinion in which they hold the new minister.[36]

In the summer of 1692, Arnauld again thought it might be possible to return to France, but when the matter was brought to Pomponne's attention, the minister again insisted that his uncle would only be permitted to return home if he promised not to write on controversial subjects.[37] Frustrated by his nephew's response, the theologian again decided that the freedom that was his in exile was worth far more than a life of semi-imprisonment on his native soil. To numerous friends he wrote that he was prepared to die abroad, and to Pomponne he wrote one last letter in December 1693, expressing his pleasure at learning that the king had asked about him and confirming his undying loyalty to his sovereign.[38]

Arnauld had much better relations with Pomponne's three sons than with the marquis himself. He had seen something of them at Pomponne during the 1670s, and after he left France he followed their development. Two of his nephews, Nicolas-Simon and Antoine-Joseph, both in the military, attempted to see him during the French campaign in the Spanish Netherlands in 1691, but their uncle declined to receive them on the grounds that they might compromise themselves by such an encounter. He was much distressed upon learning that Antoine-Joseph had died of a fever at Mons, where his regiment was stationed, and wrote the young man's father a letter of condolence, knowing how devoted he and his wife were to their children.

Arnauld was especially interested in Pomponne's third son, Henri-Charles, whose godfather he was. Henri-Charles decided on a career in the Church not so much because of any particular vocation but because of the benefices he would acquire through his father's influence. Although his uncle was critical of his multiple benefices, which he himself had given up as a young man, he nevertheless took an interest in the boy's education. Through his connections in Rome, he was able to monitor a trip his nephew made to the ancient city in 1694 accompanied by a tutor believed by Arnauld to be *"fort savant et fort pieux"* (very learned and very devout). To the tutor Arnauld wrote that it was important for the young man to learn about the structure and function of the papacy as well as to master canon law. He also recommended that his great-nephew learn Italian "so that he can read the memoirs of Cardinal Bentivoglio, who was a particular friend of the bishop of Angers. There he will learn many things of interest about the court of Rome under the pontificate of Clement VIII."[39]

The bishop of Angers, Henry Arnauld, the last but one of the children of Antoine and Catherine Arnauld, died in June 1692. "The bishop of Angers is dead at the age of ninety-nine [he was actually ninety-five]," announced his younger brother to a friend several days later. "One has reason to believe that he will receive his recompense from God for a long life devoted to his diocese . . . and for never having abandoned the truth."[40] After his arrival at Angers in 1650, Henry never left his diocese, devoting his entire time to its needs. He worked hard to improve the quality of the clergy by improving the curriculum in the seminaries in his diocese, he toured its parishes on a regular basis, and he made every effort to place the regular clergy under episcopal jurisdiction. In a very real sense his activities as a bishop were an extension of the reforming activities of his older sister Angélique, and he earned the reputation of being one of the major figures in the Catholic reform movement during the latter half of the seventeenth century. Although he never returned to Port-Royal after his consecration, he always remained in touch with the community. During the crisis over the formulary, Henry made every effort, together with a handful of other bishops, to protect the Jansenist movement. His activities met with some resistance from those who opposed his reforms in the diocese. The Jesuits objected to his efforts to place the order under his control, and the King objected to his insistence on maintaining the distinction between *droit* and *fait* after the Peace of the Church.

Within the family he was a source of constant support: to Andilly, with whom he lived for many years in the rue de la Verrerie and at Pomponne; to his brother Antoine, whose guardian he became after their mother entered Port-Royal; to Simon de Pomponne, who learned much about the art of diplomacy from him; to the abbé Arnauld, ignored by his father; and to his sisters and nieces at Port-Royal, who looked to him for protection. Although a member of the community in spirit, he chose in death to remain apart from it as he had since becoming a bishop in 1650, preferring to be buried in the cathedral at Angers rather than among so many other members of the family at Port-Royal.

At the time of his brother's death Antoine Arnauld was beginning to feel the effects of his eighty years. His eyesight was failing, and he had difficulty working for any length of time. Like his sister Agnès and his niece Angélique de Saint-Jean, he thought of the advantages of death, *"le bonheur de la mort chrétienne."* Resigned to ending his life on foreign soil, he succumbed to a brief illness in August 1694. His close friend and protégé, Pasquier Quesnel, described the event in a letter to the former *solitaire* Lancelot: "I should add that he died by the grace of Jesus Christ with pen in hand, in defense of what he was called by God to undertake. It seems as though God arranged all the disputes in which he became involved so that the faithfulness with which he performed the ministry to which he had been called would shine forth even in his last days."[41] According to the terms of his will, his body was buried in Brussels but his heart at Port-Royal-des-Champs, to where it was smuggled.

Among the Arnauld family papers at the Bibliothèque de l'Arsenal is a letter to Pomponne from an admirer who had never met *le grand Arnauld* but admired his work. "His [Arnauld's] life was a perpetual struggle against worldliness, error and vice."[42] These words constitute a fitting epitaph for the theologian, who conceived of religious life in much the same way as his sister Angélique. However, for Angélique the struggle was as much against her own worldly inclinations as it was against the world itself. For this reason she was always torn between a desire to carry on the struggle in the world and a desire to withdraw from it. She had warned her brother that public disputations were in themselves manifestations of pride and that he ought to give more thought to redeeming himself than to redeeming others, but *le grand Arnauld* seemed determined to win the laurels of victory in this world as well as in the next. Though he aspired to be one of God's elect, he undoubtedly took some satisfaction in his renown within the Republic of Letters and in his place among the group designated by Charles Perreault as *"les hommes illustres qui ont paru en France pendant ce siècle"* (illustrious persons who have appeared in France during this century).[43]

With the death of Antoine Arnauld the last of the religious reformers within the family had disappeared. The remaining Arnaulds were engaged in worldly pursuits of one sort or another, with the exception of Marie-Angélique de Sainte-Thérèse at Port-Royal and Charlotte, a daughter of Pomponne, a nun at another convent. The marquis's fortunes at court continued to rise. When he had first served as minister between 1671 and 1679, he had been somewhat isolated from his colleagues, the Le Telliers and Colbert,[44] but at the time of his second appointment, the king, who did what he could to bind his ministers to him, arranged a marriage between Pomponne's youngest daughter, Catherine-Félicité, and Colbert de Torcy, the son of Colbert de Croissy, the man who had replaced Pomponne in 1679. To the dowry of 280,000 pounds provided by her parents at the time of the marriage in 1696 the king added 100,000 pounds.[45] Five years earlier he had given the marquis a pension of 60,000 pounds to help defray the military expenses of his two oldest sons.[46]

The marquis de Torcy took his father's place in the *conseil d'en haut* upon Croissy's death in 1696. He and his father-in-law worked together in the negotiations that led to the Treaty of Ryswick (1697) that put an end to the War of the League of Augsburg, begun in 1688, and they participated in the diplomatic maneuvering that took place among the European powers over the vexing question of the Spanish succession. They also shared lodgings at Versailles. In 1698, the year his unfortunate older brother, the abbé Arnauld, died, Pomponne turned eighty. Though still in good health, he would have liked to have retired, but he could not do without the rewards of office, which he needed to support his family. While with the court at Fontainebleau in September 1699, Pomponne suffered an attack of indigestion and died on the 26th of that month.

Pomponne's reputation in that world in which he had received so many honors was best summed up by the duc de Saint-Simon: "He was an excellent man with a strong sense of what is right, just and proper, who considered well what he had to do, but without being too slow. He was a modest man, of moderation, of admirable simplicity of habit and of solid and enlightened piety. One could see a gentle character and intelligence in his eyes, and in his face, wisdom and candor." This was strong praise indeed from a man who was usually critical of people whom he knew, including Madame de Pomponne, whom he deemed *"avare et obscure."* Saint-Simon's father had been a friend of the Arnauld family, who, in the memoirist's opinion, were *"illustre en science, en piété et par beaucoup d'autres endroits.* (illustrious in their erudition, their piety and in many other things).[47] This connection may help account for the duke's high regard for the minister, but others then and since have shared that view. He was a man whose fidelity to his sovereign was unshakable, according to a contemporary,[48] a man who "represents the quality of *honnêté* so prized in the seventeenth century. Since this was a kind of constant courtesy and fair conduct in relations to one's fellow men, an equable decency in the harsh commerce of this world, perhaps Pomponne carried 'honesty' as far as it could go without violating reason of state."[49] The perception of the marquis de Pomponne as a man of integrity, loyalty, and merit shows that he was much influenced by the ideals of the *commissaire* upheld by his father and grandfather. As he reviewed his own life in his memoirs, Andilly came to believe that his real misfortune was not being able to provide the king with the service he deserved, service that placed royal interests ahead of his own. He hoped that his son would succeed where he had failed. Many of those who mourned Pomponne's death believed that he had.

Although never a Jansenist in the usual sense of the term, Pomponne may be regarded as a secular Jansenist. Like his father, Arnauld d'Andilly, Pomponne believed that there should be no conflict between service to the king and service to God as long as a man was of a proper disposition. The ideal disposition of the *commissaire* was a willingness to place the king's interests above one's own in the same way that the disciples of the abbé de Saint-Cyran insisted in placing the interests of God above all else. Just as his aunt Angélique and other members of his family believed that only loyal and obedient service to God was worthy of divine favor, Pomponne believed that such service on the king's behalf merited the king's favor.

The last of Arnauld d'Andilly's children, Marie-Angélique, died a year after her brother. She was also the last Arnauld among the nuns of Port-Royal. In 1703, the nuns were once again subjected to renewed persecution. The Jansenist controversy had flared up again during the last two decades of the seventeenth century, a time of social unrest caused by famine and the adverse impact of the War of the League of Augsburg. Signature of the formulary still remained an issue, and in some dioceses, including Angers, bishops permitted a respectful silence on the *question de fait*. Eager to put an end to the quarrel over Jansenism once and for all, Louis XIV ordered all ecclesiastics, including nuns, to sign the formulary without appending any reservations. In 1703 the archbishop of Paris, Cardinal de Noailles, commanded the nuns at Port-Royal to obey the king's order, which the nuns refused to do. Louis XIV then sought permission from the new pope, Clement XI, to disperse the nuns and to close the convent. Clement agreed on condition that the aging and infirm nuns be allowed to remain in the convent until their death. Refusing to accept this condition, the king sent the *lieutenant civil*, Argenson, to Port-Royal in October 1709, exactly a hundred years after Angélique had closed the doors of the establishment to her parents. His orders were to shut down the convent, disperse the nuns, and then empty the graves. The second marquis de Pomponne was given permission to remove the bodies of his family to Pomponne, but the other nuns were placed in a common grave a short distance away. On 22 January 1710 the *conseil d'en haut*, which then included Pomponne's son-in-law, Torcy, ordered that the buildings of Port-Royal-des-Champs be destroyed.

Louis XIV's violent action against a community of women was undertaken because he had always regarded Port-Royal as a foyer of dissent and potential subversion. Now that the convent lacked the protection of prominent personages at court, the king believed that such drastic measures would undoubtedly deter deviant religious activity in the future. Ever since the Richelieu era, various high officials of church and state had viewed with deep suspicion what they regarded as an aura of heresy that hung about the valley of the Chevreuse, an aura that encouraged men and women to conduct their religious lives on their own terms, without appropriate supervision. From the king's point of view, the nuns were more often than not inclined to resist any efforts to control them. In their efforts to defend their spiritual ideals, they earned the reputation in some circles of being witches or of being "as proud as Lucifer," an expression used by the archbishop of Paris at the time of the first expulsion of nuns in 1664. Looking back at Louis XIV's willful destruction of Port-Royal-des-Champs almost three hundred years later, it seems more than an attempt on his part to destroy what he regarded as a bastion of heresy and dissent; it seems an awesome assertion of patriarchal power at the disposal of a ruler who was determined to subjugate women to the authority of men. Louis had had enough of *frondeuses* of one sort or another: the duchesse de Chevreuse, his cousin the duchesse de Longueville, Marie de Gonzague, Angélique Arnauld and her niece Angélique de Saint-Jean. By razing Port-Royal to the ground, he hoped to prevent it from becoming a shrine to those who believed that the nuns and their supporters were martyrs. How wrong he was!

Looked at in another way the destruction of Port-Royal was the inevitable result of Angélique's conviction that religious life involved a constant struggle against the world. During the crisis over the formulary during the 1660s, both she and her niece had envisioned the physical destruction of the convent. To their way of thinking such destruction would eradicate only the external trappings of their religious life. Only by compromising their ideals would the true essence of Port-Royal be destroyed.

12

The Marquis's Children:
Jansenists in Spite of Themselves

THE CHILDREN of the marquis de Pomponne came of age
at the time when Port-Royal was in decline, the *solitaires* disbanded, and
the nuns left to grow old without the possibility of recruiting new
blood. His children were not imbued with that *mépris du monde* that had
so transformed the previous generations in the family. They had been
brought up to expect the same grace and favor that the king had bestowed on their father. The ideals to which Pomponne's sons aspired
were reflected in the *mémoires* of their grandfather, Arnauld d'Andilly,
written for the purpose of impressing them with the illustrious deeds of
their male ancestors. Pampered though they were by the king's largesse at the outset of their careers, the marquis's children were later to
encounter serious obstacles created by the Jansenist movement with
which the Arnauld family had been long associated. The last generation
to bear its name had no spiritual ties to that movement, but they were
nevertheless bound to it by familial loyalty.

The lives of Pomponne's children spanned almost a century. In 1661,
the year in which the first child was born, Louis XIV was beginning his
reign. The power of the monarchy was at its peak, resistance to it
having exhausted itself by the end of the Mazarin era. In 1756, the year
in which the last of Pomponne's children died, the power of the monarchy was again under challenge, primarily from the parlements, then in
the process of developing an alternative to the ideal of absolute monar-

chy—the ideal of government under law. The Counter Reformation had long since come to an end, its energy sapped by internecine squabbles pertaining to doctrine and jurisdictional rights and by the secular trends inherent in French culture at the end of the reign of Louis XIV.

By the time the marquis's children reached middle age, Port-Royal had been razed to the ground, but the Jansenist movement continued to be a force to be reckoned with throughout the eighteenth century despite the efforts of church and state to destroy it. In its underground newspaper, *Les Nouvelles Ecclésiatiques*, Jansenist editors continued to denounce the Jesuits, but as the century progressed, they became increasingly concerned with the ideals of the Enlightenment. Yet, ironically, the historical significance of eighteenth-century Jansenism lies not so much in the movement's adherence to religious ideals as in its political alliance with the parlements, an essentially secular alliance that opposed the absolutist pretensions of the government of Louis XV. Pomponne's children were swept up in these currents, which transformed French political culture in the decades preceding the Revolution of 1789, and their lives were significantly affected by them. Scions of a family that had played an important role in the history of the seventeenth century, the marquis's offspring never came close to matching the achievements of their forebears. However, they were proud of these achievements, and they were never reluctant to defend the family's integrity in the face of continuing efforts to impugn it.

In developing family strategies after he and his wife became parents, Pomponne faced problems not unlike those encountered by his father, Arnauld d'Andilly, and grandfather Antoine. He, like them, had to provide for a burgeoning household. As we have seen, Pomponne was haunted throughout his career by the fear that he would not be able to support his many children. Between 1661 and 1679 his wife Catherine gave birth to eleven children, six of whom survived infancy. Three were born between 1661 and 1664 while Pomponne was in exile because of his connection with the fallen minister Fouquet. By the time of his first appointment as minister in 1671, Pomponne's household included six children—four boys and two girls. Writing to his cousin, the marquis de Feuquières, in Stockholm in the spring of 1674, the minister complained of the hardship caused by children. "In four or five months I will have as many as you. As of now I am scarcely in a position to support them."[1] At the time of his dismissal from the ministry in 1679, the marquis's household included eight children, a number that ap-palled Madame de Sévigné, the mother of two. By the time of his second appointment as minister in 1691 that number had been reduced to five, three boys and two girls.

Of Pomponne's three daughters who survived infancy, two, Marie-Emmanuelle, born in 1663, and Charlotte, born in 1668, became pen-sioners at Port-Royal-des-Champs after the Peace of the Church. The third, Catherine-Félicité, the future marquise de Torcy, born in 1679, was denied the benefit of an education supervised by her aunt Angélique de Saint-Jean because in that year the crown expelled the pensioners from the convent and forbade the admission of future stu-dents. Among the three generations of Arnauld women beginning with that of Angélique and Agnès, Catherine-Félicité was the only one to have no association with Port-Royal. Because Pomponne intended that she and her oldest sister, Marie-Emmanuelle, make suitable marriages, the need to provide them with adequate dowries added to his financial burdens. In 1677 Marie-Emmanuelle became engaged to the marquis de Molac, much to Pomponne's delight. Despite the dowry of two hundred thousand pounds that Pomponne agreed to provide, the mar-riage never took place because, as Madame de Sévigné suggested, Mo-lac did not wish to become associated with a family whose reputation was controversial.[2] Marie-Emmanuelle died unmarried in 1686 at the age of twenty-three.

Marie-Emmanuelle's younger sister Charlotte became a nun at the convent of Malnoue in northern France in 1693. Angélique de Saint-Jean, who remained in touch with her niece after the expulsion of the pensioners from Port-Royal in 1679, was keenly aware of her niece's religious vocation, which she attempted to nurture, albeit from afar. Whether her parents would have permitted her to leave the convent had she not had a vocation and wished to do so is not known. The prospect of providing a dowry for a third daughter would not have been particularly pleasing to her father even though Louis XIV had show-ered him with favors in the 1680s during his years out of office. In any event, Charlotte lived a long life as a nun, about which little is known other than that her parents provided Malnoue with an annual pension of five hundred pounds for the rest of her life, that she moved from Malnoue to the convent of Chelles after her father's death in 1699, and that she died in 1746 at the age of 81. As a simple nun Charlotte achieved the obscurity that her great aunt Angélique often yearned for but never attained.[3]

The marquis's youngest daughter, Catherine-Félicité, was betrothed to Colbert de Torcy as part of the arrangement by which he was returned to the ministry in 1691. In the making of these arrangements, the young woman was a pawn not only in her father's strategy to promote the interests of his family but also in the king's strategy to bind his ministers to him. Her father-in-law, Colbert de Croissy, who strongly opposed the marriage of the daughter of his former rival to his son Torcy, managed to delay the event until after his death in 1696. According to Saint-Simon, Catherine and her husband lived together in perfect harmony. Although he was better liked than she, "she had in effect a veritable power over him in heart and in mind. She was very intelligent and knew a great deal. She was independent and incapable of hiding her feelings, characteristics that conformed to the name she bore."[4] Saint-Simon's description of Madame de Torcy calls to mind the two Angéliques, both of whom were highly intelligent, well educated, and fiercely independent. They influenced the men of the family from the cloister of Port-Royal; Catherine dominated them within the household. There was, however, a major difference between Catherine-Félicité and her aunts. As abbesses the aunts were the heads of their own household whereas Catherine, regardless of her influence within her family, remained a member of her husband's household. Her life was shaped by her husband's career and by his interests.

At court, Madame de Torcy's place was determined by her husband's rank, a fact of life that made itself abundantly clear to her one evening in 1707 at Marly where the king was in residence. According to Saint-Simon, whose amusing and often malicious accounts of life at the court of Louis XIV are not always to be believed, as the company was gathering for dinner, the marquise placed herself ahead of a duchess, a mistake that she instantly became aware of and tried without success to rectify. When the king was seated, the expression on his face indicated his displeasure to all, including Catherine. He said nothing during dinner, but later in the evening he told Madame de Maintenon

> that he had been the witness of insolent and unbelievable behavior—these were the terms he used—that made him so angry that he was unable to eat anything . . . Such behavior on the part even

of a person of high rank would have been inexcusable, but coming from a little bourgeoise, daughter of Pomponne, whose family name was Arnauld, married to a Colbert, it was enough to cause him to leave the table, which he was on the point of doing at least ten times but from which he refrained out of consideration for her husband. Thereupon he ran through the genealogy of the Arnaulds, which didn't take him much time and then passed on to the Colberts, remarking on their absurd claim to be descended from a king of Scotland.[5]

Saint-Simon, who disliked Madame de Torcy in particular and the vile bourgeoisie in general, must have taken pleasure in recounting this episode. Whether Saint-Simon's account is true or not, it reflects the continuing disdain with which the old nobility viewed the nobility of the robe.

Perhaps the king's displeasure was made all the more acute by his realization that this was not the first time that the behavior of a member of the Arnauld family had given offense. If so, Saint-Simon was unaware of it, although he speculated that Torcy's career was hampered by his wife's Jansenist connections. Torcy was dismissed from office in 1715. His ties to the Arnauld family undoubtedly affected his efforts to regain a place in the ministry. There are indications that his daughter, the marquise d'Ancezune, a great favorite of Louis XV's minister Cardinal Fleury, tried to use her influence to revive her father's career, but Fleury, who succeeded during his seventeen years in office in keeping the Jansenist movement in check, was not inclined to rehabilitate the husband of an Arnauld who did not hesitate to express her Jansenist sympathies.[6] Like so many other members of her family, Catherine-Félicité lived a long life, dying in 1755 at the age of seventy-six. She outlived all but one of her siblings, Henri-Charles, who died the following year.[7]

Henri-Charles, born in the Netherlands in 1669, was the youngest of Pomponne's three sons who survived infancy. The two older boys were Nicolas-Simon, born in 1662, and Antoine-Joseph, born in 1664. Their grandfather Andilly, who had withdrawn to Pomponne in that year, supervised the education of the two, much to the delight of their father, then ambassador to Sweden. All three of the marquis's sons were tutored by their cousin Le Maistre de Sacy, among others. Madame de

Sévigné, who often visited Pomponne, was much impressed by one of the tutors, "an admirable man, who is here to teach law to the oldest son. He is a man who knows everything, *un ésprit lumineux.*"[8] In addition to the excellent education they received, the marquis's sons benefitted from the favors bestowed on their father by his grateful sovereign during the time that he was out of office. In 1683 Nicolas-Simon was awarded an infantry regiment, Antoine-Joseph a regiment of dragoons, and Henri-Charles the abbacy of Saint-Maixent-en-Poitou. When Pomponne returned to the ministry, the king gave him sixty thousand pounds to help defray the military expenses of his two older sons.[9] Eschewing the professions of their father and grandfather or a career in the law, they chose instead—or their father chose for them—more traditional occupations. Two of the young men entered the military, and the third entered the Church.

Antoine-Joseph's military career was launched during the War of the League of Augsburg. After distinguishing himself in the campaign on the Rhine, he prepared the way for the French victory at Fleurus by leading his regiment against two heavily fortified redoubts on the Sambre, an action that made it possible for the French troops to cross the river. "I am so impressed by the magnificent and brilliant action of the chevalier de Pomponne," wrote Madame de Sévigné to her daughter in July 1690. "News of the event comes from all quarters . . . In truth tears come to my eyes when I learned what the king had to say about it."[10] The young chevalier's letters to his father from the front are full of excitement at the military undertakings that he was involved in. "Since the taking of Huy, we have talked of nothing else but conquests and victories," he boasted, "and in order to uphold the honor of our arms, we will end the campaign by taking Charlesroy [sic]." Ambitious for a promotion to the rank of brigadier, and aware of a number of vacancies at that level in several brigades, Antoine-Joseph begged his father to use his influence to secure a promotion for him.[11] He won further honors at the battle of Steinkirk, but his promising career was cut short by a fever from which he died in November 1693. He was handsome, likable, and witty, according to Saint-Simon. When his parents learned of his death, "they were inconsolable, and she [the marquise] became almost a recluse, preoccupied as she was for the rest of her long life [she died in 1711] with her grief and with her piety."[12]

Nicolas-Simon, Pomponne's oldest son who inherited his title in

1699, also took up a career in the military, and during the War of the League of Augsburg campaigned in northern Italy. In September 1690 word reached Versailles that he had been killed in action, but the king learned that it was a false report and sent someone to Pomponne to inform the marquis and his wife that their son was alive and well. When Pomponne went to Versailles to thank Louis for his concern, Louis condescended to say to him that his high regard for him extended to his sons. Despite his father's (and grandfather's) high hopes for him, Nicolas-Simon's career was not noteworthy. After his marriage in 1694 to the wealthy Constance d'Harville de Palaiseau, he gave up his military career. Nicolas-Simon was sent on a brief mission to the Elector of Bavaria in 1699, and he held the office of Lieutenant-General of the Ille de France from 1677 until 1720. More important offices and commissions may have eluded him because of his reputation of being a "dull-witted, miserly, and gloomy" person "who counted for nothing even within his family for much of his life."[13] His career, like that of his brother-in-law Torcy, was not helped by the family's association with Jansenism.

The second marquis de Pomponne spent his later years cultivating his garden at Pomponne as his grandfather had done. His love of his estate is clearly expressed in his will: "My estate at Pomponne has given much pleasure to my ancestors and to present members of my family. They have among other things enlarged the park and enhanced the beauty of the gardens. I myself have made several improvements in the orangerie, in the arrangement of the fountains and in other things, and I will continue to embellish the estate as long as I live. Because I love the place so much, I want to make certain that it will not be neglected by those who will have the possession of it in the future." He went on to specify that a certain amount of the revenues of the estate, valued at 168,000 pounds in 1712, be invested in its upkeep. In this way he sought to sustain a property that had caused his father almost as much pain as pleasure in the rebuilding of it after its destruction during the Fronde and in which his grandfather had invested almost as much time and effort as he had invested in Port-Royal.

Nicolas-Simon's heir was his daughter, Catherine-Constance-Emilie, the only one of his children to survive infancy. In 1715 she was married to the comte de Cayeux, later the marquis de Gamaches. Her father provided her with a dowry of 150,000 pounds from the sale of the *seigneurie* of Chambrais. In his will Nicolas-Simon stipulated that his daughter alone was to administer the estate because he regarded his son-in-law as incompetent. When the will was drawn up in 1721, Catherine and her husband had no children. The heir to the estate was to be Pomponne's cousin, the third marquis de Feuquières, because of the close ties that had existed between the two branches of the family. In order to inherit Pomponne, Feuquières would be required to assume the name of Arnauld.

In a codicil to the will drawn up in 1726, by which time the marquise de Gamaches had given birth to two daughters, Nicolas-Simon stipulated that at his death his daughter would have the use of the estate for her lifetime but that his granddaughter, Constance-Simone-Flore-Gabrielle, born in 1725, would inherit the estate. The marquis de Pomponne also expressed the wish that his granddaughter marry a nephew by marriage, the marquis de Tresnel. If such a marriage did not take place, a family council composed of Constance-Simone's uncles, the abbé de Pomponne and the marquis de Torcy; her cousins, Torcy's two sons-in-law; the marquis de Tresnel; and one outsider, the president de Maisons, would choose his granddaughter's husband. In any case, the bridegroom would have to assume the name of Arnauld.[14]

All of Nicolas-Simon's efforts to preserve the marquisat of Pomponne, as well his family name, were in vain. After his death in 1737 at the age of seventy-four, his daughter succeeded in obtaining from the Parlement of Paris a decree breaking her father's will and having herself made the sole heir. When the daughter Constance-Simone, by this time the marquise de Gamaches, died in 1747, the estate of Pomponne was inherited by her six children, who sold the property to an outsider, Antoine Feydeau de Brou, a wealthy *financier*, for 345,000 pounds. Feydeau de Brou was related by marriage to the Ladvocat family, which in turn was linked to the Arnaulds through the marriage of Arnauld de Pomponne and Catherine Ladvocat. There may well be some truth to Saint-Simon's assertion that Nicolas-Simon Arnauld, the second and, as it turned out, the last marquis de Pomponne, counted for nothing in his family. His grandchildren, for their own reasons, did not retain the family seat, which had been so well cared for by three generations of Arnaulds and which had become by the middle of the seventeenth century the most tangible evidence of the family's worldly achievements. Nicolas-Simon's body (which had been buried in the family chapel at Pomponne), together with his father's heart and the bodies of his relatives removed from Port-Royal-des-Champs, was taken to Palaiseau, a *seigneurie* belonging to his wife's family, not far from Versailles or, for that matter, from Port-Royal-des-Champs. *Sic transit gloria mundi.*

The most prominent of the first marquis de Pomponne's three sons was the youngest, Henri-Charles, born in the year that the Peace of the Church was promulgated. He acquired the title of abbé at the age of fourteen, when the king honored him with the usufruct of the monastery of Saint-Maixent-en-Poitou in 1683. Not satisfied with the annual income he received from this benefice, he gave it up in favor of a more lucrative one that had once belonged to Cardinal Mazarin, Saint-Médard-en-Soisson, the annual income from which was thirty thousand pounds in 1693. Never particularly scrupulous in the exercise of his priestly responsibilities, Henri-Charles did not hesitate to take advantage of the material resources of the Church in a way that would have horrified his uncle *le grand Arnauld*. It was said of him that "he neglected nothing that might increase the value of his abbeys."[15]

He, and presumably his father, hoped that he would follow in his great-uncle Henry's footsteps and, after a period of time in the diplomatic service, become a bishop. Certainly he was in an excellent position to satisfy these ambitions. He had gone to Rome in 1693 to learn the intricacies of papal politics as Henry Arnauld had done fifty years earlier. Italy, of course, had been where his father, the first marquis de Pomponne, had launched his career, also under the auspices of his uncle Henry. Not only was he well-educated in Italian affairs, but he also had the advantage of having in his father and brother-in-law two persons responsible for French foreign policy. As he embarked on his career he had every reason to expect that he would eventually receive a bishopric, all the more so because previous abbés of Saint-Médard had received episcopal appointments.

In 1698 Henri-Charles was ordained and at the same time awarded the office of *aumonier* in the household of the duke of Burgundy. After a brief diplomatic mission to Italy, in 1704 the king, at Torcy's suggestion, appointed him ambassador to Venice. There he remained for six years, trying without much success to protect French interests against expanding Hapsburg influence in northern Italy during the War of the Spanish Succession. Returning to Paris in 1711 after a brief sojourn in

Florence, the abbé de Pomponne looked forward to receiving at that time the high office that he had long wished for. Although the king had nothing against him personally and had been kindly disposed to him and his immediate family in the past, he was, according to Saint-Simon, "unalterably opposed to placing someone with the name of Arnauld in a bishop's seat"[16] at a time when the Jansenist controversy was particularly acute. It was in the previous year that the king had ordered the destruction of Port-Royal, so closely identified with the abbé's family. Despite his family's long tradition of service to the crown, and his brother-in-law Torcy's patronage, Henri-Charles received nothing more than the office of *conseiller d'état de l'eglise*, a relatively insignificant sinecure.

Over the course of his long life, the abbé de Pomponne collected other honors. In 1716 he bought the chancellorship of the Order of the Holy Spirit from Torcy, which carried with it a *brevet de retinue* of three hundred thousand pounds, and in 1743 he was elected to the *Académie des Inscriptions et des Belles Lettres*.[17] He maintained a town house in Paris,[18] as well as a country estate, and an apartment at Versailles. Although he often boasted to his acquaintances of his close ties with the king, he never seems to have been more than a peripheral figure at court. In 1723 the abbé became involved in the Club de l'Entresol, a group that included Montesquieu and other well-connected men with a keen interest in politics. According to the marquis d'Argenson, one of its members, the Entresol was a "perfectly free political society, made up of men who loved to reason about what was going on and would assemble together to speak their minds openly without fear of being compromised." The club is known to have influenced the policy of the regency government of Louis XV, which explains why the king's first minister, Cardinal Fleury, decided to dissolve it in 1730.[19] Apparently he was suspicious of the free and frank discussions that occurred at club meetings. Once again the monarchy manifested its dislike of free and open groups such as the *solitaires* and the Entresol, both of which included members of the Arnauld family.

Interested as he was in the affairs of the world, the abbé de Pomponne did not share his forebears' distaste for life at court. He was never a Jansenist in any spiritual sense but was nonetheless proud of his ancestors' achievements as the "friends of truth" as well as in the king's service. Unwilling to tolerate attacks on the religious beliefs or reputa-

tion of the family, he was a Jansenist by association rather than conviction. As such he resisted the imposition of the last of the anti-Jansenist
papal encyclicals, *Unigenitus*, promulgated in 1713.

As in the case of the previous encyclicals, *Unigenitus* was issued by
Pope Clement XI in response to pressure from Louis XIV. Determined
to suppress Jansenism once and for all, the king asked the Vatican to
condemn a particularly controversial Jansenist work, *Le Nouveau testament en français avec des réflexions morales sur chaque verset* (The New
Testament in French with Moral Reflection on each verse), written by
Pasquier Quesnel, a protégé of Antoine Arnauld. The new encyclical
condemned one hundred and one propositions from Quesnel's work,
which pertained to the doctrine of efficacious grace, the governance of
the Church, unjust excommunication, and the distinction between the
questions of *droit* and *fait*. Instead of suppressing Jansenism, *Unigenitus*
reinvigorated the movement by drawing together not only Jansenists,
but bishops—including Louis Antoine de Noailles, archbishop of
Paris—who believed that the encyclical encroached on episcopal rights,
and the parlements, which believed that the encyclical was an infringement of Gallican liberties, that is to say, on the authority of the crown.
Many of those opposed to *Unigenitus* suspected the machinations of the
Jesuits, who were invariably seen by Gallicanists as instruments of the
papacy.

Not surprisingly, the abbé de Pomponne was unalterably opposed to
Unigenitus, not only because it condemned the cherished religious beliefs of so many members of his family but also because he saw it as a
violation of those Gallican liberties of which his great-grandfather Antoine Arnauld had been the ardent champion. In a number of letters to
the archbishop of Paris after the promulgation of the encyclical, the
abbé protested against the papal claim of infallibility on matters of
doctrine, asserting the traditional Gallican argument that in these matters a universal council representing the Church as a whole should be
the ultimate arbiter.[20] In 1717 several French bishops, supported by a
significant element of the clergy, including the abbé, appealed to a
future council of the Church to rule on the orthodoxy of *Unigenitus*. In
other words, the appellants refused to submit to the encyclical, thereby
defying the authority of the king as well as the pope. In joining the
ranks of the appellants, the abbé de Pomponne became part of a move-

ment, sometimes known as political Jansenism, that by the middle of the eighteenth century was to challenge the authority of both the papacy and the monarchy.[21]

As the jealous guardian of his family's reputation, the abbé sprang to its defense when a Jesuit by the name of Pichon published a book in 1745 attacking the theology of *le grand Arnauld* as blasphemous and heretical. Appealing to the *conseil d'état*, Pomponne asked for a condemnation of the book on the grounds that it was an assault on the Catholicity of his uncle. In a letter to an acquaintance written at the time, he attacked the Jesuits in terms reminiscent of both his uncle and great-grandfather. "Let these wretched Jesuits bark at the moon in their rage against the bishops who are uniting . . . in defense of true doctrine. The entire French episcopacy must attack these unfortunate clerics who preach the most pernicious doctrine."[22] To the bishop of Auxerre, who had issued a statement condemning Pichon's work, the abbé asserted that all bishops who were not courtiers would find merit in Auxerre's condemnation. He then went on to criticize the chancellor for having authorized the publication of a work that was disrespectful to religion. Although Pichon's permission to publish the tract was to be revoked, according to Pomponne, the chancellor was unwilling to take further steps to punish Pichon. "I asked him as the chief judicial officer in the kingdom to use his authority to repair the damages done to my great uncle. I pointed out to him that you [Auxerre] were the only official who had avenged the honor of such a great personage. However all I could get from him was useless moaning and groaning about Jesuit oppression and Pichon's slanderous opinions." Everyone, it seemed, was either a friend of the Jesuits or afraid of them.[23] Finally, in 1749, the *conseil d'état*, in response to Pomponne's appeal, issued a decree condemning Pichon's work. However, under pressure from the Jesuits, who argued that Pichon was only reasserting a position taken in the seventeenth century by that bastion of orthodoxy, the Sorbonne, the decree was withdrawn, much to the abbé's consternation.

The abbé de Pomponne in 1756 experienced a final humiliation on his deathbed. The new archbishop of Paris, Christophe de Beaumont, a vehement anti-Jansenist, had recently ordered that only those furnished with a *billet de confession* declaring that they accepted the authority of *Unigenitus* were entitled to receive the last rites of the Church. The curé de Saint-Roch, in whose parish the abbé resided, initially refused to administer the sacraments to the dying man, who had consistently adhered to the view that the encyclical was an unwarranted exercise of papal authority. The fact that he was an Arnauld undoubtedly strengthened the curé's opinion that the abbé should be denied the last rites. Only after the abbé's family spoke to him "*avec hauteur et mépris*" (in a haughty and disdainful manner), according to the marquis d'Argenson, did the curé reluctantly agree to permit his parishioner to partake of the sacraments before he died at the age of eighty-seven.[24]

The abbé de Pomponne was not well thought of by many of his contemporaries. He was a "feather-brain," according to Argenson, "who knew a lot but was never able to master his ideas."[25] The duc de Luynes, whose ancestor had been for a time a *solitaire* at Port-Royal, was even more critical, asserting that Pomponne had been vain and "entirely content with himself and everything he touched."[26] Luynes asserted that

> M. l'abbé was a liar and enthralled by everything he owned and everything he did. To hear him talk, his office of Chancellor of the Ordre du Saint-Esprit was the second most important in the state even though he only had the right to enter the Louvre when their Majesties were absent. He spoke of this right in a most self-satisfied manner. His apartment at Versailles was always the most convenient [*le plus commode de tout Versailles*]. For a long time his was in the second cross gallery although he would tell everyone that it was on the same level as the king's. Every honor that he had received was superior to everyone else's. His country estate at Nogent was amply furnished, he would tell you, even though it was in fact quite sparse. He never neglected anything that would increase the worth of his abbeys. In a word his imagination made him content with everything that was his, and he communicated his self-satisfaction to his friends in terms most favorable to himself but that were suspect to others.[27]

In many ways the children of the first marquis resembled the children of La Mothe-Arnauld, the first member of the Arnauld family to receive a patent of nobility as a reward for service to the crown. The ambitions of that generation were shaped by worldly concerns—the acquisition of status, influence, and property—that they had inherited from earlier generations of Arnaulds. Three generations later, the marquis's children had attained a higher social status—although not so high as to elude the contempt of the duc de Saint-Simon, in whose eyes the Arnaulds were still "vile bourgeois"—and had acquired far greater wealth than their ancestors. Their status and wealth were, in effect, the fulfillment of the ambitions of earlier generations of the family, and their own ambitions were shaped by the same worldly concerns.

The *mépris du monde* that caused Angélique and her generation in the family to reject the values of her ancestors had little influence on the children of the first marquis de Pomponne, with the possible exception of his daughter Charlotte, who spent most of her life in an obscure monastic cell. Much as they respected the ideals of the Port-Royalists in the family, they were too much enamored of their titles, offices, and possessions to repudiate them, and they honored the achievements of their father too much to withdraw from a world that had given them much and seemed to promise them even more. Finally, they were conditioned by their upbringing to aspire to the grace and favor that the world had to offer rather than the grace and favor of a higher power.

As it turned out, the hope for further advancement for Nicolas-Simon and Henri-Charles was frustrated in part, it seems, by character flaws remarked on by their contemporaries—in the case of the second marquis a dull wit, and in the case of the abbé, pomposity and pretentiousness. Neither had the respect and admiration of their peers that had contributed to the first marquis's advancement or that had enabled members of earlier generations of the family to have an influence on the affairs of state. At the same time their association with Jansenism, albeit through family ties, constituted an obstacle to satisfying the ambitions of the two men and their brother-in-law, the marquis de Torcy.

Simon de Pomponne's children became Jansenists in spite of themselves, out of respect for the ideals of Port-Royal rather than a profound religious commitment to them. In order to make their way in the world, they might have publicly repudiated Jansenism by accepting the authority of *Unigenitus*. Instead the marquise de Torcy, her daughter, and her younger brother, the abbé, all went out of their way to defend the reputation of their Jansenist ancestors in spite of any adverse effect on them. Forced to choose between obedience to church and state and the honor of their family, they chose the latter without hesitation. For the last generation of Arnaulds, it was a matter of conscience to defend their family. In so doing, they attached themselves to the Gallican, Jansenist, and parliamentary opposition to *Unigenitus* that by the middle of the eighteenth century was able to challenge not only the authority of the papacy but also the authority of the monarchy.

❧ 13

The Arnaulds in History

$\mathcal{T}$HE STORY of the Arnauld family unfolds during a momentous period of French history. When Antoine La Mothe-Arnauld moved from the Auvergne to Paris, France was being torn apart by the Wars of Religion brought about by the Reformation. In 1756, the year that the abbé de Pomponne died, France became involved in the Seven Years' War, the burden of which contributed to the destruction of the Old Regime. La Mothe-Arnauld, his sons, and his grandsons entered the king's service at a time when the monarchy, emerging from the chaos of civil war, gradually increased its authority over the kingdom. Indeed, one of his sons, Antoine Arnauld *père*, enunciated the principle of monarchical absolutism in the clearest terms possible: that the king is "sovereign in his state, holding his power from God alone" and that "there is no power on earth whatever, spiritual or temporal, which has any authority over his kingdom, to take away the sacred nature of our kings." Less than a century and a half later, as the abbé de Pomponne lay dying in the midst of the crisis over the *billets de confession*, the parlements were laying claim to a share of the king's authority, at the same time suggesting that the king was subject to the law of the land just like everyone else. At the time when the earlier generations of the family were making their way in the world, French culture was essentially religious. By the time of the abbé de Pomponne's death, French culture was rapidly becoming secularized. What one historian has called "the desacralization of the monarchy" was under way[1] by the middle of the eighteenth century, undermining the religious foundations on which that august institution had stood for centuries. The religious beliefs that permeated French culture at the time of the Counter Reformation were facing a serious challenge from the *philosophes* of the Enlightenment, who objected to the oppressive influence of the Catholic Church. La Mothe-Arnauld and the generations of the family that followed him were much affected by these changes taking place in France between the sixteenth and the eighteenth centuries, changes which the family in various ways had helped to bring about.

A crucial event in the chronicle of the Arnauld family was the *journée du guichet* (25 September 1609), the day that marked Angélique's commitment to the Counter Reformation. Although initially opposed to the reforming efforts of the young abbess of Port-Royal, her family gradually became involved in her struggles. These struggles eventually led to a major confrontation in 1664 between the nuns of Port-Royal and the archbishop of Paris. Encouraged by the intransigence of Angélique de Saint-Jean and *le grand Arnauld*, the nuns refused to obey the archbishop's order to sign the formulary without reservation. This confrontation had a significant impact on the course of French history during the two centuries preceding the Revolution of 1789.

The confrontation was inspired by that *mépris du monde* that was the very essence of Angélique Arnauld's spirituality. *Contemptus mundi* has a long history in Christian thought. Its definition is set forth in the New Testament: "Love not the world, neither the things that are in the world. If any man love the world, the love of the Father is not in him. For all that is in the world is the lust of the flesh, and the lust of the eyes, and the pride of life, is not of the Father, but is of the world" (1 John 2:15–16). This theme is at the heart of the monastic tradition, justifying a turning away from the world, but it also had a profound influence in the Christian world beyond the cloister. "Whoever reflects upon all the adversities that are to be found on earth will find no good in them. The world is naught but misery, created by God for man in order that he suffer torment and tribulation, and there undergo punishment for his sins."[2] So wrote Bono Giamboni, a Florentine judge of the thirteenth century. In the era of the Reformation the theme is evoked to inspire reform on both sides of the religious divide by instilling in the faithful the desire to root out worldly influences within the sinner in particular and the church as a whole. Particularly affected by this sentiment was Saint Theresa of Avila, who viewed the world as "filled with lies . . . In the midst of the pleasures proposed by the demon, there is naught but sorrow, problems, and contradictions."[3] It was this *contemptus mundi*, firmly rooted in the monastic tradition and in the reforming ideals of the Counter Reformation, that caused Angélique Arnauld to launch her own program of reform.

However, Angélique's attitude toward the world was also inspired by a strong sense of guilt: the guilt that she came to feel because of the way in which her father and grandfather had acquired her office of abbess in violation of canon law and especially because of her conviction that she was not worthy of the high ecclesiastic office that she had acquired through her family's influence. As a result of her conversion experience she looked upon her former self with loathing, not just because of what she had once been but of what still lurked within her. The love of the comforts of her father's house, the admiration of her relatives' fine clothes and of their status in the world, the anticipation of marriage and children, all sentiments that she had clung to during her earliest years in Port-Royal, were sentiments that would never be removed, to her way of thinking, without an infusion of God's grace, which she in no way deserved.

The *mépris du monde* embraced by members of the Arnauld family also reflected a disillusionment with public life and a desire to enjoy the pleasures of private life and to cultivate the self. The urge for self-fulfillment, whether in undertaking penitential exercises in solitude or in engaging in philosophical and literary discussions among persons of similar dispositions, constitutes what has come to be known as individualism. A preoccupation with the self at the expense of the *res publica* was very much in evidence in France from the latter half of the sixteenth century to the end of the seventeenth century.[4] Robert Arnauld d'Andilly, his brother Henry, the bishop of Angers, and his son Simon enjoyed the blessings of private life in their homes and as members of the Rambouillet circle, where they sought refuge from the turmoils of public life. The competition for the favor of persons in high places, the lack of material resources with which to obtain favors and preferments, and the distasteful atmosphere at court were all factors that shaped the view shared by Robert Arnauld d'Andilly, Antoine Le Maistre, and others in the family that they lived in a particularly corrupt age, a view that caused them to become *solitaires*.

In response to their contempt for the world, the Arnaulds withdrew from it in various ways. Angélique the Reformer tried to isolate herself and her nuns from outside influences, including her unregenerate family. Antoine Le Maistre renounced his promising career in the Parlement of Paris for a life of prayer and solitude, a life that he shared with his brothers and others who took up residence at Port-Royal-des-Champs. Arnauld d'Andilly also withdrew to Port-Royal as an act of penance, after making arrangements for his son Simon's career. So too did his youngest brother, Antoine, after having resigned several lucrative benefices and having donated a good part of his inheritance to Port-Royal.

Withdrawal from the world proved to be as hard to achieve for the Arnaulds as it was and is for all who seek to cut themselves off entirely from it. From the time of her conversion, Angélique had been torn between her public responsibilities as an abbess and her personal religious commitments or, as she preferred to look at it, a perpetual struggle against the dominant traits of her character, pride and ambition. Her niece, Angélique de Saint-Jean, a member of a monastic community for almost her entire life, still managed to remain in close contact with the world beyond the walls of Port-Royal through her continuing contacts with her father, uncle, and brothers, to say nothing of the archbishop of Paris. Antoine Le Maistre and his *solitaire* brothers were perhaps the most successful in cutting themselves off from the world, but Le Maistre, like his aunt Angélique, struggled with his pride, refusing at first to submit to his brother Sacy's spiritual direction. He was always inclined to the heroic gesture, which the abbé de Saint-Cyran and others tried to repress. Although associated with the *solitaires*, Arnauld d'Andilly and his youngest brother, Antoine, never became one of them, suspended as they both were between the way of the world and the life of the spirit. Continued involvement in the world in one way or another made the Arnaulds all the more vulnerable to the assaults of their enemies.

Their enemies, which included not only the Jesuits but prominent officials of church and state, were among other things suspicious of an attitude of independence that marked the character of so many Arnaulds. That attitude was displayed by Angélique in the confrontation with her family on the *journée du guichet*, in her dealings with the Cistercian order, with the bishop of Langres, and with the many confessors who did not meet with her approval. That same attitude was evident in Antoine Le Maistre's decision to renounce his career not for the purpose of entering the clergy or joining a religious order but in order to conduct his life on his own terms. Arnauld d'Andilly, who admired his father's ability to be his own man, managed with some success to define the terms of his existence. Neither entirely a *solitaire* nor entirely a courtier, he was able to remain in touch with the Port-Royal community and with the court.

The Arnaulds' desire to define the terms of their existence was influenced by a spirituality that contained within it a strong sense of personal responsibility in the conduct of religious life, perhaps a vestigial remnant of the Protestantism to which their ancestors adhered. The responsible Christian, to both the Huguenot and Jansenist way of thinking, having made his or her commitment to God's purpose was compelled by conscience to defend that commitment against corrupting worldly influences within and outside of the self. This emphasis on maintaining the integrity of the self inherent in the Augustinian strain of piety is the most important similarity between Protestantism and Calvinism. Both contributed significantly to that individualism inherent in seventeenth-century culture.[5]

After 1640, the Arnaulds became involved in the Jansenist controversy, brought on by serious theological differences that divided the Catholic Church within itself almost as intensely as those dividing Catholicism from Protestantism. The efforts of both church and state to suppress Jansenism succeeded only in aggravating the controversy. The Arnauld family's attempt to defend its religious beliefs was not just in response to the arrest and imprisonment of the abbé de Saint-Cyran or the assault on the *Augustinus* of Bishop Jansen; the struggle was itself an integral part of their religious beliefs as well as a manifestation of their *mépris du monde*. Religious life, according to Angélique, consisted of a perpetual conflict between God's elect and the forces of evil. A significant indication that one was of the elect, in her opinion, was a willingness on the part of the Christian to suffer persecution at the hands of God's enemies. While the Arnaulds, along with other Jansenists, agreed that suffering and persecution was efficacious, there was some disagreement among them as to how and to what extent one should engage in the struggle. Some, most notably the Le Maistre brothers and the other *solitaires*, were inclined to suffer persecution in silence without engaging in polemics or other acts of defiance. Even so, Antoine's legal sensibilities were so offended by the papal encyclical *Ad sacram* that he was unable to prevent himself from writing a pamphlet, albeit anonymously, attacking the encyclical on the grounds that it violated Gallican liberties, so dear to parliamentary circles. Angélique was torn between her intense desire to suffer persecution without complaint and an equally intense desire to speak out in defense of the truth, as she understood it. She continually wavered between the two courses of action, sometimes rebuking her brother Antoine's defiant polemicizing, sometimes encouraging him to speak out on behalf of the ideals they both shared.

The two most defiant members of the family, *le grand Arnauld* and Angélique de Saint-Jean, had no compunctions whatsoever about engaging in public debate. Each encouraged the other to resist to the utmost any attempt to compromise the religious ideals so dear to the abbé de Saint-Cyran and the community of Port-Royal. Their *mépris du monde* as they construed it inspired them to combat the forces of evil in the world. In defense of these ideals, each displayed that attitude of independence so characteristic of the Arnaulds: Angélique de Saint-Jean by creating a religious life entirely enclosed within the self, detached from the external trappings of the mass, and Antoine by going into exile voluntarily in order to be free to speak his mind, unhampered by the authority of the king or, for that matter, his nephew Pomponne.

Two members of the family who were more inclined to seek accommodation with their adversaries than to suffer in silence or to quarrel publicly were Arnauld d'Andilly and his brother the bishop of Angers. Both were involved in the public arena in a different way than were the nuns and *solitaires*. Andilly made every effort to persuade Mazarin and others that the religious ideals of the family posed no danger to church or state, proclaiming his undying loyalty to the crown whenever the occasion arose. He also tried to persuade his youngest brother to be less intransigent by accepting the compromise on the formulary worked out by his friend, the bishop of Comminges. Not only did he fear that a continuation of the controversy would destroy his son's career, but he also believed that if the quarrel continued, Port-Royal, sacred as it was to his family, would be destroyed. Henry Arnauld shared this concern.

At the same time he believed that the intransigence of Antoine and the nuns undermined episcopal authority. Nevertheless, when confronted with the choice of submitting to the wishes of king and pope on the matter of the formulary and remaining loyal to the Port-Royal community, neither of them hesitated to decide in favor of what had become for them a family shrine.

Loyalty to family was of paramount importance to the Arnaulds. To be sure, Angélique appeared to break with her parents and oldest brother on the occasion of the *journée du guichet,* but once having made clear to them what her intentions were, she did everything in her power to make them and other relatives adopt her *mépris du monde,* thereby drawing them into her struggle against a sinful world. The reformation of the Arnauld family was undertaken as much because she needed her family's support—both financial and psychological—as she engaged in her reforming activities within and beyond Port-Royal as it was because of her concern for their immortal souls. Later on in her life she came to believe that her family had been chosen by God to defend his truth, a belief that was shared by her niece. To Angélique de Saint-Jean's way of thinking, the Arnaulds were engaged in a sacred cause that immunized them from the dishonorable treatment that they were subjected to at the hands of corrupt officials. Although she was able to achieve an extraordinary degree of spiritual self-sufficiency during the time of her incarceration in the convent of the Visitandines, she was nevertheless as dependent on her family for support and encouragement as her aunt had been. While with the Visitandines, she longed for news of her aged father, whose deteriorating physical condition worried her, and when she was made aware of the false rumor that her aunt Agnès had signed the formulary, her own resolve to resist the archbishop's command almost broke. And in spite of her disapproval of her brother Simon's successful career, her feelings toward him and his family were always affectionate.

Bonds of loyalty and affection sustained the relationship between the exiled Antoine Arnauld and his family in France. He kept in touch with Angélique de Saint-Jean at Port-Royal, and he followed from afar the progress of his great-nephews, Nicolas-Simon, Antoine-Joseph and Henri-Charles. To be sure, he disapproved of his nephew the abbé Arnauld, whose selfishness and greed prevented him from fulfilling his financial obligations to his uncle. He was also critical of the abbé's brother Simon, the marquis de Pomponne, for imposing unacceptable conditions on Arnauld's return to France. What Arnauld found inexcusable in his nephew's behavior was his refusal to defend the honor and reputation of his family when it again came under attack during the flare-up of the Jansenist controversy at the end of the seventeenth century. If Pomponne was unwilling to speak up in defense of his family because of the potential effect on his career and on the well-being of his own children, his son Henri-Charles, the abbé, whose own career had suffered because of family connections, was only too eager to do so a half a century later when *le grand Arnauld's* reputation was called into question by the Jesuit Pichon. Yet the marquis de Pomponne's family loyalty was not so weak as to prevent him from using his influence to obtain Sacy's release from the Bastille in 1669 and provide shelter for him and other refugees from Port-Royal on his estate. Nor did he hesitate to enroll two of his daughters as pensioners at Port-Royal during the Peace of the Church without regard to the effect that their association with such a controversial establishment might have on his own reputation.

Family ties notwithstanding, there were serious differences of opinion among the Arnaulds as to possible strategies to adopt in the face of persecution. These differences came to the fore during the crisis over the formulary in the 1660s. Those who were most defiant of the authority of the archbishop and the king were the nuns, led by Agnès and Angélique de Saint-Jean. Behind the walls of their convent they were able to achieve a degree of isolation that was greater than that which most of their male relatives were capable of achieving. There they were able to sustain their *mépris du monde*, so much a part of the monastic tradition. "It is certain," wrote the first Angélique, "that attachment to creatures is the greatest obstacle to our spiritual well-being. We must attach ourselves to God alone. When we distance ourselves from creatures, we approach God."[6] But even the cloister did not prevent Angélique or her niece, Angélique de Saint-Jean, from engaging with the world. Angélique, as we have seen, was torn between her desire to suffer persecution in silence and her inclination to lash out at her enemies, between the monastic ideal and her reforming zeal, between her reformed self and unregenerate self, and her public responsibilities as abbess of Port-Royal and her private needs. Only in the last few days of her life did she succeed in achieving that isolation that she always yearned after. Angélique de Saint-Jean, by contrast, was never reluctant to combat the world in defense of the religious ideals of Port-Royal. If she seemed sometimes to violate the monastic principle of isolation, she did so by invoking other ideals that were part of the monastic tradition.

Submission and obedience, attributes historically associated with monasticism—and with women—enabled Angélique de Saint-Jean and other nuns of Port-Royal, ironically enough, to defy the archbishop of Paris and other authorities because they were able to assert that they owed submission and obedience only to God and to those ecclesiastic officials who, they believed, were clearly acting in God's name. Indeed, the split between the nuns of Port-Royal who eventually agreed to sign the formulary and those who did not was caused by a fundamental disagreement over what was required of them in the way of obedience and submission. Those—the majority—who obeyed Archbishop Péréfixe did so in obedience to his authority. Those who defied that authority did so in obedience to what they believed was a higher authority. Those nuns who defied that authority did so also because they were defending their integrity as women. Women in this period were more inclined than men to define their identity and self-respect in terms of their religious beliefs. In this sense the attitude of Angélique de Saint-Jean and her sister nuns was similar to that of her cousin Anne Arnauld, the marquise de Feuquières who, in the face of considerable pressure from her husband to convert to Catholicism, was adamant in her adherence to her Huguenot convictions. In both instances, the women felt compelled by the dictates of conscience to defend themselves against the demands of a patriarchal society. In response to those dictates, Angélique de Saint-Jean, two of her sisters, her aunt Agnès, and a handful of nuns refused to submit to Archbishop Péréfixe's demand in the summer of 1664 that they sign the formulary drawn up by the king's council. Committed though they were to a life of solitude and prayer, they were drawn into the public arena, in which their act of defiance had a lasting effect.

The men of the Arnauld family, including Antoine, the theologian, remained in the public arena for other reasons. The pursuit of honor and pride of place that had fired the ambition of their ancestors was never entirely rooted out of their psyches by the *mépris du monde* that they had adopted largely under the influence of their female relatives.

Andilly's ambition for his son was at least as great as it once had been for himself. Henry, tied though he was to his diocese at Angers, remained in touch with affairs at court; and Antoine was sensitive to the prevailing political winds as well as to his growing reputation as one of the more illustrious men of letters of his time. Even the *solitaire* Sacy, incarcerated in the Bastille for his refusal to sign the formulary, was not so insensitive to political realities in 1669 as to refrain from putting pressure on Angélique de Saint-Jean and the other intransigent nuns to accept the conditions of the Peace of the Church. He and Antoine, who had been steadfast in support of Angélique's position until the terms of the Peace were being drawn up, used their considerable influence on her to accept these terms. However, Antoine was prepared in his own way to carry out the struggle in which his family had become engaged, prompted by his mother's dying wish that he defend the truth and his combative nature. Never willing to isolate himself from the world, he expressed his *mépris du monde* in the form of verbal assaults against the laxist ethics of the Jesuits and, more important, what he perceived to be unjust authority within the church.

The real significance of the struggle against a sinful world in which Angélique the elder engaged her family was the defiant attitude toward authority that belies the view that they were the innocent victims of oppression. For Angélique, the essence of religious life was conflict, through which God tested the religious commitment of the individual, a conviction on her part that shaped the *mépris du monde* that she and other members of her family espoused. In the confrontation that took place on the *journée du guichet*, the abbess challenged her parents' authority by insisting on her right to reform her convent against their wishes. Her niece and namesake defied the authority of the archbishop of Paris by insisting on her right to sign the formulary on her own terms. Antoine Arnauld defended that right in various treatises, at the same time deploring what he perceived to be "the heresy of domination" inherent in the papacy's claim to establish Catholic doctrine without the advice and consent of other authorities within the Church. As the most influential Jansenist spokesman after the death of the abbé de Saint-Cyran, *le grand Arnauld* denounced the several anti-Jansenist encyclicals issued by the Vatican as a manifestation of despotic tendencies within the ecclesiastical hierarchy, a charge that had a definite appeal to Gallican sensibilities. And by insisting on the distinction between *droit* and *fait* in the quarrel over the formulary, Arnauld sought to limit the authority of the Church to the realm of faith, thereby anticipating a major theme inherent in the Enlightenment.

The struggle in which the Arnaulds and other Jansenists engaged during the seventeenth century was essentially religious in nature—a struggle for the heart and soul of the Church. Yet the *mépris du monde* adopted by some members of the family affected their political ideals as well. In a certain sense, it reinforced the ideals of the *commissaire* cherished by Isaac Arnauld, *intendant des finances* under Henry IV and Louis XIII, the first member of his family to express himself on the subject in public. *Mépris du monde*, as Isaac Arnauld understood the term, was as much a justification of his worldly achievements and those of his family as it was a justification of his faith. If one were called upon by God to serve the king, one should do so with a Christian motivation and work hard to advance the king's interests and not one's own. These ideals were shared by Isaac's nephew and protégé, Andilly, who throughout his political career extolled loyal and disinterested service to the crown as opposed to the self-serving activities so common among the courtiers of his time. As a disciple of the abbé de Saint-Cyran, who emphasized the necessity of a penitential attitude based on love of God rather than love of self, Andilly had little difficulty in adapting the concept to justify the *commissaire's* love of the king as the basis of his service rather than self-interest. It had been the politics of self-interest engaged in by others, he believed, that had thwarted his own ambitions. However, he managed to instill in his son Arnauld de Pomponne that secularized version of *mépris du monde* that he had developed within himself. Pomponne's successful career was based on his reputation for piety, probity, and devotion to his sovereign's interests. Family members such as Isaac, Andilly, and Pomponne, and others like them, inspired by these political ideals, contributed much to the increase in monarchical power in France.

In the final analysis, however, the *mépris du monde* of the Arnaulds, which caused them to resist what they regarded as the excessive authority of popes and bishops, inevitably brought them into conflict with the crown itself. Even before the confrontation over the formulary, Andilly, critical of policies of the king's government and of the influence of favorites in that government, became ever so discreetly involved in the Fronde to the extent of publishing two *Mazarinades*. When at last he realized that Mazarin had regained his position of first minister, he did what he could to ingratiate himself with the cardinal. The crisis over the formulary was initiated by Louis XIV's decision in 1661 to circulate the document among the French clergy for the purpose of securing the obedience of each of its members, male and female. To the extent that the Arnaulds and others resisted signature, they were acting in disobedience of the king as well as the pope. Critical though they were of certain policies of the crown, Andilly, Angélique de Saint-Jean, Antoine Arnauld, and others never questioned the form of the French government itself. In no way were they involved in developing an ideology of opposition to absolutism.

Such an ideology began to emerge during the eighteenth century in the quarrel instigated by the encyclical *Unigenitus*, so offensive to significant elements within the clergy and the magistracy either because it offended the religious ideals of intransigent Jansenists or the Gallican prejudices of the sovereign courts. That quarrel extended beyond the Church to the body politic as the Parlement of Paris began to challenge the crown's anti-Jansenist policies. It came to a head in the decade of the 1750s when the archbishop of Paris, Christophe de Beaumont, ordered his clergy to obtain *billets de confession* from parishioners indicating that they had submitted to the authority of *Unigenitus*. The Parlement of Paris condemned Beaumont's action on the grounds that it violated Gallican liberties. When Louis XV rebuked the Parlement for interfering in a matter beyond its jurisdiction, the Parlement responded that as the sovereign court of the land it was the guardian of the fundamental laws of the kingdom, to which the king owed obedience as well as his subjects. By asserting the principle that the king's government was under law instead of the source of law, the Parlement appeared to be supporting a doctrine in opposition to absolutism, a doctrine subscribed to by a formidable coalition of Jansenists, Gallicans, and a significant element within the magistracy.

Among those who enrolled in that opposition were the remaining offspring of the first marquis de Pomponne, chief among whom was the abbé de Pomponne, drawn to the movement out of family loyalty rather than any spiritual affinity to Jansenism. However, the heroes of the Jansenist resistance of the seventeenth century, including members of the Arnauld family long since dead, inspired that opposition through the publication during the first half of the eighteenth century of the various memoirs, *relations*, and necrologies associated with Port-Royal. Many of these had been written or edited by Angélique de Saint-Jean for the purpose of educating future generations of nuns in the ideals of the first Angélique and her associates within the Port-Royal community.

The archives of Port-Royal, including those memoirs and necrologies, were miraculously saved from destruction by the *lieutenant de police*, Argenson, whom Louis XIV had ordered to destroy Port-Royal. Having seized the archives, Argenson, who respected the nuns of Port-Royal, gave them to a Jansenist sympathizer, Françoise-Marguerite de Joncoux. As guardian of the collection, she made it available to other sympathizers for the purpose of sustaining the memory of the Port-Royal community.[7] Despite the fact that many of these documents were intended for the nuns only, they were published during the first half of the eighteenth century not only to sustain the memory of Port-Royal but to encourage opposition to the anti-Jansenist policies of Louis XV and his ministers. Some manuscripts, including the *Relation de captivité* (1711) of Angélique de Saint-Jean, were published immediately after the destruction of Port-Royal in 1710, when Louis XIV was still alive. After the promulgation of *Unigenitus* in 1715, virtually all of the memoirs drawn up by Angélique de Saint-Jean began to appear in print: the *Nécrologe de l'Abbaye de Notre-Dame de Port-Royal des Champs* (1723), the *Mémoires pour servir à l'histoire de Port-Royal* (1734–1737), the *Mémoires pour servir à l'histoire de Port-Royal et à la vie de la Réverande Mère Angélique Arnauld de Sainte-Madeleine, réformatrice de ce monastère* (1742), *Lettres de la Réverande Mère Angélique Arnauld, abbesse et réformatrice de Port-Royal* (1742–1744), and *Réflexions de la Mère Angélique de Saint-Jean pour préparer ses soeurs à la persécution* (1737). The Arnauld family dominates the pages of these works.

The memory of Port-Royal's heroic resistance to oppression in the seventeenth century that so inspired the eighteenth century was shaped by the most intransigent member of the Arnauld family, Angélique de Saint-Jean, through the mythography that she created. After the confrontation with the archbishop of Paris in 1664, she had opposed the attempts to reach a compromise that led to the Peace of the Church in 1669, only reluctantly giving in to the appeals of her uncle Antoine and her cousin Sacy, who thought the Peace was necessary to secure the future of Port-Royal. Now after the destruction of the convent, her chronicles evoked her spirit of resistance. These writings also linked the nuns' heroic struggle against oppression at a time when Louis XIV was at the height of his power with the burgeoning opposition to monarchical absolutism during the reign of Louis XV.

Angélique de Saint-Jean's mythographic presentations focused on that *mépris du monde* that had motivated the Arnaulds and other Jansenists, innocent victims of persecution as they were made to seem, to resist the onslaughts of the forces of evil. Now, in response to *Unigenitus*, they were incorporated in a universal myth by a group of Jansenist theologians including Jacques-Joseph Duguet, a protégé of Antoine Arnauld. Duguet and his associates came to regard resistance to the encyclical as part of a continuing battle, prefigured in scripture, between the upholders of the truth and those who attempted to undermine it—a battle that manifested itself in the struggles between Essau and Jacob, Saint Augustine and Pelagius, Jansenists and Jesuits, and Port-Royal and its enemies. During the quarrel over the *billets de confession*, the conflict between the crown and parlement was interpreted by some Jansenists in light of that titanic struggle. Some of these Jansenists, closely associated with the magistracy, began to focus their attention on the illegal if not tyrannical actions of the king instead of the Church hierarchy.[8]

The dramatic struggle of the Port-Royal community against the tyranny of church and state, sustained in memory by the recently published memoirs, necrologies, and correspondence of the nuns of Port-Royal, was the ultimate consequence of Angélique Arnauld's conception of religious life. That struggle resulted, as she foresaw, in the destruction of Port-Royal. The cry of tyranny, first used by Arnauld in defense of his and his family's religious ideals against the illegal and unjust measures taken by the Catholic hierarchy, was raised by the Jansenist-Gallican opposition a century later against the very monarchy that Arnauld's ancestors had once served so well. Snatched from oblivion by the enemies of *Unigenitus*, the Arnaulds, whose destiny was transformed by Angélique's conversion and by the myth of Port-Royal to which Angélique de Saint-Jean contributed so much, rode into battle once again, phantom warriors, to avenge the destruction of Port-Royal-des-Champs as part of a campaign that less than a hundred years after its destruction would bring down the Old Regime.

Notes

Bibliography

Index

Notes

1. Introduction

1. There is no adequate English translation for *mépris du monde*. I have used the French phrase throughout the text.

2. See Catherine Maire, "Port-Royal: La fracture janséniste," in *Les Frances*, ed. Pierre Nora (Paris: Gallimard, 1989) pp. 471–529; *Jansénisme et Révolution*, ed. Catherine Maire (Paris, Chroniques de Port-Royal, 1990); Dale K. Van Kley, *The Damiens Affair and the Unraveling of the Ancien Regime* (Princeton: Princeton University Press, 1984); Dale K. Van Kley, *The Religious Origins of the French Revolution* (New Haven: Yale University Press, 1996); Dale K. Van Kley, "Church, State and the Ideological Origins of the French Revolution," *Journal of Modern History* 51 (1979): 629–666.

3. Marc Fumaroli, *L'Age de l'éloquence: Rhétorique et "res literaria" de l'époque classique* (Geneva: Droz, 1980); Lucien Goldmann, *Le Dieu caché* (Paris: Gallimard, 1959).

4. See F. Ellen Weaver, *The Evolution of the Reform of Port-Royal: From the Rule of Citeaux to Jansenism* (Paris: Beauchesne, 1978) 123–132.

2. The Early Generations

1. *Mémoires de Messire Robert Arnauld d'Andilly*, ed. C.-R. Petitot, *Collection des mémoires relatifs à l'histoire de France* (Paris: Foucault, 1824), vols. 23, 24; Pierre Guilbert, *Mémoires historiques et chronologiques sur l'Abbaye de Port-Royal des Champs* (Utrecht, 1759), 2 vols.

2. Bibliothèque Nationale (BN), Pièces Originales, vol. 100; Dossiers Bleus, vol. 32; Nouveau d'Hozier, vol. 12; Cabinet d'Hozier, vol. 14. These genealogical records contain much valuable information on noble families in early modern France.

3. Régis de Chantelauze, *Histoire des Ducs de Bourbon et des Comtes de Forez* (Paris: Champion, 1868), vol. 3, pp. 249–252.

4. BN Cabinet d'Hozier, vol. 14.

5. See George Huppert, *Les Bourgeois Gentilshommes* (Chicago: University of Chicago Press, 1977). Francois Bluche calls this social group *bourgeois de robe*. Bluche, "L'Origine social des secretaires d'état de Louis XIV 1642–1715," *XVIIe siècle* 14 (1960): 8–22.

6. BN *Fonch Français* (ff) 33004.

7. *Mémoires d'Andilly*, vol. 23, p. 383.

8. L. Delavaud, *Le Marquis de Pomponne* (Paris: Plon, 1911), p. 236; BN Cabinet d'Hozier, vol. 14.

9. Barbara B. Diefendorf, *Beneath the Cross: Catholics and Huguenots in Sixteenth-Century Paris* (New York: Oxford University Press, 1991), pp. 52, 55.

10. For information on La-Mothe Arnauld's children, see the genealogical records in the Salle des Manuscrits at the Bibliothèque Nationale cited above; *Mémoires d'Andilly*, vol. 23, pp. 305–358; Eugène and Emile Haag, *La France protestante, ou vies des Protestants français* (Paris: Slatkine Reprints, 1966), vol. 1; Louis Cognet, *La Réforme de Port-Royal 1591–1618* (Paris: Flammarion, 1950), pp. 251–260; Jacques Pannier, *L'Eglise réformée de Paris sous Louis XIII* (Paris: Champion, 1922), pp. 246–322.

11. Tallement des Réaux, *Historiettes*, ed. Antoine Adam (Paris: Gallimard, 1967), vol. 1, p. 508. Tallement des Réaux, a Huguenot, knew the Arnauld family both through the Huguenot community in Paris and the salon of the marquise de Rambouillet.

12. Dossiers Bleus, vol. 32.

13. Diefendorf, *Beneath the Cross*, p. 117.

14. *Lettres inédites des Feuquières tirées des papiers de la famille de la duchesse de Descazes*, ed. E. Gallois (Paris: Champion, 1846), vol. 1, pp. 141–142.

15. Ibid., pp. 32–33.

16. Ibid., p. 142.

17. BN ms. fr. 3773.

18. *Mémoires et relations sur ce qui s'est passé à Port-Royal des Champs depuis le commencement de la réforme de cette abbaye* (s.l., 1714), p. 125. Hereafter referred to as *Mémoires de Port-Royal*.

19. *Mémoires d'Andilly*, vol. 23, pp. 324–325.

20. Tallement des Réaux, *Historiettes*, vol. 1, p. 508.

21. *Mémoires d'Andilly* vol. 23, p. 305; BN Cabinet d'Hozier, vol. 14.

22. Pierre Guilbert, *Mémoires historiques et chronologiques sur l'abbaye de Port-Royal des Champs*, vol. 1, p. 270.

23. Fumaroli, *L'Age de l'eloquence: Rhétorique et "res literaria" de la Renaissance au seuil de l'époque classique* (Geneva: Droz, 1980), p. 44.

24. Robert Arnauld d'Andilly's account of his father's career is to be found in *Mémoires d'Andilly*, vol. 23, pp. 308–320.

25. Pierre de l'Estoile, *Journal de Pierre de l'Estoile* (Paris: Gallimard, 1948), vol. 6, p. 204.

26. *Mémoires d'Andilly*, vol. 23, p. 320.

27. Quoted in C.-A. Sainte-Beuve, *Port-Royal*, ed. Maxime Leroy (Paris: Gallimard, 1961), vol. 1, p. 141.

28. Bibliothèque de l'Arsenal, Arnauld Family Papers, 6034.

29. Quoted in J. Michael Hayden, *France and the Estates General of 1614* (Cambridge: Cambridge University Press, 1974), p. 131. See also Jeffrey K. Sawyer, *Printed Poison: Pamphlet Propaganda, Faction Politics, and the Public Sphere in Early Seventeenth-Century France* (Berkeley: University of California Press, 1990), p. 115.

30. Pierre de l'Estoile, *Journal*, vol. 1, p. 21.

31. For genealogical and biographical information on Simon Marion see BN Dossiers Bleus, vol. 429.

32. Guilbert, *Mémoires historiques*, vol. 2.

33. William Ritchey Newton, "Port-Royal and Jansenism: Social Experience, Group Formation and Religious Attitudes in Seventeenth-Century France" (Ph.D. diss., University of Michigan, 1974), vol. 2, p. 238.

34. *Mémoires d'Andilly*, vol. 23, pp. 308–309.

35. Tallement des Réaux, *Historiettes*, vol. 1, p. 505.

36. Pierre de l'Estoile, *Journal*, vol. 6, p. 217.

37. *Mémoires d'Andilly*, vol. 23, p. 323.

38. Pierre de l'Estoile, *Journal*, vol. 7, p. 26.

39. *Mémoires d'Andilly*, vol. 23, pp. 323–324.

40. Pierre de l'Estoile, *Journal*, vol. 8, pp. 79–80, 125–126.

41. *Mémoires d'Andilly*, vol. 1, pp. 322–323; see also Françoise Bayard, *Le Monde des financiers au XVIIe siècle* (Paris: Fayard, 1988), p. 409.

42. Tallement des Réaux, *Historiettes*, vol. 1, p. 507. See also Bibliothèque de l'Arsenal, Arnauld Family Papers, 6034.

43. For a discussion of the distinction between *officiers* and *commissaires*, see Daniel Dessert, *Fouquet* (Paris: Fayard, 1987), pp. 36–40.

44. Isaac Arnauld, *Mépris du monde; résolutions vertueuse de l'obéissance deue au roy; méditations sur la vieillesse* (Paris: n.p., 1618).

45. *Journal inédit d'Arnauld d'Andilly 1614–1620*, ed. Achille Halphen (Paris: Techener, 1857), pp. 62, 68. See also Hayden, *France and the Estates General of 1614*.

46. Jean-Paul Charmeil, *Les Trésoriers de France à l'époque de la Fronde* (Paris: Picard, 1964), p. 91.

47. BN Cinq Cents, Colbert ms. 81.

48. BN Dossiers Bleus, vol. 32; Pièces Originales, vol. 100 and 4o fm 21108, 26112, 26116.

49. Isaac Arnauld, *Mépris du monde*.

3. Angélique the Reformer

1. The early career of Angélique Arnauld (1591–1626) is described in detail in two books written by Louis Cognet, *La Reforme de Port-Royal 1591–1618* (Paris: Flammarion, 1950) and *La Mere Angélique et Saint François de Sales* (Paris: Flammarion, 1951).

2. BN ms. fr. 13893. "Relation de Catherine de Ste Félicité sur la vie de Madame Arnauld." See also *Mémoires pour servir à l'histoire de Port-Royal et à la vie de la Réverande Mère Angélique de Sainte-Madeleine Arnauld, réformatrice de ce monastère* (Utrecht, 1742), vol. 1, pp. 281–283, hereafter referred to as *Mémoires de Utrecht*. These memoirs constitute one of the basic sources for the history of Port-Royal.

3. BN ms. fr. 17795.

4. Elizabeth Rapley, "Women and Religious Vocation in Seventeenth-Century France," *French Historical Studies* 18 (1994): 619.

5. Sainte-Beuve, *Port-Royal*, vol. 1, pp. 124–129.

6. *Mémoires de Utrecht*, vol. 2, p. 248.

7. *Relation écrite par la Mère Angélique Arnauld sur Port-Royal*, ed. Louis Cognet (Paris: Grasset, 1949), pp. 30–31.

8. Ibid., p. 40.

9. *Mémoires de Utrecht*, vol. 1, p. 245.

10. Ibid., vol. 2, p. 420.

11. *Relation de la Mère Angélique*, p. 46.

12. Ibid., pp. 47–48.

13. Ibid., p. 50.

14. *Mémoires de Port-Royal*, p. 131.

15. *Relation de la Mère Angélique*, p. 65.

16. Ibid., pp. 79–80.

17. Jean Racine, *Abrégé de l'histoire de Port-Royal* (Paris: Crès et Cie., 1926), pp. 38–39.

18. For an account of the events that took place at Maubuisson see BN ms. fr. 17795; *Relation de la Mère Angélique*; and Cognet, *La Mère Angélique et Saint François de Sales*, pp. 15–99.

19. Augustin Gazier, *Jeanne de Chantal et Angélique Arnauld d'après leur correspondance 1620–1640* (Paris: Champion, 1915), p. 129.

20. Germaine Grebil, "La 'tentation' visitandine," *Chroniques de Port-Royal* 41 (1993): 121–147.

21. *Relation de la Mère Angélique*, pp. 121–122. For a detailed discussion of these matters see William Ritchey Newton, "Port-Royal and Jansenism: Social Experience, Group Formation and Religious Attitudes in Seventeenth-Century France" (Ph.D. diss., University of Michigan, 1974), pp. 130–376.

22. BN ms. fr. 17795.

23. Ibid.

24. *Relation de la Mère Angélique*, p. 114.

25. Ibid., pp. 129–130.

26. Ibid., pp. 124–127; BN ms. fr. 17795.

27. Bibliothèque de l'Arsenal, Arnauld Family Papers, 6626.

28. *Relation de la Mère Angélique*, pp. 140–141.

29. BN ms. fr. 17795; *Mémoires de Port-Royal*, pp. 103–127.

30. *Mémoires de Port-Royal*, pp. 114–115.

31. *Relation de la Mère Angélique*, p. 173.

32. BN ms. fr. 17795.

33. Ibid.

34. *Relation de la Mère Angélique*, p. 97.

35. Ibid., p. 142.

36. Saint-Cyran's penitential theology is summarized in Alexander Sedgwick, *Jansenism in Seventeenth-Century France: Voices from the Wilderness* (Charlottesville: University Press of Virginia), pp. 31–46. For a more detailed treatment of the subject see Jean Orcibal, *Jean Duvergier de Hauranne, abbé de Saint-Cyran et son temps* (Paris: Vrin, 1947) and Jean Orcibal, *Jean Duvergier de Hauranne, abbé de Saint Cyran et le jansénisme* (Paris: Seuil, 1961).

37. Quoted in Alexander Sedgwick, "The Nuns of Port-Royal: A Study of Female Spirituality in Seventeenth-Century France," in *That Gentle Strength: Perspectives on Women in Christianity*, eds. Lynda L. Coon, Katherine J. Haldane, and Elizabeth Sommer (Charlottesville: University Press of Virginia, 1990), p. 183.

38. BN ms. fr. 17791.

39. Claude Lancelot, *Mémoires touchant la vie de M. de Saint-Cyran par M. Lancelot pour servir à l'éclaircissement à l'histoire de Port-Royal* (New York: Slatkine Reprint, 1968), p. 325.

40. *Nécrologe de l'Abbaye de Notre-Dame de Port-Royal des Champs*, ed. Antoine Rivet (Amsterdam: Potgieter, 1723), pp. 302–311.

41. Cognet, *La Mère Angélique et Saint François de Sales*, p. 121.

42. *Relation de la Mère Angélique*, p. 132.

4. The Conversion of a Family

1. Louis Cognet, *La Réforme de Port-Royal* (Paris: Flammarion, 1950), p. 19.

2. Ibid., p. 21.

3. *Mémoires pour servir à l'histoire de Port-Royal des Champs depuis le commencement de la réforme de cette abbaye* (s.l. 1714), p. 207.

4. Ibid., pp. 314–315.

5. Ibid., p. 125.

6. BN ms. fr. 17795.

7. *Relation écrite par la Mère Angélique Arnauld sur Port-Royal*, ed. Louis Cognet (Paris: Grasset, 1949), p. 60.

8. Bibliothèque de Port-Royal, ms. 86, pp. 30–31.

9. *Relation de la Mère Angélique*, p. 61.

10. Ibid., p. 42.

11. *Relation de la Mère Angélique*, pp. 67–68.

12. Ibid., p. 69.

13. For a more detailed account of the early life of Anne Arnauld, see *Relation de la Mère Angélique*, pp. 66–73; Cognet, *La Réforme de Port-Royal*, pp. 195–213.

14. *Mémoires de Port-Royal*, p. 177.

15. Ibid., p. 120.

16. Ibid., I, 124–125.

17. Louis Cognet, *La Mère Angélique et Saint François de Sales* (Paris: Flammarion, 1951), pp. 180–194.

18. *Mémoires de Port-Royal*, p. 339.

19. BN ms. fr. 17795.

20. *Mémoires de Port-Royal*, pp. 314–315.

21. *Mémoires pour servir à l'histoire de Port-Royal et à la vie de la Réverande Mère Angélique de Sainte-Ma Arnauld, réformatrice de ce monastère* (Utrecht, 1742), vol. 2, p. 251.

22. *Mémoires de Port-Royal*, p. 316; Pierre Guilbert, *Mémoires historiques et chronologiques sur l'abbaye de Port-Royal des Champs* (Utrecht, 1759), p. 253.

23. BN Collection Dupuy (854), 156–164 contains the court decree in favor of Antoine Arnauld. See also "Factum pour Catherine Le Maistre, etc." Bibliothèque de l'Arsenal, Arnauld Family Papers, 6034.

24. Sharon Kettering, "The Household Service of Early Modern French No-

blewomen," *French Historical Studies* (forthcoming). I am grateful to Professor Kettering for allowing me to read the typescript.

25. *Lettres de la Mere Agnès Arnauld*, ed. M. P. Faugère (Paris: Duprat, 1858), vol. 1, p. 13.

26. Ibid., vol. 1, p. 17.

27. Quoted in Cognet, *La Mère Angélique et Saint François de Sales*, p. 111.

28. Augustin Gazier, *Jeanne de Chantal et Angélique Arnauld* (Paris: Champion, 1915), p. 132.

29. *Mémoires de Port-Royal*, p. 282.

30. Cognet, *La Mère Angélique et Saint François de Sales*, pp. 237–238.

31. Guilbert, *Mémoires historiques*, pp. 202–206.

32. Archives Nationales, S 4515 dossier 9 (22 January 1629).

33. *Relation de la Mère Angélique*, p. 108.

34. Bibliothèque de Port-Royal, mss. 86, 186–190.

35. Nicolas Fontaine, *Mémoires pour servir à l'histoire de Port-Royal* (Utrecht, 1736), p. 29.

36. BN ms. fr. 17795.

37. Cognet, *La Mere Angélique et Saint François de Sales*, p. 68.

38. *Relation de la Mère Angélique*, pp. 168–170.

39. *Mémoires de Port-Royal*, pp. 147, 152.

40. Ibid., p. 152.

5. The Reformation of a Family

1. BN ms. fr. 17795.

2. *Mémoires de messire Arnauld d'Andilly*, C.-R. Petitot ed., *Collection des mémoires relatifs à l'histoire de France* (Paris: Foucault, 1820–1828), vol. 23, pp. 318–319.

3. *Relation écrite par la Mère Angélique sur Port-Royal*, ed. Louis Cognet (Paris: Grasset, 1949), pp. 63, 67. See also W. R. Newton, "Port-Royal and Jansenism: Social Experience, Group Formation and Religious Attitudes in 17th-Century France" (Ph.D. diss., University of Michigan), vol. 2, p. 163.

4. BN ms. fr. 17791.

5. *Nécrologe de l'Abbaye de Notre-Dame de Port-Royal-des-Champs, Ordre de Citeaux, Institut du Saint-Sacrement*, ed. Antoine Rivet (Amsterdam: Potgieter, 1723), pp. 412–419.

6. C.-A. Sainte-Beuve, *Port-Royal*, ed. Maxime Leroy (Paris: Gallimard, 1961), vol. 1, p. 385.

7. Quoted in Jean Orcibal, *Jean Duvergier de Hauranne, abbé de Saint-Cyran et son temps* (Paris: Vrin, 1947), p. 535.

8. Pierre Guilbert, *Mémoires historiques et chronologiques sur l'abbaye de Port-Royal des Champs* (Utrecht, 1759), vol. 1, p. 4.

9. *Lettres de la Mère Agnès Arnauld, abbesse de Port-Royal*, ed. M. P. Faugère (Paris: Duprat, 1858), vol. 1, pp. 38–40, 55.

10. Nicolas Fontaine, *Mémoires pour servir à l'histoire de Port-Royal* (Utrecht, 1736), pp. 69–71.

11. Ibid., p. 68.

12. Ibid., p. 13.

13. Ibid., p. 14.

14. Ibid., pp. 36–37.

15. Ibid., p. 39.

16. Ibid., p. 71.

17. Sainte-Beuve, *Port-Royal*, vol. 1, p. 404. See also Alexander Sedgwick, "La famille Arnauld à travers le 'Port-Royal' de Sainte-Beuve," *Chroniques de Port-Royal* 42 (1993): 251–259.

18. Fontaine, *Mémoires*, pp. 80–81.

19. Ibid., pp. 270–271.

20. Usually referred to as Port-Royal-des-Champs as distinct from Port-Royal-de-Paris.

21. AN Gallois LXXV 116. The Le Maistre brothers gave the sum total of 40,000 livres to Port-Royal on 4 March 1654 in return for annual incomes each of 850 livres.

22. Two brothers of Le Maistre, Sainte-Elme and Vallemont, remained in the world. One of Sainte-Elme's daughters became a pensioner at Port-Royal.

23. Fontaine, *Mémoires*, pp. 118–119.

24. Ibid., p. 117.

25. In 1636 Saint-Cyran became involved in a literary quarrel with a Jesuit scholar as the result of the publication of his work *Somme des Fautes et faussetés de Père Garasse* (1622). Earlier, in 1632, he had attacked the order in his so-called Petrus Aurelius writings. See Alexander Sedgwick, *Jansenism in Seventeenth-Century France: Voices from the Wilderness* (Charlottesville: University Press of Virginia), pp. 22–23.

26. The importance of learning to the *solitaires* is illustrated by the size of the library that they collected at "Les Granges," the little farm next to Port-Royal-des-Champs, now a national museum. The collection was built around the library of Antoine Le Maistre. See Odette Barenne, *Une Bibliothèque de Port-Royal* (Paris: Etudes Augustiniènes, 1985).

27. "Supplement du nécrologie de Port-Royal," Bibliothèque de Port-Royal ms. 39.

6. Robert Arnauld d'Andilly

1. *Mémoires de messire Arnauld d'Andilly*, C.-R. Petitot ed., *Collection des mémoires relatifs à l'histoire de France* (Paris: Foucault, 1820–1828), vol. 23, p. 358.

2. BN Dossiers Bleus, vol. 32.

3. *Mémoires d'Arnauld d'Andilly*, vol. 23, pp. 360–365.

4. On the nature of these offices see Richard Bonney, *Political Change in France under Richelieu and Mazarin* (Oxford: Oxford University Press, 1978); and Orest Ranum, *Richelieu and the Councillors of Louis XIII* (Oxford: Oxford University Press, 1963), pp. 45–99.

5. *Mémoires d'Arnauld d'Andilly*, vol. 23, pp. 403–404.

6. Ibid., vol. 24, pp. 14–15.

7. Ibid., vol. 23, p. 325.

8. Ibid., vol. 24, pp. 17–18.

9. Ibid., vol. 24, p. 27.

10. For an account of the intrigues in Gaston's household see Georges Dethan, *Gaston d'Orléans, conspirateur et prince charmant* (Paris: Fayard, 1959).

11. *Mémoires d'Arnauld d'Andilly*, vol. 23, pp. 404–405.

12. Robert Arnauld d'Andilly, *Lettres de Monsieur Arnauld d'Andilly* (Paris: J. Camusat, 1645), p. 18.

13. *Mémoires d'Arnauld d'Andilly*, vol. 23, p. 37.

14. *Lettres d'Arnauld d'Andilly*, p. 31.

15. *Lettres chrestiennes et spirituelles de Messire Jean Du Verger de Hauranne, Abbé de Saint-Cyran* (Paris, 1645), vol. 1, p. 249. This edition of Saint-Cyran was edited by Andilly as a memorial to his friend.

16. Quoted in C.-A. Sainte-Beuve, *Port-Royal*, ed. Maxime Leroy (Paris: Galimard, 1961), vol. 1, pp. 315–316.

17. BN ms. fr. 17790.

18. Ibid.

19. Ibid.

20. Ibid.

21. *Lettres de la Mère Agnès, abbesse de Port-Royal*, ed. M. P. Faugère (Paris: Duprat, 1858), vol. 1, p. 59.

22. Bibliothèque de l'Arsenal, cartons 5179–5185, "Journal autographe d'Arnauld d'Andilly."

23. *Lettres d'Arnauld d'Andilly*, p. 106.

24. See, for example, Andilly's letter to the marechal de Brézé, 10 November 1630, ibid., p. 130.

25. Anon., *La Vie de M. le duc de Montausier Pair de France, Gouverneur de Monseigneur Louis Dauphin, ayeul du Roy à présent regnant, ecrite sur les mémoires de Madame la Duchesse d'Uzès sa fille* (Paris, 1729), vol. 2, p. 160.

26. Ibid., vol. 1, p. 44.

27. *Lettres d'Arnauld d'Andilly*, p. 31.

28. *Lettres de la Mère Agnès*, vol. 1, p. 35.

29. *Mémoires d'Arnauld d'Andilly*, vol. 24, p. 37.

30. *Lettres de la Mère Agnès*, vol. 1, p. 66.

31. BN ms. fr. 17790.

32. Ibid.

33. Ibid.

34. *Mémoires d'Arnauld d'Andilly*, vol. 24, p. 73.

35. *Lettres d'Arnauld d'Andilly*, p. 230.

36. *Mémoires de l'abbé Arnauld*, vol. 1, p. 187.

37. *Lettres inédites des Feuquières tirées des papiers de la famille de Madame la duchesse Descazes*, ed. E. Gallois (Paris, Champion, 1845–1846), vol. 1, pp. 293–294.

38. *Lettres d'Arnauld d'Andilly*, p. 290.

39. "Mémoire pour faire voir à mes enfants de quelle sorte j'ai ménagé mon bien et le leur," Bibliothèque de l'Arsenal, Arnauld Family Papers, 6034. The memoir is also to be found in L. Delavaud, *Le Marquis de Pomponne, 1618–99* (Paris: Plon, 1911), pp. 194–198.

40. BN Dossiers Bleus 32; ms. fr. 33004.

41. *Mémoires de l'abbé Arnauld*, vol. 1, p. 123.

42. BN ms. fr. 1058.

43. BN ms. fr. 17790.

44. *Mémoires de l'abbé Arnauld*, vol. 1, pp. 144, 146.

45. Ibid., vol. 1, p. 160.

46. *Lettres inédites des Feuquières*, vol. 1, p. 230.

47. *Mémoires de M. de Coulanges suivis de lettres inédites de Mme de Sévigné, de son fils, de l'abbé de Coulanges, d'Arnauld d'Andilly, d'Arnauld de Pomponnne, etc.* (Paris: Champion, 1820), p. 509.

48. *Mémoires de l'abbé Arnauld*, C. R. Petitot ed., *Collection des mémoires relatifs à l'histoire de France* (Paris: Foucault, 1820–1828), vol. 240, pp. 180–182.

49. Bibliothèque de l'Arsenal, Arnauld Family Papers, 6626.

50. Ibid., 6034.

51. *"Nécrologe de Port-Royal,"* Bibliothèque de Port-Royal, ms. 85.

52. Bibliothèque de l'Arsenal, Arnauld Family Papers, 6034.

53. BN ms. fr. 3777.

54. BN ms. fr. 3778.

55. *Mémoires de l'abbé Arnauld*, vol. 24, pp. 246–247.

56. The *mémoires* are entitled "Avis à la reine pour attirer la bénédiciton de Dieu sur la France" and "Mémoire pour un souverain," both written in 1643. Bibliothèque de l'Arsenal, Arnauld Family Papers, 6034.

57. *Mémoires d'Arnauld d'Andilly*, vol. 24, p. 75.

58. *Mémoires de l'abbé Arnauld*, vol. 24, p. 214.

59. *Lettre de M. le President Gramont à Philarque* (Toulouse, 1644).

60. *Lettres d'Arnauld d'Andilly*, p. 540.

61. *Mémoires d'Arnauld d'Andilly*, vol. 24, p. 98.

62. Conrart's verses are to be found in manuscript form in the Bibliothèque de l'Arsenal, Arnauld Family Papers, 6034.

63. *Confessions de Saint Augustin*, ed. Philippe Sellier, trans. Odette Barenne (Paris: Gallimard, 1993), p. 249.

64. Ibid., p. 94.

65. Ibid., p. 168.

66. See Philippe Sellier's introduction, ibid., p. 18.

67. Tallement des Réaux, *Historiettes*, ed. Antoine Adam (Paris: Gallimard, 1967), vol. 1, p. 511.

68. Nicolas Fontaine, *Mémoires pour servir à l'histoire de Port-Royal* (Utrecht, 1759), p. 290.

69. Claude Lancelot, *Mémoires touchant la vie de l'abbé de Saint-Cyran* (New York: Slatkine Reprints, 1968), pp. 127–128.

70. Fontaine, *Mémoires*, p. 290.

71. BN ms. fr. 17795.

72. BN Dossiers Bleus 32. For a brief account of the life of Henry Arnauld see Isabelle Bonnot, *Hérétique ou Saint? Henry Arnauld éveque janséniste d'Angers au XVIIe siècle* (Paris: Nouvelles Editions Latines, 1984), pp. 93–102. This work is primarily an account of Arnauld's career as bishop of Angers, 1649–1692. See also the earlier work of Claude Cochin, *Henry Arnauld, éveque d'Angers* (Paris: Picard, 1921). This biography is incomplete.

73. *"Mémoire pour servir à la vie de M. Henry Arnauld, Evêque d'Angers,"* Bibliothèque de l'Arsenal, Arnauld Family Papers, 6042.

74. BN ms. fr. 3773.

75. BN ms. fr. 37777.

76. BN ms. fr. 37771.

77. BN ms. fr. 17795. See also *Mémoires pour servir à l'histoire de Port-Royal et à la vie de la Réverande Mère Angélique de Sainte-Madeleine Arnauld, réformatrice de ce monastère* (Utrecht, 1742), vol. 3, p. 302.

7. Le Grand Arnauld *and the Origins of Jansenism*

1. Nicolas Fontaine, *Mémoires pour servir à l'histoire de Port-Royal* (Utrecht, 1759), pp. 127–288. For a brief account of Antoine Arnauld's relationship with his family, see Alexander Sedgwick, "Le Grand Arnauld en Famille," *Chroniques de Port-Royal* 44 (1995): 11–18.

2. Ibid., p. 129.

3. Ibid., p. 127.

4. BN ms. fr. 17798.

5. This issue is discussed in greater detail in Sedgwick, *Jansenism in Seventeenth-Century France: Voices from the Wilderness* (Charlottesville: University Press of Virginia), pp. 28–30.

6. The best summary of Jansen's *Augustinus* is to be found in Nigel Abercrombie, *The Origins of Jansenism* (Oxford: Oxford University Press, 1936). See also Louis Cognet, *Le Jansénisme* (Paris: PUF, 1960); and for a very brief account of the doctrinal issues involved, see Sedgwick, "Prophets without Honor? Jansen and the Jansenists," *History Today* 50 (July 1990): 36–42. For Saint-Cyran's role in the Jansenist movement see Jean Orcibal, *Jean Duvergier de Hauranne, Abbé se Saint-Cyran et son temps* (Paris: Vrin, 1948), 2 vols.

7. Claude Lancelot, *Mémoires touchant la vie de Monsieur de Saint-Cyran* (New York: Slatkine Reprints, 1968), vol. 1, p. 325n.

8. These letters are to be found in BN ms. fr. 17802.

9. Ibid.

10. Antoine Arnauld, *Apologie de Monsieur Jansenius evesque d'Ipres* (s.l., 1644).

11. Antoine Arnauld, *Seconde apologie de Monsieur Jansenius evesque d'Ipres et de la doctrine de S. Augustine* (s.l., 1645).

12. Antoine Arnauld, *De la fréquente communion* (Paris, 1643). For an account of the origins of this work as well as of the early education of Antoine Arnauld see Jean Lesaulnier, "*La Fréquente communion* d'Antoine Arnauld," *Chroniques de Port-Royal* 44 (1995): 61–82.

13. Archives Nationales MC LXXV 116.

14. *Supplement au nécrologie de l'Abbaye de Notre-Dame de Port-Royal des Champs*, ed. Antoine Rivet (Amsterdam: Potgieter, 1723), p. 250.

15. *Supplement*, pp. 258–259.

16. Fontaine, *Mémoires*, p. 348.

17. Ibid., p. 347.

18. BN ms. fr. 17790.

19. These undated letters are to be found in BN ms. fr. 17790.

20. BN ms. fr. 17791.

21. Ibid.

22. Ibid.

23. BN ms. fr. 17795.

24. Ibid.

25. For more on Arnauld's views on the autonomy of theologians see Sedgwick, *Jansenism in Seventeenth-Century France*, pp. 111–112.

26. The five propositions translated into English are to be found in Sedgwick, *Jansenism in Seventeenth-Century France*, p. 68.

8. The Arnauld Family during the Fronde

1. See, for example, Léonard de Marandé, *Inconvéniens d'estat procedans de jansénisme* (Paris, 1654).

2. BN ms. fr. 17791.

3. Ibid.

4. BN ms. fr. 17792.

5. Ibid.

6. BN ms. fr. 17793, which contains all of Angélique's letters to the queen of Poland.

7. Nicolas Fontaine, *Mémoires pour servir à l'histoire de Port-Royal* (Utrecht, 1759), p. 17.

8. BN ms. fr. 17793.

9. BN ms. fr. 17793.

10. Ibid.

11. Jean Racine, *Abrégé de l'histoire de Port-Royal par Jean Racine*, ed. Augustin Gazier (Paris: Le Musée du Livre, 1908), pp. 91–92.

12. Ibid., p. 121.

13. BN ms. fr. 17795.

14. BN ms. fr. 3771.

15. Valentin Conrart, *Mémoires de Valentin Conrart, premier secretaire perpetuelle de l'Académie Française*, ed. L. J. N. Monmerqué (Paris: Foucault, 1826), p. 223.

16. Claude Lancelot, *Mémoires touchant la vie de M. de Saint-Cyran par M. Lancelot pour servir l'éclaircissement à l'histoire de Port-Royal des Champs* (New York: Slatkine Reprints, 1968), vol. 1, p. 163n.

17. For an account of the political role of the Bouthillier family see Orest Ranum, *Richelieu and the Councillors of State* (Oxford: Oxford University Press, 1963). See also A. J. Krailsheimer, *Armand-Jean de Rancé, Abbot of La Trappe* (Oxford: Oxford University Press, 1974). Rancé was a member of the Bouthillier family.

18. *Mémoires de l'abbé Arnauld*, C. R. Petitot ed., *Collection des mémoires relatifs à l'histoire de France* (Paris: Foucault, 1820–1828), vol. 24, pp. 285, 290.

19. Ibid., vol. 24, p. 290.

20. Quoted in Isabelle Bonnot, *Hérétique ou Saint? Henry Arnauld, éveque janséniste d'Angers au XVIIe siècle* (Paris: Nouvelles Editions Latines, 1984), p. 112.

21. Ibid., p. 113.

22. Quoted in Douglas C. Baxter, *Servants of the Sword: French Intendants of the Army 1630–70* (Urbana, Illinois: University of Illinois Press, 1976), p. 130.

23. *Mémoires de l'abbe Arnauld*, vol. 24, pp. 276–277.

24. For an account of Fabert's life see Jules Bourelly, *Le Maréchal de Fabert (1599–1662)* (Paris: Didier, 1881), 2 vols.

25. Bibliothèque de l'Arsenal, Arnauld Family Papers, 6035.

26. Valentin Conrart, *Mémoires de Valentin Conrart* (New York: Slatkine Reprints, 1971), p. 225.

27. These *Mazarinades* were, of course, published anonymously, but the identity of their author has been clearly established. See Hubert Carrier, "Port-Royal et la Fronde. Deux Mazarinades inconnues d'Arnauld d'Andilly," *Revue d'Histoire Littéraire de la France* 75 (1975): 1–29. See also Alexander Sedgwick, *Jansenism in Seventeenth-Century France: Voices from the Wilderness* (Charlottesville: University Press of Virginia, 1977), pp. 63, 215 n. 19.

28. BN ms. fr. 3770.

29. Robert Arnauld d'Andilly, *Lettres d'Arnauld d'Andilly* (Paris: J. Camusat), p. 163.

30. For a discussion of the issues relating to the religious Fronde see Richard M. Golden, *The Godly Rebellion: Parisian Curés and the Religious Fronde 1652–1660* (Chapel Hill, NC: University of North Carolina Press, 1981).

31. Jean Brisacier, *Le Jansénisme confondu* (Paris, 1651), p. 6.

32. BN ms. fr. 17793.

33. *Lettre à une personne de condition* and *Seconde lettre à un duc et pair,* both ostensibly addressed to the duc de Luynes, a patron of Port-Royal, but in fact addressed to the public at large.

34. Quoted in Sedgwick, *Jansenism in Seventeenth-Century France,* p. 73.

35. BN ms. fr. 17795.

36. BN ms. fr. 17783.

37. Ibid.

38. BN ms. fr. 17795.

39. BN ms. fr. 17790.

40. BN ms. fr. 17798. The words in Latin are similar to those used by Pope Leo X in his encyclical condemning Luther.

41. Ibid.

42. Ibid.

43. Ibid.

44. P. Jansen, *Arnauld d'Andilly, Défenseur de Port-Royal (1654–59). Sa correspondance inédite avec la cour conservée dans les archives du Ministère des Affaires Etrangères* (Paris: Fayard, 1973), p. 37.

45. Ibid., p. 38.

46. Ibid., p. 101.

47. Antoine Arnauld, *Oeuvres de messire Antoine Arnauld* (Brussels: Culture et Civilisation, 1964–1966), vol. 3, p. 54. Referred to hereafter as *Oeuvres.*

48. BN ms. fr. 10587.

49. Bibliothèque de l'Arsenal, Arnauld Family Papers, 6626.

50. BN ms. fr. 17793.

51. Ibid.

52. Bibliothèque de l'Arsenal, Arnauld Family Papers, 6036.

53. Arnauld, *Oeuvres,* vol. 21, p. 65.

54. Anne's letter and Andilly's reply may be found in L. Delavaud, *Le Marquis de Pomponne, 1618–1699* (Paris: Plon, 1911), pp. 24–30.

55. BN ms. fr. 17795.

56. Arnauld, *Oeuvres,* vol. 1, p. 16.

9. The Confrontation

1. Andilly's letter to the king may be found in BN ms. fr. 10587 and in the Bibliothèque de l'Arsenal, Arnauld Family Papers, 6626.

2. *Mémoires for the Instruction of the Dauphin,* ed. and trans. Paul Sonnino (New York: Free Press, 1965), p. 54.

3. Quoted in Alexander Sedgwick, *Jansenism in Seventeenth-Century France: Voices from the Wilderness* (Charlottesville: University Press of Virginia), p. 108.

4. Quoted in ibid., p. 109.

5. *La Correspondance de Martin de Barcos, Abbé de Saint-Cyran,* ed. Lucien Goldmann (Paris: Presses Universitaires de France, 1956), p. 358.

6. For more on the various Jansenist reactions to the demand for signature, see Lucien Goldmann, *Le Dieu caché* (Paris: Gallimard, 1959).

7. Antoine Arnauld, *Oeuvres de messire Antoine Arnauld* (Brussels: Culture et Civilisation, 1964–1966), vol. 1, pp. 317–321.

8. Ibid., vol. 1, pp. 326–327.

9. Ibid., vol. 1, pp. 350–351.

10. Ibid., vol. 1, p. 341.

11. Ibid., vol. 1, pp. 361–362.

12. Ibid., vol. 1, p. 359.

13. Ibid., vol. 1, pp. 243–244.

14. Ibid., vol. 1, p. 254.

15. Ibid., vol. 1, p. 277.

16. BN ms. fr. 17795.

17. BN ms. fr. 17792.

18. BN ms. fr. 17795.

19. BN ms. fr. 13894.

20. Nicolas Fontaine, *Mémoires pour servir à l'histoire de Port-Royal* (Utrecht, 1759), p. 21.

21. *Lettres de la Mere Agnès Arnauld, abbesse de Port-Royal,* ed. M. P. Faugère (Paris: Duprat, 1858), vol. 1, p. 511.

22. BN ms. fr. 19738.

23. *Mémoires et relations sur ce qui s'est passé à Port-Royal des Champs depuis le commencement de la réforme de cette abbaye* (s.l. 1716), pp. 501–505.

24. Quoted in the introduction to *Relation de la captivité d'Angélique de Saint-Jean Arnauld d'Andilly,* ed. Louis Cognet (Paris: Gallimard, 1954), p. 10. This introduction provides a brief account of Angélique's life.

25. *Nécrologe de l'abbaye de Port-Royal des Champs,* ed. Antoine Rivet (Amsterdam: Potgieter, 1723), pp. 54–55.

26. Victor Cousin, *Jacqueline Pascal* (Paris: Didier, 1877), p. 371.

27. Odette Barenne, *Une bibliothèque de Port-Royal* (Paris: Etudes Augustiniènes, 1985), pp. 11–20.

28. Quoted in F. Ellen Weaver, *The Evolution of the Reform of Port-Royal* (Paris: Beauchesne, 1978), p. 127.

29. J. LeSaulnier, "Relation de la Mère Angélique," *Chroniques de Port-Royal* 42 (1992): 7–92.

30. Bibliothèque de Port-Royal (hereafter referred to as BPR), manuscript collection, Lettres de la Mère Angélique de Saint-Jean à partir de 1653.

31. Weaver, *The Evolution of the Reform of Port-Royal*, pp. 127–128.

32. BPR, Angélique to Luzancy, 19 July 1659.

33. Ibid., Angélique to Angélique de Saint-Jean, April 1657.

34. Ibid.

35. Jean Racine, *Abrégé de l'histoire de Port-Royal* (Paris: Crès et Cie., 1926), pp. 235–236.

36. Bibliothèque de l'Arsenal, Arnauld Family Papers, 6038.

37. BN ms. fr. 10583.

38. *Mémoires de Port-Royal*, vol. 3, pp. 550–551.

39. BPR, Angélique de Saint-Jean to Henry Arnauld, 7 June 1661.

40. Ibid., Angélique de Saint-Jean to Antoine Arnauld, 5 November 1661.

41. Ibid., Angélique de Saint-Jean to Antoine Arnauld, 12 November 1661.

42. Ibid., 28 November 1661.

43. See, for example, Arnauld's *Apologie pour les religieuses*, written in 1665. *Oeuvres*, vol. 23, pp. 320–350.

44. BPR, Angélique de Saint-Jean to Antoine Arnauld, 28 November 1662.

45. Ibid.

46. Ibid., Angélique to Andilly, 10 July 1664.

47. Ibid., Angélique to Arnauld, 17 January 1664.

48. BN ms. fr. 10587.

49. Angélique describes the scene and her ensuing captivity in *Relation d'Angélique de Saint-Jean Arnauld d'Andilly*, ed. Louis Cognet.

50. Ibid., p. 31.

51. BN ms. fr. 10587.

52. *Relation d'Angélique de Saint-Jean d'Andilly*, p. 31.

53. Ibid., p. 38.

54. Ibid., pp. 51–52.

55. Ibid., p. 55.

56. BPR, Angélique to Arnauld, 23 May 1667.

57. *Relation d'Angélique de Saint-Jean d'Andilly*, p. 65.

58. Ibid., pp. 113–114.

59. Ibid., p. 79.

60. Ibid., p. 93.

61. Ibid., pp. 77, 93.

62. Ibid., p. 45.

63. Ibid., p. 133.

64. Ibid., pp. 109–110.

65. Ibid., pp. 228–229.

66. Ibid., p. 156.

67. *Divers actes, lettres et relations des religieuses de Port-Royal* (Utrecht, 1735).

68. BPR, Angélique to Arnauld, July 1666.

69. Ibid., Angélique to Arnauld, 5 November 1665.

70. *Texte provenant de Port-Royal et qui semble bien être de la Mère Angélique de Saint-Jean*. See F. Ellen Weaver, *The Evolution of the Reform of Port-Royal*, p. 151.

71. *Relation d'Angélique de Saint-Jean d'Andilly*, p. 197.

72. BPR, Angélique to Arnauld, 23 May 1665.

73. *Divers actes*, vol. 1. See Sedgwick, *Jansenism in Seventeenth-Century France*, pp. 130–131.

74. BPR, Angélique to Arnauld, 17 May 1668.

75. *Choix de lettres inédites de Louis-Isaac Le Maistre de Sacy (1650–1683)*, ed. Geneviève Delassault (Paris: Nizet, 1959), pp. 108–113.

76. *Divers actes.*

77. BPR, Angélique to Luzancy, 27 September 1669.

10. Pomponne

1. Robert Arnauld d'Andilly, *Mémoires d'Arnauld d'Andilly*, C. R. Petitot ed., *Collection des mémoires relatifs à l'histoire de France* (Paris: Foucault, 1820–1828), vol. 24, p. 98.

2. See Chapter 5 and BN Dossiers Bleus 32. Pomponne inherited his father's pension of three thousand pounds from the king and the pension of four thousand pounds from Gaston d'Orleans. In 1644 he was appointed a *conseiller au roi*, a nonvenal office that carried with it an annual income of three thousand pounds.

3. The marriage contract of 8 May 1660 may be found in L. Delavaud, *Le Marquis de Pomponne* (Paris: Plon, 1911), pp. 157–158.

4. Bibliothèque de l'Arsenal, Arnauld Family Papers, 6035.

5. *Mémoires de l'abbé Arnauld*, C. R. Petitot ed., *Collection des mémoires relatifs à l'histoire de France* (Paris: Foucault, 1820–1828), vol. 24, p. 317.

6. BPR, Angélique de Saint-Jean to Pomponne, 29 August 1662.

7. BPR, Pomponne to Angélique, 30 July 1661.

8. These letters are to be found at the Bibliothèque de l'Arsenal (BA), Arnauld Family Papers, 6036.

9. Both quotations are in Herbert H. Rowen, "Arnauld de Pomponne," *American Historical Review* 61 (1956): 534.

10. BA, Arnauld Family Papers, 6036.

11. *Mémoires de M. de Coulanges suivis de lettres inédites de Madame de Sévigné, de son fils, de l'abbé de Coulanges, d'Arnauld d'Andilly, d'Arnauld de Pomponne etc.* (Paris: Champion, 1820), p. 473.

12. Ibid., pp. 475–480.

13. Ibid., p. 481.

14. BA, Arnauld Family Papers, 6037.

15. Pomponne to Colbert, 4 February 1667, in *Archives de la Bastille*, ed. François Ravaisson-Mollien (New York: Slatkine Reprints, 1975), vol. 3, p. 43. In his impressive biography, *Fouquet* (Paris: Fayard, 1987), Daniel Dessert points out that far from enriching himself at the crown's expense, Fouquet lost most of his fortune in the king's service.

16. BA, Arnauld Family Papers, 6037.

17. BA, Arnauld Family Papers, 6036.

18. Delavaud, *Pomponne*, p. 178.

19. BA, Arnauld Family Papers, 6037.

20. Quoted in Rowen, "Arnauld de Pomponne," *American Historical Review* 61 (1956): 535.

21. BA, Arnauld Family Papers, 6037.

22. Pomponne to Andilly, 12 February 1667, in Delavaud, *Pomponne*, p. 17.

23. Pomponne's diplomatic memoirs were eventually published in 1860.

24. *Mémoires d'Arnauld d'Andilly*, vol. 24, p. 301.

25. BA, Arnauld Family Papers, 6037.

26. Pomponne to Andilly, 8 January 1667, in *Mémoires de Coulanges*, p. 417.

27. Ibid., pp. 510–511.

28. In 1666, for example, Pomponne wrote his father asking him to greet his eldest son affectionately when the two met at the christening of one of his daughters. See *Mémoires de Coulanges*, p. 509.

29. *Mémoires d'Arnauld d'Andilly*, vol. 24, p. 319.

30. Ibid., vol. 24, p. 100.

31. Ibid., vol. 24, p. 95.

32. Ibid., vol. 24, pp. 103–104.

33. Pomponne to Luzancy, 10 September 1667, in *Mémoires de Coulanges*, pp. 528–529.

34. BA, Arnauld Family Papers, 6037.

35. Ibid., Pomponne to Le Peletier, 3 July 1666.

36. Pomponne to Andilly, 4 June 1667, in *Mémoires de Coulanges*, p. 524.

37. For further discussion of French diplomacy in this period see Rowen, "Arnauld de Pomponne," *American Historical Review* 61 (1956); Herbert Rowen, *The Ambassador Prepares for War, the Dutch Embassy of Arnauld de Pomponne 1669–1671* (The Hague, 1957); and Paul Sonnino, *Louis XIV and the Origins of the Dutch War* (Cambridge: Cambridge University Press, 1988).

38. BA, Arnauld Family Papers, 6037.

39. Ibid.

40. Ibid.

41. Pomponne, "Relation de Suède 1671," quoted in Rowen, "Arnauld de Pomponne," *American Historical Review* 61 (1956): 541.

42. *Mémoires de Coulanges*, p. 535.

43. *Lettres inédites des Feuquières tirées des papiers de la famille de la duchesse de Descazes*, ed. E. Gallois (Paris: Champion, 1846), vol. 2, p. 35.

44. Ibid., vol. 2, pp. 156–157.

45. Ibid., vol. 3, p. 72.

46. *Correspondance de Madame de Sévigné*, ed. Roger Duchêne (Paris: Gallimard, 1972), vol. 1, p. 344.

47. BPR, Andilly to Pomponne, 5 September 1671.

48. *Mémoires de l'abbé Arnauld*, C. R. Petitot ed., *Collection des mémoires relatifs à l'histoire de France* (Paris: Foucault, 1820–1828), vol. 24, p. 337.

49. BA, Arnauld Family Papers, 6626, "Relation de mon voyage à Versailles lors que j'allay remercier le Roy d'avoir honoré mon fils de la charge de secretaire d'état 10 septembre 1671."

50. BA, Arnauld Family Papers, 6037.

51. BPR, Angélique de Saint-Jean to Luzancy, 8 September 1671.

52. BPR, Angélique to Madame Périer, the sister of Pascal, 18 October 1671.

53. BPR, Angélique to Pomponne, 12 February 1672.

54. BPR, Angélique to Luzancy, 18 December 1671.

55. BA, Arnauld Family Papers, 6037.

56. BPR, Angélique to Andilly, undated letter.

57. BPR, Angélique to Andilly, 8 May 1673.

58. *Lettres de la Mère Agnès, abbesse de Port-Royal*, ed. M. P. Faugère (Paris: Duprat, 1858), vol. 2, p. 366.

59. *Correspondance de Madame de Sévigné*, vol. 1, p. 681.

60. BA, Arnauld Family Papers, 6038.

61. *Mémoires de l'abbé Arnauld*, vol. 24, pp. 206–207.

62. BPR, Angélique to Madame de Fontpertuis, 23 October 1674.

63. BPR, Angélique to M. Hermand, 13 October 1674.

64. Ibid.

65. BPR, Angélique to Madame de Fontpertuis, 17 May 1674.

66. BPR, Angélique to Mlle Le Maistre, 13 March 1676.

67. Antoine Arnauld, *Oeuvres de messire Antoine Arnauld* (Brussels: Culture & Civilisation, 1964–1966), vol. 32, p. 103.

68. BN Collection Baluze 20 (fol 181), Arnauld to Pomponne, 14 June 1677.

69. Emile Jacques, *Les Années d'exile d'Antoine Arnauld (1679–1694)* (Louvain: Publication Universitaires de Louvain, 1976), pp. 34–36. This book provides an exhaustive account of Arnauld's life in those years.

70. BN ff 17800, Arnauld to Pomponne, May 1679.

71. Jacques, *Les Années d'exile*, pp. 43–78.

72. BPR, Angélique de Saint-Jean to unknown, 24 January 1679.

73. BPR, Angélique to Henry Arnauld, 20 May 1679.

74. BPR, Angélique to Henry Arnauld, 25 May 1679.

75. *Lettres inédites des Feuquières*, vol. 2, p. 320.

76. Ibid., vol. 2, p. 110.

11. *Toward the Destruction of Port-Royal*

1. *Correspondance de Madame de Sévigné*, ed. Roger Duchène (Paris: Gallimard, 1972), vol. 2, pp. 739–742.

2. *Lettres inédites des Feuquières tirées des papiers de la famille de Madame la duchesse Descazes*, ed. E. Gallois (Paris: Champion, 1845–1846), vol. 5, pp. 26–27.

3. Ibid., vol. 5, p. 38.

4. BNP, Angélique de Saint-Jean to duchesse de Luynes, 23 November 1679.

5. BNP, Angélique to Mlle de Courcelle, 21 September 1681.

6. Bibliothéque de l'Arsenal, Arnauld Family Papers, Angélique de Saint-Jean to Pomponne, 21 September 1681.

7. BNP, Pomponne to Angélique de Saint-Jean, 26 November 1681.

8. BNP, Angélique de Saint-Jean to Charlotte de Pomponne, 1680.

9. BNP, Angélique de Saint-Jean to Madame de Fontpertuis, 14 April 1680.

10. BNP, Angélique de Saint-Jean to Luzancy, 4 July 1680.

11. BNP, Angélique de Saint-Jean to M. de Fourmant, 5 September 1680. Fourmant was an aide to Pomponne.

12. BNP, Angélique de Saint-Jean to Madame de Fontpertuis, 16 November 1681.

13. BNP, Angélique de Saint-Jean to Madame de Fontpertuis, 18 August 1682.

14. BNP, Angélique de Saint-Jean to Luzancy, 4 July 1680.

15. Nicolas Fontaine, *Mémoires pour servir à l'histoire de Port-Royal* (Utrecht, 1759), p. 528.

16. C.-A. Sainte-Beuve, *Port-Royal*, ed. Maxime Leroy (Paris: Gallimard, 1961), vol. 3, p. 229.

17. BN ff 17800, Arnauld to Angélique de Saint-Jean, 22 April 1680.

18. Emile Jacques, *Les Années d'éxile d'Antoine Arnauld* (Louvain: Publications Universitaires de Louvain, 1976), p. 342.

19. Antoine Arnauld, *Oeuvres de messire Antoine Arnauld* (Brussels: Culture & Civilisation, 1964–1966), vol. 2, p. 415.

20. Quoted in Alexander Sedgwick, *Jansenism in Seventeenth-Century France: Voices from the Wilderness* (Charlottesville: University Press of Virginia, 1977), p. 153.

21. For further discussion of the relationship between Arnauld's ideas and the Enlightenment, see Alexander Sedgwick, "Seventeenth-Century Jansenism and the Enlightenment," in *Church, State and Society under the Bourbon Kings of France*, ed. Richard M. Golden (Lawrence, Kansas: Coronado Press, 1982), pp. 125–147.

22. These issues are discussed in greater detail in Sedgwick, *Jansenism in Seventeenth-Century France*, pp. 153–156.

23. Arnauld, *Oeuvres*, vol. 37, p. 10.

24. Jacques, *Les Années d'exile*, p. 18.

25. Arnauld, *Oeuvres*, vol. 2, p. 142.

26. Quoted in Jacques, *Les Années d'exile*, p. 246.

27. Ibid., p. 246.

28. BN ff 17800, Arnauld to Angélique de Saint-Jean, 28 May 1682. For a more detailed account of Antoine Arnauld's finances, see Ellen Weaver-Laporte, "Angélique Crespin du Vivier, Madame de Fontpertuis," *Chroniques de Port-Royal* 44 (1995): 19–30.

29. Jacques, *Les Années d'exile*, p. 433.

30. BN ff 19723, Arnauld to Elector of Trier, 14 August 1686.

31. Arnauld, *Oeuvres*, vol. 3, p. 70.

32. Ibid., vol. 3, p. 501.

33. *Correspondance de Madame de Sévigné*, vol. 2, p. 881.

34. The marquise d'Ancezune's account of her grandfather's life is to be found in L. Delavaud, *Le Marquis de Pomponne* (Paris: Plon, 1911), pp. 1–18.

35. *Correspondance de Madame de Sévigné*, vol. 3, p. 974.

36. BN ff 19727, Arnauld to Vaucel, 3 August 1691.

37. Jacques, *Les Années d'exile*, p. 539.

38. Arnauld, *Oeuvres*, vol. 3, p. 698.

39. BN ff 19726.

40. BN ff 19726.

41. Quoted in Jacques, *Les Années d'exiles*, p. 701.

42. Bibliothèque de l'Arsenal, Arnauld Family Papers, 6039.

43. The title of a work published by Charles Perrault in 1698.

44. Sonnino, *Louis XIV and the Origins of the Dutch War* (Cambridge: Cambridge University Press), pp. 180–181.

45. The marriage contract is to be found in Delavaud, *The Marquis de Pomponne*, p. 159.

46. Ibid., p. 98.

47. *Mémoires de Saint-Simon*, ed. Gonzague Truc (Paris: Gallimard, 1953), vol. 2, pp. 667–673.

48. Bibliothèque de l'Arsenal, Arnauld Family Papers, 6040.

49. Herbert Rowen, "Arnauld de Pomponne," *American Historical Review* 61 (1956): 548.

12. The Marquis's Children

1. Quoted in L. Delavaud, *Le Marquis de Pomponne* (Paris: Plon, 1911), p. 66. At that time Madame de Pomponne was expecting a child, Catherine, who was born in October but who lived for only twenty-four hours.

2. *Correspondance de Madame de Sévigné*, ed. Roger Duchène (Paris: Gallimard, 1972), vol. 2, pp. 570, 575, 990n.

3. Delavaud, *Pomponne*, 168. See also Pierre Varin, *La Vérité sur les Arnauld* (Paris: Champion, 1845), vol. 2, p. 360.

4. *Mémoires de Saint-Simon*, ed. Gonzague Truc (Paris: Gallimard, 1953), vol. 3, pp. 957, 999.

5. Ibid., vol. 2, pp. 518–521.

6. *Mémoires du duc de Luynes sur la cour de Louis XV* (Paris: Didet frères, 1860), vol. 1, p. 422, vol. 2, p. 284; *Mémoires de Saint-Simon*, vol. 4, pp. 180, 630.

7. The marquis de Torcy died in 1746.

8. *Correspondance de Madame de Sévigné*, vol. 3, p. 989.

9. Bibliothèque de l'Arsenal, Arnauld Family Papers, 6626.

10. Delavaud, *Pomponne*, pp. 14–15.

11. *Correspondance de Madame de Sévigné*, vol. 3, p. 910n.

12. *Mémoires de Saint-Simon*, vol. 1, p. 673.

13. Ibid., vol. 1, p. 673.

14. *Testament et codiciles de Messire Nicolas-Simon de Pomponne*, BN Ln27 649. See also Delavaud, *Pomponne*, pp. 123–128.

15. *Mémoires du duc de Luynes*, vol. 15, p. 113.

16. *Mémoires de Saint-Simon*, vol. 2, p. 406, vol. 3, p. 1105.

17. BN, Cabinet d'Hozier, Dossiers Bleus, 32.

18. The abbé de Pomponne also inherited the family house in the rue de la Verrerie, which he rented out as his father had done.

19. *Journal et mémoires du marquis d'Argenson*, ed. E. J. B. Rothery (New York: Johnson Reprints, 1968), pp. 91–111. For a brief discussion of the Club de l'Entresol see Nannerl O. Keohane, *Philosophy and the State in France* (Princeton, NJ: Princeton University Press, 1980), pp. 362–363. See also Robert Shackleton, *Montesquieu: A Critical Biography* (Oxford: Oxford University Press, 1961), pp. 63–66.

20. BN ff 23222.

21. For more extensive discussions of these issues see Dale Van Kley, *The Damiens Affair and the Unraveling of the Old Regime 1750–70* (Princeton, NJ: Princeton University Press, 1984) and Jacques Parguet, *Le Bulle Unigenitus et le jansénisme politique* (Paris, Picot, 1976).

22. Quoted in Delavaud, *Pomponne*, pp. 89–90. See also BN Pieces Originales, 100.

23. Bibliothèque de l'Arsenal, Arnauld Family Papers, 6626.

24. *Journal et mémoires du marquis d'Argenson* (Paris, 1860), vol. 5, p. 181.

25. Ibid., vol. 9, p. 286.

26. Ibid., vol. 1, pp. 95, 105; *Mémoires du duc de Luynes*, vol. 15, p. 113.

27. *Mémoires du duc de Luynes*, vol. 15, pp. 139–140.

13. The Arnaulds in History

1. Jeffrey W. Merrick, *The Desacralization of the French Monarchy in the Eighteenth Century* (Baton Rouge: Louisiana State University Press, 1990).

2. Quoted in Jean Delumeau, *Sin and Fear: The Emergence of a Western Guilt Culture 13th-18th Centuries*, trans. Eric Nicholson (New York: Saint Martin's Press, 1990), p. 22. This work provides an interesting account of the development of *mépris du monde* in Western culture, among other things.

3. Quoted in Delumeau, *Sin and Fear*, p. 19.

4. For further discussion of individualism in early modern France, see the important work of Nannerl O. Keohane, *Philosophy and the State in France: The Renaissance to the Enlightenment* (Princeton, NJ: Princeton University Press, 1980).

5. Alexander Sedgwick, *Jansenism in Seventeenth-Century France: Voices from the Wilderness* (Charlottesville: University Press of Virginia, 1977), pp. 46, 199.

6. Augustin Gazier, *Jeanne de Chantal et Angélique Arnauld* (Paris: Champion, 1915), p. 147.

7. The preservation of the memoirs, necrologies, etc., from the archives of Port-Royal, their publication, and their impact on eighteenth-century Jansenism are described in the important article by Catherine Maire, "Port-Royal: La fracture janséniste," in *Les Frances*, ed. Pierre Nora (Paris: Gallimard, 1989) pp. 471–529. For further discussion of eighteenth-century Jansenism see Dale K. Van Kley, *The Damiens Affair and the Unraveling of the Ancien Regime* (Princeton, NJ: Princeton University Press, 1984); Dale K. Van Kley, *The Religious Origins of the French Revolution* (New Haven, CT: Yale University Press, 1996); and Dale K. Van Kley, "Church, State and the Ideological Origins of the French Revolution," *Journal of Modern History* 51 (1979): 629–666.

8. Figurism is discussed in further detail in Maire, "Port-Royal." See also Maire, "Les sources de Sainte-Beuve ou la mise en mémoire de Port-Royal," *Chroniques de Port-Royal* 42 (1993): 87–98.

Bibliography

Manuscript Sources

ARCHIVES NATIONALES (AN)

Minutier Central des Notaires de Paris.
Etude LXXV (Gallois), laisses 98–152.
Série S.
4515 *Donation de Catherine Marion Arnauld à Port-Royal 1629.*
Archives du Ministère des Affaires Etrangères.
1593–1594 Letters of Robert Arnauld d'Andilly to Madame Bouthillier.

BIBLIOTHÈQUE DE L'ARSENAL (BA)

5180–5185 *Journal de Robert Arnauld d'Andilly.*
6034–6040 Arnauld family papers.
6549 Letters of Antoine *(le grand)* Arnauld to the duc de Luynes.

BIBLIOTHÈQUE NATIONALE (BN)

Collection généalogique.
Cabinet Hozier 14.
Nouveau d'Hozier 12.
Dossiers Bleus 32, 429.
Pièces Originales 100.
Fonds francan 33004 Analyse des titres de la famille Arnauld.
Cinq Cents de Colbert 81.
Mélanges de Colbert 80.

Nouvelles Acquisitions (na)
3771–3778 Letters of Henry Arnauld to the President Barillon 1639–1643.
4820, 6210 Copies of letters of Chancellor Séguier.
Manuscrits francan (ms. fr.)
10583 Letters of Madame de Sablé.
10587 Letters of Robert Arnauld d'Andilly.
13893 Relation de Catherine de Ste.-Félicité Arnauld.
13894 Letters of Angélique Arnauld.
15595 Mélanges jansénistes including *le grand Arnauld's* last will and testament.
15610–15611 Letters of President Barillon 1639–1642.
17411 vol. 11, Séguier's letters.
17750 Mélanges jansénistes including letters of Arnauld family.
17790–17795 Letters of Angélique Arnauld.
19705 Letters of the duchesse de Longueville.
19720 Relation of the captivity of Angélique de Saint-Jean Arnauld.
19723–19727 Letters of *le grand Arnauld.*
19734 Letters of the Arnauld family.
19738 Account of the life of Angélique de Saint-Jean Arnauld.
20972 Abbé de Pomponne's complaint against Père Pichon S.J. 1748.
23222 Abbé de Pomponne's letters to the Cardinal
de Noailles on the subject of *Unigenitus.*

BIBLIOTHÈQUE DE PORT-ROYAL (BPN)

Letters of Angélique de Saint-Jean Arnauld, 1653–1684.
Mémoires pour servir à la vie de plusieurs personnes recommendables par leur vertu et
   mortes en grande odeur de piété. Recueillées en 1707.

Printed Primary Sources

Anonymous. *La Vie de Monsieur le duc de Montausier, pair de France.* 2 vols. Paris,
   1725.
Arnauld, Agnes. *Lettres de la Mère Agnès Arnauld, abbesse de Port-Royal.* Ed. M. P.
   Faugère. 2 vols. Paris, 1850.
Arnauld, Angélique. *Lettres de la Mère Angélique Arnauld, abbesse et réformatrice de*
   Port-Royal. 3 vols. Utrecht, 1742. *Relation écrite part la Mère Angélique Arnauld*
   sur Port-Royal. Ed. Louis Cognet. Paris, 1948.
Arnauld, Angélique de Saint-Jean. *Relation de captivité d'Angélique de Saint-Jean*
   Arnauld d'Andilly. Ed. Louis Cognet. Paris, 1954.
Arnauld, Antoine *(l'avocat). Antiespagnol.* 1592. *Le France et véritable discours au roy*
   sur le rétablissement qui luy est demandé par les Jésuites. 1603. *Utile et salutaire*
   advis au roy pour bien regner. n.d.
Arnauld, Antoine *(le grand). Apologie de M. Jansenius, eveque d'Ypres.* Paris, 1644. *De*
   la fréquente communion. Paris, 1643. *Oeuvres de Messire Antoine Arnauld, docteur*
   de la maison et société de Sorbonne. 42 vols. Paris-Lausanne, 1755–1783. *Seconde*
   apologie de M. Jansenius, eveque d'Ypres. Paris, 1645. *Seconde lettre de M. Arnauld,*
   docteur de la maison et société de Sorbonne à un duc et pair de France. Paris, 1655.

Arnauld, Antoine (abbé de Chaumes). *Mémoires. Collection des mémoires relatifs à l'histoire de France.* Ed. C.-R. Petitot. Vol. 24. Paris, 1824.

Arnauld, Isaac. *Mépris du monde; résolution vertueuse de l'obéissance deu au roy; Meditations sur la veillesse.* Paris, 1618.

Arnauld, Pierre. *Propositions au roy sur la réformation de l'état.* Paris, 1618.

Arnauld d'Andilly, Robert. *Confessions de Saint Augustin.* Eds. Odette Barenne, Philippe Selliers. Paris, 1993. *Journal inédit d'Arnauld d'Andilly (1614–20).* Ed. Achille Halphen. Paris, 1857. *Lettres de Monsieur Arnauld d'Andilly.* 2 vols. Paris, 1645. *Mémoires. Collection des mémoires relatifs à l'histoire de France.* Ed. C.-R. Petitot. Vols. 23, 24. Paris, 1824. *La Manière de cultiver les arbres fruitiers.* Paris, 1652.

Arnauld de Pomponne, Simon. *Relation de mon ambassade en Hollande 1669–71.* Trans. Herbert H. Rowen. Utrecht, 1955.

Barthélemy, Edouard de, ed. *Les Amis de la marquise de Sablé. Recueil des lettres des principaux habitués de son salon.* Paris, 1865.

Brisacier, Jean. *Le Jansénisme confondu.* Paris, 1651.

Clémencet, Charles. *Histoire générale de Port-Royal.* 10 vols. Amsterdam, 1757.

Conrart, Valentin. *Mémoires de Valentin Conrart, premier secretaire perpetuel de l'Académie Française.* Ed. J. N. Monmerqué. Paris, 1826.

Delassault, Geneviève, ed. *Choix des lettres inédites de Louis-Isaac Le Maistre de Sacy (1650–83).* Paris, 1959.

Divers actes, lettres et relations des religieuses de Port-Royal du Saint Sacrement touchant au sujet de la signature du formulaire. 3 vols. Utrecht, 1736.

Duchène, Roger. *Correspondance de Madame de Sévigné.* Paris, 1972.

Fontaine, Nicolas. *Mémoires pour servir à l'histoire de Port-Royal.* 2 vols. Utrecht, 1736.

Gallois, E., ed. *Lettres inédites des Feuquières tirées des papiers de la famille de la duchesse de Descazes.* 5 vols. Paris, 1846.

Gazier, Augustin. *Jeanne de Chantal et Angélique Arnauld d'aprés leur correspondance.* Paris, 1915.

Goldmann, Lucien, ed. *La correspondance de Martin de Barcos, abbé de Saint-Cyran.* Paris, 1956.

Guillebert, Pierre, ed. *Mémoires historiques et chronologiques sur l'abbaye de Port-Royal-des-Champs.* 2 vols. Utrecht, 1758.

Haag, Eugène and Emile. *La France protestante ou vies des protestants français.* 10 vols. Paris, 1846–1854.

Jansen, Paule, ed. *Arnauld d'Andilly, défenseur de Port-Royal, 1654–59. Sa correspondance inédites avec la cour conservée dans les archives du Ministère Etrangère.* Paris, 1953.

La Guilande de Julie. Paris, 1641.

Lancelot, Claude. *Mémoires touchant la vie de M. de Saint-Cyran par M. Lancelot pour servir l'éclaircissement à l'histoire de Port-Royal.* 2 vols. Cologne, 1738.

L'Estoile, Pierre de. *Mémoires-journaux de Pierre de l'Estoile.* Ed. G. Brunet et al. 11 vols. Paris, 1888–1896.

Le Maistre, Antoine. *Lettre d'un avocat au parlement à un de ses amis.* Paris, 1657.

Lesaulnier Jean, ed. *Port-Royal insolite.* Paris, 1992.

Lettre de Monsieur le Président de Gramond à Phlarque. Toulouse, 1644.

Marandé, Léonard de. *Inconveniens d'estat procedans de jansénisme*. Paris, 1654.

Mémoires et relations sur ce qui s'est passé à Port-Royal-des Champs depuis le commence-ment de la réforme de cette abbaye. s.l. 1716.

Mémoires pour servir à l'histoire de Port-Royal. Ed. Abbé Goujet. 3 vols. Paris, 1734–1737.

Mémoires pour servir à l'histoire de Port-Royal et à la vie de la Réverande Mère Angélique de Sainte-Madeleine Arnauld, réformatrice de ce monastère. Utrecht, 1742–1744.

Nécrologe de l'Abbaye de Notre-Dame de Port-Royal des Champs, ordre de Citeaux. Ed. Antoine Rivet. Amsterdam, 1723.

Quesnel, Pasquier. *Histoire de la vie de M. Arnauld*. Liège, 1697.

Racine, Jean. *Abrégé de l'histoire de Port-Royal*. Ed. Pierre Gandon. Paris, 1926.

Rapin, René. *Histoire de jansénisme depuis ses origines jusqu'en 1644*. Paris, 1861.

Saint-Cyran, Jean Duvergier de Hauranne, abbé de. *Lettres chrestiennes et spirituelles de Jean Du Verger de Hauranne, Abbé de Saint-Cyran*. Ed Robert Arnauld d'Andilly. 2 vols. Paris, 1645–1647. *Lettres chrestiennes et spirituelles de M. de Saint-Cyran qui n'ont point été imprimées jusqu'à présent*. 2 vols. Paris, 1744. *Lettres inédites de Saint-Cyran*. Ed. Annie Barnes. Paris, 1962.

Sonnino, Paul, ed. and trans. *Mémoires for the Instruction of the Dauphin*. New York, 1970.

Tallement des Réaux. *Historiettes*. Ed. Antoine Adam. 2 vols. Paris, 1960.

Tavenaux, René. *Jansénisme et politique*. Paris, 1965.

Index